HISTORY

OF

TRIAL BY JURY

BY

WILLIAM FORSYTH, M.A.

LATE FELLOW OF TRINITY COLLEGE, CAMBRIDGE, AND AUTHOR OF "HORTENSIU OR HISTORY OF LAWYERS."

SECOND EDITION, PREPARED BY

JAMES APPLETON MORGAN, Esq.

AUTHOR OF "THE LAW OF LITERATURE," ETC., ETC.

THE LAWBOOK EXCHANGE, LTD.
Clark, New Jersey

ISBN 9780963010681 (hardcover)
ISBN 9781616192624 (paperback)

Lawbook Exchange edition 1994, 2012

The quality of this reprint is equivalent to the quality of the original work.

THE LAWBOOK EXCHANGE, LTD.
33 Terminal Avenue
Clark, New Jersey 07066-1321

*Please see our website for a selection of our other publications
and fine facsimile reprints of classic works of legal history:*
www.lawbookexchange.com

Library of Congress Cataloging-in-Publication Data

Forsyth, William, 1812-1899.
   History of trial by jury / by William Forsyth. – 2nd ed./
prepared by James Appleton Morgan.
     p. cm.
   Originally published: London: J.W. Parker, 1852.
   Includes bibliographical references and index.
   ISBN 0-9630106-8-9 (acid-free paper)
   1. Jury—History. 2. Jury—Great Britain—History. I. Morgan,
Appleton, 1845-1828. II. Title.
K2292.F67   1996
347'. 052'09—dc20   96-14505
[342.75209]   CIP

Printed in the United States of America on acid-free paper

HISTORY

OF

TRIAL BY JURY

BY

WILLIAM FORSYTH, M.A.

LATE FELLOW OF TRINITY COLLEGE, CAMBRIDGE, AND AUTHOR OF "HORTENSIU
OR HISTORY OF LAWYERS."

SECOND EDITION, PREPARED BY

JAMES APPLETON MORGAN, Esq.

AUTHOR OF "THE LAW OF LITERATURE," ETC., ETC.

JERSEY CITY:
FREDERICK D. LINN & COMPANY,
PUBLISHERS.

PREFACE.

IN his preface to the present work its author observes that, "It is remarkable that no History of Trial by Jury has ever yet appeared in this country. Several learned essays on its origin have, indeed, from time to time been written, but chiefly in reviews, and the fugitive literature of the day. In Germany the subject of the Jury has of late years occupied much attention, and has been investigated with laborious accuracy. I would especially mention the works of Rogge, Phillips, Gunderman, Welcker, Mittermaier, and Gneist. But no English lawyer has hitherto devoted himself to the task of giving a full and historical account of the rise and growth of the Jury System, although it would be unjust not to acknowledge some valuable contributions by the late Mr. Starkie, in articles written by him in the *Law Review* and elsewhere; and Sir Francis Palgrave has, in his *Rise and Progress of the English Commonwealth*, thrown much light on the nature of the earliest form of Jury Trial known to our ancestors.. And yet the subject is one which

PREFACE.

can be properly discussed by those only who possess competent legal knowledge; and it might have been thought that it would have attracted the curiosity, and exercised the pen of our legal writers. But it was, many years ago, made a reproach against us by the late great American jurist, Mr. Justice Story, that we confine ourselves too much to the technicalities of our profession. He says:

"'There is a remarkable difference in the manner of treating juridical subjects between the foreign and the English jurists. The former, almost universally, discuss every subject with an elaborate theoretical fullness and accuracy, and ascend to the elementary principles of each particular branch of the science. The latter, with few exceptions, write practical treatises which contain little more than a collection of the principles laid down in the adjudged cases, with scarcely an attempt to illustrate them by any general reasoning, or even to follow them out into collateral consequences. In short, these treatises are but little more than full indexes to the reports, arranged under appropriate heads; and the materials are often tied together by very slender threads of connection.'

"But in truth we can hardly be surprised at this. An English lawyer has small encouragement to write anything else but a 'practical treatise.' That is the only kind of literature in which he can safely appear as an author, or which gives him a chance of attaining what is supposed to be the great object of his existence—professional success. And the

PREFACE. v

public care little for historical inquiries, except such as are of a popular and amusing kind. I am by no means sanguine that the subject I have chosen will excite sufficient interest to secure it a favorable hearing; and therefore I can hardly be disappointed in the result. But I am not without hopes that readers, if few, yet fit, may be found, who will care to know something of the origin and development of a system so important in a national point of view as that of the Jury. To such I commend my labors. I have traveled over too wide a field not to fear that I have committed some errors; but I trust they are neither numerous nor important. And they who best know the difficulties of the inquiry will be the most lenient in their censure."

In the present edition I have taken the liberty of adding a few notes to Mr. Forsyth's text, and of correcting one or two inaccuracies in his chapter upon "Juries in the United States."

JAMES APPLETON MORGAN.

July 1, 1875,
229 BROADWAY, NEW YORK.

CONTENTS.

CHAPTER I.
THE NATURE OF THE JURY SYSTEM.
SECT.					PAGE
I. Various Theories respecting the Origin of the Jury	.	.	.	.	1
II. Causes of mistaken Views on the Subject	.	.	.	.	5

CHAPTER II.
THE ANCIENT TRIBUNALS OF SCANDINAVIA. 13

- I. The Norwegian Laugrettomen 16
- II. The Swedish Nämbd 19
- III. The Danish Tingmænd, Nævninger, and Sandemænd . . 23
- IV. The Icelandic Tólftar-Quidr 26

CHAPTER III.
LEGAL TRIBUNALS OF ANCIENT GERMANY

- I. Constitution of the old German Courts of Justice . . . 32
- II. The Mode of Proof in the ancient Courts of Germany . . . 40

CHAPTER IV.
THE JUDICIAL SYSTEM OF THE ANGLO-SAXONS.

- I. Trial by Jury unknown to the Anglo-Saxons . . . 45
- II. The Wergild 48
- III. The Fridborh 50
- IV. The Anglo-Saxon Courts 52

SECT.		PAGE
V.	Examples of Anglo-Saxon Civil Trials	58
VI.	Of the Compurgators	61
VII.	Of the legally appointed Witnesses in the Anglo-Saxon Law	70
VIII.	Results of the Investigation	76

CHAPTER V.

THE ANGLO-NORMAN PERIOD.

I.	On the legal Changes introduced by the Normans	78
II.	Modes of Trial in Civil Suits in the Anglo-Norman Times	82
III.	The Meaning and Nature of the Judicium Parium	91
IV.	The Courts established by the Assises de Jerusalem	95

CHAPTER VI.

THE JURY IN THE TIME OF THE PLANTAGENETS.

I.	On the Assize as established by Henry II.	101
II.	What suggested the idea of Trial by Assize	110
III.	Subsequent History of the Assize	112
IV.	On the Trial by the *Jurata*, and the meaning of the expression Assisa vertitur in Juratam	115

CHAPTER VII.

THE JURY CEASING TO BE WITNESSES BECOME JUDGES OF EVIDENCE.

I.	Mode of Trial where Witnesses were named in Deeds	125
II.	Mode of Trial per Sectam	128
III.	On the personal knowledge of the Jury as distinct from the Evidence	130

CHAPTER VIII

JURY SYSTEM IN CIVIL TRIALS.

I.	The Jury Process	135
II.	On Special Juries	143
III.	On Challenges	145
IV.	On Attaints and New Trials	149

CONTENTS.

CHAPTER IX.

JURY IN CRIMINAL CASES.

Sect.	Page
I. Ancient Mode of presenting Offenses	159
II. Rise and Growth of the Jury System for the Trial of Accusations	165
III. Trial by Jury in Criminal Cases in Jersey	172

CHAPTER X.

THE GRAND JURY, AND OTHER MATTERS RELATING TO CRIMINAL TRIALS.

I. The Grand Jury	178
II. The Coroner's Jury	186
III. The Jury de Medietate Linguæ	189
IV. Challenges in Criminal Trials	191
V. Question of new Trial in Cases of Conviction of Felony	193

CHAPTER XI.

REQUIREMENT OF UNANIMITY IN THE JURY.

I. Origin of the Rule as to Unanimity	197
II. Question of the Reasonableness of the Rule considered	203

CHAPTER XII.

ON THE PROPER PROVINCE OF THE JURY.

I. Powers and Duties of Juries in England	216
II. Distinction between the Office of the Judge and that of the Jury	235
III. Mixed Questions of Law and Fact	242
IV. Presumptions of Law and Fact	243
V. Utility of Written Pleadings	246

CHAPTER XIII.

THE JURY SYSTEM IN SCOTLAND.

I. Jury Trial in Civil Cases	249

CONTENTS.

SECT.   PAG
II. The Assize in Criminal Trials 27
III. The Verdict of Not Proven 28

CHAPTER XIV.
THE JURY IN THE UNITED STATES. . 28

CHAPTER XV.
TRIAL BY JURY IN FRANCE AND OTHER PARTS OF THE CONTINENT.

I Trial by Jury in France 29
II. The Jury in other parts of the Continent. 31

CHAPTER XVI.
INTRODUCTION OF TRIAL BY JURY INTO THE CRIMINAL PROCEDURE IN GERMANY.

I. System of Criminal Procedure which Trial by Jury was intended to supersede 31
II. Introduction of the Jury Trial in Criminal Cases . . . 32

CHAPTER XVII.
ILLUSTRATIONS OF TRIAL BY JURY IN THE CASE OF ENGLISH STATE PROSECUTIONS. 3:

CHAPTER XVIII.
THE JURY CONSIDERED AS A SOCIAL, POLITICAL AND JUDICIAL INSTITUTION. 3!

HISTORY

OF

TRIAL BY JURY.

CHAPTER I.

THE NATURE OF THE JURY SYSTEM.

SECTION I. *Various Theories respecting the Origin of the Jury.*

THE rise and growth of the Jury system is a subject which ought to interest not only the lawyer but all who value the institutions of England, of which this is one of the most remarkable, being until recently a distinctive feature of our jurisprudence.

In the following pages an attempt is made to investigate its origin and trace its history, until it assumed the well-defined form and office with which we are so familiar, but which long excited the admiration and envy of the nations of Europe, until at last, by slow degrees and to a partial extent, many of them have succeeded in adopting it themselves. The inquiry is more difficult than may at first sight appear. Trial by Jury does not owe its existence to any positive law:—it is not the creature of an Act of Parliament establishing the form and defining the functions of the new tribunal. It arose, as I hope to show, silently and gradually, out of the usages of a state of society which has forever passed away, but of which it is necessary to have a clear idea, in order to understand how this mode of trial first came into existence.

Few subjects have exercised the ingenuity and baffled the research of the historian more than the origin of the jury. No long time has elapsed since the popular opinion was—and perhaps it even now prevails—that it was an institution established by Alfred the Great; and we prided ourselves on the idea that this was one of the legacies of freedom bequeathed to us by our Anglo-Saxon ancestors.[1] An enlightened spirit of historical criticism applied to the subject has, however, of late years done much to dissipate this delusion; and it would be unjust not to acknowledge how greatly in this country we are indebted for more correct views to the labors of Reeves, Palgrave, Starkie, and Hallam. But the jurists of Germany also deserve the praise of having investigated the question with profound learning and searching accuracy, and the frequent reference made in the course of this treatise to their works will prove how fully I appreciate the services they have rendered in the elucidation of the present inquiry.

Numerous have been the theories as to the birth and parentage of this the favorite child of the English law. Some writers have thought the origin so lost in the darkness of antiquity, as to render investigation hopeless. Thus Bourguignon says,[2] "Its origin is lost in the night of time;" and the late Chief Commissioner Adam declares that "in England it is of a tradition so high that nothing is known of its origin; and of a perfection

---

[1] Amongst the cartoons exhibited as designs for the decoration of the new Houses of Parliament, one of those which obtained a prize was called the First Trial by Jury. We see there the culprit brought before twelve Saxon jurors sitting in the presence of a judge in the open air. The picture well deserves its reputation as a work of art; but as the representation of an historical fact it is untrue.

[2] Son origine se perd dans la nuit des temps. Mémoire sur le Jury.

so absolute that it has remained in unabated rigor from its commencement to the present time."[1] Spelman was uncertain whether to attribute the origin of the system to the Saxons or the Normans. Du Cange and Hickes ascribed its introduction to the Normans, who themselves borrowed the idea from the Goths. Blackstone calls it "a trial that hath been used time out of mind in this nation, and seems to have been coeval with the first civil government thereof;" and he adds, "that certain it is that juries were in use among the earliest Saxon colonies." In his learned work on "The Origin and Progress of the Judicial Institutions of Europe," Meyer regards the jury as partly a modification of the Grand Assize established by Henry II., and partly an imitation of the feudal courts erected in Palestine by the Crusaders; and he fixes upon the reign of Henry III. as the æra of its introduction into England.[2] The theory of Reeves in his "History of the English Law" is, that when Rollo led his followers into Normandy they carried with them this mode of trial from the North. He says that it was used in Normandy in all cases of small importance, and that when the Normans had transplanted themselves into England they endeavored to substitute it in the place of the Saxon tribunals. He speaks of it therefore as a novelty introduced by them soon after the Conquest, and says that it may be laid down with safety that the system did not exist in Anglo-Saxon times.[3] Turner, on the other hand, in his "History of the Anglo-Saxons," thinks that it was then in use, "although no record marks the date of its commencement;"[4] and he ought to have added, or "notices the fact of its existence." Sir Francis Palgrave says, that a tribunal of sworn witnesses elected out of the popular courts and employed

---

[1] Treatise on Trial by Jury in Civil Causes (in Scotland).
[2] Orig. et Progrès des Inst. Judic. tom. II. c. 11.
[3] Hist. English Law, I. c. 1; II. c. 2.
[4] Hist. Ang.-Saxons, III. 223.

for the decision of rights of property, may be traced to the Anglo-Saxon period; but that in criminal cases the jury appears to have been unknown until enacted by the Conqueror.[1]

The opinion of one of the latest and ablest of our legal writers, Mr. Sergeant Stephen, seems to coincide with that of Reeves, for he says, "The most probable theory seems to be that we owe the germ of this (as of so many of our institutions) to the Normans, and that it was derived by them from Scandinavian tribunals, where the judicial number of twelve was always held in great veneration."[2] He refers also to the Grand Coustumier as justifying the idea that the jury is of Norman origin. But we may remark in passing, that this work was written later than the year 1215; so that whatever may be the similarity of usage between the two countries which we find therein mentioned, it is more probable that the Norman was derived from the English.

Some writers, especially amongst the Germans, attribute the origin of the English Jury to a national recognition of the principle that no man ought to be condemned except by the voice of his fellow-citizens. And as the ancient courts of justice amongst the Teutonic nations were nothing more than assemblies of freemen, met together for the purpose of deliberating on whatever affected the interests of the gau or district of which they were the inhabitants, including the punishment of offenses and the settlement of civil claims, it has been thought that here is to be found the assertion of the same principle as pervades the jury-trial, and that therefore the latter is derived from and only a modification of the former.

But if this be so, how can we account for the fact that in England alone the system was developed into its modern

---

[1] Rise and Progress of Eng. Commonwealth, I. 256.
[2] Comment. III. 349.

form, and that while amidst all the freedom of Anglo-Saxon institutions it was unknown, it first assumed a distinct and historical character under the reign of a Norman king? We shall see, unless I am mistaken, in the course of our inquiry, that the jury does not owe its existence to any preconceived theory of jurisprudence, but that it gradually grew out of forms previously in use, and was composed of elements long familiar to the people of this country. Where such diversity of opinion prevails, and so many learned men have professed their inability to pierce the darkness that surrounds the early history of the subject, it well becomes a writer to be diffident of his own view; but I can not help feeling persuaded that the rise of the jury system may be traced as a gradual and natural sequence from the modes of trial in use amongst the Anglo-Saxons and Anglo-Normans,—that is, both before and after the Conquest,—and that therefore in order to understand how it arose, we have only to make ourselves fully acquainted with those modes of trial and the state of society on which they so intimately depended.

SECTION II. *Causes of mistaken Views on the Subject*

In endeavoring to trace the origin of any institution which has come down to us from remote antiquity, we must carefully consider under what aspect it appears when first noticed by contemporary writers. This often differs widely from the form and character which it acquires in the slow growth of years, and yet its identity may be proved with as much certainty as that of the river whose well-head is a spring oozing out of a grassy bed, and which swells into a broad expanse of waters before it loses itself in the ocean. We shall only be deceived if we fix our attention upon its maturity rather than its infancy; upon its end rather than its beginning. In constitutional history this is eminently true. We must deal with institutions as philology does with words. To ascertain the derivation of the latter we resolve them into their earliest known forms, and these are often the only clue whereby we can discover the stock from which they sprung, and the meaning they primarily bore.

So in the case of Trial by Jury:—we must determine the point of time when it is first mentioned as an historical fact, and see what were then its characteristic features. We must know its primitive form, and observe in what point of view it was looked upon by the writers of the early ages. The subsequent changes it has undergone will not throw much light upon its origin—nay, they rather tend to mislead us by suggesting false analogies and wrong points of comparison; and many a specious but mistaken theory on the subject would have been avoided, if due attention had been paid to the accounts of the true nature of the tribunal which we find in the pages of Glanvill and Bracton, and of which we find incidental notice in contemporary annals and records.

Again, we must be careful not to attach too much importance to seeming analogies, or mistake partial resemblances for complete identity. It is this which has led so many writers to espouse conflicting views respecting the origin of the jury. By fixing their attention on particular points of two systems, and finding that these in a great measure correspond, they have imagined that the one must have been copied from the other. Thus some think that they discover the archetype of the jury in the Teutonic and Saxon compurgators, who were generally twelve in number, and whose oaths were conclusive of the matter in dispute. Others derive it from the Rachinburgen or Scabini of the continental nations; others from the sectatores and pares of the ancient county and feudal courts in this country.

One important feature of the institution is by no

means peculiar to it. I mean the fact that it is a sworn tribunal—that its members decide under the solemn sanction of an oath. This was the case with the Dicasts at Athens and the Judices at Rome, and the same principle prevailed in the old Norse THING and German MALLUM, when the right of all the inhabitants of the gau or mark to be present at the judicial proceedings of these periodical assemblies, became in practice limited to a few, as the representatives of the community.

But sufficient attention has not been paid to what is the distinctive characteristic of the system; namely, that the Jury consists of a body of men taken from the community at large, summoned to find the truth of disputed facts, who are quite distinct from the judges or court. Their office is to decide upon the effect of evidence, and thus inform the court truly upon the question at issue, in order that the latter may be enabled to pronounce a right judgment. But they are not the court itself, nor do they form part of it; and they have nothing to do with the sentence which follows the delivery of their verdict. Moreover, they are not members of any class or corporation, on whom, as distinct from the rest of their fellow-citizens, is imposed the task of taking part in judicial inquiries. They are called upon to serve as the particular occasion arises, and then return to their usual avocations and pursuits, so as to be absolutely free from any professional bias or prejudice.

Few writers, when speculating on the rise of the jury, have kept this principle of its being separate from the court and employed solely to determine questions of fact, steadily in view. They have generally confounded the jurors with the court, and have thus imagined an identity between the former and those ancient tribunals of Europe where a select number of persons—often twelve—were taken from the community and appointed to try causes, but who did so in the capacity of Judges, and when satisfied of the evidence awarded and pronounced the doom.

These are the Geschwornen-Gerichte to which the jurists of Germany of late years have been so fond of appealing, as the model upon which they wish to reform their modern courts of judicature, and which they assume to have been in principle the same as the English Jury.[1]

But a little reflection will convince us that this is not so, and that the distinction above insisted on, is not a mere formal one, but of a radical and important kind. It involves, in fact, the question of the possibility of the tribunal continuing to exist. A court of justice where the whole judicial authority is vested in persons taken from time to time from amongst the people at large, with no other qualification required than that of good character, can only be tolerated in a state of society of the most simple kind. As the affairs of civil life become more complicated, and laws more intricate and multiplied, it is plainly impossible that such persons, by whatever name they are called, whether judges or jurors, can be competent to deal with legal questions. The law becomes a science which requires laborious study to comprehend it; and without a body of men trained to the task, and capable of applying it, the rights of all would be set afloat—tossed on a wide sea of arbitrary, flunctuating, and contradictory decisions. Hence in all such popular courts as we are describing, it has been found necessary to appoint jurisconsults to assist with their advice, in matters of law, the uninstructed judges. These at first acted only as assessors, but gradually attracted to themselves and monopolized the whole judicial functions of the court. There being no machinery for keeping separate questions

[1] See Rogge, Gerichtswesen der Germanen, and Staats Lexicon, vol. VII art. Jury

of law from questions of fact, the lay members felt themselves more and more inadequate to adjudge the causes that came before them. They were obliged perpetually to refer to the legal functionary who presided, and the more his authority was enhanced, the more the power of the other members of the court was weakened, and their importance lessened, until it was seen that their attendance might without sensible inconvenience be dispensed with altogether. And of course this change was favored by the crown, as it thereby gained the important object of being able, by means of creatures of its own, to dispose of the lives and liberties of its subjects under the guise of legal forms. Hence arose in Europe, upon the ruins of the old popular tribunals, the system of single judges appointed by the king, and deciding all matters of fact and law, and it brought with it its odious train of secret process and inquisitorial examinations. But the result was inevitable. The ancient courts of Scandinavia and Germany carried in their very constitution the element of their own destruction, and this consisted in the fact that the whole judicial power was in the hands of persons who had no special qualifications for their office.

Far otherwise has been the case in England. Here the jury never usurped the functions of the judge. They were originally called in to aid the court with information upon questions of fact, in order that the law might be properly applied; and this has continued to be their province to the present day. The utility of such an office is felt in the most refined as well as in the simplest state of jurisprudence. Twelve men of average understanding are at least as competent now as they were in the days of Henry II. to determine whether there is sufficient evidence to satisfy them that a murder has been committed, and that the party charged with the crime is guilty. The increased technicality of the law does not affect their fitness to decide on the effect of proofs.

Hence it is that the English jury flourishes still in all its pristine vigor, while what are improperly called the old juries of the continent have either sunk into decay or been totally abolished.

A near approximation indeed to the proper functions of the jury is to be found in the proceedings of criminal state trials amongst the ancient Romans, although we may be quite certain that the English institution is in no way copied from them.[1] There we find a presiding judge, who was either the prætor or a judex quæstionis specially appointed by him, and a body of judices taken from a particular class, at one time the equestrian, and at another the senatorial, whose duty it was to determine the fact of the guilt or innocence of the accused.[2] At the close of the evidence they were said to be missi in consilium by the judge, that is, told "to consider their verdict," and to each were given three tablets marked respectively with the letters A. for Absolvo, C. for Condemno, and N. L. for Non Liquet, one of which he threw into an urn, and the result of the trial was determined by the majority of the letters that appeared. If the fatal C. prevailed, the prætor pronounced the sentence, with which the judices did not interfere.[3] So far the course of procedure seems closely analogous to our own. But

[1] This, however, was not the opinion of Dr. Pettingall, who wrote an ingenious treatise in 1769 to show that the English jury was probably derived from the Greeks and Romans.

[2] It is difficult to convey to an English reader the precise import of foreign terms of jurisprudence, without using an awkward periphrasis—and for this reason, that the words nominally equivalent have acquired by usage a different sense amongst us. Thus, although it seems quite correct to render "judices" by "judges," we are so accustomed to associate with the name of the latter our own notions of their peculiar functions, that we are misled when we apply it to the Roman judices, who in many respects corresponded more nearly to our jurymen. So with regard to the Scabini—Schöppen—and Urtheiler of the Teutonic system. They were the "members of the courts" who determined both law and fact, and gave judgment—combining thus the functions of both judge and jury.

[3] See Heinecc. Antiq. Rom. Syntagma, lib. IV. tit. 18.

the important difference is this. The Roman judices might, without any breach of legal duty, acquit in spite of the most conclusive evidence of guilt; for they were entitled as representing the sovereign people to exercise the prerogative of mercy, and their verdict in that case implied and was equivalent to a pardon. Their functions therefore were not, like those of the jurymen of later times, restricted to the mere finding of facts, but extended to the exercise of a power which, with us, is lodged in the supreme executive of the state. We may further add, that when the prætor announced the verdict of the majority, if it was condemno he used the words Videtur Fecisse or Non Jure Videtur Fecisse; if it was absolvo, the words Non Videtur Fecisse, or Jure Videtur Fecisse; and perhaps the last form was adopted not only when the facts had been proved against the accused, and there was a legal excuse for the deed, but also when the prætor saw that the acquittal was intended as an act of mercy and a pardon.

I believe it to be capable almost of demonstration, that the English jury is of indigenous growth, and was not copied or borrowed from any of the tribunals that existed on the continent. In order to prove this, it will be necessary to examine what those tribunals in ancient times really were, and show wherein the difference between them and our own system consisted; a difference, in my opinion, of so essential a kind, that writers never could have been so misled as to confound them, if they had not occupied themselves rather with what the jury now is, namely, the sole judge of the effect of evidence produced, and the arbiter of compensation for contracts broken and injuries received—with what it originally was, when its verdict was nothing more than the conjoint testimony of a fixed number of persons deposing to facts within their own knowledge.

Let us therefore now turn our attention to the primæval courts of justice on the continent, and consider first those of Scandinavia, where the system in many points bore such resemblances to our own, as to have induced some authors to maintain that the latter must have been derived from it.

CHAPTER II.

THE ANCIENT TRIBUNALS OF SCANDINAVIA.

A DANISH jurist, Professor Repp of Copenhagen, published some years ago a very learned treatise on the forensic institutions of Scandinavia,[1] which deserves to be better known in this country than it is. It supplied a chasm in juridical literature, for previously to its appearance the most crude and imperfect views were held respecting the old Norse tribunals, and Blackstone and other writers were content to take their scanty information from Saxo Grammaticus, Stjernhook, and the Leges Saxonum, a Latin copy of the latter having been discovered in the library of Fulda in the middle of the sixteenth century. Repp, however, has investigated the subject with diligence and accuracy. He examined about forty ancient codes of law in the original languages, and has thrown much light upon what has hitherto been one of the darkest regions of forensic history. Even now it may be said to be still a terra incognita to the English lawyer; and yet the resemblances that occur between the primæval courts of justice of the Northmen and our own at the present day, are such as might well provoke curiosity, even if they did not secure a careful and discriminating inquiry. Repp, indeed, is so im-

[1] Historical Treatise on Trial by Jury, Wager of Law, and other co-ordinate forensic institutions formerly in use in Scandinavia and Iceland, 1832. This work is now very scarce, and it was with great difficulty that I was able to procure a copy.

pressed with this that he does not hesitate throughout his work to speak of the usual mode of trial amongst them as trial by jury; and with referenee to the Norwegian tribunals, says, that the analogy is so strong as to exclude every doubt in regard to the common origin of the laws respecting "juries" in both countries. I venture, however, to think that he is mistaken in this point, and that his error has arisen from a twofold cause —first, from not sufficiently distinguishing the functions of a judge from those of a juryman in the modern sense of the word; and, secondly, from not knowing or not remembering that the jurymen of England were originally nothing but witnesses. In the course of the present chapter I shall have occasion to point this out more fully, when the different courts of Scandinavia come separately under our consideration.

But it may be here stated generally, that throughout the whole of that region the characteristic of the legal tribunals was, that they were composed of twelve persons, taken from time to time from amongst the people, who determined questions in dispute upon oath, and whose judgment or verdict was decided by the majority.

With reference to this mode of trial, Repp says that its antiquity can not now be determined. We discover it with the earliest dawn of Northern history; and even at that early period, as an ancient institution. We can trace the undoubted existence of juries (in this sense) as far back as one thousand years; before that period the history of Northern Europe is wrapped in Cimmerian darkness, and we can not expect to find authentic records respecting juries, where all other records fail. The use of this tribunal, however, in Scandinavia was not so frequent before the beginning of the tenth century as afterwards. In earlier times it was frequently superseded by trial by battle, which was deemed the most honorable mode of settling disputes; and as that began to decline on the introduction of Christianity, it was succeeded by compurgation and the ordeal, which last is said to have been first established in consequence of Bishop Poppo, in the year 950, thrusting his hand into a red-hot iron glove, and drawing it out unscathed, to prove to the Jutlanders that the religion which he preached was divine. The people seeing this, rushed in crowds to the baptismal font, and in future adopted the ordeal as a means of appealing to Heaven to determine disputed rights.

The most ancient codes, however, do not sanction any other mode of trial than that by sworn judges. In none—not even in those of the tenth century—is the trial by battle mentioned, and very few allude to the ordeal. But they abound with notices of the various forms of trial by jurors; they contain minute and elaborate regulations respecting its form, its application, and its contingencies, and prescribe its use in almost every page.[1]

The jurors, however, of the old Saxons were nothing but compurgators. This was the only mode of trial in use amongst them. If a man were accused of a crime, he either paid the legal fine, or proved his innocence by his own oath and that of a certain number of friends proportioned to the nature of the offense.[2] But no mention is made of any tribunal of sworn juries or others, acting in a judicial capacity. And this is an important fact, when we consider that from them came the invaders and occupants of Britain, to whom, under the name of Anglo-Saxons, we trace up so many of our most cherished rights and customs as freemen.

[1] Repp, Histor. Treatise.
[2] The Saxon laws are full of such enactments as the following, De ictu nobilis xxx. Solid. vel, si negat, tertia manu juret. De Vulneribus.

Section I. *The Norwegian Laugrettomen.*

In Norway it was different. There causes were determined and offenses tried by a body of sworn jurymen in the most ancient times. We have a full account of the constitution of this tribunal in the code or law of Gulathing, published by King Magnus, in the year 1274. But this did not establish the court:—it merely introduced some changes in an institution which had existed long before. In Norway there were two solemn meeting or THINGS held periodically—the one in the North, called FROSTA-THING, and the other in the South, called GULA-THING. The latter assembled in the Island of Guley, where there was a sacred place in which the court was held in the open air. Three persons holding different offices under the crown were authorized by law to nominate a certain number of deputies (called Nefndarmen, or "named-men") from each district, who attended the Things. In the Gula-thing there were one hundred and thirty-nine of these deputies; and at the opening of the assembly each of the officers who returned them had to take an oath in the following form: "I certify, laying my hand on the holy book, and I appeal to God, that I nominated such men for Gula-thing as I considered most able and discreet according to my conscience, nor did I therefore receive any gift or favor." From amongst the deputies were chosen (but in what manner is left in uncertainty) thirty-six men to act as jurors, who took their seats within the sacred inclosure, in a space marked off by staves and ropes, called Laugretta, and the jurors themselves were called LAUGRETTOMEN,[1] which literally means, "Law-amendment-men." This name seems at first sight to imply that they had legislative rather than judicial functions to perform, but this

---

[1] From Laug lex and retta emendatio.

was not so. In those simple times, the written laws generally specified particular cases, and the consequence was, that others were constantly occurring which the code had left unprovided for. To adjudicate upon such causes was therefore like making new laws, and hence the jurors derived their name. The Thing was presided over by a Lögmann or Law-man, one of whose qualifications for the office in old times was, that he could recite by heart the laws of the land; but he had anciently no voice in the decision of the causes that were tried, until an innovation in this respect was introduced by King Magnus. The following are some passages taken from his code:

"The Thing shall last so long as the Lawman chooses, and during such time as he, with the consent of the jury, deems necessary for adjudging the causes which then are to be heard. Their number is three times twelve; their nomination must be so managed that some fit men be chosen from every district. Those who are chosen to be jurors shall, before they enter the court, swear an oath after the following form:

"'I protest before God that I will give such a vote in every cause, as well on the side of plaintiff as defendant, as I consider most just in the sight of God, according to law and my conscience; and I shall always do the same whenever I shall be chosen as juror.'

"This oath every man is to swear before he enters the court, the first time he serves on a jury, but not a second time, though he should be chosen. Every man must go fasting into court, and make his appearance there while the sun is in the east, and remain in the court till noon. No man must bring any drink into court, neither for sale nor in any other way. If those who are outside the sacred cords make there such noise and disturbance that the jurors are prevented from hearing cases, or those from pleading who have obtained leave from the lawman and the jurors, they shall pay a fine of an ore silver, when detected and convicted, having been previously admonished.

"Those who are chosen to serve as jurors shall judge according to law, in all causes that in a lawful manner and course are hither (that is to Gula-thing) appealed. But in all cases that the code does not decide, that is to be considered law which all the jurors agree upon. But if they disagree, the lawman prevails with those who agree with him; unless the king with the advice of the most prudent men shall otherwise decide."

Previously to the promulgation of this code the Lögmann had merely presided and acted as the legal adviser of the jurors, they being the judges to all intents and purposes. They were not, however, bound to consult him, as they were fully entitled to decide cases according to their own view of the law. Here, however, he was invested with a most important judicial power, as in the event of any disagreement in opinion among the jurors, he could, by giving his vote on that side, make the judgment of the minority prevail. During the season of the year also when the Thing was not sitting, he was empowered to act as supreme judge, and hear and decide causes alone.

Now, although Repp in his learned work constantly speaks of the proceedings before this tribunal as "trial by jury," and draws attention to the analogy between it and the English jury, we must not allow ourselves to be deceived by the apparent resemblance. The Laugrettomen were in all respects judges, and not merely jurymen, as the word is usually understood. They decided both law and fact, and awarded the sentence which the law prescribed. So far they resembled English juries, that they were not a class of men holding any permanent judicial office, but chosen from time to time, amongst the people, to attend the Thing and administer justice. But this was no more than happened, as we shall see, in the case of the Rachinburgen of the Teutonic, and the Arimannen of the Lombard nations. They were a court of judges popularly constituted, but their functions were manifestly different from those of a body of men summoned merely to determine for the court disputed questions of fact, by their own previous knowledge of the case, or upon the evidence of witnesses before them.

The Norwegian king, Magnus, seems to have disliked the popular element in this court of the Laugrettomen, and he gave his countenance to trial by wager of law or compurgation, the meaning of which will be hereafter explained. This rendered the use of the court less frequent, although it continued to subsist in a modified form for many ages afterwards; and remains of it are discovered in the code of King Christain V. of Denmark, which was enacted in the year 1683.

SECTION II. *The Swedish Nambd.*

In Sweden a similar tribunal existed from time immemorial. In the ancient codes of that country it is most frequently called Nämbd;[1] and there were several kinds of it. Thus we find mention of the Konungz Nämbd, or King's Jury, the Lawman's, the Bishop's, and the Hundred's jury. The first was a court of appeal from the Lawman's court, as that was from the Hundred. Causes and offenses of every kind were tried before these courts, and whenever any case of importance occurred, which required judicial investigation, it was the duty of the magistrate to summon an extraordinary Thing or meeting, and nominate a Nämbd to take cognizance of it. For it was only at a Thing that the

---

[1] Solemnis fuit et adhuc est Hyperboreis nostris Nembdæ usus, cujus officium ante fuit de facto tantum cognoscere, examinare, statumque causæ exponere, uti constat ex jure nostro. Welt, Themis Romano-Svecica, quoted by Repp. Nämbd, is sometimes spelt Nämnd and Nämd.

court could sit as in Norway. It was, in fact, in the nature of a committee chosen out of the deputies who attended the assembly; and the Thing was a meeting at which all the judicial business was transacted by the Nämbd. In the Landslagh the king's Nämbd is spoken of as if it had only criminal jurisdiction; but according to Repp, civil causes also came before it. The words of the code are: "Now offenses may happen to be committed against the king and the law laid down in the king's BALK; therefore there shall be twelve men ordered in every Lawman's jurisdiction, agreed upon, chosen, and nominated by the king and the natives of this country. They shall attentively and diligently seek out and discover, each in that district in which he is ordered to maintain justice, all those that, contrary to this law, disturb or molest the people. And they have to swear the following oath." The code then gives the oath, which is, that they will not make any man guilty who is innocent, nor any man innocent who is guilty, and proceeds: "Whomsoever these twelve, or seven of their number, convicted before the king himself, or those who judge under his commission in a court of inquisition, or in a Landsthing, let him be cast and lose his hand, head, life, and goods or money, to the king or the prosecutor and the district, according to the nature of the offense. Whomsoever they discharge, let him be discharged. Against this jury (or court) there is no appeal."

Repp says that we are not to suppose from the words of the law that the jurors were a kind of officers, or commissioners of the peace, or even a sort of public prosecutors. They were jurors to all intents and purposes, and to them lay an appeal from the inferior courts in all causes. As to the mode of nomination of jurors, we are left in some doubt. One code (the Oestgotha-Lagh) says, the magistrate of the district was to appoint a jury, and both the contending parties were to be present and approve of those who were nominated. And it says, "True men[1] are to sit on the Nämbd, and not parties in the cause, nor their friends or relatives. According to the Westgotha-Lagh, the king was to appoint a Nämbd for himself.[2]

It must be admitted that between the Swedish Nämbd and the English jury there appear many curious points of resemblance—and especially so, if we can put implicit faith in the passage which I have already quoted in a note from Laurens Welt, who wrote in the year 1687, and who says that the office of the former, in early times, was de facto tantum cognoscere. When an offense had been committed, the magistrate of the district was to convoke a Hundreds-thing, and in the words of the law, "the nämbd shall investigate and ascertain the truth in that cause. If there be witnesses, let them appear before the jury, and let each man swear the oath prescribed to him; and the magistrate of the district shall dictate the oath."[3] "If a man ravishes a woman —is caught in the act—and twelve men prove the fact by their evidence, then the magistrate shall instantly issue circulars,[4] and summon a Thing, and sentence him to be executed by the sword without delay."

Still, however, I believe that the nämbd was the whole court, notwithstanding what Welt says as to their deciding only upon fact, and that in early times the whole

---

[1] Sanninda män, which literally means "truth-speaking men." The term is Icelandic.

[2] In the Uplandzlagh occurs a provision which makes twelve men nominate the judges: "When judges are to be chosen, the magistrate shall rise and nominate twelve men from the hundred: these men shall nominate two men to be judges. The king shall invest them with authority to judge. These judges shall be present at the Thing every Thing-day."

[3] Edzöris Balk of Landslagh. Repp, 96.

[4] Literally "cut up the chip of message." Repp, 105.

judicial power, both of judge and jury, was lodged in its hands. This view is confirmed by Repp himself, who yet speaks of it always as a jury. He says that "in ancient courts juries were everything, and judges were functionaries of only secondary importance, and that authority and power originally vested in the juries, have, under the progressive development of monarchy, been transferred from them to the judges." In other words, the judges were originally mere presidents of a court consisting of sworn members, who exercised full judicial powers. The latter were from time to time chosen from amongst the people, and their number was twelve; but still they were not "jurymen" in the modern sense of the term, and altogether different from the probi homines of the vicinage in England, summoned for the purpose of giving the court the benefit of their testimony upon some disputed claim or question of guilt.

In Friesland a single judge named asega[1] pronounced the sentence or doom (tuom). But he had frequently assessors to aid him, who seem to have had, when they attended, a voice in the judgment. Their number was seven,[2] or twelve, and hence they are often spoken of as "the twelve"[3] (tolef, zwölfe), or "the seven of the twelve." Sometimes also they are called "the king's orkennen" (witnesses), a fact which must not be lost sight of, when we come to speak of the English jury in its earliest form. They had to execute the decree of the asega or president, and discharged many of the duties of the modern sheriff and police.

---

[1] Asega literally means legem dicens, juridicus.—See Grimm, Deutsche Rechts Alterthümer.

[2] Septem suffragiis reus vel vincit vel vincitur. Stjernhook, 59.

[3] The old Norse name of this tribunals was tolfmanna-domr, "the doom of twelve men." A more expressive term for a verdict could hardly be found.

SECTION III. *The Danish Tingmænd, Nævninger, and Sandemænd.*

In Denmark the modes of trial by compurgation (there called Lov),[1] and the ordeal, existed in full vigor; but concurrently with these, before the administration of the law fell into the hands of regular judges, causes were decided by persons who were called either Tingmænd, Nævninger, or Sandemænd, according to the nature of the court they attended. Of these let us speak briefly in their order.

And first of the TINGMÆND.[2] These were not necessarily jurors. They were the members who constituted the Thing, of whom, according to the law of King Waldemar, seven made a quorum. But they did not originally adjudicate upon causes, except when no other jurors had been appointed—their proper business being to form the Thing at which the public affairs of the district were transacted—and they were therefore more like a municipal council than a court of justice. At a later period, however, by the law of King Erik, a special jurisdiction was given to them.

Next of the NÆVN, or NÆVNINGER.[3] These were the proper jurors or sworn judges of Denmark, being so called from nævn, "to name." The appellation therefore signifies that they were the named or nomination men. They existed in very ancient times, and long anterior to any of the extant Danish codes.[4] Their number was origi-

---

[1] The literal meaning of Lov in Danish is "law."

[2] Ting is the same as Thing in the other Scandinavian languages, the Danes being unable to pronounce the h. Mænd is the plural of mand, man. The Tingmænd therefore are persons attending or serving at a Thing or court.

[3] Instead of nævn we often find the word spelt nefnd, which is the Icelandic form.

[4] Saxo Grammaticus indeed says, Hist. Dan. lib. IX. that Ragner Lod-

nally twelve, and they were chosen by the inhabitants of the district; although in some criminal cases the prosecutor, and in others the magistrates, might nominate them. The latter also had this power in default of a nomination by the community. In Jutland they were appointed annually by the inhabitants for trying all causes within the year. In Scania fifteen were nominated at first, as the accused or defendant was entitled to challeng three. In later times the number varied according to the nature of the offenses they had to try, but still twelve was the basis on which each tribunal was formed. Almost all the laws that exist respecting them have reference to their functions as criminal judges; and Repp says that it is evident the office was in Denmark held to be an odious one. In certain cases they were required to be related to one of the parties, and were hence called Köns-Nævninger, or Kions-neffn (kindred-jurors). This occurred chiefly in causes in which family questions had to be decided, as whether a child had been born alive? whether it had been baptized? or whether it had survived its father or mother?

In Denmark a cause was decided by the majority of the jurors; but the bishop, together with the best eight men of the district, had the power of confirming or rejecting their judgment; and an ancient code provides that if they are all unanimous they shall forfeit their property when they have given a judgment contrary to the opinion of the plurality of the best men of the district. In criminal cases it appears that no man could compel another to submit to a trial before the Nævn unless he either brought witnesses in support of his charge, or

brok, who reigned over Denmark between 750 and 790, instituted the trial by twelve men. Ut omnis controversiarum lis, semotis actionum instrumentis, nec accusantis impetitione nec rei defensione admissa, DUODECIM PATRUM AP PROBATORUM JUDICIO mandaretur, instituit. But according to Repp, Professor Ancher, in his Dansk Lovhistorie, has satisfactorily shown that the institution is of much older date.

swore to its truth by an oath called the asworen eth. And it was the province of the juries to decide upon the preliminary proofs whether they would allow the trial to proceed or not. In this proceeding we may trace a faint resemblance to our own grand-jury system, the principle in both being the same, namely, that a man ought not to be put upon his trial unless there is a prima facie case of guilt made out against him.

The SANDEMÆND[1] were peculiar to Jutland. They were sworn judges, eight in number, two being nominated by the king for each division of the country. They took an oath to judge on the spot where the deed had been committed, or, if a right of land was in dispute, then where the property is situated. They received half a mark of silver for horse-hire from the party who employed them, whatever the result of their judgment might be, and their verdict was determined by a majority; but subject, as in the case of the nævn, to be annulled by the bishop and his eight coadjutors. The oath they took was to the effect that they would state nothing but what they knew to be most right and true (SANDESTE), and they had cognizances of all personal injuries and disputes respecting land and church-property.

It is needless to repeat here what has been already said respecting the Norwegian and Swedish juries. The Danish nævn and sandemænd were in principle exactly the same—namely, in persons whom the whole judicial power, in the particular case, was vested. They were therefore the court itself, pro hac vice, and may with as much propriety be called judges as jurors. True it is they were not learned judges—that is, not men trained in the study of the law, and appointed permanently by the crown: but in the simplicity of ancient

---

[1] From sand (true), or sande (to prove). The word is translated by the Danish lawyers veridici.

times this was not necessary, for the law itself was too brief and plain, and the causes of too clear a nature, to require an apprenticeship to qualify a man for the office of a judge. But because this was so, and men taken from the ranks of the people were, from time to time, chosen to try cases and determine both law and fact, this does not render them less judges, in the strict sense of the word, than the learned occupants of the judicial bench were who afterwards supplied their place.[1]

All traces of this system have long since vanished in Denmark. The nævn are not summoned, although the institution has never yet been formally abolished. The business of courts of justice there, except in the high court of appeal in Copenhagen, is carried on with closed doors. A single judge presides, assisted by learned colleagues, and no part of the proceedings transpires until their conclusion, except such as the parties themselves choose to make public. In the high court which is open to the public, a chief justice presides, with twelve assessors, and here alone the pleadings are verbal, eight advocates being privileged to speak in it: but there is no jury for them to address.

SECTION IV. *The Icelandic Tólftar-quidr.*

Iceland was anciently divided into thirty-nine provinces, or shires, each of which was called a Godord, and three of these made a Thing, or judicial district, in which the Varthing, or court for that district, was annually

[1] Repp, in his Treatise, p. 132, finds fault with Vogt for speaking of the Sandemænd in his Comment. de Homicidio as judges. He says: " He (Vogt) could not conceive the possibility of a court without them. The trial by jury in its ancient form—the primæval simplicity of the northern courts —was unintelligible to him." But surely the idea of courts of justice without judges would be an absurdity. It matters not, as respects the name by which the members ought to be called, whether they are learned lawyers or not. They are, to all intents and purposes, judges.

held.[1] There were, therefore, thirteen of these Things. Over each shire presided a magistrate called Godi, and three of these nominated for each Varthing twelve judges, who tried causes in the first instance. From these lay an appeal to the Fiordungs-dóm, a court held about Midsummer at the Althing,[2] and composed of thirty-six judges nominated by nine Godar (plural of Godi) for each quarter of Iceland. From this a cause might be appealed to the Fimtar-dóm, the fifth court, so called because it was the fifth in number of the courts held at the Althing. This was the tribunal of last resort, and the judges were nominated by the Godar, twelve for each quarter of the island, so that they nominally amounted to forty-eight. The law, however, required that the plaintiff should reject six of these, and the defendant another six; so that the number who actually sat to try a cause was reduced to thirty-six, or three times twelve, which was considered a doubly sacred number. But besides these regular courts, civil and criminal cases were tried by jurors in sets of five, nine, or twelve, according to the nature of the case. The last was called Tólftar-quidr (a nomination of twelve), and was much employed in cases of dispute between the Godars and their Thingmen. In such instances the Godi nominated eleven, and the other party the twelfth, who, however, was obliged to be one of the other two Godar who bore office in that Thing. But this tribunal was not confined to such causes alone. In other cases, eleven of the jurors were always nominated by the Godi, and he himself was the twelfth. And those were held to be the best qualified to serve, who were the nearest neighbors to the place where the cause of trial arose. If they did not agree, the judgment of the majority was binding,

---

[1] Our knowledge of Icelandic law is chiefly derived from the Grágás the Grey-Goose code.

[2] That is, All-thing, general court.

and it was determined by lot who should first declare his opinion.

Now according to the expression of Repp these different bodies of jurors " were employed for judging of facts," and this may seem to imply that, as in the case of English jurors, their province was confined to this. But this does not seem to be his meaning, for in another part of his work, when speaking of the limited nature of the Lawman's authority, he says: "Still he was entirely dependent on the Thingmen (deputies of the legislative assembly) in his judgments, and on the juries as a select body or committee of the Thingmen; or, rather, the judgment was theirs, and not his. Such was the case in Iceland." If so, then the Icelandic jurors had exactly the same office as those of Norway or Denmark; and what has been already said of the latter will equally apply to them. The truth, however, is, that questions of law and fact in those early ages, were generally so simple as to render a separation between them unnecessary. A decision upon the latter involved certain legal consequences which were definite and clear, and which were as well known to the members of the Thing as to the professed lawyer. The jurors, therefore, in determining the facts of the case, also applied the law, and were thus both judge and jury combined.

Legal process, however, in Iceland was by no means deficient in intricacy. It may be interesting to quote one or two cases from the Niáls Saga,[1] to show that in those primitive times, as well as in our own day, justice was sometimes defeated by technical objections. An eminent lawyer, named Asgrim, had a suit at the Althing against Ulf Uggason, and " there happened to Asgrim a thing which rarely occurred in any cause in which he

[1] Repp, Historical Treatise, 167.

was concerned; he was nonsuited for mistaking a point of law. He had nominated five jurors instead of nine. This was pleaded in defense." In another case, Odd Ofeigson prepared his cause for the Althing, and summoned nine jurors out of the district; but it so happened that one of them died, and Odd instantly summoned another in his place out of the district. Against this, an objection was made by two lawyers, Styrmir and Thorarin, who observed: "We do both of us perceive that Odd has here mistaken a point of law in the preliminaries of this cause, summoning a juror out of the district in place of the deceased, for this he ought to have done at the Thing; he must accordingly be nonsuited." One of them then went up to the court and spoke as follows: " Here are men ready to defend Ospak (the defendant) in this cause. Thou (addressing Odd) hast made a mistake in the preliminaries, and thou must be nonsuited; thou hast to choose one of two things: either give up the matter entirely, and proceed no further, or we will put in our plea, and avail ourselves of the circumstance, that we are a little more versed in the law than thou art." They at the same time stated to him wherein the error lay, whereat, says the Saga, Odd was astonished and greatly vexed, and left the court.

Odd's father, Ofeig, was a lawyer of a less formal school; and he spoke as follows: "How does it happen that Ospak is not outlawed? Are there not sufficient grounds to condemn him? Has he not, in the first place, committed theft, and then slain Vali?" To this the court answered: "All this is not denied; nor is it pretended that this issue of the cause is grounded in justice or equity; but there was an informality in the preliminaries of the process." Ofeig replied, " What informality could there be of greater moment than the crimes which this man has committed? Have you not made an oath that you will in your judgments adhere to justice and truth and the laws? But what can be more just and equitable than outlawing and depriving of all means of supporting life a most heinous culprit, who has deserved such a condemnation? As to that part of your oath by which you are enjoined to judge according to law, you ought, indeed, on the one side to be mindful of the laws of process: but, on the other, not forgetful of equity and justice; this ought to be your firm purpose when you take the oath, to condemn such as have deserved it, to punishment, and not to incur the heavy responsibility of suffering them to escape with impunity."

Such, then, were the ancient courts of justice in Scandinavia, and it has, I think, in the course of the inquiry, been proved that they were essentially different from our own jury. But independently of the reasons which have been already urged against the theory, that it was derived from them, the following consideration seems to be entitled to great weight. If the old tribunals of the North were the archetype of the jury, how could we have failed to discover the existence of their leading and peculiar features in the juridical system of the Anglo-Saxons? The Jutes and Angles and Saxons and Danes, who at various times overran and occupied England, came from the countries where the institutions of which we have been speaking prevailed, and if they had transplanted them to the land of their adoption, we must have found them noticed amongst the numerous laws and customs of the Anglo-Saxon period, of which records are still preserved. The existence of a nämbd would have been as distinctly marked in them as it is in the Scandinavian codes.

It is, in my opinion, the most improbable of theories to suppose that courts constituted like those of Norway and Sweden, with their twelve jurors and presiding Lawman, should have been introduced into Britain by the invading Northmen some centuries before the Norman

Conquest, and have become the common tribunals of the country, without leaving any record or trace of their existence until the reign of Henry II. And yet this must have been the case if the hypothesis is true, that the jury was copied from the courts of Scandinavia. For I hope to show that the form of our jury trial was then first established; and it is not pretended that the Norman king sent commissioners like the Decemviri to collect the laws and customs of the North, before he instituted the Grand Assize. If that mode of trial was taken from those countries, it must have gained footing here at the time when the migrating hosts who landed on our shores retained the liveliest recollection of the usages of the nations of which they had so recently formed a part. If an identity between the institutions is supposed to be proved by their resemblance, let those who maintain that theory explain why, the more we examine the periods following the Saxon and Danish immigrations into Great Britain, the more certainly we can prove that this mode of trial had then no existence.[1]

[1] The most remarkable approximation to our own institution seems to have existed at an early period in Russia for the trial of criminal cases. In the French translation of M. Karamsin's Histoire de Russie, we find the following: Le plus ancien code des lois russes porte que douze citoyens assermentés discutent suivant leur conscience les charges qui pèsent sur un accusé, et laissent aux juges le droit de determiner la peine.

CHAPTER III.

LEGAL TRIBUNALS OF ANCIENT GERMANY.

SECTION I. *Constitution of the old German Courts of Justice.*

THE earliest courts of the various German tribes were very much alike.[1] The basis of the Teutonic polity, and what may be called the unit of the system, was the division of the country into districts, called marken, several of which made up a gau. At the head of each gau was a territorial lord, who led forth the military array in war, and sat as president of the courts of justice within his jurisdiction. Thus, so late as the year 1299 the Archbishop of Mayence presided over the landgericht of his province. But as the increasing frequency and number of the tribunals rendered it impossible for the suzerain to attend all in person, presidents were appointed, who were at first chosen by the community at large,[2] but afterwards nominated by the king, until in many instances the office became a kind of hereditary right. The name we find usually applied to

---

[1] For the acccount here given of the old German tribunals, my authorities are chiefly Savigny's Geschichte des Romischen Rechts, Rogge's Gerichtswesen der Germanen, and Grimm's Deutsche Rechts Alterthümer. The latter work is a mine of antiquarian legal lore.

[2] Eliguntur in iisdem conciliis et principes, qui jura per pagos vicosque reddunt. Tac. Germ. c. 12.

these persons is grafio or graf,[1] for which the Latin equivalent comes, frequently occurs: other appellations, such as vogt, tunginus, missus regis, missus comitis, are also used; but at a later period these were superseded by the more general word richter.

The meetings at which judicial as well as other proceedings took place were of two kinds, called "unbidden" (ungebotene), and "bidden" (gebotene); or, as we should say, ordinary and extraordinary. The ordinary were held at stated times, once, twice, or thrice every year, according as the usage varied in different places. This was the "mallum legitimum" of the Franks and the gemot of the Anglo-Saxons. No notice was required in order that the freemen of the district might attend, for the day or days of meeting were known to all; and if they did not appear, they were liable to a fine. The extraordinary, however, were only summoned when there was some special business to be transacted; and previous notice was given of the time and place of meeting. Here, too, it seems that the absentees were fined.[2]

The presiding "comes" or "missus" had, however, no voice in the decision; and his duties, like those of the archon at Athens and prætor at Rome, were merely ministerial. The members of the court (urtheiler or schöffen) had the right to determine all questions of law and fact; and, with the assistance of witnesses in the early ages, no doubt did so. But as the law became

[1] This word has been usually derived from grau, canus, as though the idea of age or seniority were implied. But Grimm suggests the derivation ravo tignum (rafter), doms. Hence gfravo, contubernalis, comes. Gerefa, from which we have scir-gerefa, or sheriff has the same root as graf.

[2] Grimm, Deuts, Rechts Alterthümer. These meetings or courts had various names, derived (1) from the district, or (2) from the presiding officer, or (3) from the persons who attended them. Thus we find them called (1) landgericht, gaugericht, markgericht, stadtgericht, (2) grafen gericht, vogtsgericht, probstgericht, (3) rittergericht, lehengericht, mann gericht.

more technical, and the transactions of mankind more complex, the want of assistance from those who had applied themselves to legal studies would soon be felt Accordingly we find mention of such persons under the name of Sachibarone, whose office it was to act in the capacity of legal assessors or advisers to the uninstructed members of the court. But when, instead of a certain number of freemen, taken indiscriminately, selected persons were, as we shall presently notice. appointed judges, whose office required them to acquaint themselves with the law, the Sachibaro was superseded in his functions, and the name almost entirely disappears.[1]

The presiding officer held a staff or wand in his hand, and sat on a chair (stuhl) which was frequently of stone; while the other members of the court were seated beside or beneath him on a bench.[2]

These, who were in reality the judges, consisted originally, as we have seen, of all the freemen of the community, whose duty it was to attend the meeting;[3] and as it was necessary that every sentence, if not unanimous, should be determined by a majority, three freemen at least must be present to constitute the court. It was in order to obviate the occurrence of either one of two opposite evils, namely the absence of a sufficient number, or

---

[1] This is the view which Grimm takes of the meaning of Sachibaro. Deuts. R. Alter. 783. One of the old Bavarian laws was the following: Comes vero secum habeat judicem, qui ibi constitutus est judicare, et librum legis, ut semper rectum judicium judicet. Rogge thinks that this appointment of a judex was peculiar to the Bavarians and Alamanni. See his Gerichtswesen Germ. ch. iii. § 14.

[2] It seems that the president of the tribunal sat cross-legged, to signify the repose and gravity proper to his office. An old law prescribed that he should sit "like a grim-looking lion, with the right foot crossed over the left." See Grimm. D. R. A. 763.

[3] Hence they were called dingpflichtige and dingmänner, *i.e.* men whose duty it was to attend the ding or court. It deserves notice that the Latin equivalent for these words used by the old writers, is veridici.

the conflux of too many at these meetings, that a new custom was introduced.

The president, or perhaps in some instances the parties themselves, chose beforehand certain freemen, who were required to form a court for the hearing of the particular case. Their number varied, but was generally seven, and never, for the reason before given, less than three. The name by which those who were thus nominated to act in a judicial capacity were known amongst the old Franks was Rachinburgen.[1] Savigny applies this term to all the freemen, who, in contradistinction to the numerous body of the unfree (unfreien), had the full civic franchise; but Rogge and Grimm think it was restricted to those who were from time to time chosen to discharge judicial functions, and who did not form a separate class in the community, any more than our own jurymen. Perhaps, however, there is no great difference between these two views; for as all the freemen were competent to fill the office of judges, they were all in one sense Rachinburgen, or, at all events, might at any time become so by attending the courts.

Amongst the Lombards the corresponding name was Arimannen;[2] and they are both rendered in old charters

---

[1] One of two derivations has usually been given of the first two syllables of this word: (1) from racha, *i.e.* sache, causa, whence comes recht; (2) from rek or reiks, nobilis, implying the free members of the community, which Savigny prefers. Grimm, however, rejects both these, and derives the word from the Gothic ragin, which he says is employed merely to strengthen the idea of the word with which it is compounded. He thinks therefore, that the true interpretation of rachinburgen must be found in the meaning of burgen, which he derives either from burg, oppidum, so that a rachinburg would be civis optimo jure; or from burg, vadimonium, with reference to the system of mutual suretiship that prevailed amongst the Germans and Anglo-Saxons, as will be afterwards explained.

[2] Thus we find in a grant of the Emperor Henry IV. (A. D. 1084) the words donamus insurper... monasterio liberos homines quos vulgo Arimannos vocant habitantes in castello S. Viti. Savigny Gesch. i. c. 4. This writer inclines to the derivation of Arimannus from Ehre, signifying not honor in the restricted sense of nobility, but full rights of citizenship, the

and legal documents by the Latin equivalent of *boni homines,* "good men and true."

Before giving judgment, the members of the court retired from the presence of the presiding officer in order to consider their decision, or verdict, as it may be not improperly called.[1]

Such, then, were the Germanic courts of justice in their earliest form. They were composed of the freemen of the district, and presided over by the Graf, or Count. All had a right to attend and take part in the judgment, which therefore, as we may well suppose, was sometimes of a tumultuous character.[2] At a later period it was different, and we find judges duly appointed to the office, and called Scabini,[3] who, however, did not at first exclude the freemen, but seem to have sat with them as joint members of the court. The chief difference between them was, that it was optional to the latter to attend or not, as they pleased, except at the stated yearly meetings, while the Scabini were obliged to sit by virtue of their office. This change seems to have been introduced by or about the time of Charlemagne; for the name does not occur in any documents of an earlier

---

caput of the Romans. The word would thus have the same meaning as Rachinburgen, according to the etymology of the latter, which Savigny prefers. And certainly the examples which he adduces strongly bear out the correctness of his view, that both words were applied to the class of freemen generally.

[1] The existence of this practice, so curiously similar to that of a modern jury, is established by Grimm, who quotes from old annals and records a great variety of instances. D. R. A. 786.

[2] Of this we have an instance in the early part of the seventh century: Comes quidam ex genere Francorum cognomine Dotto, congregatâ non minima multitudine Francorum, in urbe Torndeo, ut erat illi injunctum ad dirimendas resedrat actiones. Tunc....præsentatus est quidam reus, quem omnis turba acclamabat dignum esse morte. Bouquet, 3, 533, cited by Savigny, I. c. 4, art. 2.

[3] Scabinus is derived by Grimm from scapan, "to order or decree." The Italian scabino, Spanish esclavin, and French echevin, are all the same word.

date,¹ but they are frequently used in the capitularies of that monarch. They were chosen by the presiding "comes," or "missus," with the assent of the people generally;² and the number required to form a court was seven: "ut nullus ad placitum banniatur (summoned)... exceptis scabineis septem qui ad omnia placita præesse debent;"³ but on solemn and important occasions they were increased to twelve.⁴ Grimm remarks that there is an unmistakable relation between these two numbers so applied—for as seven is the smallest majority that can exist amongst twelve, it was therefore necessary that seven at least should be agreed, to enable the court to pass sentence.⁵ But to entitle this argument to weight, it ought first to be shown, that in order to pronounce a valid judgment, the seven, in ordinary cases, were required to be unanimous. Otherwise there seems no reason why any other number greater then seven should not have answered the purpose equally well. Eight or ten admit of majorities consisting of five or six, which would be as efficient as one of seven, unless it were a fundamental rule that seven at least must, in all cases, concur in a decision. This, however, Grimm has not shown, nor do I believe it to have been the fact.

While noticing the many points of resemblance between the Scabini, or judges of the Teutonic courts, and the English jury, Savigny mentions one important difference, that the former decided all questions of law and fact alike; whereas the latter are restricted wholly to the finding of facts, and the law applicable to the case is

---

[1] Savigny, Ib.
[2] Ut missi nostri, ubicunque malos scabineos inveniunt, ejiciant, et totius populi concensu in loco eorum bonos eligant, et cum electi fuerint, jurare faciant, ut scienter injuste judicare non debeant. Capit. ann. 829.
[3] Capit. ann. 803.
[4] Capit. ann. 819.
[5] Deuts. Rechts. Alter. 777. Sometimes, but not often, we find the number of the court consisting of a multiple of seven or twelve.

laid down by the presiding judge.[1] He observes that this is analogous to the proceedings of the Roman tribunals, where the prætor directed the judices as to the law; and he declares himself unable to account for an agreement between the two systems in a practice in which they both differed from the custom of the Teutonic courts, with which the jury has so much in common.

But when we come to consider what were the original and proper functions of the English Jury, we shall see that the difficulty felt by Savigny vanishes at once. It never was intended that they should determine any questions of law. They had in fact no judicial duty to perform. They were summoned to inform the court, which was distinct from themselves, of certain facts of which they had peculiar means of knowledge, and then their office was at an end. The Scabini, on the contrary, were both court and jury. They determined the question of innocence or guilt, or whatever fact might be in dispute, and they also awarded and pronounced the judgment.

But, moreover, Savigny is not quite correct in saying in this sense, that amongst the Romans the question of law was for the prætor, and that of fact for the judices. In civil causes the parties went before the prætor, who seems to have settled what the law was, supposing the facts proved, and he then appointed a judex to try the case, who might, if he thought fit, call in as assessors persons learned in the law to assist him with their advice; and as they sat not as magistrates on the tribunal, but on benches, as it were ad pedes judicis, they were called Judicis Pedanei. This is the meaning of the passage in

[1] Gesch. Rom. Rechts, 1. c. 4, art. 2, Die Schöffen. Bernardi, in his Origine de la Legislation Francaise, has confounded the distinction between the Scabini and the Rachinburgen, and imagines that the boni homines were persons chosen to represent the whole community at a trial, and were the judges of fact, while the Scabini were judges of law. If this were so, the tribunal would closely resemble that of the modern jury. But Savigny has clearly shown that this view is erroneous.

Aulus Gellius: Finally, to prevent all danger of determining questions of law by persons not learned in the law, they used to appoint one or more assessors, learned in the law, by whose advice they (the judges) were bound to determine all questions of law;[1] which Mr. Starkie, by mistake, applies to the judices presided over by a prætor at the public criminal trials, who do, as before noticed, present some curious features of resemblance to a modern jury.[2]

The nearest approach among ourselves to such a tribunal as the Scabini, is the House of Lords when it sits as the High Court of Parliament to try a peer, or, in the case of an impeachment, a commoner; on which occasions the Lord High Steward acts as president, but the peers are judges both of law and fact. This, however, is only during the sitting of parliament; for when such a trial takes place during the recess, it is the court of the Lord High Steward, to which the peers are summoned,

---

[1] Denique ut tanto minus esset periculi ne imperiti judicarent, solebant aliquando iis unus aut plures judicii socii jurisperiti adjungi, quorum consilio omnia agerent. Noct. Att. xii. 13. See Heinecc. Antiq. Rom. Syntag. iv. tit. 5, 17.

[2] In his Law of Evidence, I 5, n (d), Mr. Starkie says: "The principal and characteristic circumstance in which the trial by a Roman differed from that of a modern jury, consisted in this, that in the former case, neither the prætor, nor any other officer distinct from the jury, presided over the trial to determine as to the competency of witnesses, the admissibility of evidence, and to expound the law as connecting the facts with the allegations to be proved on the record; but in order to remedy the deficiency, they resorted to this expedient: the jury generally consisted of one or more lawyers, and thus they derived that knowledge of law from their own members which was necessary to enable them to reject inadmissible evidence, and to give a correct verdict as compounded both of law and fact." The expressions "jury" and "verdict," here used by Mr. Starkie, tend only to mislead. He mistakes the calling in of assessors by a judge in civil causes, for the addition of lawyers to the panel of judices, who in criminal trials at Rome determined the question of guilt or innocence, and who were, in many respects, analogous to modern jurymen; but we never find any jurisperiti added to them.

and he is then the sole judge of matters of law, while they are triers of matters of fact.[1]

SECTION II. *The Mode of Proof in the Ancient Courts of Germany.*

We have next to consider the mode of proof by which questions were decided amongst the ancient Germans; and the inquiry deserves particular attention from the important bearing which it has upon the origin of trial by jury amongst ourselves, as it will be hereafter explained. But so much as relates to the use of compurgation as a means of determining questions of innocence or guilt, as well as other disputes, may be conveniently deferred until we speak of the judicial system of the Anglo-Saxons, of which it was a prominent feature. Here it will be sufficient to notice the character and functions of witnesses, not called like the compurgators merely to assert their belief in the credibility of a party, but to depose to certain facts supposed to be within their own cognizance.

But it will be necessary to remember that our attention is here directed to a state of society entirely different from any which now exists in Europe; and we must endeavor, as far as possible, to divest ourselves of the ideas and prejudices derived from modern systems of judicature. One of the most striking characteristics of the olden time was the unbounded confidence placed in the oath or word of a freeman legally competent as a witness. It was in general conclusive of a matter in dispute, and when called for in due form, had all the effect of a decision by a court of justice.[2] But all freemen were not equally competent to give evidence in all cases. Only those who were associated as inhabitants of the same mark (markgenossen) could be witnesses for or against

---

[1] See 19, State Trials, 962-964.
[2] See Rogge, Gerichtsw. der Germ. 93-131. Grimm., Deuts. Rechts. Alter.

each other. And of these the competency varied according to the subject-matter of their testimony. With respect to such things as might well be presumed to be of public notoriety within the district, such as the right to the possession of land, as proved by acts of ownership, or offenses against the peace of the community, every one of the markgenossen who possessed a certain amount of property might give evidence, although he had not actually seen what had occurred.[1] Nearness of neighborhood in such cases was deemed sufficient to qualify a man for being a witness, for he could hardly in those times be ignorant of matters of common repute around him. Here we see what credit was given to the testimony of the vicinage; a principle which had such an important influence upon our own early jurisprudence.

But besides circumstances and events of general interest to the community, to prove which all the free members were competent witnesses, there were, of course others of a private nature to which the same presumption of public knowledge could not apply. To attest these, therefore, the attendance of persons was required who might be able, when called upon afterwards, to declare what had taken place in their presence. Thus, where the right of succession in a father to a wife's property depended on the birth of a living child, witnesses were summoned to be present at the lying-in[2]—a custom which still exists in this country when children are born to the reigning sovereign. So also in the case of entering upon an inheritance (or "being served heir," according to the expression of the Scotch law), the alienation of lands,

---

[1] Ille homo qui hoc testificare voluerit, commarchanus ejus debet esse, et debet habare sex solidorum pecuniam et similem agrum. Leg. Bainv. T. 16, c. 1, § 2. Sanè si eos (caballos) in re sua damnum sibi facientes invenerit clauseritque. vicinis suis et consortibus contestetur. Leg. Burg. T. 49, c. 3.

[2] —hæreditas materna ad patrem ejus pertineat, eo tamen si testes habet pater ejus quod vidissent illum infantem oculos aperire ut potuisset culmen domus videre et quatuor parietes. Leg. Alam. T. 92.

the manumission of a serf, the buying and selling of chattels, the payment of debts, and contracts generally. And where homicide was committed, even in self-defense or from any other justifiable cause, it was necessary for the slayer immediately to make known what had happened, to the nearest persons he could find, that their testimony as to his conduct and demeanor immediately after the event might exonerate him from guilt. Common prudence, indeed, would dictate to every man the same course at the present day.

Among the ancient Germans the credibility of all competent witnesses was the same. Their testimony was deemed of equal weight, nor was the character of the witness taken into account. Indeed, with one exception, no kind of crime disqualified him or affected his legal credit. The offenses of which society then took cognizance were almost entirely those of violence against persons or property. But these could be all atoned for by the payment of a pecuniary compensation or fine, and when this was satisfied there was an end of the matter, and no stain rested upon the character of the offender. The exception to which I allude was the crime of having borne false witness: a person guilty of this was incapable of giving testimony again.[2] At a later period, however, as in the time of Charlemagne, we find it laid down that a witness ought to be one cui ille, contra quem testimoniare debet, nullum crimen possit indicere.[3]

Except amongst the Lombards, all evidence was given upon oath, and as a natural consequence from what has been already said, it had the same effect as a judgment of the court. It was, in fact, the judgment pronounced by the mouths of witnesses; for, in most cases, all that was required was to ascertain the truth of the matter in dispute

---

[1] Leg. Rothar. c. 16. Leg. Bainv. T. 8, e. 5.
[2] See Rogge, Greichts. Germ.
[3] Capit. lib. iii. c. 32.

—and this their testimony declared. Hence, no formal judgment on the part of the members of the court (schöffen) was required, and where the law had clearly prescribed what consequences were to flow from proved or admitted facts, their office was superfluous. The facts were found by the witnesses, and their evidence was equivalent to a judicial decision of the question.[1] Hence, also, we find that their number, like that of the judges, was usually seven,[2] and at a somewhat later period they are spoken of as associated with the presiding missus, or comes, in the trial of causes; ut adjutores Comitum sint ad justicias faciendas.[3] And even when it became customary for a defendant to adduce counter evidence on his part, so that there arose a conflict of testimony, this was not weighed and determined by the court, but the credibility of either side was decided by the combat, as an appeal to the God of Truth. Nothing can more clearly prove that the evidence was regarded in the nature of a verdict or judgment, for usually the court itself, in convicting an offender, did no more than sentence him to undergo the ordeal, which gave him still a chance of escape; and amongst the old Saxons of the continent the judges (in number seven) might[3] themselves be challenged to fight by the culprit and six of his friends.[4]

Moreover, the witnesses not only deposed to facts, but also gave evidence with respect to value, where an injury to property had been committed, or payment of a debt had been withheld. In other words, they determined the amount of damages. For their testimony was conclusive, and the court did not attempt to interfere.[5]

[1] This explains what Malblanc says in his Doctrina de Jurejurando: Id enim observavi, olim præsertim inte Germanos difficulter judices s. arbitros a testibus discerni potuisse. Hence, the witnesses were said to adjudicate, as in an example from an old record quoted by Grimm, testes qui, præsentes fuerunt, et hanc causam dijudicaverunt. Deuts. R. Alter. 859.

[2] Grimm, ubi supra.   [3] Capit. Louis, ann. 812.
[4] Sachsenspiegel, ii. art. 12. Rogge, Gerichtsw. Germ. 89.
[5] Rogge, Gerichtsw. Germ. c. iv. § 28.

Now when we come to consider the earliest constitution of the jury, we shall see some striking points of resemblance between its functions and those of the old German witnesses. Indeed they so far coincided that it is remarkable that in this country alone, that institution was developed from a state of things so nearly similar. Why it should have been unknown on the continent, and yet have flourished with so much vigor in England, is a problem of which the solution, I believe, is to be found in the fact of the institution in Germany of the Scabini under Charlemagne. These were the sole judges of fact as well as law. They absorbed the whole judicial functions of the court, and therefore there was no room for another body distinct from them, whose office should be conclusively to determine questions of fact for them. And when the principle was once established of thus making the court consist entirely of a limited number of duly qualified judges, the transition to which I have before adverted to single judges, nominated by and dependent on the crown, who decided without the intervention of a jury, was a natural and almost necessary consequence.

CHAPTER IV.

THE JUDICIAL SYSTEM OF THE ANGLO-SAXONS.

SECTION I. *Trial by Jury unknown to the Anglo-Saxons.*

IN his admirable edition of Blackstone's "Commentaries,"[1] Mr. Sergeant Stephen says, that "When the Anglo-Saxon memorials are carefully scrutinized, we find them to be such as even to justify a doubt whether trial by jury (in any sense approaching to our use of that term) did actually exist among us at any time before the Norman Conquest." This statement is, I believe, short of the truth. It may be confidently asserted that trial by jury was unknown to our Anglo-Saxon ancestors; and the idea of its existence in their legal system has arisen from a want of attention to the radical distinction between the members or judges composing a court, and a body of men apart from that court, but summoned to attend it in order to determine conclusively the facts of the case in dispute. This is the principle on which is founded the intervention of a jury; and no trace whatever can be found of such an institution in Anglo-Saxon times.[2]

[1] Vol. III. 588, n. (z).
[2] In "The Chronotype—an American Memorial of Persons and Events" —New York, April, 1873. Vol. I. No. 4—we find on page 117, the following

" In Woodward's ' History of Wales from the Earliest Times,' accounts are given of several sovereign Welsh princes and kings of the name of Morgan

If it had existed, it is utterly inconceivable that distinct mention of it should not frequently have occurred in the body of Anglo-Saxon laws and contemporary chronicles which we possess, extending from the time of Ethelbert (A. D. 568–616) to the Norman Conquest. Those who have fancied that they discover indications of its existence during that period have been misled by false analogies, and inattention to the distinguishing features of the jury trial which have been previously pointed out. While, however, we assert that it was unknown in Saxon times, it is nevertheless true that we can recognize the traces of a system which paved the way for its introduction, and rendered its adoption at a later period neither unlikely nor abrupt. This is, indeed, just what we might expect. Our early jurispru-

---

warlike, and who constituted themselves formidable barriers against Anglo-Saxon domination and encroachment, some of them living as far back as A. D. 400. To one of these ancient kings—Morgan of Gla-Morgan—about A. D. 725, is accredited the invention and adoption of the Trial by Jury, which he called 'the Apostolic Law.' 'For,' quoth our regal and pious namesake, 'as Christ and his twelve Apostles were finally to judge the world, so human tribunals should be composed of the king and twelve wise men! And this, it seems, was a century and a half prior to the reign of Alfred the' Great, to whom is generally accredited the honor of originating this form of trial."

We find other reference to Woodward's History, but have been unable to procure a copy of the book itself. The Morgan of Gla-Morgan here referred to, was an early chief or king of Wales, who took up arms against Edward II., who laid heavy imposts upon the Welsh to support his war in France. He is referred to as prominent in the records of that country in a black-letter volume in the Astor Library, New York. " The historie of Cambria, now called Wales, written in the British language above two hundred years past : translated into English by H. Floyd, gentleman : corrected, augmented, and continued out of records and best approved authors, by Daniel Powell Doctor in Divinitie. Imprinted at London by Rafe Newberie and Henrie Denham cum priveligio Regiæ magistratis: 1584, pp. 71, 79, 122, 380, 382. His province of Gla-Morgan was captured in A. D. 987, by Meredyth, another Welsh king, and despoiled, "so that no place was free from sword and fire"—Id. And see also Warrington's " History of Wales, p. 337.

dence was too imperfect not to be in a transitionary state. Its history is analogous to that of our constitution which has been formed by the slow growth of ages, and is the result of experience rather than the offspring of theory. But if this be true of our political, it is still more so of our judicial, institutions. The prejudice against any sudden change in them is great. They are interwoven with the usages and customs of the people, whose rights seem to be endangered when the mode of maintaining or enforcing them is altered.

It has been well said, that " by far the greatest portions of the written or statute laws of England consist of the declaration, the re-assertion, the repetition, or the re-enactment, of some older law or laws, either customary or written, with additions or modifications. The new building has been raised upon the old groundwork; the institutions of one age have always been modeled and formed from those of the preceding, and their lineal descent has never been interrupted or disturbed."[1]

The proof of the non-existence of the jury amongst the Anglo-Saxons must depend upon a careful consideration of their judicial system, so far as we are able to understand it; and this, therefore, must be the subject of our inquiry. But in order to obtain an accurate idea of that system, it is necessary, first, to notice two remarkable features of their society, not indeed peculiar to them, for we find that they existed on the Continent as well as in England, but which seem to have been more fully developed, and to have had more influence upon the national institutions here than elsewhere. These were the Wergild and Frithborh, both intimately connected with each other—upon which it will be useful to say a few words.

[1] Palgrave's English Commonw 1. 6.

Section II. *The Wergild.*

The wer-gild (called also man-bot) was a composition in money to be paid for personal injury done to another, according to the value which the law set upon his life.[1] For amongst the Saxons, and indeed all the nations of the Teutonic family, every freeman was deemed to possess a certain pecuniary value, which varied according to his rank; and this determined the amount of compensation which he was entitled to receive for a wound or a blow.[2] We find it mentioned in the earliest Anglo-Saxon laws extant—those of King Ethelbert—which are full of minute regulations on the subject. Every bodily injury, from the loss of a nail to the destruction of life, had its appropriate price, which must be paid by the offender; and it was only on failure of this payment that he could be punished for his wrongful act. A regular tariff of penalties was thus established, which, as will be hereafter noticed, gave rise to appellations by which different classes were distinguished. The king had his wergild as well as the lowest ceorl.[3]

The great object of this system of pecuniary compensation for acts of violence, was to prevent the wild justice of revenge, and put a check upon the right of feud which was cherished amongst the Teutonic nations as one of the inalienable rights of freedom. When a member of a family was slain, all his surviving relations felt themselves called upon to avenge his death, and they immediately

---

[1] Wer signifies "man," and therefore wer-gild, or wer-geld, means the worth or payment of a man.

[2] Luitur enim homicidium certo armentorum vel pecorum numero. Tac. Germ. c. 21. By one of the Ripuarian laws, leg. ii. tit. xxxvi. De diversis interfectionibus, it was provided, that animals might be given instead of money as a wergild, their various values being computed in solidi. Thus, si quis weregildum solvere debet, bovem cornutum videntem et sanum pro duobus solidis tribuat.

[3] See "Ancient Laws and Institutes," tit. Wergilds.

became the enemies of, and in a state of feud (fǎ) with the person who had inflicted the wound.[1] It was therefore provided that, instead of this lex talionis, so destructive of the peace and well-being of the community, the injured party if he survived, or his relations if he died,[2] should be content with a money-payment as a compensation, or damages for the wrong done to him; and by a law of Alfred, if any man attempted private redress by vengeance before he had shown his readiness to accept the wergild if offered to him, he was to be severely punished. If, however, the offender refused to pay the legal compensation, he was exposed to the vengeance of the injured party and his friends; and this alternative was expressed by an old Anglo-Saxon proverb, Bicge spere of side other bere, "Buy off the spear or bear it."[3]

It appears, also, that if an affray took place and several were killed on both sides, an account was taken and balance struck of the amount of slaughter, and of the numbers and value (wer) of the slain. If on both sides these were equal, then no vengeance could be taken, or demand made of compensation; but if one side had sustained greater loss that the other, it was entitled to compensation (wer) or bot or vengeance to the extent of the overplus or excess.[4]

---

[1] Thus Tacitus tell us of the ancient Germans, Suscipere tam inimicitias seu patris seu propinqui quam amicitias necesse est. De Moribus Germ. c. 21.

[2] —recipitque satisfactionem universa domus. Id.

[3] Leg. Edw. Conf. 12. Amongst the Lombards, females were not entitled to share in the compensation because they could not "bear the feud." Quia filiœ ejus, eo quod fœmineo sexu esse probantur, non possunt ipsam faidam levare, ideo prospeximus ut ipsam compositionem non recipiant. Leg. Luitpr. Lang. ii. c. 7. The law seems to have been different elsewhere Et quia fœmina cum armis defendere nequiverit, duplicem compositionem accipiat. Leg. Bainv. iii. c. 13. Perhaps, however, these laws refer to different wergilds; the first to payment of compensation in the case of a relative, the last to payment for injury done to the woman herself.

[4] See Oaths, Anc. Laws and Inst. p. 183. Leg. Hen. I. c. 70, § 9. S.

But besides the payment to the injured party there was a penalty due to the state, which was called wite. "All crimes were by the Anglo-Saxons considered in a twofold light; first, as a damage or mischief done to the individual; next, as an offense against the peace of the whole state; the punishment, therefore, was apportioned in a twofold ratio. The injured person, or his relations or gild-brothers, received compensation for the injury done to him or them, in the shape of damages. The state, or those to whom as an especial privilege the state had delegated this power, received the fine for the breach of the peace."[1]

Section III. *The Frithborh.*

In the absence of anything like an organized police for the prevention and punishment of crime, the Anglo-Saxons, in common with all the Teutonic nations, endeavored to secure some of the blessings of a more settled state of society through the medium of the system known in later times by the name of Frank-pledge. This word, however, is incorrect, and suggestive of error, for it is derived from Frithborh, the pledge or guarantee of peace—which was corrupted into Freoborh, and translated by the Norman jurists, who were imperfectly, if at all, acquainted with Anglo-Saxon, into liberum plegium, instead of pacis plegium. It means, therefore, a "peace-pledge," the mutual guarantee by which every member of a tithing as well as of a mæg, or family, became a pledge or surety (borh) to the other members, as well as to the state, for the maintenance of the public peace.

se invicem occidant liberi, vel nativitate vel casu servi, unus pro alio jaceat. Si superabundat aliquis eorum in genitura, quærant parentes ejus Weræ vel vindictæ superplus. Si unius dignitatis et paritatis sint, in eo consistat.

[1] Kemble's Introduction to the Codex Diplomaticus Ævi Saxonici, lvii A most valuable dissertation upon parts of the Anglo-Saxon law.

In the collection of laws called Leges Edwardi Confessoris, there is a full account of this universal system of bail. "Another peace the greatest of all there is, whereby all are maintained in former state, to wit, in the establishment of a guarantee which the English call Frithborgas, with the exception of the men of York, who call it Tenmannetale, that is, the number of ten men. And it consists in this, that in all the vills throughout the kingdom all men are bound to be in a guarantee by tens, so that if one of the ten men offend, the other nine may hold him to do right."[1]

These members of a tithing were fellow-gildsmen, who if a crime were committed by any of their body, were to arrest him and bring him to justice. If they thought him innocent, they were to clear him by their oaths—or if he were convicted and sentenced, they were to pay the wergild and wite—and if he fled from justice they were to make oath that they had no guilty participation in his escape; which if they failed to prove, they had to pay a penalty proportioned to the offense. So, on the other hand, they were entitled to receive a part of the compensation paid by a wrongdoer, for any injury inflicted on a member of their gild or tithing.[2]

We find also amongst the same laws an enactment which might with some advantage perhaps be revived at the present day in some parts of Ireland, where, owing to connivance or intimidation, the detection of crime has in many districts become so difficult. This provided that the hundred which did not within a month and a day discover the slayer of a person murdered within their boundary, should pay a sum of forty-six

---

[1] Leg. Edw. Conf. 20, and see Leg. Edg. II, 6; Cnut, 20; Gul. Conq. iii. 14.

[2] Si quis occidat hujusmodi qui parentes non habent, compositionis medietas solvatur Regi et medietas gildonibus. Leg. Alf. Chron. Bromton apud Twysden, p. 825.

marks, of which forty went to the king, and the remaining six went to the relations of the slain, if the murderer were not found and brought to justice within a year.[1]

The original of these societies must be sought for in family unions afterwards extended beyond relationship by blood to connection by neighborhood. At first the mægas or members of the same family were alone responsible for the conduct of each other, and a law of Ethelbert provided that in the event of a homicide fleeing the country, the family (mægas) should pay half the wergild, called there leod, of the slain man. The first mention of gildsmen occurs, I believe, in the laws of Alfred, where it is provided that "if a man kinless of paternal relations fight and slay a man, then, if he have maternal relations, let them pay a third part of the wer; his fellow-gildsmen a third part; and for a third part let him flee (be banished). If he have no maternal relatives let his fellow-gildsmen pay half, and for half let him flee."

SECTION IV. *The Anglo-Saxon Courts.*

The different kinds of Anglo-Saxon courts will next occupy our attention; but the information we possess respecting them is too scanty to furnish materials for a very satisfactory inquiry.[2]

We have seen that the frithborh was a system of mutual bail for the preservation of the public peace. The smallest subdivision for this purpose was the tithing (teothing), consisting of ten families, the members of which were responsible for the good conduct of each other, and, on this account, the society was sometimes called wer-borhe or sureties for the payment of the "wer." The head-man of this community was named

[1] Leg. Edw. Conf. 15.
[2] See some remarks as to the origin of courts, in Morgan's Law of Literature, vol. II., chapter on Legal Reports.

teothings-ealdor, or tienheofod; and he seems to have acted as a kind of arbitrator in settling disputes about matters of a trifling nature; but whether he had actually a court for administering justice, does not very clearly appear.[1]

Next in order came the Hundred (hundrede), which in its original constitution consisted of ten tithings, or a hundred families, associated together by a similar bond of mutual responsibility. In some parts of England the territorial division was called a Wapentake[2] instead of Hundred. The head-man was called the hundredes-ealdor, or simply gerefa,[3] which was the generic name for the officer or reeve of any district. He acted as the presiding officer of the hundred-court, which met once at least every month,[4] and had both civil and criminal jurisdiction. The bishop, however, of the diocese had co-ordinate authority with him, and the court had cognizance of ecclesiastical causes, which were entitled to

---

[1] Speaking of the Rolls in the Rotuli Cur. Reg. of the tenth year of Richard I., for Hertford, Essex, and Middlesex, Sir F. Palgrave says, in his Introduction to that collection: "These rolls are amongst the earliest connecting links between the Anglo-Saxon law and the English common law, properly so called. From them we learn, that in those counties which corresponded with the ancient kingdom of Essex, the tithing was not a division of territory, but an organization of the inhabitants. The Decenna, Decania, or Frankpledge, answered by its Headborgh: he was the leader and chieftain of the band."

[2] The ordinary derivation of this word is from wappen, arms, and tæcan, to touch, signifying that the inhabitants of each hundred did homage to their headman, by touching his spear with their weapons. See Leg. Edw. Conf. c. 33. Phillips, however, in his Gesch. des Angles. Rechts, thinks that the word denotes the mode in which the different hundreds were distinguished by the painting of their arms, taking tæcan in the sense of "to mark."

[3] This term, however, is not found earlier than the Leges Edw. Confessoris. In the Leg. Hen. I. c. 91, § 1, he is called "aldremannus hundreti." The origin of the word gerefa has been already explained; see ante, p. 33, note.

[4] Ic wille that acle gerefa haebbe a gemot ymbe feower wucan. "I will that each reeve hold a court always (once) in four weeks." Leg. Edw.

precedence over any other business. Trials by ordeal seem most frequently to have taken place there. Sometimes it was formed by a union of two or more hundreds, as in the case where the litigant parties belonged to different hundreds, or there was a deficiency in the numbers requisite to constitute a court.[1]

Besides this, there was a scir-gemot, or court of the shire or county, which was held twice every year, or oftener, if occasion required.[2] It was convened by the shire-reeve (sometimes called ealdor-man), who presided over it, assisted by the bishop. Here causes were decided and business transacted which affected the inhabitants of several of the hundreds.

The highest court of all was that of the king, in which he himself was present attended by his councilors, or witan. We are not, however, to suppose that this was a permanent or fixed tribunal. It was held as occasion required, and wherever the king happened to be. Of this several instances occur in the Saxon Chronicle and the monkish histories of the time. But it was in general only a court of appeal; for it was a rule of Anglo-Saxon law that no man should apply for justice to the king unless he had first sought it in vain in the inferior courts, or, as it was expressed, he had become "nanes rihtes wyrthe innan his hundrede."[3]

Such were the different Anglo-Saxon courts. But with respect to those of the tithing and hundred a question naturally occurs, how territorial divisions founded upon numerical proportions of the inhabitants could be maintained? Constant fluctuations would necessarily take place from the increase of families and the migration of

[1] Si aliquid in Hundredis agendorum penuria judicum vel casu aliquo transferendum sit in duas vel tres vel amplius Hundredas. Leg. Hen. I. c. 7.

[2] Leg. Edg. II. 5; Cnut. II. 17; Edw. Conf. 35. There were also small town-courts, burhgemote, with limited jurisdiction.

[3] Leg. Cnut. II. 16.

residents; and we should imagine that in the course of a very few years an arrangement previously made on this system would be disturbed, and the names derived from the number of families within a given district rendered inappropriate. This difficulty seems to have been provided for by a periodical adjustment in the following manner. It was the duty of all the freemen of a hundred to meet twice a year and examine into the state of the tithings to see whether they had their full complement of members, and whether there was a deficiency or excess of numbers.[1] If this happened, we must suppose, although it is not so expressly stated, that a fresh numerical arrangement was made from time to time.

It is, however, important to notice that this provision for the meeting of the hundred twice a year does not occur in any of the Saxon laws now extant. But we must not conclude that because it is first mentioned in the Leges Henrici Primi the custom did not prevail before the time of that monarch. These Leges are nothing more than a collection of laws and usages which existed in Anglo-Saxon times; and as the greater part of them continued in force after the Norman invasion, they are spoken of in the present tense as still existing. The compilation seems to have been made by some private person, and must not be regarded as a code of laws published by the authority of the State.[2]

Although originally, and perhaps always in strict right, the whole of the free male adults of a district might at-

---

[1] Speciali tamen plenitudine, si opus est, bis in anno conveniant in hundretum suum quicunque liberi, tam hudefest quam folgarii, ad dinoscendum, scilicet, inter cetera, si decanie plene sint, vel qui. quomodo, qua ratione, recesserint, vel super-accreverint. Leg. Henrici I. c. viii. § I. The tam hudefest quam folgarii, mean "as well householders as mere retainers;" hudefest is a corruption of heorthfest—men who had a dwelling or hearth of their own: folgarii, retainers who lived in the house or on the premises of their lord. See Glossary to Ancient Laws and Inst.

[2] See Phillips, Eng. Reichs u. Rechtsgeschichte, I. 202.

tend and form the monthly or half-yearly court held for that district, yet it is by no means improbable that in practice this became limited to a smaller number. The analogy of what took place in the continental tribunals, is, as we have seen, in favor of this supposition, and Grimm seems to be clearly of opinion that there was such a class of judges amongst the Anglo-Saxons; but he says that it can not be affirmed with certainty whether they were designated by any particular name.[1]

There are several passages to be found amongst the Anglo-Saxon laws which throw light upon this question. Thus one of the laws of Ethelred provided, "Let doom stand where thanes are of one voice: if they disagree, let that stand which VIII. of them say;[2] and let those who are there outvoted pay each of them VI. half-marks." And an order respecting the " Dunsætas," or dwellers in Wales, ran thus: " XII. lahmen[3] shall administer the law (or, explain it, riht tæcan) to the British and English VI. English and VI. British (Wylisce). Let them forfeit all they possess if they administer it wrongly, or let them clear themselves that they know no better."

Another law of Ethelred[4] enacted, that a "gemot (or

---

[1] His mistake in thinking that the term "witnesses" (gecorene to gewitneese) was applied to them will be pointed out hereafter. At a later period after the Norman Conquest, we find those who attended the hundred, county, and manorial courts, to try offenses and determine disputes there, called secta and sectatores; and the obligation to attend was in the nature of a tenure, for neglect of which they might be distrained to appear. Fleta II. c. 53–65.

[2] In the compilation known by the name of Leges Henrici Primi, we find the following law: Vincat sententia meliorum et cui justitia magis acquieverit. Unless we consider meliorum as equivalent to plurimorum, and indicating a majority, this would open a wide door to cavil and dispute. Allen, in his notes to Leg. Hen. I. (Anc. Laws and Inst.), assumes it to mean a majority, and to be a substitution for the two-thirds, or eight, of the law of Ethelred, and he asks whether justitia here means the king's justiciary? This interpretation is at least doubtful.

[3] Lah-man means jurisconsultus, judex.

[4] Le_. Ethel. III. 3.

meeting) be held in every wapentake; and the XII. senior (yldastan) thanes go out and the reeve with them, and swear on the relic that is given to them in hand, that they will accuse no innocent man, nor conceal any crime."[1]

Now this may possibly mean that the thanes here spoken of were to act as the judges of the gemot, or court; and such is the opinion of Dufresne, Brady, and Hicks, who think that they correspond to the scabini of the Franks. In this sense also the passage is taken by Phillips, in his able and accurate work, the Geschichte des Anglesachsischen Rechts. But the more general, and perhaps preferable, view is, that the thanes were in the nature of inquisitors of crimes committed within the district; and accordingly Sir Francis Palgrave,[2] speaking of this law, says, "If the wapentake, or hundred, impeached the offender, the suitor spake by the twelve chief thanes, who together with the gerefa were sworn that they would not accuse any innocent man, nor conceal any crime. . . The resemblance of the twelve thanes to a grand jury is sufficiently obvious; and the principal difference between the Anglo-Saxon echevins[3] and the modern inquest of the shire, seems to have consisted in the greater stability of the ancient magistracy, who, judging from the analogies afforded by the burghs, held their offices for a definite period." I hope, however, to be able to show in the course of this chapter, that the functions of the twelve thanes, considered in this point of view, did not materially differ from those of the court itself at that time—so that the two theories are hardly at variance with each other.

[1] Nænne sacleasan man forsecgean ne nænne sacne forhelan. Phillips (Gesch. Ang. Rechts) translates forsecgean, "condemno." Mr. Thorpe (Anc. Laws and Inst. I. 295) renders ne nænne sacne forhelan, " nor conceal any guilty one." But this is incorrect, for sacne means a thing, not a person.

[2] English Commonwealth, I. 213.

[3] Sir F. Palgrave here applies the term echevins to the Thanes. It is the French form of scabini, whose office has been previously explained.

So far, therefore, as the extant laws give us any information, it seems not improbable that the usual number of numbers composing the court was twelve. But we find mention in the old chronicles of causes decided amongst the Anglo-Saxons by twenty-four judges. Thus in the following passage from the Historia Eliensis:[1] "Tandem veniens Ægelwinus Alderman ad Grantebrucge habuit ibi grande placitum civium et Hundretanorum coram XXIV. judicibus." In this case we may suppose that there was a union of two hundreds, which probably happened because the suit was one of importance. At the same time I do not think that the right of all the freemen of the district to attend these courts in the capacity of judges was taken away.[2] But it came to be looked upon rather as a burden than a privilege, and as such it is spoken of by Bracton and Fleta, when they discuss the duty of the secta or sectatores to appear in the county and baronial courts.

SECTION V. *Examples of Anglo-Saxon Civil Trials.*

Before quitting this part of the subject it will be useful to give one or two instances of trials which took place before these primitive tribunals.[3] They will help us to understand the system better than a more lengthened disquisition.

A large meeting or court (magna concio) was held at Witlesford, in Cambridgeshire, over which Ægelwin the ealdorman presided. When all were seated, one Wensius a relation of Wulfric, rose and laid claim to two hydes of land at Swaffham, of which he said that he and his

---

[1] I. 34, and see Ib. 13.

[2] Thus at the court mentioned in the text, held at Witlesford in Cambridgeshire, we are told that Ægelwinus Aldermannus et omnes meliores concionatores de comitatu Grantebrycge were present. Hist. Eliens. I. 45.

[3] Hist. Eliens. I, 45.

kinsmen had been unjustly deprived, and had not been paid their value. Upon this Ægelwin, the president, asked the assembly if there was any one present who knew how Walstun, the party in possession, had become the owner of the land. Alfric of Wicham answered, that Wulstan had bought it from Wensius, the claimant, for eight pounds, which he paid him in two sums, at two different times, and that the last of these sums was sent to him by the hands of Leofwin, the son of Ædulph, who gave him the money in the presence of eight hundreds, in the southern part of Cambridgeshire, where the lands in dispute lay.[1] To prove the truth of this assertion, Alfric vouched as witnesses the inhabitants of those eight hundreds (VIII. hundretas traxit in testimonium); and the court having heard their evidence decided against the claimant.

The next case is taken from the Historia Ramesiensis.[2] Some land at the same place, Swaffham, in the possession of the monastery of Ramsey, was claimed by Alfnoth, who summoned Œdnoth, the sub-prior, and others of the monks, to appear at Wendlebury before judges (coram judicibus). These judges were, Aylwyn

---

[1] —dedit illi pecuniam in una cyrotheca involutam coram VIII. Hundretis, in quibus prædicta forte jacebat. It is difficult to conceive how the land in dispute, which we are told was two hydes, could have been situated in eight hundreds, unless we assume the hyde to have contained a greater number of acres than seems possible. Mr. Kemble, in his "Saxons in England," Bbk. I, c. 4, has fully investigated the subject, and he says, that "the hypothesis of the hide having comprised from thirty to thirty-three acres, is the only one which will answer the conditions found in various grants;" and "that it is entirely impossible for the hide to have reached 120, or even 100 acres." But if this writer is correct in his computation, then 66 acres (two hydes) must have lain in no less than eight hundreds. But in another passage (bk. I, c. 9) he assumes it as probable that our present hundreds nearly represent the original in number and extent, and if so, it is plainly impossible that the two hydes which were the subject of dispute could have contained only 66 acres.

[2] Cap. 47.

the sheriff (Aldermannus), and Edric, an officer appointed by the king (regis præpositus), who presided over the court, which consisted of a number of principal men of the county. After some progress had been made in the inquiry, it was suggested and agreed that the dispute should be decided by thirty-six persons, half of whom were to be chosen from the friends of one party, and half from the friends of the other, qui causam judiciali sententia inter eos dirimerent. These were named, and they retired from court to examine into the case. In the meantime, however, and during their absence, Alfnoth, the plaintiff, asked Œdnoth, and another monk who was in his company, whether they would venture to make oath that they were entitled to the land, and thus terminate the dispute? Œdnoth answered that they were ready to do so: but the sheriff refused to allow this, saying, that it was not right that the clergy should be sworn before a secular tribunal; whereupon the court unanimously agreed that the oath was unnecessary, that the monastery ought to keep the land, and that Alfnoth, for his false claim, should forfeit his property to the king.

It will be sufficient to quote one more example of these suits. A son having laid claim to some lands in his mother's possession, sued her in the county court, and, as he was opposed by a relative who appeared on her behalf, three of the thanes took horse and rode to her, to inquire into the facts of the case. The lady, in a moment of anger, formally disinherited her undutiful son, and made Leoflæd, a female relative, her heir, in the following terms: "Here sitteth Leoflæd, my kinswoman, unto whom I grant both my land and my gold, both gown and dress, and all that I possess after my own day." The thanes returned and testified to the court that these words had been spoken; upon which, judgment was given against the son, and a record made that Leoflæd's husband was entitled to the property, of course, after the death of the testatrix.[1]

Of the exact mode in which trials were conducted in these courts we know little; but the Anglo-Saxon laws, and contemporary annals, make frequent mention of two classes of witnesses who play a most important part in the judicial proceedings of the time, and of whom it is necessary to speak somewhat in detail.

These consisted, 1, of compurgators, who supported by their oaths the credibility of a party accused of a crime, or engaged in a suit; and, 2, of persons appointed to attest transactions, in order that their evidence might be available afterwards in case of dispute. We proceed first to consider the former.

Section VI. *Of the Compurgators.*

Amongst the Anglo-Saxons there was what we may call a graduated scale of oaths, and legal credit was attached to them according to the rank of the witness. And this rank was estimated by the amount of "wergild" or value set upon his life according to the principle which has been previously explained. Thus the oath of a twelfhyndes-man (*i.e.*, a person whose wer was twelve hundred shillings) was equal to that of six ceorls or twyhyndesmen; and the reason assigned for this by a law of Athelstan, was, because the homicide of a twelfhyndes man could only be fully atoned for by taking vengeance on six ceorls, and his wergild was equal to that of six ceorls.

On the same principle we find oaths sometimes designated by the number of hydes of land possessed by the party taking them. Thus the expressions occur, be hund twelftig hyda, and be sixtig hyda, the meaning of which is this: Whoever was the owner of five hydes of land

---

[1] See Kemble's Introduct. to Cod. Dip. Ævi Sax.

had a wergild of six hundred shillings, and was called a sixhyndes man. Hence the oaths of twelve sixhyndesmen were the oaths of twelve persons owning each five hydes of land, so that they represented sixty hydes, and the aggregate value of their oaths was, in Anglo-Saxon parlance, called be sixtig hyda. In like manner as the twelfhyndesman had a legal value double that of the sixhyndesman, his worth was that of twelve hundred shillings, which represented ten hydes. Twelve such persons, therefore, represented $12 \times 10 = 120$ hydes of land, and the aggregate value of their oaths or legal credibility was expressed by be hund twelftig hyda.

It is, perhaps, hardly correct to call the compurgators witnesses, for they did not make their appearance in court to testify that they had witnessed anything relating to the facts in dispute, but merely to vouch for the trustworthiness of the party on behalf of whom they came forward. But, even now, we use the expression "witnesses to character," and we may, therefore, with equal propriety apply the term to the compurgators, whose office was so closely analogous. They resembled, in some respects, the laudatores of the Roman law.

The chief difference between these and the compurgators of the English law consisted in this, that the former were produced to show the improbability that a person so supported in his adversity by friends could have been guilty of the crime imputed to him,—while the latter pledged their belief on oath that the accused had not sworn falsely in denying the charge brought against him; and if a sufficient number could be found to do this, he was entitled to an acquittal. For, in the times of our Anglo-Saxon ancestors, such regard was paid to the sanctity of an oath, and such a repugnance was felt to the idea, that a man of good repute amongst his neighbors could be willfully forsworn, that if, when charged with a debt or a crime, he denied it on oath in a court of justice, and could get a certain number of persons to swear that they believed him, he had judgment given in his favor, unless the opposite party could produce more compurgators on his side.[1]

The oath taken by the accused was as follows:

" By the Lord, I am guiltless both in deed and counsel of the charge of which N. accuses me."

That by the compurgators was:

" By the Lord, the oath is clear and unperjured which M. has sworn."[2]

If a man was accused of an offense and ran away, and any one charged the lord (hlaford) with having counseled or been privy to his escape, the law was that the lord should " take to him five thanes and he himself the sixth, and clear himself thereof by oath."[3] If the purgation succeeded, the lord was entitled to the wer (*i.e.* amount of legal compensation due for the crime), but if it failed (*i.e.* if a sufficient number of proper compurgators could not be found), the lord was obliged to pay the wer to the king, and the man who had fled became an outlaw.[4]

But the usual number of compurgators was twelve. Thus in the articles of peace between Guthrum, king of

---

[1] The system of compurgation was by no means peculiar to the Anglo Saxons. It was in use amongst all the various nations of the Teutonic family, and twelve seems to have been with them the favorite number of compurgators, although more were often required: Ingenuus, nobilis homo ingenuus—cum duodecim ingenuis se purget. Concil. Tribur. ann. 895. See Bernardi, De l'Orig. de la Legislation Franc. 82, and Rogge, Gerichtswesen der Germanen, Chap. 5.

[2] Anc. Laws and Inst. tit. Oaths.

[3] Leg. Ethel. 1; Cnut, Sec. 30, 31; Henr. I. 41. § 6.

[4] Id. The expression in the various laws on this subject is wer, as given in the text: but I apprehend that it is used loosely for wite, which means the penalty due to the king or lord for the public wrong done by crime. The wer belonged properly to the injured party, or his relatives and gildsmen if he were dead; but it is not unfrequently put for the whole amount payable by the wrongdoer, and then it includes the wite.

the invading Danes, and Alfred, about the year 880, we find the following provision:[1] "If a king's thane be accused of man-slaying, if he dare to clear himself, let him do that with XII. king's thanes. If any one accuse that man who is of less degree than the king's thane let him clear himself with XI. of his equals and with one king's thane. And so in every suit which may be for more than four "mancuses."[2] And if he dare not, let him pay for it threefold, as it may be valued."

One of the laws of William the Conqueror declared that if a man were accused of robbery and bailed to appear and answer the charge, and in the meantime fled from justice, his bail was to swear with eleven compurgators (si jurra sei duzime main) that at the time he offered himself as bail he did not know that the man had committed the robbery, and that he had not been privy to his escape.[3] So also by another law of the same monarch, if a man were charged with theft who had hitherto borne a good character, he might clear himself by his own single oath; but if he had been previously convicted or accused (e hi blasme unt este), he was to make oath "with the twelfth hand;" and for this purpose fourteen persons were to be named, out of whom he was to choose eleven, making himself the twelfth.—If, however, they refused to swear, he had to undergo the ordeal.[4]

But we must now notice an important feature in this system, which seems to have been intended as a check upon its liability to abuse. Experience must have soon shown that when a man was allowed to choose his own compurgators, it was not difficult for him to select out of a large body of relations or neighbors a sufficient number who would be willing to swear that they believed

---

[1] Anc. Ll. and Inst. 155.
[2] The mancus was equal to thirty pence.
[3] Leg. Gul. Conq. 3.
[4] Id. 14. See also 15.

him, whatever his character might be. The oath taken by friends thus rallying round him at his call, was known by the name of ungecorene-ath, or rim-ath, "the unchosen oath;" because the witnesses were not chosen or nominated by the opposite party. But afterwards the accused was allowed to name persons of the proper class (*i.e.*, kinsmen or fellow-gildsmen of the accused), and out of these the accused or defendant was obliged to choose his compurgators. This was called the cyre ath, or "chosen oath," because the oath of the accused was supported by the oaths of persons chosen by his adversary; and we may well imagine that the latter took care to nominate persons who were least likely to be tampered with, or to be influenced by undue feelings of compassion.[1]

It seems also that in some cases a certain number of compurgators were named by the reeve of the district, consisting of relatives and neighbors of the accused, and out of these he was obliged to choose the number required for his compurgation.[2] This form of procedure was equally called the cyre ath. Here, too, the number out of which the compurgators were to be chosen was generally twelve, or some multiple of twelve, and they were called the equals or peers (gelican) of the accused. If he was a man of bad character, a triple number of per-

---

[1] See Gunderman, Enstehung der Jury, n. 55. Phillips, Anglesachs. Recht. 182.

[2] This was exactly in accordance with the custom that prevailed amongst the nations of the continent, where we find that numerous laws existed, regulating the mode of appointing compurgators, who in the Latin versions of those laws are called sacramentales legitimi, or simply sacramentales. Thus: Si qualiscunque causa inter homines liberos evenerit et sacramentum landum fuerit, si usque ad XX. solidos fuerit causa ipsa aut amplius, ad Evangelia sancta juret cum XII. aliis suis, id est sacramentalibus. Ita ut VI. Ili nominentur ab illo qui pulsat, et septimus sit qui pulsatur, et quinque juales voluerit reus, liberos tamen, ut sint XII.—Leg. Rothar. c. 364. Et cum XII. sacramentalibus juret, cum quinque nominatis et septem advocatis Leg. Alam. tit. 77.

sons were named, out of whom he was to choose a triple number of compurgators, or if they were not named, and he was unable to procure the required number to vouch for him, he was obliged to undergo the triple ordeal.[1]

But it was not in all cases that compurgation was allowed. In some crimes of open violence, or when a man was taken in the mainour with the red hand, or other proofs of guilt upon him, he could not clear himself by adducing persons to swear to their belief in his innocence. The process in this case was different. It was no longer a contest of oath against oath—*i.e.*, the oath of the accuser against the oaths of the accused and his compurgators. The former, indeed, swore to the truth of the charge, and in this he was supported by the oaths of a competent number of friends, but the latter was obliged to submit to the ordeal in order that by the judgment of God his guilt or innocence might be made manifest.

An accusation thus fortified by oath was called vorath, or forath;[2] and we may now perceive that it makes little difference whether we consider the "twelve senior thanes," mentioned in the law of Ethelred, which has been previously noticed,[3] members of a court of justice, or merely inquisitors to accuse of crime. Their functions in either case would be very nearly, if not altogether, the same.

If we regard them as "accusers," they were obviously equivalent to kind of public vorath—that is, to persons who supported their charge against the accused by jointly pledging their oaths to its truth—in which case we

---

[1] Northumb. Presb. Leges, c. 51; Leg. Ethel. I. 1; Leg. Gul. Conq. c. 17.

[2] In the old Danish law it was known as the asworen eth, "sworn oath." In the Salic law it is called wedredum. See Gunderman, Enst. der Jury. 35.

[3] *Ante*, pp. 56, 57.

have seen that compurgation was not allowed where the accusation related to certain specific acts of violence, and the accused was obliged to resort to the ordeal to clear himself. The vorath was in fact taken as a primâ facie proof of guilt, and so might be regarded as a judgment of a court condemning the suspected person to undergo the ordeal, in order that the God of Truth might interpose and ultimately decide the question of innocence or guilt. If so, then the functions of the thanes as accusers were not dissimilar to those of judges, whose doom in such a case would in Anglo-Saxon times have been the same, namely, that the culprit must abide the issue of the ordeal. And this view is strengthened by the following provision of the same law of Ethelred, which ordains, "And let every one (accused) buy himself law with XII. ores, half to the lord (landrica), and half to the wapentake; and let every man of previous bad character (tiht-bysig) go to the threefold ordeal, or pay fourfold."

The ordeal was also to be undergone in the following cases: 1. Where a person accused was unable to adduce a sufficient number of compurgators; 2. Where he had been notoriously guilty of perjury on a previous occasion; 3. Where he was not a freeman; unless his hlaford, or lord, swore to his belief in his innocence, or bought him off by paying the wergild. But it seems that even when the ordeal was requisite, the accused was obliged previously to take an oath that he was innocent in the sight of the law (mid folcrihte unscyldig).[2]

The ordeal was of three kinds: 1. The ordeal of hot iron, in which the accused had to take up and carry for a certain distance a mass of hot iron of a pound weight; 2. The ordeal of hot water, in which he had to take out of a pitcher of boiling water a stone hanging by a string, at a depth equal to the length of his own hand. In some

---

[1] From tihtle (accusation), and bysig (implicated, busied).
[2] Leg. Athelst. I. 23.

cases he had to undergo the triple ordeal (pryfeald lada), in which the iron was increased to three pounds weight, or the stone was sunk in the water to the depth of his elbow.[1] 3. The Corsnæd,[2] or ordeal of the accursed morsel. This consisted in making the accused person swallow a piece of bread, accompanied with a prayer that it might choke him if he were guilty. Godwin, the powerful Earl of Kent, and father of Harold, was currently believed to have died in the act of attempting to swallow the corsnæd.[3]

If a party was unable to vouch a sufficient number of compurgators, he was deemed to have taken a false oath, and lost his suit in a civil case, or was convicted in a criminal.[4] But even if he did produce the requisite number, his opponent might (in some cases at all events) overpower the force of their testimony by calling compurgators on his side, whose oaths were of preponderating legal value. These, again, might be met by the accused in the same manner, and so on, until either party prevailed in the amount of legal value of the witnesses who supported him with their oaths. Sometimes the number of compurgators was so great as to form a large

---

[1] Leg. Ina. 77, App. Duncange v. Lada.

[2] From cor, proof, and snaed, morsel or crumb. It was also called nedbread, or bread that must (ned) be taken.

[3] In the year 1194 (temp. Rich. I.), when the Justices in Eyre for the county of Kent came to Canterbury, it was testified before them that the Abbott of St. Augustines ought to have, and his ancestors had always had, libertatem legis, scilicet judicii aquæ et ignis et duelli. Chron. Thorne apud Twysden, fo. 1841. And we find from another chronicler, that in the following year the ordeal was put in force in Canterbury, Mense Decembri Justiciæ qui vocantur errantes missi per Angliam ab Archiepiscopo Cantuariensi fuerunt apud Cantuariam, ibique per ministros regis judicio aquæ mundati sunt vel perierunt criminosi, qui ad regiam pertinebant coronam. Gervase, ann. 1195.

[4] An instance of the former occurs in the Hist. Eliens. I, 44: Cui omnia illata deneganti et contradicenti ut cum jurejurando se purgaret, quod cum facere nequibat, nec qui secum jurare debuerant habere, poterat, decretum est, ut eo expulso Brihtnodus Alderman utrisque hydis uteretur.

assembly. Thus, in one case, we read of upwards of a thousand attending.[1]

"Perjury," says Mr. Hallam, "was the dominant crime of the middle ages; encouraged by the preposterous rules of compurgation, and by the multiplicity of oaths in the ecclesiastical law."[2] Now it is obvious that such a system as that of compurgation could be of real efficacy in promoting the ends of justice, only where unbounded reverence was paid to the sanctity of an oath. But we may be very sure that it must at all times have been a most fallacious test of innocence, and have favored, to an alarming extent, the escape of the guilty. This was at last discovered; and the only wonder is, that such a mode of trial was allowed to linger so long amongst us. It gradually, however, fell into disuse, and was ultimately restricted to actions of debt, where, until a very recent period, the defendant was allowed "to wage his law," that is deny upon oath the debt, and vouch eleven compurgators in support of his credibility. The consequence of this was, that plaintiffs avoided, when they could, that form of action, for, as Sir Edward Coke says of his own time, "Men's consciences do grow so large specially (in this case passing with impunity), as they choose rather to bring an action upon the case upon his, the defendant's, promise, wherein, because it is trespass sur. le case, he can not wage his law, that an action of debt."[3]

Certain points of resemblance between the compurgators and the jury, and especially the coincidence in point of number, have led several authors to the conclusion, that the latter was derived from the former, and was in truth only a modification of the ancient usage in this re-

---

[1] Tunc Ulnothus adduxit fideles viros plus quam mille, ut per juramentum illorum sibi vindicaret eandem terram. Hist. Eliens. 1, 35.
[2] Midd. Ages. Suppl. Notes, p. 260.
[3] Co. Litt. 295. b. The party himself was sworn de fidelitate, and the eleven compurgators, de credulitate.

spect.[1] But this is, I believe, entirely a mistake, founded on a misconception of the original nature of the office of jurymen. We shall show, indeed, hereafter that they were witnesses, but not to character, only to facts. Compurgation was one mode of trial; the jury was another. Each was distinct from the other, and both might, and in fact did, co-exist together, although, as experience taught men the immense advantage which the latter had over the former as a means of discovering the truth, trial by compurgators gradually fell into disuse.

SECTION VII. *Of the legally appointed Witnesses in the Anglo-Saxon Law.*

We must next notice a class of witnesses appointed by law to attest bargains, whose existence has not hitherto attracted the attention it deserves, with reference to the subject of our inquiry. They seem to have stood in the place of modern public notaries, for the purpose of supplying evidence of transactions, and so preventing perjury and fraud. We have already had occasion to describe them as they existed amongst the old Germans, and the Anglo-Saxon laws enable us to give a more particular account of their functions.

The earliest mention of these witnesses occurs, I believe, in one of the laws of Athelstan (A. D. 924-940), which enacted that there should be named in every reeve's jurisdiction[2] as many men as were known to be unlying, that they might be for witness in every suit. "And be the oaths of these unlying men according to the worth

---

[1] Amongst others, Rogge has advanced this opinion with great confidence, in his learned and useful treatise, Greichtswesen der Germanen, chap. viii. § 44; and Turner, in his Hist. of the Anglo-Saxons, has altogether confounded the compurgators with the jury.

[2] The original is manung, which seems to have comprised all who resided within the jurisdiction of the reeve, and owed obedience to his summons. See Anc. Laws and Inst. p. 223.

IV.] OF LEGALLY APPOINTED WITNESSES.

of the property without dispute." They were also liable to punishment if they bore false testimony. "But if it be found that any of these (the appointed witnesses) have given wrongful witness, let his witness never again stand for aught, and let him also give XXX. shillings as wite (or penalty.")[1]

But the most explicit information on the subject is contained in the laws of Edgar, which provided as follows:[2]

"This then is what I will; that every man be under surety within the towns (burgs) and without; and let witness be appointed to every town and to every hundred.

"To every town let there be chosen XXXIII. as witnesses (gecorene to gewitnesse).[3]

"To small towns and in every hundred XI., unless ye desire more.

"And let every man with these witnesses buy and sell every of the chattels he may buy or sell, either in a town or in a wapentake; and let every of them when he is first chosen as witness give the oath that he never, neither for love nor for fear, will deny any of those things of which he was witness, nor declare any other thing in witness save that alone which he saw or heard; and of such sworn men let there be at every bargain two or three as witness.

"And he who rides in quest of cattle, let him declare to his neighbors about what he rides; and when he comes home, let him also declare with whose witness he bought the cattle."

In the simple state of society which existed in the time of our Saxon forefathers, transactions between man

---

[1] Leg. Athels. I. 10.
[2] Leg. Edg. Supp., and see Leg. Edw. I. 5; Edm. Conc. Culint. 5; Ethelr. I. 3; Cnut, Secul. 24; Edw. Conf. 38; Gul. Conq. I. 45; III. 10.
[3] These are the gewitnesse, whom Grimm confounds with the members of the court. See ante, page 56, note 1.

and man were conducted with a publicity and openness of which we have now no example. Sir Francis Palgrave has well and eloquently described the mode in which evidence was thus perpetuated in early times.[1] "The forms, the festivities, and the ceremonies accompanying the hours of joy, and the days of sorrow, which form the distinguishing epochs in the brief chronicle of domestic life, impressed them upon the memory of the people at large. The parchment might be recommended by custom, but it was not required by law; and they had no registers to consult, no books to open. By the declaration of the husband at the church-door the wife was endowed in the presence of the assembled relations, and before all the merry attendants of the bridal train. The birth of the heir was recollected by the retainers who had participated in the cheer of the baronial hall; and the death of the ancestor was proved by the friends who had heard the wailings of the widow, or who had followed the corpse to the grave." Payments were made in the presence of the Hundred court, that all the district might be able afterwards to testify to the fact,[2] and the charters and deeds were usually witnessed by a number of persons the most interested in the grant, and therefore the most likely to remember it. On one occasion when a hyde of land was given by the monastery of Ely to Œdnoth, a monk of Ramsey, for his good offices in terminating a troublesome dispute, he cut off four pieces of turf, and laid them on the altar of Gregory in his convent, in the presence of a crowd of witnesses, in hujus meræ donationis argumentum.[3] Secrecy and concealment were deemed to be almost conclusive evidence of fraud or crime—and as such they were treated by the

---

[1] English Commonwealth, I. 248.
[2] —dederunt ei eandem pecuniam apud Brandune coram testimonio totius Hundreti in quo illa terra jacet. Hist. Eliens. I. 46.
[3] Hist. Rames. c. 42,

Anglo-Saxon law. Thus if a person being on a journey were to make a bargain suddenly without any previous intention (unmyndlunge), and without having declared it when he rode out, he was to make it known on his return, and if it was for live stock, he was with witness of his township to bring it to the common pasture. And if he did not do this before five days he was to forfeit the cattle, "because he would not declare it to his neighbors," even although he had really bought them in the presence of legally named witnesses, and the ealdor of the hundred were satisfied that this was true.[1] So also if a man from afar, or a stranger, were to go out of the highway into some by-path or wood, and did not then shout or blow a horn, he was to be accounted a thief, either to be slain, or redeemed with his wergild.[2]

And so late as the reign of Henry II., in cases of rape the woman was to go to the nearest town immediately after the outrage, and make known to trustworthy persons the injury she had suffered—showing the marks of violence and state of her clothes if torn. She was then to go before the headman of the hundred and do the same, and also publicly declare the ill-usage she had received at the next county court.[3]

In all this, the usage of the Anglo-Saxons corresponded closely with that of the Teutonic nations of the Continent. And, although I am not aware that there is extant amongst the laws of the former any distinct statement that hundredors generally were competent witnesses with respect to matters of common interest or notoriety within the hundred, as we have seen was the case with respect to the markgenossen of Germany, this may, I think, be inferred with sufficient certainty from the whole tenor of those laws, as well as from incidental

---

[1] Leg. Edg. Supp. 8, 9, 10; and see Leg. Gul. Conq. 10.
[2] Legg. Withræd, 28; Ine, 20.
[3] Glanv. Tract. de Leg. XIV. c. 6.

mention of such testimony in the old chronicles. And what has been before said on the subject of the conclusiveness and legal effect of the evidence thus given, applies with equal force to the Anglo-Saxon witnesses. Their testimony was decisive of the matter of dispute. It was a verdict not to be questioned or gainsaid.[1]

When one of the legally appointed witnesses appeared in court to give evidence respecting a transaction which he had attested, he took the following oath:[2]

"In the name of Almighty God! as I here for N. in true witness stand, unbidden and unbought, so I with my eyes oversaw, and with my ears overheard, that which I with him say."

And the defendant was himself obliged to take an oath, corresponding to the plea of nil debet, in the following form:

"In the name of the living God, I owe not to N. scot (sceatt) or shilling, or penny or penny's worth; but I have discharged to him all that I owed him so far as our verbal contracts were at first."

It may be asked whether there was not also an oath denying the alleged contract altogether (corresponding to the plea of nunquam indebitatus); for that which has just been cited amounts merely to a plea that whatever contract may have been made has been satisfied by payment. We find no such form, and perhaps for the following reason. The onus of proof lay upon the plaintiff, who to establish his demand must have called the attesting witnesses to the transaction. If he had none, then the requisition of the law had not been complied with,

---

[1] Postea vero evoluto tempore, et defuncto Rege ædgaro, visus est idem Leonricus subdola calliditate, omnem conventionem, quam cum Episcopo fecerat, annullare si posset, sed legales viri ædricus Rufus et Leonricus de Berle et Sivirthus vecors, qui huic rei intererant et testes fuerant. ejm convictum reddiderunt.—Hist. Eliens. I. 6.

[2] Anc. Laws and Inst. Oaths, p. 181.

and he failed in his suit.[1] If he had, the mere denial of the defendant would avail nothing, as it would be very difficult, if not impossible, for him to call witnesses to prove a negative; that is, that there never had been such a contract as the plaintiff alleged.

Although we have no express information on the point, we may reasonably conclude that compurgation was not allowed in cases where the plaintiff could prove his demand by calling the legal witnesses who had attested the contract. Otherwise the absurdity would follow, that the oath of a defendant, backed by relatives or friends whom he vouched for a belief in his integrity, would be sufficient to discredit the positive testimony of those whom the law had appointed as trustworthy witnesses. And this view is confirmed by what we know of wager of law in later times. This was not permitted when the debt claimed was secured by a deed or other specialty which spoke for itself, but only, as Coke says,[2] " when it groweth by word, so as he may pay or satisfy the party in secret, whereof the defendant having no testimony of witnesses may wage his law."

In his "Geschichte des Angelsachsischen Rechts,"[3] Phillips considers these witnesses as having judicial functions to perform; and indeed treats them as identical with the court which took cognizance of disputes arising out of transactions which they had attested. I can not, however, think that this view is correct. The passages which he cites from the Anglo-Saxon laws are those which

---

[1] If, for instance, the ownership of cattle were in dispute, and the party who asserted that he had bought them could not produce the requisite number of legal witnesses, he was obliged to restore them to the former proprietor. Leg. Sec. Cnut, 24, and compare Leg. Gul. Conq. 1: Quod si aliquis rem postmodum calumniatus fuerit et nec testes habuerit nec warrantum, et rem reddat et forisfacturam cui de jure competit.

[2] Co. Litt. 294, b.

[3] Sect. 50. Grimm also confounds the witnesses with the court in his Deuts. Rechts Alter. 779. See ante, p. 71.

have been already quoted or referred to; and they certainly do not prove it. They nowhere say that the witnesses had to act as judges; and in the following instance at least they are spoken of as different and distinct: Aluricus igitur eandem terram Brihtnoto Abbati liberavit in manu primum coram XXIV. Judicibus in prædicto loco, deinde etiam similiter fecit coram testibus legalibus.[1] In so far, however, that their evidence was conclusive, it may be taken to have been equivalent to a judicial sentence, and this has perhaps misled Phillips and others to suppose that they did pronounce such a sentence in the character of judges.

Originally, indeed, there may have been no difference between these two characters; for when all the freemen of the hundred attended the gemot, or court, they necessarily included those who could give evidence upon the matters that came before it. These were as much members of the court as the rest; and their testimony, therefore, on a disputed question was the judicial decision upon it. But afterwards, when the court consisted of a limited number, the judges and witnesses must have been different persons, although the effect of the evidence of the latter remained the same.

SECTION VIII. *Results of the Investigation.*

Let us now see at what point we have arrived in the investigation of the judicial system of the Anglo-Saxons.

1. We find that courts existed presided over by a reeve, who had no voice in the decision, and that the number of persons who sat as judges was frequently twelve, or some multiple of that number. 2. The assertions of parties in their own favor were admitted as

[1] Hist Eliens. I. 13.

conclusive, provided they were supported by the oaths of a certain number of compurgators; and in important cases the number was twelve, or, at all events, when added to the oath of the party himself, made up that number. 3. The testimony of the neighborhood was appealed to, for the purpose of deciding questions which related to matters of general concern. 4. Sworn witnesses were appointed in each district, whose duty it was to attest all private bargains and transactions, in order that they might be ready to give evidence in case of dispute. 5. Every care was taken that all dealings between man and man should be as open and public as possible; and concealment or secrecy was regarded as fraud, and in some cases punished as guilt. When we come to consider the "Assise," as established by Henry II., and fully understand the principle of that mode of trial, we shall see how, out of these different elements, which continued in full force under the Anglo-Normans, was produced at last the institution of the jury. As yet it had no visible existence, but the idea was implied in the requirement that disputed questions should be determined by the voice of sworn witnesses, taken from the neighborhood, and deposing to the truth of what they had seen or heard. What was wanting was to mold this procedure into a formal shape, which it did not attain until a century after the Norman Conquest.

CHAPTER V.

THE ANGLO-NORMAN PERIOD.

SECTION I. *On the legal Changes introduced by the Normans.*

IN his History of the English Law, Reeve says:[1] "The accession of William of Normandy to the English throne makes a memorable epoch in the history of our municipal law. Some Saxon customs may be traced by the observing antiquary, even in our present body of law, but in the establishment made in this country by the Normans are to be seen, as in their infancy, the very form and features of English law. It is to the Conquest, and to the consequences of that revolution that the juridical historian is to direct his particular attention. A new order of things then commenced."

This is, I believe, a great mistake, arising from a want of sufficient knowledge of the legal system of the Anglo-Saxons. It would be much nearer the truth to say, that that system was unaffected by the Conquest—and continued in all its vigor for many years after that event.

With reference to the right which the victory at Hastings might be supposed to confer on William to alter the laws and institutions of the country which he had successfully invaded, we must not be misled by the use of the word "Conqueror." This, in legal parlance, signified

[1] Vol. I. chap. 2.

merely that he had acquired the throne by "purchase," and not by descent, not that he had vanquished the nation over which he began to reign, so that he could impose laws upon the people, jure belli.[1]

Nor does it militate against this view, that we find William asserting an "hereditary" title, which at first sight seems opposed to a claim by "purchase." The fact is, that William, conscious of the weakness of his title, resorted to every possible means of strengthening it; and therefore claimed the crown both as heir of the Confessor, designating himself in his charters, "Ego Wilhelmus Rex Anglorum hereditario jure factus," and as having had it bequeathed to him by that monarch. But this anxiety to make out a legitimate title, proves that he did not wish to rely upon the right of conquest, which would of course have superseded and been paramount to any other. At the same time it must be admitted that the words armis conquisivit are applied by old writers to his acquisition of the throne.[2]

There can be no doubt that it was the intention of William I. that his English subjects should continue to enjoy the rights and usages to which they had been accustomed under the laws of their Anglo-Saxon king of the line of Cerdic. But it is equally certain that much injustice and oppression were practiced by his Norman followers, who knowing nothing of these laws were disposed to trample upon the Anglo-Saxons as a conquered race; and we can easily conceive how often, in the insolence of successful invasion, might must have triumphed over right, and caused an apprehension on the part of

---

[1] See this question fully discussed by Sir Matthew Hale, Hist. of Common Law, I. c. 5. Spelman, Gloss. title Conquestus, defines the word, id quod a parentibus non acceptum, sed labore pretio vel parsimonia comparatum possidemus. Hinc Gulielmus I. dicitur, qui Angliam conquisivit i. e. acquisivit "purchased"; non quod subegit.

[2] See Hickes's Thes. Diss. Epist. p. 31.

the English, that they would soon lose their dearly-cherished customs, and be subject in all things to the (to them) unknown laws and caprice of their Norman tyrants. They therefore fondly looked back to the time of Edward the Confessor, the last of their legitimate sovereigns, as that when they enjoyed their natural rights and customs without foreign interference, and were loud in their clamors to William to restore to them the laws of that king—meaning thereby, as I conceive, not any particular code enacted by him—but the laws which prevailed in his reign, and which had been handed down for generations from their forefathers, and were the inheritance of every Anglo-Saxon freeman.

This view agrees with the expressions used by William in the proclamation or charter addressed by him in 1070, to "William, Bishop, and Godfrey, Portreeve, and all the burgers in London, French and English," in which he says, that his will is that they all should have the laws which they possessed in the days of King Edward.

And the statutes which he afterwards promulgated, and which are known by the name of Leges Gulielmi Conquestoris, are headed by the following preface, or title: Cez sont les leis e les custumes que li reis Will grantad al pople de Engleterre apres le cunquest de la terre: iceles meimes que li reis Edward, sun cusin, tint devant lui.

Accordingly, we find the distinguishing features of Anglo-Saxon jurisprudence retained by the Norman king. Of these we may mention the wergild, or manbot, for bodily injuries; the system of mutual suretyship (frithborh, improperly rendered frank-pledge); the prohibition of suits before the king, unless there was first a failure of justice in the hundred, or county court; the necessity of purchases and sales being made in the presence of legal witnesses: and the use of compurgation and the ordeal.[1]

---

[1] In proof of this see the Leges Gul. Conq. in the "Ancient Laws and Institutes," published by the Record Commissioners.

V.] LEGAL CHANGES OF THE NORMANS.

The most important changes in our judicial system made by the conqueror were, 1, the separation of the spiritual and temporal courts; 2, the introduction of the combat, or duel, as a means of determining civil suits and questions of guilt or innocence; and, 3, the appointment of justiciars, to administer justice throughout the realm.

With regard to the second of these, however, Sir Francis Palgrave thinks, that notwithstanding the silence of Anglo-Saxon laws and records on the subject, trial by battle may have existed in England before the Conquest. He says:[1] "It must be admitted that an Anglo-Saxon duel can not be adduced; but the argument which rests upon the absence of trial by battle in the courts of Anglo-Saxon origin, is not entirely correct. Immediately after the Conquest, the 'witnesses' of the church of Worcester offered to become the champions of St. Mary, and to defend the rights of Bishop Wulstun by combat against the claims of the abbot of Evesham. It was in regular course, according to the common law, to join battle in the county court, when the cause was not removed into a superior tribunal. If we reject the subtleties, the distinctions, and, above all, the technical expressions which unquestionably were due to the Anglo-Norman lawyers, and invented, or perfected, under the Anglo-Norman sovereigns, the principles which govern the proceedings of judicial battle are so nearly identified with those which are to be collected from the Teutonic codes, as to afford a probability that they were parts of the Anglo-Saxon law, preserved by the usage and traditions of the people."

With respect to the justiciars, it has been generally supposed that justices in eyre (justitiarii itinerantes) were first established in 1176, by Henry II., for we find it recorded that in that year, in a great counsel held at Northampton, the king divided the realm into six parts, and

[1] English Commonw. I. 224.

appointed three traveling justices to go each circuit, so that the number was eighteen in all.[1] Three years afterwards, in 1179, a fresh arrangement was made, and the six circuits were reduced to four, which were distributed amongst fifteen judges.[2] But although the formal division of the kingdom into separate circuits may have been first made by Henry II., yet there is no doubt that single justiciars were appointed by William I., a few years after the Conquest, who visited the different shires to administer justice in the king's name, and thus represented the curia regis as distinct from the hundred and county courts.[3]

SECTION II. *Modes of Trial in civil Suits in the Anglo-Norman Times.*

The same remark which has already been made, with reference to the absence of all mention of the form of jury trial in the Anglo-Saxon laws, applies equally to the first hundred years after the Conquest. It is incredible that so important a feature of our jurisprudence, if it had been known, would not have been alluded to in the various compilations of law which were made in the reigns of the early Norman kings. These consist of the Leges Gulielmi Conquestoris, Leges Henrici Primi, and Leges Edwardi Confessoris,[4] and in none of them is a hint given of the existence of the jury.

But although the jury, properly so called, does not

---

[1] Spelman, Codex. [2] Ibid.
[3] Misit autem dehinc rex potentissimus justitiarios per unamquamque scyram. Hen. Hunting. 18, Will. I.
[4] With respect to these last, we not must be mislead by the name into a supposition that they were laws enacted by the Saxon Edward. They were a collection of such as existed in his time, compiled most probably in the reign of Henry II., in order that the English might possess a record of their old laws, and a guarantee for their continuance. See Phillips, Eng. Reichs u. Rechtsgeschichte.

yet seem to have been in existence, we find in the narratives of several suits, which came before the courts in those reigns, distinct traces of a mode of trial which easily paved the way for the introduction of that system. In order to satisfy ourselves on this important point it will be necessary to notice each of these briefly in chronological order.

First, then, we find a writ directed by William the Conqueror to Archbishop Lanfranc, Roger Earl of Moreton, and Bishop Galfrid, requiring them to summon all the shires which were present at the plea of lands of the church of Ely held before the last departure of the Queen to Normandy. To these were to be added such of the barons as could conveniently appear who held lands of the same church, and who had been present at the trial. And when the assembly met, several (plures) Englishmen were to be chosen out of those who knew in whose tenure and possession the lands lay at the time of the death of Edward the Confessor, and they were to confirm their statements by an oath (jurando testentur).[1] The register of Domesday Book was, in fact, compiled from evidence of this kind given upon the inquests held under the general survey ordered by the Conqueror.

In the famous placitum held on Pennenden Heath in the same reign, when Lanfranc, archbishop of Canterbury, reclaimed the lands belonging to his see which had been seized by Otho, the Bishop of Bayeux, William's natural brother, during the vacancy that intervened after the deposition of Stigand, the matters in dispute were determined by the men of the whole county, whom the king summoned to attend, and especially those native English who were best versed in the old laws and customs. This great cause detained the assembly three whole days (eâ causâ totus comitatus per tres dies fuit ibi detentus), and

---

[1] Dugdale's Monasticon, 1. 478, cited in Palgrave's Proofs and Illustrations, English Commonwealth.

was decided in favor of the archbishop. They also adjudged (fuit ibi diracionatum, etiam a toto comitatu concordatum et judicatum) that the Archbishop of Canterbury held the lands in his demesne as free and quit of all manner of services, as the king held his own lands.[1]

We have an account of one other important suit in the same reign, which deserves particular attention, from the fact that in order to decide it recourse was had to the oaths of twelve men; and this has been eagerly seized on as a proof that trial by jury was introduced by the Conqueror. It will be found, however, when carefully considered, by no means to warrant that assertion; and the apparent resemblance vanishes when the true nature of the intervention of the twelve in this case is properly understood. Pichot, the sheriff of Cambridgeshire, had dealt with some land as belonging to the king which Gundulf, Bishop of Hrof, in Kent, asserted to be the property of the Church.[2] They both appealed to the king, who ordered that all the men of the county should be assembled, in order that the question might be determined by their judgment. Otho, Bishop of Bayeux, presided over the court, the members of which were sworn to say the truth;[3] but dreading the power of the sheriff, they decided unjustly in favor of the king's title. Otho, not being satisfied, required them to choose out of their whole number twelve, who should upon their oaths confirm the judgment which they all had given. This was done, and as the names of six of the "jurors" have been recorded, it may be interesting to mention them. They were Edward of Chippenham, Harold and Leofwine of Exninge, Eadric of Giselham, Wulfwine of Landwade, Ordmer of Berlingham, and six others of the best men of the county. They retired together for a short time,

[1] Hickes's Thes. Dissert. Epist.
[2] Textus Roffensis apud Hickes, Thes. Dissert. Epist. p. 33.
[3] It is clear from the context that the homines comitatus were sworn.

and on their return into court swore that the judgment given was right and true. Soon afterwards, however, a monk named Grim, having occasion to visit Bishop Gundulf, and hearing of the decision, declared that the whole body was perjured, as he had himself formerly received the rents and services from the land in question as agent or bailiff on behalf of the Church. Upon this, Gundulf went to the Bishop of Bayeux, and told him what the monk had said. Otho first examined the man himself, and then sent for one of those who had taken part in the judgment; and this person at once, with much apparent contrition, confessed, that he had perjured himself. Another was sent for, who made the same confession. The bishop then ordered the rest of the court, and also the twelve who had upon oath confirmed the judgment, to meet him in London, where he summoned many of the principal barons of the kingdom to come and form a court. These adjudged that the whole of those who originally decided the cause had committed perjury, and the land was restored to Bishop Gundulf. But, inasmuch as twelve of them asserted that they had not agreed in the judgment of the others, Otho ordered that they should clear themselves by the ordeal of hot iron, and when they failed in this, they were, with the rest of the county, obliged to pay a fine to the king.

It is extraordinary that the true nature of this proceeding has escaped the penetration of previous writers. They have assumed it to be the first authentic instance of a trial by jury in this country. Even Sir F. Palgrave speaks of the jury in the above case giving their verdict against Gundulphus.[1] And Turner, in his "History of the Anglo-Saxons,"[2] says, "It is not contested that the institution of a jury existed in the time of the Conqueror. The document which remains of the dispute between Gundulf, the bishop of Rochester, and Pichot,

---

[1] Eng. Comm. I. 253.   [2] Vol. I. p. 535.

the sheriff, ascertains the fact." But so far from this position being not contested, it would, I believe, be much more correct to say that the jury trial in its form of an inquest by twelve men summoned to determine by their verdict a disputed fact, was unknown in the time of the Conqueror. And the above-cited trial proves nothing in favor of the opposite view.

In reality the twelve on this occasion were merely compurgators, called upon by the president of the court to support upon oath the suspected judgment, or rather testimony (for it was nothing more), of their fellows. It is true that they differed from ordinary compurgators, inasmuch as they here affirmed testimony which they had themselves given; but this was an exceptional case. It was not possible to find compurgators distinct from the court, for it was supposed to consist of the whole county, and therefore Otho was obliged to make a portion of the members perform that office. And he might not unreasonably suppose that by thus diminishing the number, he increased the sense of responsibility, and had a better chance of arriving at the truth. I am satisfied that this is the right view of the case, and that except as regarded their number, the duodecim de melioribus comitatus, here mentioned, had nothing in common with the assize or recognition by jurors of a later period. We see at once why they were twelve, for that was the ordinary number required in compurgation on grave occasions.

In the year 1090, in the reign of William Rufus, when the citizens of London disputed the title of the convent of St. Augustine's at Canterbury to the vill of Stonor, we are told that it was decided in the same vill by the justiciars (diracionatum est per justiciarios), that the abbot and his monastery were entitled to it and all rights thereunto pertaining.[1] From the way in which

[1] Chron. Gul. Thorne de rebus gestis Abbatum Sti Augustini Cantuariæ, apud Twysden. fo. 1793.

the chronicler, who was himself a monk of St. Augustine's, tells us that the king favored the side of the abbot, we may suspect that the royal pleasure was not without influence on the decision of the justices. But no hint is given that there was any intervention of the men of the county in giving judgment in this case. It was tried and determined by the justices alone.

In the same reign occurs a writ addressed to the sheriff requiring him to assemble the shire of Hamton, and decide by its judgment whether the land of Isham, in the time of the king's father, paid rent to monks of St. Benedict. And it is clear that this inquest was taken on the oaths of the men of the shire; for afterwards a writ was issued to the sheriff ordering him to restore Isham to the abbot, "as he proved his claim to it in Hamton, and as it was testified and sworn."[1]

But it was not only with regard to land that such inquests were taken, for we find a writ in the name of Prince William, the son of Henry I., addressed to the sheriff of Kent requiring him to summon "Hamo the son of Vital, and the probi vicini of Sandwich whom Hamo shall name," to say the truth respecting the freedom from toll of a vessel belonging to the abbot of St. Augustine's which seems to have been seized for non-payment of dues. Subsequently, the sheriff was directed to restore the vessel to the abbot, according to the recognition of the good men of the county (sicut recognitum fuit per probos homines comitatus).[2] And in the reign of Henry II. we have a writ addressed to Richard de Lucy and the foresters of Windsor to take a recognition, "by the oaths of lawful men of the hundred," as to a right of pannage for hogs claimed by the abbot of Abingdon.

[1] Brady, Pref. xlix. cited in Palgrave's Proofs and Illustrations.

[2] Bib. Cott. Julius, D. Id. This instance is important, as being one of the earliest, if not the first, where mention is made of the probi vicini being summoned to determine a dispute.

In the year 1121, Henry I. ordered that a complaint of the monks of St. Stephen, at Caen, against the king's tenants of Bridport, for unlawfully taking possession of some lands of the manor of Bridton, which they claimed in right of their abbey, should be heard before judges, and determined by the affirmation of the men of four townships of that neighborhood. On the day appointed Warine, the sheriff of Dorset and Somerset, assembled seven "hundreds," and the cause was heard before them. Sixteen men, consisting of three from Bridport, three from Bridton, and ten from the neighborhood, took an oath that they would affirm the truth in the inquisition; and their testimony was, that the land was of old time appurtenant to Bridton, and ought to belong to whoever was the owner of that manor. The names of these jurors have been preserved, and amongst them we find one mentioned as Alwine Bacon, their foreman (qui erat præpositus).[1]

In a county court held in the reign of Stephen (A. D. 1153), a cause was tried between the monks of Christ's Church, Canterbury, and the sheriff, Radulf Picot, as to the right of the latter to levy certain imposts on their lands. Picot himself presided, and the case was decided in favor of the monks by the judgment of the whole county.

In the Chronicle of Battle Abbey we find mention made of several actions brought to recover manors and lands belonging to the monastery; but nothing is there said of a jury, or even a recognition by an assize, although the narrative is carried down nearly to the end of the reign of Henry II.[2] The causes were heard before the king himself in council, or one of his justiciars, and determined by the evidence of charters and other documents. In one case, Abbot Walter prosecuted a claim to some land at Bernehorne, which he alleged to have been purchased

[1] Chartul. St. Stephen's at Caen, Id.
[2] See the Chronicon Monasterii de Bello.

by a former abbot, in the reign of Henry I., and of which the monastery had been unjustly deprived. The king (Henry II.) appointed a day for the parties to appear before him at Clarendon, and thither accordingly they came, and the cause was tried in the presence of the king. The abbot produced his deeds, and judgment was given in his favor (unanimi consensu totius curiæ adjudicatum est), and a writ was issued to the four knights who then held the office of sheriff of Sussex, commanding them to restore the land to the abbey, having first ascertained its metes and bounds "by the oaths of twelve trustworthy men of the neighborhood who knew the boundaries."[1]

The last instance we need quote occurred in the reign of Henry II. There was a dispute between the inhabitants of Wallingford and the Abbot of Abingdon respecting the right of the latter to a market in their town. The king accordingly issued a writ to Robert, Earl of Leicester, Justiciar of England, and ordered him to summon the whole county of Berkshire, and cause twenty-four of the elder inhabitants, who remembered the times of the king's grandfather, Henry I., to be chosen, that they might upon their oaths declare whether they had seen a full market held at Abingdon in those days. Accordingly the sheriff, under the instructions of the earl, convoked the meeting, and the twenty-four chosen jurors swore that they had seen and attended a full market there. The townsmen, however, suggested to the king that the statement was false, and that some of the jurors were retainers of the abbey. He therefore ordered that a fresh inquest should be held at Oxford, in the presence of his justices, and that the jurors should be chosen by both sides out of the county of Berkshire, and the towns of Wallingford and Oxford. The result was, that they

---

[1] Chronicon Monasterii de Bello, pp. 105–110.

were divided into three parties, each of whom asserted a different right of market; and the Earl of Leicester, who was present, seeing that it was hopeless to expect them to agree, left the meeting and went to the king, who was then at Salisbury, and having informed him of what had happened, told him that he himself remembered, when he was a boy, seeing a full market at Abingdon so long back as the reign of King William. This satisfied the king; who thereupon ordered that the full right of market should be confirmed to the abbot, and the townsmen who came to him with their complaint were dismissed roughly from his presence.[1]

It is from a careful consideration of these narratives that we must derive our knowledge of the judicial system under the Anglo-Norman kings. And they throw considerable light upon the subject of our inquiry. Although the form of the jury did not then exist, the rudiments of that mode of trial may be distinctly traced, in the selection from the neighborhood where the dispute arose, of a certain number of persons, who after being duly sworn testified to the truth of the facts within their own knowledge. This is what distinguishes the proceeding from what took place amongst the Anglo-Saxons— namely, the choosing a limited number of probi homines to represent the community, and give testimony for them. When we come to describe the original constitution of the jury, as it appears in the treatises of Glanvill and Bracton, we shall see how easy was the transition from the mode of procedure which we have just considered to that of the assize, or rather that the latter was merely a modification of the former. But first it will be necessary to say a few words respecting the judicium parium, about which a good deal of misconception still prevails.

[1] Bib. Cott. Claud. B. vi. 178. Palgrave, clxxx.

SECTION III. *The Meaning and Nature of the Judicium Parium.*

It is a common but erroneous opinion, that the judicium parium, " or trial by one's peers," had reference to the jury. This expression has misled many, and amongst others Reeves, and one of the greatest of our legal authorities—Blackstone—who thought that in that palladium of the early liberties of England, Magna Charta, trial by jury was provided for, because it was there declared that every freeman should be tried by the legal judgment of his peers, or by the law of the land.[1] He says: "The truth seems to be, that this tribunal was universally established among all the northern nations, and so interwoven in their very constitution, that the earliest accounts of the one give us also some traces of the other. Its establishment, however, and use in this island, of what date soever it be, though for a time greatly impaired and shaken by the introduction of the Norman trial by battle, was always so highly esteemed and valued by the people, that no conquest, no change of government, could ever prevail to abolish it. In Magna Charta it is more than once insisted on as the principal bulwark of our liberties; but especially by chap. 29, that no freeman shall

---

[1] Reeves says, after quoting these words, " that is, by a lawful trial : either that by jury which it was intended to promote and patronize; or by the ancient modes long known to the law of the land." Blackstone might have suspected that the judicium parium must mean something different from trial by jury, for he adds to the passage quoted in the text the words " a privilege which is couched in almost the same words with that of the Emperor Conrad two hundred years before: nemo beneficium suum perdat, nisi secundum consuetudinem antecessorum nostrorum et per judicium parium suorum." Comm. III. c. 23. But he seems to have thought that the institution existed everywhere, for he goes on to say, " And it was esteemed in all countries a privilege of the highest and most beneficial nature." This may be true of the judicium parium, but certainly is not of trial by jury.

be hurt in either his person or property, nisi per legale judicium parium suorum vel per legem terræ." [1]

But the same expression occurs in a compilation of our laws of earlier date than Magna Charta. We find it in the Leges Henrici Primi. Thus, unusquisque per pares suos judicandus est et ejusdem provinciæ. The pares, however, here spoken of have no reference to a jury. They may possibly include the members of the county and other courts, who discharged the function of judges, and who were the peers or fellows of the parties before them. In a stricter and more technical sense, however, they mean the homage or suitors of the baronial courts, which had seignorial jurisdiction, corresponding to the hallmotes of the Anglo-Saxons, and in some degree to the manorial courts of the present day. And the words above quoted, from the laws of Henry I., were taken by the compiler from the capitularies of Louis IX. of France, where we know that no such institution as the jury existed until the period of the first Revolution.

It may, indeed, be fairly doubted whether the words judicium parium could ever with propriety have been applied to the verdict of a jury. It will be hereafter shown how limited its functions were from the first; and we shall see that the jurors were merely witnesses deposing to facts with which they were acquainted. And it is difficult to understand how their sworn testimony in court could have been called a judicium. This implies the decision of a judge, and such the magna assisa, or

---

[1] In his observations on Magna Charta, Barrington having noticed the correspondence of the 29th Chapter with a Norman Charter nearly contemporaneous, says, "I should therefore conceive that the trial per pares in the 29th Chapter of Magna Charta, was meant chiefly to relate to the trial of the barons by their peers, though it hath, fortunately for the liberties of this country, been expounded to extend to the trial of all persons by a jury." It is certainly, however, a mistake to suppose that by the pares are meant peers in the limited sense of peers of parliament. The latter term is derived from the former, but at the time of Magna Charta it had a much wider signification.

jurata patriæ, never gave. They came to the court to state upon oath their knowledge of certain facts, but they were not a part of it, and, therefore, could not be said to pronounce a judgment. In the Rotuli Curiæ Regis, the entries clearly point out the distinction between the verdict of the jury and the judgment of the court. The former commences with the words Juratores dicunt, the latter is headed Judicium. And Glanvill, when he speaks of the conclusive finding of the juries, says, stabit veredicto visineti; but when of the decision of the court consequent upon that finding, he uses the expression secundum dictum visineti judicabitur.[1]

In one sense, indeed, the jury may be said to discharge judicial functions, and always to have done so from the earliest period at which they appear in our forensic annals, when they were strictly witnesses. For the peculiarity by which their evidence was then distinguished was, that it was conclusive of the facts in dispute. The veredictum of a jury was always an estoppel against any averment to the contrary, unless they could be convicted or manifest perjury and fraud—and this could only be done by a subsequent proceeding. As regarded the trial in hand, their testimony (for in old times their verdict was nothing more) was taken to be literally and absolutely true. Now every court of justice has obviously two distinct functions to perform—one of which is to determine the facts, and the other to apply the law. The former is the appropriate province of a jury, the latter of the judge; but inasmuch as the conclusive finding of facts is a judicial act, the term judicium may,

---

[1] Tract. de Leg. II. 6; v. 4; XIII. 7, 11. In one passage, Bracton may seem at first sight to apply the term judicium to a verdict. He says that in a certain case the jury do not commit perjury; licet faciunt fatuum judicium, quia loquuntur secundum conscientiam, quia falli, possunt in judiciis suis sciat ipse justitiarius, fo. 289 (a). But judicium here means the judging faculty of the mind, which determines it to a particular conclusion.

perhaps, be allowed in that sense to apply to the verdict.

Some writers have supposed that the term judicium parium was applied to the decisions of the freemen of the old German courts, before the feudal system sprung up in Europe; and that the pares spoken of were the genossen, or associated members of the different districts, into which each territory was divided. These they imagine to have sat and judged in classes, according to the rank or occupation of the person to be tried. Thus the nobles would judge the noble, the peasants the peasant, and so on. But this theory is not borne out by the documents and records we possess. On the contrary, it may be safely asserted that no such distinction prevailed in those times, but the whole body of freemen of the gau or mark formed the court, and were the triers and judges of all persons and cases whatever.

But to return from this digression.—By one of the laws of William I., if there was a dispute between a lord and his vassal respecting any agreement about holding land, the vassal was to prove his case by the testimony of his peers (par ses pers de la tenure meimes), for in such a case he could not vouch a stranger.[1]

To do suit (sectam) at a county or other inferior court was in fact one of the common tenures by which land was held, and the suitors, called sectatores, or sometimes at a later period pares, where therefore bound to give their attendance. Hence when the tenant was entitled to claim exemption as being a minor, and in ward to the king, or on any other ground, he obtained a writ pro exoneratione sectæ ad curiam comitatus vel baron. And this was said to lie " where the tenant holdeth his land to do suit at the county-court, hundred, or other court-baron or wapentake or leet, and he who ought to do suit is in ward unto the king or his committee, and the lord

[1] Leg. Gul. Conq. 23.

of whom he holdeth by such service will distrain him to do his suit at his court during the time he is in ward unto the king or his committee."[1]

The lord had no voice in the decision come to by the homage: he simply presided, and carried into effect the judgment.[2] According to the feudal law of Europe, if a vassal had neglected to perform the military service due from him, he was tried by his compeers, his fellow-vassals,[3] and lost his fief, si de vocatione legitima a domino suo convinci per compares suos poterit.[4] And in case of a dispute between a lord and his vassal, if any member of the court knew the truth of the fact he was obliged to make it known; Notandum est quod de omni controversia quæ inter dominum et vasallum oritur, si pares veritatem noverint omino cogi debent a dominio et paribus dicere veritatem.[5] Here we see, as in many other instances, the office of trier and witness blended together, but no trace of the intervention of third parties corresponding to a jury.

SECTION IV. *The Courts established by the Assises de Jerusalem.*

We have very scanty information on the course of procedure in these feudal courts in Europe, but the defect is supplied in a great measure by the invaluable work the "Livre des Assises de Jerusalem," which is an account of the courts established in Palestine by the Crusaders after Godfrey Duke of Bouillon had ascended

---

[1] Fitzherbert, Nat. Brev. 158.
[2] Le coustume de Beauvoisins est tele que li seigneurs ne jugent pas en leur cour, mes les homes jugent. Coutumes de Beauvaisis, c. 57.
[3] Meyer says, that the first mention of the right of vassals to be judged by their peers, occurs in a capitulary of Charles the Bald in 856. Institut. Judic. I. 459.
[4] Feudorum Lib. ii. tit. 54.
[5] Id. tit. 58.

the throne of the kingdom of Jerusalem, when that city had been rescued from the Saracens in the year 1099.[1] Feudal courts were then established on the model of those that existed in the countries from which the crusaders came; and as the great majority of the soldiers of the cross were from France, the law of that kingdom was the one which chiefly regulated their procedure. It will be useful to consider what this was, that we may see how far writers are mistaken who think that trial by jury may have been derived from it.

Godfrey of Bouillon established two secular courts of justice in his new kingdom, one called La Haute Cour, the High Court, of which he himself as suzerain was the chief justiciary; and the other La Cour des Bourgeois, or Court of the Burgesses, called also the Viscount's Court, presided over by one of his feudal lords. The judges of the High Court were the chevaliers who held by tenure of knights' service in capite, and of the Burgess Court the townsfolk of the city, "the most upright and wise to be found therein."

The great barons had feudal courts of their own upon the model of La Haute Cour at Jerusalem. To these they summoned their tenants, just as they were summoned to attend the high court presided over by the king himself, and within the limits of their seignories they had the privilege of coining money. The same rights were enjoyed by the patriarch, the archbishops, and bishops, for they held fiefs attached to their churches.

In the feudal courts were determined all questions in which the lord and his vassals were interested, except matters relating to heresy, marriage, and wills, of which the Church took exclusive cognizance. No one, how-

---

[1] There is a very full and accurate account of the Assises de Jerusalem, and the courts of Palestine, in Wilkens's Geschichte der Kreuzüge, Vol. I. c. 13, and Beilage, III. Id. p. 17.

ever, had the right to hold a court within his fief to whom the privilege had not been granted by the superior lord. If any tenant who was himself a mesne lord (for sub-infeudation was practiced to a great extent as in England, until it was prohibited by the statute Quia Emptores) usurped such jurisdiction improperly, he was held to have forfeited his allegiance, and was liable to severe punishment. The vassals of those lords who were entitled to hold courts resorted to them, and the vassals of those who had no such privilege preferred their claims in the court of the king or some lord paramount.[1] The lord himself presided, or he might appoint a deputy, and it was his office to fix the time and place of meeting, when and where it was the duty of his vassals to attend.[2] The sentence was executed but not determined by him. This devolved upon the vassals whom he summoned to his court, and all his tenants who might happen even though not summoned to be present, might be called upon, if the lord thought fit, to take part in the judgment.

In the Haute Cour, where the king himself or his substitute presided, the assessors of the inferior feudal courts might be summoned to sit, for they were not less the vassals of the crown, because they held their fiefs from mesne lords. The rights of the sovereign were paramount over all. But in the court of a crown vassal only his own tenants might sit, unless special permission was obtained from the suzerain to call in the tenants of another vassal in cases where it was deemed advisable to have the benefit of their advice and assistance as judges.

When a complaint was made, or as we should say, an action commenced in court, the defendant was summoned by an officer (banier) to appear in person. He might, if he had a valid excuse for absence, commission

---

[1] The words of the Assize are: "il se doit clamer au seignor de qui il tient le fié, se il a court ; et se il n'a court, au chef seignor. Ch. 259.

[2] Les barons et seignors du royaume de Jerusalem qui ont court et cours et justice, doivent estre sages, léaus, droituriers, et bons justiciers. Ch. 6.

an agent to state this for him, but the latter was obliged to make oath that he had been empowered by the party for that purpose. If, however, the complainant (plaintiff) asserted that the excuse was feigned, a second summons was brought to him by three vassals, one of whom represented the president, and the others the judges of the court. This summons was peremptory, and the party must either accompany the messengers, or affirm with an oath the truth of the excuse which he had previously sent. If this excuse was that he was sick or had received a wound, the plaintiff waited for a time until he was able to inform the court that his adversary had recovered, or his wound was cured, upon which three members of the court (paires) were sent to him accompanied by a physician or surgeon sworn to speak the truth; and if the defendant persisted in saying that he was still unable, from his malady or wound, to attend, the former examined his body to ascertain whether the statement was true.[1] If found to be true, he was allowed to absent himself as long as he kept his house (tant com il demora en son hostel); if false, he was ordered to follow them to the court immediately, or if he refused, the complainant was forthwith put in possession of the disputed property.

If the defendant appeared, the plaintiff or his advocate repeated his complaint: and in most cases the former was allowed to claim a delay (demander jour) of fifteen days, at the expiration of which period both parties were bound to attend at the appointed place before sunset, or at all events before the stars appeared in the sky, and thrice proclaim, in the presence of the lord, if he had arrived, and of three of his vassals, their readiness to do right in the matter. The plaintiff then repeated his complaint, and he was obliged to be careful that he did not vary from his original statement, for if he did, the

---

[1] If it was an internal malady of which the party complained, it was the duty of the physician taster son pos et vei· ·n orine.

defendant might demand a fresh delay on the ground that it was a new plaint (nouviau claim).

If only one of the two parties appeared at the expiration of the period (which in old legal parlance in this country would have been called the essoign day) he waited until the stars were visible in the sky, and then called out to the vassals or homage in attendance, to observe them. He next applied to the lord to grant him a certificate, or record of the court, that he had kept his day, and to put him in possession of the property claimed if he was the plaintiff, or do him right if he was the defendant. This was accordingly done, and the other party was concluded in his right, unless he could prove that he had been detained by imprisonment, sickness, or some other valid and sufficient cause.

The modes of proof were, 1, the oral evidence of members of the court (recort de court), or of witnesses who were sworn to speak the truth; and if the subject-matter in dispute was of the value of a mark of silver, they were obliged to make good their testimony by combat, if challenged by the opposite party; and 2, the production of documents.

The members of the court themselves gave evidence in cases of disputes about the right to the possession of real property; and to entitle the demandant to recover it was necessary that two of them, at least, should state, if appealed to by him, that they had seen him or his ancestors in possession of the property, or knew that it had been granted to him by the rightful owner.

In criminal cases, witnesses, and the judicial combat with the accuser or his champion, seem to have been the admissible kinds of proof.

But we must notice one remarkable law, whereby, if all other means failed, an accused party was allowed to assert his innocence. This was by charging the court itself with falsehood (fausser la court), and challenging every one of its members to mortal combat. But this was a step of imminent peril; for if he did not fight with them all, one after another, he was beheaded, and if he did not vanquish them all in a single day, he was hanged (il sera pendu par la goule).[1]

In many respects different courts had, as we might expect, different usages; and Jean d'Ibelin tells us that it was the custom for two or more members of the court to state what the usage in former times had been, and this served for a precedent on the particular occasion.

There were also burgess courts in the different towns, corresponding to the Cour de Bourgeois at Jerusalem; over these an officer presided, called a vesconte (vicecomes), and the court was composed of him and twelve jurés, but nothing is known of their mode of appointment. This, however, is certain, that they were a permanent tribunal, and sat as the sworn judges of the court;[2] so that their constitution differed little if at all from that of the Scabini in Europe, of whom we have already spoken.[3] But it was not necessary that the whole twelve should sit, for three or even two were sufficient to form a quorum. The nature of their duties is shortly summed up in a passage of the Assizes: Les jurés puisque ils sont asis en la cort, deivent oyr et escouter la clamor et le repons et bien entendre; et sur ce que ils oront et connoistront, doivent faire droit jugement à lor essient sans faucer.[4]

[1] Upon the chances of success in such an undertaking, Jean d'Ibelin well observes: il me semble que nul home, si Dieu nefaisoit apertes miracles pour lui, qui la faussast en dit, la faussast en fait. Ch. 112.
[2] See Assises de Jerusalem, par Beugnot, tom. II. Introduct. p. XX. XL. Liv. des Assises, chap. VII. et seq.
[3] In a charter granted to the inhabitauts of Acre in 1231, we find the following: Jurare debent Choremanni (*i.e.* Jurati) primo jus Ecclesiæ, se servaturos, jus etiam abbatis et ecclesiæ sancti Bernardi; jura viduarum et orphanorum pauperum et divitum, et omnium hominum tam extraneorum quam juratorum suorum super causis quœ coram ipsis venerint et ad juramentum suum pertinuerint, jus et legem dicere, nec omittere propter gratiam vel timorem odium vel amorem. Id. p. 25. n. (d). [4] Chap. ix.

CHAPTER VI.

THE JURY IN THE TIME OF THE PLANTAGENETS.

SECTION I. *On the Assize as established by Henry II.*

WE now come to speak of the Assize which was established in the reign of Henry II., and is called by Glanvill, a contemporary and the earliest of our juridical writers, regale quoddam beneficium clementia principis de consilio procerum populis indultum. In another passage he mentions it as regalis institutio; so that there seems to be no doubt that it owed its existence not to custom and usage, but to a positive enactment of the king with the advice and consent of his nobles. In it we first find the jury in its distinct form, but the elements of which it was composed were all familiar to the jurisprudence of the time, and we shall see that, except as regards its definite constitution, it involved no idea novel to the minds of our ancestors.

The assisa, or magna assisa, as it was usually called,[1] was a mode of trial confined to questions concerning (1) the recovery of lands of which the complainant had been

---

[1] The word assisa means nothing more than statute or enactment. Thus Glanvill says that in some cases inferior courts were made courts of record per assisam de consilio regni inde factam. Tract. de Leg. x. c. 10. And one of our old statutes is entitled Assisa panis et cervisiæ, "an ordinance respecting bread and beer." Hence the recognition by jurors was called an assize, because it was established by an assisa, or statute of Henry II.

disseized; (2) rights of advowson; and (3) claims of vassalage affecting the civil status of the defendant.

In cases of disseizin the demandant and tenant, corresponding to the modern plaintiff and defendant, having duly appeared in court, the former "declared" in the following plain and straightforward manner:

"I claim against A. two carucates of land in the town of B. as my right and inheritance, of which my father (or grandfather) was seized in his demesne as of fee in the time of king Henry I. (or after the coronation of our lord the king), and of which he has taken the profits to the value of five shillings at the least. And this I am ready to prove by (the body of) this my freeman C., and if any mischance happens to him, then by another, D."

It is important to notice that the person thus offered as the champion of the demandant must be one who could, from his own knowledge, testify to the justice of the claim. He was, in fact, one whom the plaintiff vouched as a witness of the truth of his assertion with regard to the seizin of his ancestor.—But it was sufficient if he could give hearsay evidence on oath, derived from a trustworthy source:[1] and hence the "declaration" sometimes concluded thus:—"And this I am ready to prove by this my freeman N., whose father on his deathbed enjoined him, if at any time he heard of a dispute about this land, to give evidence of what his father saw and heard respecting him."

Sometimes it happened that a hired champion was named, but this was contrary to law, and the other side might object to his competency; for the principle of the combat was that the champion should be a "witness of the truth" of the side on which he fought; and he gave the strongest possible evidence of the sincerity of his conviction by exposing his life to peril in the cause.[2]

---

[1] Glanville says he must be a person qui hoc vidit vel audivit.
[2] Sir Edward Coke assigns a more technical but unsatisfactory reason

And as it was supposed that God interfered on behalf, of right a defeat was regarded as a proof of the falsehood of that side which sustained it; and hence not only did the party whose champion was vanquished lose his suit, but the champion was himself punished as guilty of the offense of having borne false witness. At a later period, in the reign of Edward I., the statute of Westminister provided that the champion of the demandant should not be obliged to swear, de visu et auditu, as to what he had seen and heard, "because it seldom happens but that the champion of the demandant is forsworn, in that he sweareth that he or his father saw the seizin of his lord or his ancestor, and his father commanded him to deraign that right."

But the tenant (defendant) was not obliged to accept the combat thus offered. He might, unless a valid objection were taken by his adversary, avail himself of the enactment of Henry II., and choose the trial by assize, magna, assisa domini regis.[1] Such an objection was relationship:—if both parties were descended from a common ancestor to whom the land in dispute once belonged. This, if asserted by the plaintiff, might be denied by the defendant; but if the fact were admitted, the next question was, which of the two was the nearest

He says (Litt. 294 b.): "In the writ of right neither the tenant nor demandant shall fight for themselves, but find a champion to fight for them: because if either the demandant or tenant should be slain, no judgment could be given for the lands or tenements in question. But in an appeal the defendant shall fight for himself, and so shall the plaintiff also; for then if the defendant be slain, the plaintiff hath the effect of his suit, that is the death of the defendant."

[1] It seems to have been called magna, from the importance of the questions it was called upon to decide, and the superior station of the milites who served on it. Glanvill points out the advantages of the assize over the combat, the latter of which was exposed to many tedious delays and technicalities, and was, after all, only a proof of the sincerity of a single witness, the champion; cum enim ex unius jurati testimonio procedat duellum, duodecim ad minus legalium hominum exigit ista constitutio juramenta. II: c. 7.

in blood to the common ancestor, and what circumstance, if any, had happened to deprive him of his primâ facie right to the property, *e.g.* whether there had been a sale, gift, exchange, or forfeiture for felony. In pursuing this inquiry, as any issue of fact arose between the parties it was determined by bodily combat.

If, however, the defendant denied altogether that he and the plaintiff were descended from a common ancestor, the relations of each party were summoned into court and examined as to the fact; and if notwithstanding their assertion that a common relationship existed between them, the defendant still denied it, recourse was had to the neighborhood (decurrendum erit ad vicinetum) whose verdict (veredictum vicineti) was conclusive. And if the relationship were thus proved, the trial then proceeded in the same way as if it had been originally admitted.

But if the contrary were proved, the plaintiff was punished for his unjust attempt to deprive the defendant of his assize, and lost his cause.

If, however, no objection of this kind were raised, the next step was to issue a writ of prohibition to the inferior court, if the suit respecting the lands had been there commenced;—on the ground that the curia regis had cognizance of the cause, and it was to be determined by the assize. A writ was then addressed to the sheriff commanding him to summon four knights of the neighborhood where the disputed property lay, who were, after being duly sworn, to choose twelve lawful knights, who were most cognizant of the facts (qui melius veritatem sciant); and who were upon their oaths to determine which of the litigant parties was entitled to the land. The defendant was also to be summoned to hear the election of the twelve jurors made by the four knights, and he might except to any of them for the same reasons and in the same way as witnesses might be objected to in the courts Christian. When the twelve were duly chosen, they were summoned by writ to appear in court and testify on oath the rights of the parties. They swore that they would not say anything false, nor knowingly conceal the truth; and by knowledge, says Glanvill, was meant what they had seen or heard by trustworthy information. He then adds, what shows in the clearest light how entirely they were regarded as mere witnesses, and how different the idea of their functions then was from what it is now. When they met to try the case, either they all knew who was the rightful claimant, or some of them did and some did not; or they were all ignorant. In the last case they testified this in court, and then others were chosen who were acquainted with the facts in dispute.[1] If, however, some did and some did not know them, the latter only were removed, and others summoned in their place, until twelve at least were found who knew and agreed upon the facts. Also if the jurors when chosen were not unanimous, others were to be added to the number until twelve at least agreed in favor of the one side or other.—This was called afforcing the assize.

The concurrent testimony, or verdict of the jury, was conclusive; and there could be no subsequent action brought upon the same claim; for it was a legal maxim, that lites per magnam assisam domini Regis legitimè decisæ nulla occasione rite resuscitantur imposterum.[2]

If the jurors swore falsely, and were convicted, or confessed their crime, their punishment was severe. They were

---

[1] Assisa venit recognitura si Adam de Greinvill et Willielmus de la Folie dissaisaverunt injustè et sine judicio Willielmum de Weston de libero tenemento suo in Suto, post priman coronationem Domini Regis. Juratores dicunt quod non viderunt unquam aliam saisitum de tenemento illo, nisi Willielmum de la Folie. Et quod nesciunt si Willielmus de la Folie dissaisisset eum inde vel non, Consideratum est quod alii juratores eligantur qui meilus sciant rei veritatem. Dies datus est eis ad diem Mercurii.—Plac. Ab. 11, Wiltesir.

[2] Glanv. II. c. 18.

deprived of all their personal property, and imprisoned for a year at least. They became infamous, and incompetent to act as witnesses or compurgators in future (legem terræ amittunt), but were allowed to retain their freeholds.

We see then that this proceeding by assize was nothing more than the sworn testimony of a certain number of persons summoned to give evidence upon matters within their own knowledge. It is needless to multiply proofs of an assertion which does not admit of denial or controversy. It will be sufficient to give a single instance, taken from one of the chroniclers of the time: Cumque inde summonita esset recognitio duodecim militum in curia regis facienda, facta est in curia abbatis aqud Herlavam per licentiam Ranulfi de Glanvilla, et juraverunt recognitores SE NUNQUAM SCIVISSE illam terram fuisse separatam ab ecclesia.[1] This corresponds to a trial at the present day, respecting ancient boundaries or manorial customs, where the evidence of the oldest inhabitants, as to what they have known in their time, generally determines the verdict. The difference, however, is, that in the reign of Richard I., when the dispute mentioned in Jocelin's chronicle occurred, the jury were themselves the witnesses, whereas now they derive their information from the witnesses, and give their verdict accordingly.

In the Rotuli Curiæ Regis, published by the Record Commissioners, we find numerous entries of these "Assizes" and their verdicts, in the following form:

Assisa venit recognoscendum si Robertus filius Walteri injuste et sine judicio dissaisavit Ysabel de Benninton de libero tenemento suo in Benninton infra assisam.

---

[1] Chron. Jocelina de Brakelonda, p. 45, published by the Cambridge Society. Jocelin wrote the annals of the Monastery at Bury St. Edmund's, from the year 1172 to 1202. In claiming the right to an adowson, the plaintiff, in his oral demand before the court, said et si quis hoc voluerit negare, habeo probos homines, qui hoc viderunt et audierunt, et parati sunt hoc dirationare.—Glanv. Tract. IV. c. 6.

Juratores dicunt, quod non dissaisavit eam ita. Judicium. Robertus teneat in pace; et Ysabel pro falso clamore sit in misericordia.

So entirely did the verdict of the recognitors proceed upon their own previously-formed view of the facts in dispute, that they seem to have considered themselves at liberty to pay no attention to evidence offered in court however clearly it might disprove the case which they were prepared to support. As an example of this, we may take the following narrative from the Chronicle already quoted, which contains many curious and interesting illustrations of the manners and customs of the period.

Thomas de Burg had obtained the wardship of the only daughter of Adam de Cokefield, from the abbot of the monastery to whom she had been left in ward by her father; and he claimed in her right livery of seizin of three manors to which the convent asserted that they had a title; with respect to two of these, they relied upon a declaration made by Robert de Cokefield, the grandfather, on his death-bed, that he had no estate of inheritance in them, and on a deed solemnly executed in open court by Adam, the father, in which he acknowledged that he held the two manors of the convent by agreement only for his life. Thomas de Burg thereupon applied for a writ to summon twelve knights to meet at Theocesberie (Tewkesbury), and take their oaths in the presence of the king. The assize met, and the deed was publicly read in open court; but it had no effect,—because, as the chronicler says, "they were all against us" (tota curia erat contra nos). The knights on their oaths said that they knew nothing of chartularies, or private agreements (juramento facto, dixerunt milites se nescire de cartis nostris, nec de privatis conventionibus) · but that they believed that Adam and his father and grandfather, for a hundred years back, had held the manors in fee one after the other. "And so," says Jocelin, "we were disseized by the judgment of the court, after much trouble and heavy expense, though we kept the old yearly rents." This was certainly a flagrant instance of common repute being allowed to outweigh positive evidence; but we must not suppose it to be by any means a solitary case.

As the names of the jurors who were to form the assize were known beforehand, the temptation became great to endeavor to secure a favorable verdict by bribes, and the practice seems to have prevailed to a considerable extent, for no less than three statutes were passed in the reign of Edward III. which prohibited the offense under severe penalties. Jocelin de Brakelonde also gives an example of the corruption of the times, and the danger of not propiating the knights who served in the assize. The church of Boesford was vacant, and the abbot claimed the advowson. An assize was summoned, and five of the knights who were in the panel came to the abbot and offered to swear in any way he wished if he would pay them. He however refused, and bade them when they were sworn to speak the truth according to their conscience. Upon this they left him in anger, and declared upon their oaths in court that he was not entitled to the advowson.

Although twelve was the most usual, it was not the unvarying number of the jurors of assize for some years. In the infancy of the institution the number seems to have fluctuated according as convenience or local custom required. An instance of the former is mentioned in Jocelin's Chronicle. A fine had been imposed upon the counties of Norfolk and Suffolk, and the monastery of Bury St. Edmund's was called upon to pay its proportion. The abbot, however, hastened to the king (Henry II.) who was then with his court at Clarendon, and exhibited a royal charter of exemption from all fines and imposts granted by King Edward the Confessor to the lands of the convent. Writs were thereupon issued to summon six knights of the county of Norfolk, and six of the county of Suffolk, to appear before the barons of the exchequer, and "recognize" whether the lands of the monastery ought to bear part of a general fine imposed upon the county; and because they had lands in both counties, and "in order to save trouble and expense," only six knights were chosen, who went to London, and there gave their verdict in favor of the abbot, which was enrolled by the justices.[1] On another occasion, when there was a question of jurisdiction between the abbot and the Archbishop of Canterbury, the former in the presence of the king offered to put himself upon the verdict of the two counties of Norfolk and Suffolk, that he and his convent had always had possession of the disputed franchise. The archbishop, however, said that the men of those counties had great veneration for St. Edmund (the patron saint of the monastery), and a large part of the lands in them were under the abbot's sway, so that he was unwilling to abide by their decision.[2] We find also in the same Chronicle that a verdict was taken by consent from sixteen lawful men of the hundred respecting the moiety of an advowson.[3] Indeed, it is tolerably clear from Glanvill's treatise that the law on this subject was by no means settled in his time, for he puts as a difficulty the case of there being no knights of the vicinage or county, or fewer than twelve acquainted with the facts in dispute, and he asks, without determining the point whether, supposing in such an event those who were thus qualified as witnesses to be on the jury, were to offer to prove their assertion by the combat, it would be

[1] Justiciarii autem assidentes verumdictum illorum inrollaverunt. Chron Joc. de Brakel. p. 48.
[2] Ibid. pp. 37, 38. [3] Ibid. p. 45.

allowed?[1] In the case of an assise de mort d'ancestor, if the question were raised whether one of the parties was a minor or not, it was determined by the recognition or verdict of eight jurors.[2]

SECTION II. *What suggested the idea of trial by Assize?*

The question now occurs, what gave rise to this institution of the assise, and whether it was developed from any modes of procedure previously existing? The theory of Phillips, a German writer, who has investigated the history of our early jurisprudence with much learning and ability, is ingenious, and may be shortly stated as follows.[3]

Owing to the removal by William I. of ecclesiastical causes from the cognizance of lay judges, and the gradual increase of the jurisdiction of the Curia Regis, the provincial courts, such as those of the hundred and shire, lost much of their importance. The number of causes there diminished, and the chief amount of business was monopolized by the king's court.[4] But as upwards of a century elapsed from the arrival of the Normans before Justices in Eyre were regularly appointed to visit the counties and administer the law in the king's name, great inconvenience would in the meantime be felt in at-

---

[1] Tract. de Legg. II. c. 21. In the manor of Penryn Farrein, in Cornwall, there was a custom to try an issue with six jurors, but this was in 1652 adjudged to be no good custom. By the statute 34 and 35 Hen. VIII. c. 26, concerning Wales, it was provided that trials in the shire and hundred courts of the principality should be by verdict of six men.

[2] Ibid. XIII. c. 15. The course of practice in the baronial, county, and other inferior courts, varied greatly. Ibid. XII. c. 6, 23.

[3] See his Englische Reiche und Rechts Geschichte, II. § 50.

[4] While writing this sentence it is impossible not to be reminded that, owing to the recent establishment, or, perhaps we should more properly say, restoration of the county courts, the converse of the statement would now be true.

tending the Curia Regis under the old system of procedure. This court followed the king's person, whose movements were uncertain, and as the judicial combat, which was the usual mode of settling disputes, was hampered with many formalities and delays, parties often found themselves obliged to travel from place to place before they could obtain legal redress. Besides this, they would feel the want of judges to decide at the trial, who, like those in the country courts, were familiar with the parties and their cause of quarrel. Hence would arise a wish to provide if possible a tribunal similar to the king's court. The judicial members of the county court could not all be summoned to attend, for they had causes to try at home. Who, then, could be found to supply their place? It had, as we have seen, been the practice for the plaintiff, or, in some cases, the reeve, to nominate what may be called a panel of relations and neighbors, out of whom the defendant was to choose his compurgators; and, under the altered circumstances of the time, it seemed an obvious course to choose a similar panel from amongst the members of the court of the district in which the litigant parties dwelt. The number named would be sufficient to admit of valid exceptions being taken by the defendant against some of them, and yet leave upon the panel twelve to coincide with the number of the judges constituting the county court, whose substitute and representatives they were.

Such is the theory of Phillips, but it is, upon the whole, unsatisfactory, and, in some points, too refined to be likely to be correct. According to him the assize was a modified form of the county court summoned to attend the Curia Regis, and deliver its judgment or verdict there. But this is altogether unsupported by authority; nor do I think there is any necessity for resorting to such a supposition. It seems to me that the matter admits of a much more simple explanation. In the instances already given of suits respecting lands in the reigns of the early Norman kings, we have seen that the constant practice was to decide the controversy by appealing to the knowledge of the neighborhood where the parties resided and the lands lay; and frequently a limited number of persons were sworn who represented the vicinage, and who stated on oath to whom the property belonged. These were called the probi et legales homines, and their verdict was conclusive of the question in dispute. Such were the inquests, of which examples have been already given in the preceding chapter; and when we come to speak of the Jurata we shall have occasion to consider the subject more fully. There was no difference whatever in principle between those inquests and the recognitions by the knights of assize; and it seems to me to be almost as clear as demonstration that the idea of the latter was derived from the former. In both cases the verdict was the testimony of witnesses cognizant of the matter in dispute; and if we substitute a determinate number of knights for the probi homines of an ordinary inquest, we have at once the assize.

SECTION III. *Subsequent History of the Assize.*

The first mention of the trial by assize in our existing statutes occurs in the Constitutions of Clarendon, A. D. 1164, where it was provided that if any dispute arose between a layman and a clerk as to whether a particular tenement was the property of the Church or belonged to a lay fief, this was to be determined before the chief justiciary of the kingdom, by the verdict of twelve lawful men (recognitione duodecim legalium hominum). And if they decided that it belonged to the Church, then any further plea concerning it was to be held in the spiritual court; but if to a lay fief, then in the King's Court.

VI.] SUBSEQUENT HISTORY OF ASSIZE. 113

This was followed by the Statute of Northampton, A. D. 1176, which directs the justices, in case a lord should refuse to give to the heir the seizin of his deceased ancestor, " to cause a recognition to be made by means of twelve lawful men as to what seizin the deceased had on the day of his death;" and also orders them to inquire in the same manner in cases of novel disseizin.

It was one of the articles of Magna Charta (A. D. 1215), that legal suits should no longer follow the ambulatory royal court, but be tried in some fixed place, and that recognitions by assize should be taken in the counties where the lands lay; for which purpose the king was to send into each county two justiciaries four times a year, who, with four knights of the same county, chosen by the county, were to take the assize, and no one else was to be summoned by them except the jurors and the parties (nisi juratores et duæ partes).[1] The expression "take the assize," here means "summon the assize" in the manner specified by Glanvill, and already mentioned.

The next legal writer after Glanvill is Bracton, who lived in the middle of the thirteenth century, and we find in him a clear account of the form in which this mode of trial was conducted in his time.[2]

If no exception could be taken to the assize, and the defendant denied the disseizin complained of, the first point to consider was, whether all or any of the recognitors could be objected to. And as a general rule the same causes disqualified a man from being on the assize, as disqualified him from giving testimony as a witness.

---

[1] Articuli Cartæ, § 8. These articles were sealed by King John, and afterwards drawn up in the form of a charter, to which he also affixed his seal, and so drawn up they constitute the Great Charter. The alterations and additions are pointed out by Blackstone in his Law Tracts, pp. 299–301.

[2] Bract. IV. c. 19.

Such was conviction for perjury, which made him no longer law-worthy, as was expressed by the old English maxim:

He ne es othes worthe that es enes gylty of oth broken.

Other causes were serfdom, consanguinity, affinity, enmity, or close friendship. When the objections had been disposed of, and the panel was complete, one of the recognitors took the prescribed oath, and the others then, each for himself, adopted it. The prothonotary of the court next read to the jury the issue which they were to try, saying,—"Ye shall declare on the oath which ye have taken, if N. has unjustly and without judgment disseized M. of his tenement in such a vill, since such a time, or not."

The jury were then to retire to some private place to consider their verdict, and no one was allowed to have access to them until it was delivered. If, however, they could not agree, other recognitors were empanelled, in number equal to the dissentient minority, provided it consisted of at least four; and these either joined the former jury and discussed the matter with them, or they might deliberate apart; and the conclusion to which they came was considered the verdict, which agreed of course with the view of one of the two parties into which the jury had been divided. Judgment was then given in conformity with this verdict.[1] But if any of the jurors said that they were ignorant of the facts of the case, others were added who knew the truth, until the requisite number was obtained.

---

[1] There is, however, a passage in Bracton which seems to imply that it was the duty of the judge to satisfy himself of the truth of the verdict of the assize: Sed cum ad Judicem pertineat justum proferre judicium et reddere, oportebit eum diligenter deliberare et examinare si dicta juratorum in se veritatem contineant, et si eorum justum sit judicium vel fatuum, ne si continyat eum judicem eorum dicta sequi et eorum judicium, ita falsum faciat judicium vel fatuum. iv. c. 19 § 6.

In the treatise called "Fleta," which was written in the reign of Edward I., the practice appears substantially the same. When a party complained of a disseizin a writ was issued to the sheriff, and it was his duty thereupon to convene a number, not exceeding twenty-four, of " free and lawful men " of the vincinage, out of whom in the presence of the parties (if they chose to attend) he nominated twelve indifferent persons, who then either all, or to the number of seven at least, proceeded to view the property in dispute. After having done this, their names were enrolled, and they were then summoned by two freeholders to appear at a fixed time and place before the justices of assize, ready to make recognizance: that is, try the question of disseizin.[1]

In modern times the grand assize has been now and then summoned by a writ of right; and I believe the last recorded instance of it occurred in 1834, which led to two trials, the second of which took place in 1838, when four knights girt with swords and twelve other recognitors acted as the jury in a trial at bar in the Court of Common Pleas, and were addressed by Chief Justice Tindal in summing up, as " Gentlemen of the grand inquest," and " Recognitors of the grand assize."[2] The writ of right, and all proceedings by the assize, were finally abolished by Stat. 3 and 4 William IV. c. 27.

SECTION IV. *On the trial by the Jurata, and the meaning of the expression Assisa vertitur in Juratam.*

So far we have been considering the assize, which we see was in its original constitution nothing more than a body of twelve knights empaneled to determine by their testimony a disputed question of seizin of land, right to an advowson, or villenage. But we find in Bracton and Fleta and other old legal writers, a distinction drawn be-

---

[1] Fleta, II. c. 5.   [2] Davies *v.* Lowndes, 5 Bing. N. C. 161.

tween the assize and jurata, to which it is necessary carefully to attend. What is the meaning of such expressions as these: "Utrum recognitio procedere debeat in modum assisæ vel juratæ." "Capitur assisa in modum assisæ, quod quidem non esset si caperetur ut jurata."[1] "Cadit assisa et vertitur in juratam."[2] "Capienda erit assisa in modum assisæ, secus vero si in modum juratæ?"[3] And in both the above-named authors we have chapters entitled Qualiter assisa vertitur in juratam.

The subject is involved in an obscurity which perhaps cannot now be wholly removed. This arises from the absence of any precise information respecting the mode in which the jurata was first formed, and how it came into existence. No account of this has been transmitted to us by contemporary writers to whom its use was familiar, and we are left to find our way through the darkness, relying upon the aid of analogy, and probable conjecture drawn from the incidental notices of the subject that occur in our old chroniclers and legal writers.

The theory of Meyer is that the jurata, as distinguished from the assisa, is the real jury of modern times, and that it is derived from the Cour-Basse of the kingdom of Jerusalem, the knowledge of which was brought to England by the numerous crusaders and pilgrims who visited the Holy Land. His argument, however, is chiefly based on the assumption that the word jurata, as a mode of trial, first occurs in Bracton, who wrote a century after Glanvill, and after the Crusades had in the interval taken place.[4] But this is a mistake; for although Bracton is the first writer who discusses the precise question in what cases the assisa vertitur in juratam, Glanvill distinctly notices the jurata as existing in his time. He mentions

---

[1] Bract. iv. c. 19.   [2] Id.   [3] Fleta, iv. c. 9.
[4] Dans cet ouvrage (Glanvill)....il ne se rencontre ni le nom de jury, ni la chose meme, quoiqu'il y soit souvent question de l'assise. Origine des Inst. Judic. II. 169.

it when treating of purprestures, that is, trespasses or encroachments committed against the public, as, for instance, in building upon the king's highway;[1] and says that inquisition is to be made of these before the justices per juratam patriæ sive visineti, and whoever is convicted is to be in the king's mercy; which Glanvill explains to mean a fine imposed by the oath of legal men of the neighborhood.

The problem is to discover what was the origin and constitution of the jurata of which Glanvill speaks;—and it seems to me that the solution is to be found in the early forms of procedure resorted to determine disputes concerning land or other property, such as we have seen took place in the ancient suits, of which several instances have been previously given.

It has been sufficiently shown that in those cases the mode originally adopted in the Anglo-Saxon times was to refer the question to the knowledge of the comitatus or county, and afterwards, in the Anglo-Norman, as a more convenient method, to allow the neighborhood to be represented by a certain number of the inhabitants probi et legales homines, who stated upon oath on whose side the right lay.[2] These, therefore, were called the jurato patriæ, or often simply the patria, as representing the country, whose decision this verdict was deemed to be. They spoke of matters within their own knowledge —being, in fact, nothing more than witnesses who testified to the truth of matters notorious in their district. Of such a jurata patriæ the Chronicle of Jocelin de Brakelonde affords several good examples. On one occasion the Abbot of St. Edmund's offered that the question of

---

[1] Tract. de Leg. IX. c. 11.

[2] The Great Charter (A. D. 1215) provides that amercements or fines shall be made in due proportion to the nature of the offense (secundum modum delicti), and assessed per sacramentum proborum hominum de visneto. Art. Chart. § 9.

disputed right to an advowson should be determined by the oath of the party claiming adversely to the convent. He, however, refused to swear; and it was then agreed on both sides that the matter should be decided by the oaths of sixteen lawful men of the hundred, and these declared on oath that the title was in the abbot. Another instance of the same number of jurors is mentioned in the Chronicle in the case of an affray attended with bloodshed. An oath was administered to sixteen lawful men, and when they had given their verdict, or attestatio, as it is called by Jocelin (auditis eorum attestationibus) the abbot excommunicated the offenders. And we frequently find in Glanvill the expression decurrendum erit ad visinetum, or words to the same effect; which mean that recourse must be had to the knowledge of the neighborhood where the parties dwelt, to determine some question of fact asserted on one side, and denied on the other. But it does not appear from him that there was any number limited for this purpose, although we may suppose, from analogy to the assize, that twelve would be the most usual. The testimony thus borne by the neighbors was called their testimonium or veredictum.[1]

Hence I conclude that, in the earliest times, disputes respecting lands were decided by the voice of the community of the county or hundred, as the case might be, where the parties lived; that afterwards a select number was substituted for the whole, who gave their testimony upon oath, and, therefore, were called the "jurata;" and that this suggested to Henry II. and his councillors the idea of the assize, which was nothing but the jurata in a technical form, and limited to milites, or knights, who were summoned by a writ of the sheriff in virtue of a precept from the king.

But the term "assize" had a technical meaning, and was applied only to those proceedings, the direct object

---

[1] Tract de Leg. II. c. 6, § 4; V. c. 4; IX. c. II, § 2; XIV. c. 3, § 5.

of which was either the recovery of land or realty in some shape, or the determination of the fact of villenage. In these cases the verdict of the recognitors was confined solely to the question of the rightful seizin of the land, or the civil status of the individual, but in the course of the inquiry many other issues might be raised; as, for instance, whether the plaintiff was entitled to proceed by way of assize, on account of not being a freeman, but a "villain;" or whether a particular deed had been executed or not. It became necessary to determine these questions; but the jury in doing so could not act in their capacity of recognitors of assize, in which they were limited to the single duty of deciding the issue of seizin or disseizin. Hence in such cases the expression was used, assisa vertitur in juratam, or, with perhaps less accuracy, the questions were said to be decided per assisam in modum juratæ.[1] I can not, however, quite satisfy myself whether the same assize went on with the inquiry in the new character of jurata, or a fresh process issued, and proceedings commenced de novo where questions arose in the progress of the suit which did not fall properly within the province of an assize of recognitors to determine. I think, however, that the former is the preferable view, and this is assumed by Reeves in his account of the matter.[2] He says, that when any issue arose upon a fact in a writ of novel disseizin, mort d'ancestor, and the like actions, which fact the parties agreed should be inquired of by a jurata, nothing was more natural, nor, indeed, more commodious, than that, instead of summoning other recognitors, as in Glanvill's time, the assisa summoned in that action should be the jurors to whom they might refer the inquiry. This was generally the case; and then the lawyers said, cadit assisa et vertitur in juratam; the as-

---

[1] See Fleta, IV. c. 16.
[2] Hist. English Law, I. c. 6.

size was turned into a jury, and the point in dispute was determined by the recognitors, not in modum assisæ, but in modum juratæ.[1]

As an illustration of the principle on which the distinction between the assisa and the jurata proceeded, may be mentioned the case of actions brought, where the subject-matter of dispute was consecrated land or buildings. Here there could be no right of private ownership,[2] and therefore there could be no disseizin, which always meant the ouster of the rightful owner. Hence, if any trespass or encroachment was committed upon such tenements, an assize did not lie, but a jurata was empaneled to inquire concerning the trespass. In such cases, to use the expression of the legal writers of that age, Cadit assisâ et non breve, et vertitur assisa in juratam, ad inquirendum de transgressione, si facta fuerit in re sacra, quia nulla ibi est disseisina ut per juratam emendetur transgressio.[3] So also in the case of any public building, a wrongful occupation of it was not considered a disseizin, but a purpresture or trespass, and the same rule prevailed.

Where a question arose whether the tenement claimed by the plaintiff lay in the vill and county named in the writ, and the jurors were unable to determine it, it was the duty of the judge, with the consent of both parties, to order a preambulation; and this was designated by the expression cadit assisa in perambulationem.[4] And if a deed attested by witnesses were pleaded in bar of the right claimed, then the rule was, that the parties must proceed by an assize taken in the form of a jurata, and by the witnesses named in the written instrument.[5]

---

[1] Et ita eo ipso remanet assisa, et placitum super exceptione ipsa inter ipsos litigantes deinde esse poterit. Super hac autem exceptione recognitionem desiderare potest alteruter litigantium, et eam habere poterit. Glanv. XIII. c. 20.

[2] Coke says that burglary may be committed in a church as being the domus mansionalis of Almighty God. 3 Inst. c. 14.

[3] Fleta, IV. c. 14.   [4] Id. IV. c. 15.   [5] Id. c. 16.

It seems to have been usual, if not necessary, that both parties should give their consent to enable the proceeding to take place in technical form, per juratam, and on this account, even if the verdict were erroneous, no attaint or conviction of the jury could follow, quia non erit locus convictioni propter consensum. In such case the jury were looked upon as arbitrators chosen by the litigants to decide their controversy, whom therefore it would be unjust to punish for a mistaken finding.[1] Nay, more than this, when a man put himself upon the jurata to determine a disputed issue, it was looked upon as his own mode of proof, voluntarily chosen, and therefore he had no right to quarrel with the result, whatever it might be: quia si quæ partium venire vellet contra dicta juratorum, ita diceret probationem suam esse falsam:[2] But yet Bracton tells us, that if the objection of villenage were taken in order to deprive the plaintiff of his right to the assize (for no villain could proceed by that mode of trial), and the jury found the fact against him, they might be convicted if they were wrong, provided the plaintiff could prove this, either by another jury of twenty-four, or by the testimony of his relations.[3] But in all cases where the trial was by way of "assize," and not "jurata," the jurors might be attainted for a wrong verdict, quia assisa capta est in modum assisæ, et non juratæ.[4]

An ancient statute, the date of which is uncertain, provided that in cases where land of trifling extent and value, such as an acre or toft, was claimed, the justices might

---

[1] Utraque pars facit juratam quasi judicem per consensum et per juratam terminabitur negotium siene aliqua convictione. Bract. IV. c. 23. En plusurs maneres sount assises chaunges ascuns jesques en temps ascuns a toutes jours par assent des partes jesques en jures...Si chet l'assise (cadit assisa) et pur assent des parties soient les jurours faits come juges arbiters.—Britton, c. 51.

[2] Bract. IV. c. 34.   [3] Id. IV. 23.

[4] A jurata, however, might be attained if it gave a wrong verdict in a matter which touched the King.—Bract. 290.

award a jury of twelve free men une jurre de XII. franks hommes, instead of the grand assize, to spare the service of twelve knights, par espargnir le travaille de XII. chivaliers, and these were to take an oath to speak the truth sans dire a lour ascient, that is, without being obliged to say that it was of their own knowledge.[1] The meaning of this seems to be, that they were not restricted to giving evidence of what they had seen or actually known themselves, but might deliver their verdict upon such information as they believed to be true. This was a step towards the reception by the jury of evidence from witnesses in court. Gradually the justices appointed to hold the assize were directed to entertain other questions than those concerning land. And special judges seem to have been from time to time nominated for this purpose distinct from the regular justices of the bench, and these visited the counties, traveling circuit as at the present day. Thus by Stat. 13 Edw. I. c. 30. (A. D. 1285), it is provided that to avoid the delay and expense of bringing parties to Westminster, inquisitions of trespass and other pleas, wherein small examination is required, shall be determined before the justices of assize, and the writ to the sheriff for summoning the jury is to be in the following form :

Præcipimus tibi quod venire facias coram justiciariis nostris apud Westmonasterium in Octabis sancti Michaelis nisi talis et talis tali die et loco ad partes illas venerint, duodecim, &c.[2]

In 1306 we find the word assisa applied to a trial of an action of trepass and false imprisonment.[3]

---

[1] Cotton. MS. Appendix to Statutes.

[2] It is deserving of notice, that although the statute is entitled "Of the authority of Justices of Nisi Prius," the word prius does not occur in the writ of venire facias there given and addressed to the sheriff. It was not inserted until afterwards.

[3] Rot. Parl. I. 206

VI.] *ASSISA VERTITUR IN JURATAM.*

The machinery for this mode of inquiry was ready in the existence of the jurata, so familiar to the people, in the sense here explained, in the decision of disputes. And the assisa supplied the model of the form in which it was thenceforth to appear. The transition from a varying number of neighbors assembled at a county or other court, to that of a fixed number, namely twelve, summoned to the assize court, was easy and slight; and the verdict of the jury was originally neither more nor less than the testimony of the latter.[1]

[1] The earliest record extant of a trial by a regularly constituted jurata is, I believe, that of an action of ejectment between Edward I. and the Bishop of Winchester in 1290, respecting the right to the custody of the Hospital of St. Julian at Southampton. It is found in the Rot. Parl. I. 19. It may be interesting to give the names of the jurors who gave their verdict for the king, "in cujus rei testimonium" they affixed their seals. Thomas Peveril, Henry Attecruche, John de Langele, John Pers, Thomas de Vyneter, Walter de Letford, Nicholas Gese, Adam le Horder, Hugh Sampson, Henry le Lung, John Wrangy, and John Page. At this time the pleadings in an action were identical with those at the present day. See an action of trespass brought by the parson of Chipping Norton against another parson, for turning him out of his house on a Snnday. Rot. Parl. I. 96. There the sheriff is directed to summon twenty-four jurors.

CHAPTER VII

THE JURY CEASING TO BE WITNESSES, BECOME JUDGES OF EVIDENCE.

SECTION I. *Mode of Trial where witnesses were named in Deeds.*

THE inquiry in which we have been engaged has made it abundantly clear that the verdict of the jurata, as well as the assize, was founded on the personal knowledge of the jurors themselves respecting the matter in dispute, without hearing the evidence of witnesses in court. But there was an exception in the case of deeds which came into controversy, and in which persons had been named as witnessing the grant or other matter testified by the deed. And as this seems to have paved the way for the important change whereby the jury ceasing to be witnesses themselves, gave their verdict upon the evidence brought before them at the trials, the subject deserves attentive examination.

In Glanvill's time the usual mode of proving deeds the execution of which was denied, was by combat, in which one of the attesting witnesses was the champion of the plaintiff. If the name of no attesting witness was inserted in the deed, the combat must be maintained by some other person who had seen or knew of the execution.[1] Another mode of proof was by a comparison of the disputed deed with others admitted or proved to

---

Tract de Leg. x. 12, § 3.

have been executed by the party;—but this, which would at the present day be entirely a question for the jury, was determined then by the court.[1] In the case of contracts, where the creditor could produce no deed or mortgage, or other security in support of his claim, the temporal courts took no cognizance of the matter; but the question was treated as one of broken faith, and referred to the spiritual tribunal (Curia Christianitatis).[2]

At a later period, when Bracton wrote and the judicial combat in civil suits was falling into disuse, disputes arising out of deeds and charters to which there were attesting witnesses were determined by their evidence. And it has been the general opinion that they were included in the jury and formed part of it. Thus Sir F. Palgrave says,[3] when a charter was pleaded, the witnesses named in the attesting clause of the instrument, and who had been present on the Folkmoot, the shire or the manor-court when the seal was affixed by the donor, were included in the panel; and when a grant had been made by panel, the witnesses were sought out by the sheriff and returned upon the jury." And there are two old statutes the language of which obviously favors this interpretation. The first of these is the 52 Hen. III. c. 14 (A. D. 1267), which after mentioning the exemption from serving "in assizes, juries, and inquests," enjoyed by those who had obtained grants or charters to that effect, provides, that "if their oaths be so requisite that without them justice can not be ministered, as in great assizes, perambulations, and in deeds of writings of covenants, where they be named as witnesses, or in attaints and in other cases like, they shall be compelled to swear, saving to them at another time their foresaid liberty and exemption." Next follows the Statute of Westminster, 13 Edw. I c. 38 (A. D. 1285), which enacts that if assizes and juries be taken out of the shire, no

---

[1] Tract. de Leg. x. 12, §. 4.   [2] Ibid. § 1   [3] Eng. Comm. 1

one shall serve upon them who hold a tenement of less than the value of forty shillings yearly, except such as be witnesses in deeds and other writings, whose presence is necessary, so that they be able to travel (laborandum).[1] Now, certainly, if we confine our attention to these statutes, the view above mentioned seems to be the true one. But it may perhaps be doubted whether it is correct, and whether it is right to say that the attesting witnesses were included in the panel of jurors. There are two valuable chapters in Fleta on the subject of the proof of deeds, which throw considerable light upon the question. We there find the testes clearly distinguished from the patria, juratores, and recognitores. Thus, "si testes et juratores dicant quod cartam illam nunquam viderunt."—"Cum autem testes et recognitores in curiæ comparuerint."—"Probari enim poterit carta alio modo quam per testes et per patriam sicut per collationem sigillorum."[2]—The writs to the sheriff directing him to summon recognitors, beyond doubt included the attesting witnesses; but it does not therefore follow that the latter sat as part of the jury. Their attendance was necessary, and therefore it was the duty of the sheriff to have them in court. And as their evidence really determined the question at issue, parties might not improperly be said to be tried by them as well as by the jury, or in the language of the times, "to put themselves upon the witnesses and the county"—se ponere super testes in carta nominatos et super patriam.[3] The form of writ to the sheriff in such a case was the following:

[1] The original is, non ponatur in eis aliquis qui minus tenementum habeat quam, &c. In the Statutes at Large, this passage is rendered, "none shall pass in them but such as shall hold a tenement of less than the value," which is directly contrary to the sense. See Fleta, IV. c. 5.

[2] De fide cartarum, c. 33; De probatione cartarum, c. 34.

[3] Fleta, lib. VI. cap. 33. It is upon this form of expression that Sir Francis Palgrave seems to rely in support of assertion that the witnesses were included in the jury. Compare Bracton, IV. c. 15.

Rex Vicecomiti salutem.

Summone, &c. A. B. &c. testes nominatos in cartâ quam D. in curiâ nostrâ protulit, &c. Et præterea tot et tales tam milites quam liberos et legales homines de visneto, quod sint coram, &c. ad recognoscendum super sacramentum suum si, &c.

With respect to the tot et tales, here mentioned, it appears that the number of the jurors or patria, as distinct from the witnesses on these occasions, varied in different cases. We find a writ for summoning nine; and it is deserving of notice that here only three attesting witnesses are specified,[1] which looks as though they were to be added to the jurors at the trial, and thus make up the number twelve. Sometimes the recognition was made, or, in other words, the verdict was given by the witnesses alone.[2] But the most usual number of jurors summoned besides the witnesses was twelve;[3] and if we are to suppose that the latter sat with them, then the jury frequently consisted of a greater number than twelve; which is certainly contrary to the general opinion, and to the preponderating weight of precedent and authority.[4]

And the language of the statute 12 Edward II. c. 2 (A. D. 1318) seems to me to be more consistent with the view which I had ventured to take of the separation of the attesting witnesses from the jurors, than with that which supposes them to have formed part of that body. The words are, "Also it is agreed that when a deed, release, acquittance, or other writing, is denied in the king's court wherein witnesses be named, process shall be awarded to cause such witnesses to appear as before 'hath

---

[1] Summone, &c. A. B. C. testes nominatos, &c. et præter illos 9 tam milites quam alios, &c. ad recognoscendum, &c. Ibid. § 3.
[2] Ibid. § 3.   [3] Ibid. § 2, 5.
[4] It must, however, be admitted that there are passages in Fleta which favor the opposite view. Thus, probetur carta et conventio per testes, licet domestici sint, simul cum aliis de jurata, vel per collationem, vel alio modo. C. 16.

been used. Yet the taking of the inquest shall not be deferred by the absence of such witnesses." If the witnesses in such cases formed part of the jury panel, we should hardly expect to find a statue so worded which seems to contemplate a special process to compel their attendance.

In reality, however, since the jurors themselves were originally mere witnesses, there was no distinction in principle between them and the attesting witnesses; so that it is by no means improbable that the latter were at first associated with them in the discharge of the same function, namely, the delivery of a verdict, and that gradually, in the course of years, a separation took place. This separation, at all events, existed in the reign of Edward III.; for although we find in the Year Books of that period the expression, " the witnesses were joined to the assize," a clear distinction is, notwithstanding, drawn between them. Thus, in a passage where these words occur, we are told that a witness was challenged because he was of kin to the plaintiff; but the objection was overruled on the ground that the verdict could not be received from witnesses, but from the jurors of assize. And it was said that when the witnesses did not agree with the verdict in an inquest, or, in other words, when the verdict was against evidence, the defeated party might have an attaint.[1]

SECTION II. *Mode of Trial per Sectam.*

Besides the trial by an assize or jurata, Bracton notices another mode of determining disputes. This was when a party made a claim, et inde producit sectam. The meaning of this is, that the claimant offered to prove his case by vouching a certain number of witnesses

[1] 23 Assis. 11.

VII.] MODE OF TRIAL PER SECTAM.

on his behalf who had been present at the transaction in question. The defendant, on the other hand, rebutted this presumption by producing a larger secta, that is, a greater number of witnesess on his side whose testimony, therefore, was deemed to outweigh the evidence of his opponent. This was called the defense par legem; and the suit was terminated without any intervention of a jury.[1]

Inasmuch, however, as the evidence of defendant's sacta was not deemed to be an absolute proof, but merely raised a presumption in his favor sufficient to countervail the presumption on the other side, he was not allowed to resort to this mode of rebuttal where the complainant could produce evidence of a different character, such as a deed or charter. If this was denied, the case was to be tried per patriam, or per patriam et testes in carta nominatos. But if the plaintiff produced his secta, and the defendant had none, but was obliged to rely upon his own denial, he was not (at all events in the instance given by Bracton of an action for dower (unde nihil habet) allowed to put himself on the country, but the plaintiff recovered by force of the secta,[2] or the defendant was called upon to wage his law; that is, he was obliged to bring forward double the number of witnesses adduced by his opponent until twelve were sworn. It seems that if he could procure that number to swear for him he succeeded in resisting the demand. Here there was no interposition of a jury at all, but the dispute was decided solely by the witnesses, according as the requisite number preponderated. An exception, however, was made in the case of merchants and traders,

---

[1] Bract. 290, b.

[2] If neither side had a secta, then, in the words of Bracton, de veritate ponunt se super patriam, pro defectu sectæ, vel alterius probationis, quam ad manum non habuerint.

for they were allowed to prove a debt or payment per testes et patriam.¹

The proceeding per sectam appears to have been unknown in Glanvill's time; at least he does not mention it, but says, as we have already noticed, that in cases where the plaintiff could produce no written document in support of his claim, the spiritual court alone took cognizance of the matter, and dealt with it as a sin committed on the one side or the other, either in the demand or the denial. It is, however, easy to see that the principle of the procedure is the same as prevailed in compurgation. There the plaintiff or accuser, as the case might be, supported his assertion by the rim-ath, that is, the oaths of persons who swore to their belief in its truth; and the party attacked defended himself by the cyre-ath, or oaths of compurgators, who swore that they believed in his denial. This mode of compurgation was known as the lex manifesta; but it was provided by one of the articles of Magna Charta that no man should be allowed to put another to such a defense by his own bare assertion, unsupported by trustworthy witnesses.²

SECTION III. *On the personal knowledge of the Jury as distinct from the Evidence.*

As the use of juries became more frequent, and the advantages of employing them in the decision of disputes

---

¹ Bract. fo. 315, b. Fleta, II. c. 64. This secta must not be confounded with the suitors of the county and baronial courts, who were also called secta. On the latter, see Flet. II. c. 65, and *ante*, p. 56, n. 1.

² Nullus ballivus de cætero ponat aliquem ad legem manifestam nec ad juramentum simplici loquela sua sine testibus fidelibus ad hoc inductis. There is some difficulty as to the proper translation of this passage. Ponere aliquem ad legem manifestam no doubt means putting a defendant to his compurgation; but as the loquela is the statement of the plaintiff, and the sua must refer to aliquem, I believe the sentence to be elliptical for nullus ballivus (sinat) aliquem ponere (alium) ad legem, &c. And this view is confirmed by Fleta.

more manifest, the witnesses who formed the secta of a plaintiff began to give their evidence before them, and, like the attesting witnesses to deeds, furnished them with that information which in theory they were supposed to possess previously respecting the cause of quarrel. The rules of evidence now became more strict, and except as regards the right of the jury to found their verdict upon their own private knowledge, of which we shall speak presently, the trial was conducted on much the same principles as at the present day. Thus in the eleventh year of Henry IV. we find the judges declaring, "que le jury apres ceo que ils furent jurés, ne devient veier, ne porter ovesque eux nul auter evidence, sinon ceo que a eux fuit livrere par le court, et per le party mis en court sur l'evidence monstre," that is, that the jury, after they were sworn, ought not to see or take with them any other evidence than that which was offered in open court.[1]

The occasion of this statement was where a plaintiff had privately put a juror in possession of a document which had not been tendered in evidence, and this was shown by the latter to his fellows when they were considering their verdict, which was given in favor of the plaintiff. When, however, the matter was brought under the notice of the court, they reproved the plaintiff for his conduct as improper, and refused to let him sign judgment.

In the time of Fortescue, who was lord chancellor in the reign of Henry VI., with the exception of the requirement of personal knowledge in the jurors derived from near neighborhood of residence, the jury system had become in all its essential features similar to what now exists. This will be plainly seen from a perusal of the following passages taken from Fortescue's celebrated treatise De Laudibus Legum Angliæ:

"Whensoever the parties contending in the king's

[1] Year Book, 2 Hen. IV.

courts are come to the issue of the plea upon the matter of fact, the justices forthwith, by virtue of the king's writ, write to the sheriff of the county where the fact is supposed to be, that he would cause to come before them, at a certain day by them appointed, twelve good and lawful men of the neighborhood where the fact is supposed, who stand in no relation to either of the parties who are at issue, in order to inquire and know upon their oaths, if the fact be so as one of the parties alleges, or whether it be as the other contends it, with him. At which day the sheriff shall make return of the said writ before the same justices, with a panel of the names of them whom he had summoned for that purpose. In case they appear, either party may challenge the array, and allege that the sheriff hath cited therein partially and in favor of the other party, viz., by summoning such as are too much parties in the cause and not indifferent; which exception if it be found to be true upon the oath of two men of the same panel, pitched on by the justices, the panel shall immediately be quashed, and then the justices shall write to the coroners of the same county, to make a new panel; in case that likewise should be excepted against, and be made appear to be corrupt and vicious, this panel shall also be quashed. Then the justices shall choose two of the clerks in court, or others of the same county,[1] who, sitting in the court, shall upon their oaths make an indifferent panel, which shall be excepted to by neither of the parties; but being so impaneled, and appearing in court, either party may except against any particular persons, as he may at all times and in all cases by alleging that the person so impaneled is of kin, either by blood or affinity, to the other party, or in some such particular interest, as he can not be deemed an indifferent person to pass between the parties; of which sort of

---

[1] These are called Elisors.

exceptions there is so much variety as is impossible to show in a small compass."

"Twelve good and true men being sworn, as in the manner above related, legally qualified, that is, having over and besides their movables, possessions in land sufficient (as was said) wherewith to maintain their rank and station, neither suspected by, nor at variance with, either of the parties; all of the neighborhood; there shall be read to them in English, by the court, the record and nature of the plea, at length, which is depending between the parties; and the issue thereupon shall be plainly laid before them, concerning the truth of which those who are so sworn, are to certify the court: which done each of the parties, by themselves or their counsel, in presence of the court, shall declare and lay open to the jury all and singular the matter and evidences, whereby they think they may be able to inform the court concerning the truth of the point in question; after which each of the parties has liberty to produce before the court, all such witnesses as they please, or can get to appear on their behalf; who being charged upon their oaths, shall give in evidence all that they know touching the truth of the fact concerning which the parties are at issue; and, if necessity so require, the witnesses may be heard and examined apart, till they shall have deposed all that they have to give in evidence, so that what the one has declared shall not inform or induce another witness of the same side, to give his evidence in the same words, or to the very same effect. The whole of the evidence being gone through, the jurors shall confer together, at their pleasure, as they shall think most convenient, upon the truth of the issue before them; with as much deliberation and leisure as they can well desire, being all the while in the keeping of an officer of the court, in a place assigned them for that purpose, lest any one should attempt by indirect methods to influence them as to their opinion, which they are to give in to the court. Lastly, they are to return into court and certify the justices upon the truth of the issue so joined, in the presence of the parties (if they please to be present), particularly the person who is plaintiff in the cause; what the jurors shall so certify, in the laws of England is called the verdict. In pursuance of which verdict, the justices shall render and form their judgment."

Here we see that the jury were still required to come from the neighborhood where the fact they had to try was supposed to have happened; and this explains the origin of the venue (vicinetum), which appears in all indictments and declarations at the present day. It points out the place from which the jury must be summoned.

This is well illustrated by Arundel's case, which occurred in the reign of Elizabeth.[1] He was indicted for murder, alleged to have been committed "in the city of Westminster, in the county of Middlesex, to wit, in a certain street there called King Street, in the parish of Saint Margaret in the same county of Middlesex," and the jury was returned de vicineto civitatis Westmonasterii. He was found guilty, and it was moved in arrest of judgment that the venue ought to have been out of the parish, and not out of the city. The judges met at Sergeants' Inn, and "after many arguments" solemnly determined that every trial should be out of such place which by presumption of law can have the best and most certain knowledge of the fact; and because the parish shall be intended to be more certain than the city, inasmuch as when it is alleged to be in a city, it shall be taken in law to be less than the city, the trial was held to be insufficient, and a venire de novo was awarded to try the issue again, on the ground that the life of the prisoner was never in jeopardy.—And on the trial of Reading in the reign of Charles II., where the prisoner objected to a

[1] 6 Co Rep. 14.

juror on the ground that he was on terms of friendship and intimacy with the prosecutor, the Lord Chief Justice of the Common Pleas, Sir Francis North, said, "And do you challenge a juryman because he is supposed to know something of the matter? For that reason the juries are called from the neighborhood, because they should not be wholly strangers to the fact."[1]

It was in consequence of this principle of the original constitution of the jury, that it was for a long time held that their private knowledge of facts might influence their verdict as much as the oral and written evidence which was produced in court.[2] And therefore they might bring in a verdict, although no proofs were offered on either side. "For," says Blackstone, "the oath of the jurors to find according to their evidence was construed to be, to do it according to the best of their own knowledge."[3] And it was said by the court of Common Pleas in Bushell's case[4] (A. D. 1670), that the jury being returned from the vicinage whence the cause of action arises, the law supposes them to have sufficient knowledge to try the matters in issue, "and so they must, though no evidence were given on either side in court;" —and the case is put of an action upon a bond to which the defendant pleads solvit ad diem, but offers no proof; —where, the court said "the jury is directed to find for the plaintiff, unless they know payment was made of their own knowledge, according to the plea." This is the meaning of the old legal doctrine, which is at first sight somewhat startling, that the evidence in court is not binding evidence to a jury.[5] Therefore, acting upon their own knowledge, they were at liberty to give a verdict in direct opposition to the evidence, if they so

---

[1] 7 State Tr. 267.
[2] So also with the Dicasts of Athens: οὐδὲν γὰρ οἶμαι δοκεῖ προσδεῖσθαι ὑμῖν λόγων οὐδὲ μαρτυρίας ὅσα τις σαφῶς οἶδεν αὐτός. Æsch. Con. Timarchum.
[3] Comm. III. 374.   [4] Vaughan, Rep. 135.   [5] Ibid. 152.

thought fit. Thus we find Sir R. Brooke, who was recorder of London in the reign of Edward VI., laying down the law as follows :[1]

"As to that which has been said by the king's attorney, that there ought to be two witnesses to prove the fact, it is true that there ought to be two witnesses at least where the matter is to be tried by witnesses only, as in the civil law; but here the issue was to be tried by twelve men, in which case witnesses are not necessary, for in many cases an inquest shall give a precise verdict, although there are not witnesses, or no evidence given to them. As, if it be found before the coroner, super visum corporis, that I. S. killed the dead person, and he is arraigned and acquitted, the inquest shall say who killed him, although they have no witnesses; so that witnesses are not necessary, but where the matter is to be tried by witnesses only. For if witnesses were so necessary, then it would follow that the jurors could not give a verdict contrary to the witnesses; whereas the law is quite otherwise, for when the witnesses for trial of a fact are joined to the inquest, if they can not agree with the jurors, the verdict of the twelve shall be taken, and the witnesses shall be rejected."

One reason for allowing this sort of discretion to the jury seems to have been that they might escape the severe penalties of an attaint, which they did if they could show, by any additional proof, that their verdict was according to the fact, although not according to the evidence produced before them in court; and the law charitably presumed that this additional proof was known to them at the time of giving their verdict.[2]

When, however, attaints fell into disuse and the practice of new trials was introduced, juries were no longer

---

[1] Reniger v. Fagossa, Plowd. Comm. 12.
[2] Blackst. III. 374.

allowed to give verdicts upon their own knowledge: and it was laid down as a rule, that where they were acquainted with any facts material to be known, they ought to inform the court, so that they may be sworn as witnesses; and it has been said that "the fair way is to tell the court before they are sworn that they have evidence to give."[1]

And now, so different is the principle on which the jury find their verdict, that it would be a reason for a new trial if they were told by the presiding judge to take into account and be guided by their own knowledge of facts derived from any source independent of the evidence before them. In one case[2], within the present century this was made the ground of an application for a new trial. An information was filed against a party for publishing a malicious and seditious libel relating to the Luddite riots; and the judge who tried the case was alleged to have told the jury in the course of his summing up that, with respect to certain acts of outrage which were averred in the information, they were at liberty to refer to their own personal knowledge, if they saw any of those acts committed. A motion was made for a new trial upon this and other grounds; and the judgment of Lord Ellenborough shows that, if the jury had been told to consider their own previous knowledge as any evidence of the facts, it would have been a fatal misdirection. He said, "The material objection upon which the rule was obtained was founded upon a supposed misdirection of the learned judge at the trial, viz., that he had referred, in aid of some defect of evidence, to the personal knowledge which the jurors might possess for proof of the fact that outrages had been committed at Nottingham; for, as to their having been also

---

[1] 1 Salk. 405. For an instance of a juryman being sworn to give evidence, see 18 State Tr. 123, and see note to Vol. 6. 1012.

[2] R. v. Sutton, 4 M. and Sel. 540.

committed in the neighborhood of Nottingham, I do think that it is material to prove both. It now appears, however, from the report, that the judge did not lay any stress on the personal knowledge which the jury might be supposed to possess in order to aid any defect of evidence. On the contrary, it appears that he considered the evidence as fully sufficient to establish a verdict in favor of the crown; only he made the observation with reference to what they knew, as a matter of illustration, that it formed a part of the history of the county, that such outrages had been committed, as if he had said, every one must be aware of what had passed before their own eyes, and at their own doors; but he did not advise them to rely on that as a source of information on which they were to found their verdict, but only that it might make the proof more satisfactory to their minds, if they knew what had passed, because no one can have any reason to doubt what he knows and sees. It is conclusive, I think, upon the report, that the judge did not leave this to the jury as forming a branch of evidence of itself."

It was on account of the principle of personal knowledge being required in the jury that it was, in old times, a good ground of challenge that they were not hundredors of the district where the cause of action arose. The Stat. 27 Eliz. ch. 6, however, enacted that it should be sufficient if two hundredors were on the jury for the trial of issues joined in any personal action; and now, by 6 George IV. ch. 50, the jurors need only be good and lawful men of the body of the county.

CHAPTER VIII.

JURY SYSTEM IN CIVIL TRIALS.

SECTION I. *The Jury process.*

AS it was an essential principle of the jury trial from the earliest times, that the jurors should be summoned from the hundred where the cause of action arose, the court, in order to procure their attendance, issued in the first instance a writ called a venire facias, commanding the sheriff or other officer to whom it was directed, to have twelve good and lawful men from the neighborhood in court upon a day therein specified, to try the issue joined between the parties. And this was accordingly done, and the sheriff had his jury ready at the place which the court had appointed for its sitting.

But when the Court of Common Pleas was severed from the Curia Regis, and became stationary at Westminster (a change which took place in the reign of King John, and was the subject of one of the provisions of Magna Charta), it was found to be very inconvenient to be obliged to take juries there from all parts of the country. And as justices were already in the habit of making periodical circuits for the purpose of holding the assize in pleas of land, it was thought advisable to substitute them for the full court in banc at Westminster, in other cases also. The statute 13 Edw. I. c. 30, was therefore passed, which enacted that these justices should try other issues, " wherein small examination was required," or where both parties desired it, and return the inquests into the court above. This led to an alteration in the form of the venire; and instead of the sheriff being simply ordered to bring the jurors to the courts at Westminster on a day named, he was now required to bring them there on a certain day, "nisi prius," that is, unless before that day the justices of assize came into his county, in which case the statute directed him to return the jury, not to the court, but before the justices of assize.

Still, however, a practical hardship remained; for as the sheriff was not obliged to return the writ of venire until the day on which he brought the jurors into court where the justices were sitting, the parties had no means of knowing anything of them beforehand, or ascertaining whether they had any just cause of exception against them. This led to the passing of the Statute 42 Edw. III. c. 11, which provided that no causes should be tried at nisi prius until the sheriff had returned the names of the jurors to the court. Another change now took place in the venire. That part relating to nisi prius was taken out, which was thus restored to its original form; but the sheriff purposely delayed to comply with its exigency, and the juries not being summoned by him, did not attend on the day named in the writ. He, however, returned their names in a panel or slip of parchment to the court, so that the parties had an opportunity of seeing them, and making the necessary inquiries.[1] A fresh writ was then issued in consequence of the seeming neglect of the sheriff, called a distringas, or in the Common Pleas habeas corpora juratorum, which commanded him peremptorily

---

[1] Stat. 6 Geo. IV. c. 50, directs the sheriff to return the names, abodes, and descriptions of a number of jurors, not less than forty-eight nor exceeding seventy-two, taken from the "Jurors' Book," which is annually made up for each county from lists returned from each parish therein of persons qualified to serve as jurors. The original reason for inserting the abodes and descriptions of the jurors is stated in Stat. 27 Eliz. c. 6, to be, that the sheriff might know accurately upon whom to levy the "issues," or fines for non-attendance.

to have the bodies of the jurors in court on a day therein named, unless before that day (nisi prius) the justices of assize should come into his county. And such is the present form in daily use. The first mandate in the venire, with respect to the day when the jury are to appear, is invariably disobeyed, and the distringas is the writ which really determines the time and place of the trial. Whether it is advisable thus to encumber the process by a fiction may well admit of doubt. It has too long been the disgrace of the English law that it pertinaciously adheres to forms which are inconsistent with truth. Nor can any reason be assigned for doing so, except the unsatisfactory one, that the falsehood deceives nobody. But surely it is better to make the form correspond with the reality, and not accustom ourselves to the use of language which is either unmeaning or untrue, and in some cases both.

In the Third Report of the Common-Law Commissioners (1831) they say, " It is indeed very difficult to show sufficient reason for having any writ of venire facias, distringas, or habeas corpora juratorum, issued with reference to the individual cause. The statute which requires the same panel to be returned for all the common jury causes tried at any assizes or sitting of nisi prius, has, in effect, virtually superseded these writs, and their only effect is to inflict expense and inconvenience upon the parties."

That an ill use was sometimes made of the knowledge which the return to the venire affords, is tolerably clear from passages that occur in the Plumpton correspondence in the reign of Henry VII.[1] In one instance[2] the writer, John Pullan, who dates his letter from "Lyncolns Inne at London," says with reference to a trial which

---

[1] Published by the Camden Society.
[2] p. 131. For other instances see the same Correspondence, pp. 132, 134, and 161.

was about to take place, "The copie of the retorne and pannell I send to you inclosed herein for more suretie, as tother letter is delivered. Sir, to speak of the labour I made to the contrary, I have written the circumstance thereof in my master letter, and surelye it was to the uttermost of all my power. It is so now I understand, they will have a habeas corpora againe the jurors retornable octabis Trinitatis, so that they may have a distress with a nisi prius againe Lammas Assise. Therefore, Sir, between you and my lady, ye must cause speciall labour to be made, so it be done privily, to such of the jurours as ye trust will be made friendly in the cause." It seems that in this case, for some reason, the Court of Common Pleas awarded a new venire, directed to the coroners, upon which Pullan wrote to Sir Robert Plumpton, urging him as follows: "I would your mastership made special labour to have one indifferent pannell of the coroners; they must be laboured by some friend of yours."[1]

We see here that mention is made of a panel to be returned by the coroners, and the reason is this. The officer whose ordinary duty it is to provide jurors for the trial of all matters, whether civil or criminal, is the sheriff of the county where the venue is laid. But if at the time of awarding the writ of venire facias, that is, the precept directing the jury to be summoned, it is known that the sheriff is not indifferent between the parties, the venire is not directed to him, but to the coroners. If any valid exception lies against these, the writ is directed to two clerks of the court, or to two persons of the county nominated by the court and sworn. These are called elisors, or choosers, and it is their duty to return the jury when neither the sheriff nor coroners are competent to do so.

If a sufficient number of jurors returned by the sheriff do not appear, the deficiency is made up by empaneling

[1] Ibid. p. 141.

bystanders present in court. This is called a tales de circumstantibus, the first mention of which occurs in Stat. 35 Hen. VIII. c. 6, where it is enacted that in civil causes the justices, upon request made by the party, plaintiff or defendant, shall have authority to command the sheriff to name and appoint, as often as need shall require, so many of such other able persons of the county then present at the assizes, or nisi prius, as shall make up a full jury, which persons shall be added to the former panel, and their names annexed to the same. And by 4 and 5 Phil. and Mary, c. 7, the same rule was extended to criminal trials and actions upon penal statutes. The proceedings in respect of a tales de circumstantibus are now regulated by Stat. 6 Geo. IV. c. 50, § 37.

SECTION II. *On special Juries.*

It has been said by authority that it can not be ascertained at what time the practice of appointing special jurors for trials at nisi prius first began, but that it probably arose out of the custom of appointing jurors for trials at the bar of the courts at Westminster, and was introduced for the better administration of justice, and for securing the nomination of jurors duly qualified in all respects for their important office.[1] The first statutory recognition of their existence occurs so late as in the Act 3 Geo. II. ch. 25. But the principle seems to have been admitted in early times. We find in the year 1450 (29 Hen. VI.) a petition for a special jury, that is jurors "who dwell within the shire, and have lands and tenements to the yearly value of xx*l*.," to try a plea

[1] R. *v.* Edmonds, 4 Barn. and Al. 477. In the oldest book of practice in existence, Powell's Attorney's Academy, 1623 (cited by Bentham in his Art of Packing Special Juries), no such term as special jury occurs. Eightpence a head is there stated as the fee allowed to jurres at *Nisi Prius* in London and fourpence to talesmen: By 24 Geo. II. c. 18, the fee for each special juryman was fixed at one guinea.

which it was supposed might be pleaded in abatement on a bill of appeal of murder.[1] The statute of George II. speaks of special juries as already well known, and it declares and enacts that the courts at Westminster shall, upon motion made by any plaintiff, prosecutor, or defendant, order and appoint a jury to be struck before the proper officer of the court where the cause is depending, "in such manner as special juries have been and are usually struck in such courts respectively upon trials at bar had in the said courts." And although Section 17 provides for the return of properly qualified jurors, and the attendance of the sheriff in any cause arising in any city, or county, or town, it says nothing as to the qualification of the jurors, or the attendance of the sheriff in causes arising in a county at large; "leaving that to be enforced according to antecedent practice, which may well be supposed to have been more perfectly established in the cases of counties at large than in smaller districts, by reason of its more frequent occurrence."[2]

The practice with respect to forming or "striking," as it is technically called, a special jury at the present day is as follows: Each party is entitled to have the cause tried by such a jury, and the attorneys on both sides, and the under-sheriff or his agent attend before the proper officer of the court with the special jurors' list, which, under the provisions of 6 Geo. IV. ch. 50, the sheriff is directed annually to make out from the jurors' books; and from among these described in that book as Esquires, or as persons of higher degree, or as bankers or merchants; and tickets corresponding with the names

---

[1] Rot. Parl. V. 213.

[2] R. v. Edmonds, 4 Barn. and Al. 477. A rule was made in Trinity Term, 8 Will. III. that when the master is to strike a jury, viz. forty-eight out of the Freeholders' Book, he shall give notice to the attorneys of both sides to be present, and if the one comes and the other does not, he that appears shall according to the ancient course, strike out twelve, and the master shall strike out the other twelve for him that is absent. See 1 Salk. 405.

of the jurors on the list being put into a box and shaken, the officer takes out forty-eight, to any of which names either party may object for incapacity; and supposing the objection to be established, another name is substituted. The list of forty-eight is next, and at a subsequent period, reduced by striking off, before the same officer, the names of such twelve jurors as either party shall in his turn wish to have removed; and the names of the remaining twenty-four are then inserted in the writ of distringas as the jurors to be summoned for the cause, which persons are then summoned by the sheriff to attend the trial.[1]

Section III. *On Challenges.*

The right of challenge is almost essential for the purpose of securing perfect fairness and impartiality in a trial. It was in use amongst the Romans in criminal cases, and the Lex Servilia (B. C. 104) enacted that the accuser and the accused should severally propose one hundred judices, and that each might reject fifty from the list of the other, so that one hundred would remain to try the alleged crime. In this country the right has existed from the earliest times. The tenant in Glanvill's time might object for good cause to any of the recognitors of the assize.[2] And Bracton tells us that a person put upon his trial might, if he had just cause to suspect any of the jurors to be influenced by improper feeling toward him, object to their being on the inquest, and cause them to be removed.[3]

But not only jurors, but the judge himself, might be refused for good cause, according to the old law of Eng-

---

[1] Stephen's Blackstone, III. 591. The average cost of a special jury is about £25.
[2] Excipi autem possunt juratores ipsi eisdem modis quibus et testes in curia Christianitatis juste repelluntur.—Glanv. II. c. 12.
[3] Bract. III. c. 22.

land.'¹ And this corresponds with the recusatio judicis mentioned in the code of Justinian.² But it soon ceased to be allowed in our courts, and on that account the four knights who elected the grand assize were not challengeable; "for that," as Coke says,³ "they be judges to that purpose, and judges or justices can not be challenged." And he adds, "that is the reason that noblemen, that in case of high treason are to pass upon a peer of the realm, can not be challenged, because they are judges of the fact." But this seems a very inconclusive reason, for the same would apply to ordinary jurymen, who are judges of the fact, and yet may be challenged.

The true ground of the rule with respect to peers sitting as the High Court of Parliament to try such a case is that they are then judges of the law as well as the facts, and are, therefore, no more challengeable than the judges of the courts of common law and equity. But this does not apply to peers sitting during the recess of parliament in the court of the Lord High Steward, who is then, as has been already noticed, the sole judge of matters of law; and the only reason that can be given for the rule that even there they can not be challenged, seems to be the unsatisfactory one assigned at the trial of Lord Audley in 1631, namely, "because they are not upon their oath, but upon their honor, and a challenge is tried whether he (*i.e.*, the juror) stands indifferent, being unsworn."⁴

Challenges are of two kinds: 1. to the array; 2. to the polls. 1. We have previously mentioned the cases in

---

[1] Bract. v. c. 15. Fleta, VI. c 37.
[2] Liceat ei, qui suspectum judicem putat, antequam lis inchoetur, eum recusare, ut ad alium curratur, libello recusationis ei porrecto. Cod. III. tit. I. 16.
[3] Litt. 249, a.
[4] 3 State Trials, 402. See also Co. Litt. 156, b.

which the writ of venire is directed to the coroners, or elisors, instead of the sheriff, and a challenge to the array is always grounded upon some matter personal to the officer by whom the jury has been summoned, and their names arrayed or placed upon the parchment or panel, whereon they are returned in writing to the court. Upon trials for felony this panel is not published or made known until the sitting of the court at which the trial takes place, and therefore that sitting necessarily furnishes the first opportunity of making any objection to it. Upon other trials, and in the superior courts, the parties have notice of the jurors chosen by the sheriff when he makes his return to the venire, as has been explained in the section on the jury process. But it is an established rule that a challenge to the array or to the polls can not be made until the actual appearance of a full jury; and no party therefore has an opportunity of making it, until the cause has been called on for trial. If twelve of those named in the original panel do not appear, a tales must be prayed, and the appearance of twelve obtained before any challenge can be made.[1]

There can, however, be no challenge of the array when the process has been directed to elisors, because, says Sir Edward Coke, they were appointed by the court; but the party may have his challenge to the polls.[2] The array may be challenged, that is, the whole of the jurors returned may be objected to, either by way of "principal" challenge, or challenge "to the favor." The former occurs where the sheriff (or coroners, if the venire has been directed to them), is a party to the suit, or related by blood or affinity to either of the parties. Until a late period if a peer of parliament were one of the parties, and no knight were returned upon the jury, he might challenge the array. But this cause of objection has been re-

---

[1] See R. *v.* Edmonds, 4 Barn. and Al. 471.
[2] Co. Litt. 158, a.

moved by statute.¹ Also if none of the jurors were returned from the hundred in which the venire was laid, and in which therefore the cause of action was supposed to have arisen, this was formerly a ground of challenge to the array. But successive statutes have gradually abolished the necessity of having hundredors upon the jury.

A challenge to the favor is founded upon circumstances which create a probability or suspicion of bias or partiality in the returning officer; as that the son of the sheriff has married the daughter of one of the parties, or the like.

The difference between these two kinds of challenge seems to be this: "that the first, if sustained in point of fact, must be allowed as of course; the allowance of the latter is matter of discretion only. If the challenge be controverted by the opposite party, it is left to the determination of two persons to be appointed by the court; and if these persons, called triors, decide in favor of the objection, the array is to be quashed, and a jury impaneled by the coroner,"² or the elisors, as the case may be.

Every challenge, either to the array or to the polls, ought to be propounded in such a way that it may be put at the time upon the nisi prius record, and thus become open to examination on a writ of error.³

2. Challenges to the polls (capita) are exceptions to the individual jurors, and are classed by Coke under four heads: (1) propter honoris respectum; (2) propter defectum; (3) propter affectum; (4) propter delictum. (1) Propter honoris respectum; as where a lord of parliament is impaneled on a jury. (2) Propter defectum; as in the case of an alien born, who is therefore incompetent; or the want of sufficient estate to qualify the juror. (3) Prop-

---

¹ See 34 Geo. II. c. 18; 6 Geo. IV. c. 50.
² Steph. Blackst. III. 597, and the authorities there cited.
³ R. v. Edmonds, 4 Barn. and Al. 471.

ter affectum; on well-grounded suspicion of bias or partiality. This, like the challenge to the array, is either by way of principal challenge, or "to the favor;" and it depends upon the same kind of distinction as has been previously explained with respect to the array. If the challenge is a principal one, it may be tried by the court, and the juror himself may be examined as to the cause of challenge, but is not compelled to answer if the matter tends to his discredit. But in both cases the usual way is to determine the question by triors. These, in case the first man called be challenged, are two indifferent persons named by the court; and if they try one man, and find him indifferent, he shall be sworn, and then he and the two triors shall try the next: and when another is found indifferent and sworn, the two triors shall be superseded, and the first two sworn on the jury shall try the rest.[1] (4) Propter delictum; where a juror has been convicted of some offense that affects his credit, and renders him infamous.

Section IV. *On Attaints and New Trials.*

In considering the comparative advantages of different systems of judicial inquiry, an important point to notice is the provision made for remedying wrong decisions. Man is so fallible in his opinions, so liable to be deceived by evidence, and so apt to draw mistaken inferences from facts, that if in all cases the verdict of a jury in the first instance were final, and subject to no revision, great hardship and injustice must necessarily ensue. And yet such was the rule in this country for many centuries, while the proceeding by attaint was in force. But this does not seem to have been the case originally. The attaint was, I believe, at first in the nature of a new trial, and the punishment of the previous jury, only one of the con-

[1] Blackst. Comm. III. 363.

sequences of the verdict of the jury of attaint. The latter was in form empaneled, not to try the former jurors, but simply the question of the wrongful disseizin; and if their verdict differed from that of the first jury, this amounted to a conviction of that body. This is proved by the form of the writ summoning the second set of twenty-four jurors.[1]

Rex Vic. salutem.

Si talis fecerit te securum de clamore suo prosequendo, tunc summoneas per bonos summonitores XXIV legales homines de visneto de tali villa quod sint coram justiciariis nostris ad primam assisam cum in partes illas venerint parati recognoscere si talis injuste et sine judicio disseisivit prædictum talem de libero tenemento suo ......unde talis queritur quod juratores assisæ novæ disseisinæ, quæ inde summonita fuit et capta inter eos coram justiciariis nostris ultimo itinerantibus in comitatu tali, falsum fecerunt sacramentum. Et interim diligenter inquiras qui fuerunt Juratores illius assisæ, et eos habeas ad præfatam assisam coram præfatis justiciariis.[2]

At the day of trial the record of the former assize was read in the presence of the twenty-four and the former twelve jurors, and the complainant was asked to specify in what points the latter had sworn falsely. When he had done this, each of the twenty-four took an oath that he would speak the truth as to all that should

---

[1] Bract. 291.

[2] In Rot. Parl I. 56, (18 Edw. I.) we have an instance of a petition for and grant of an attaint: Emma quæ fuit uxor Willelmi Spillewque, pauper, mulier, petit attinctam super Inquisitionem redisseisinæ versus Abbatem de Tewkesbury et Ballivos suos, qui contra eam dixit ob favorem Abbates et Ballivorum suorum. Rex concessit quod veniat recordum assisæ et novæ diss. et inquis. rediss. et vocatis partibus coram Justic. de Banco fiat ibi justicia

be required of him; and the judge then explained to them the matter in dispute, and if he thought fit he might call upon each to declare the grounds of his verdict; and according as this was in favor of the one side or the other, acquittal or condemnation followed. The mode also in which their verdict was enrolled shows that they discharged the office of trying the former jury by deciding the question which had been previously submitted to that body. Jurata viginiti quatuor ad convincendum XII. venit recognitura si injust et sine judicio disseisivit, &c. Now, this, I think, must surely mean that if their verdict contradicted that of the jury of twelve, the latter was annulled. And as the verdict of the second jury was final, and there could be no attaint against them, Bracton tells us that they ought to be carefully examined by the justices, and give good reasons for their verdict; "for," he says, "twenty-four are often deceived as well as twelve, and sometimes commit perjury, or are mistaken, and sometimes speak false where the twelve have spoken truth."[1]

If they could not agree, they were to be afforced by the addition of other jurors, as in an assize in the first instance. If their verdict was opposed to the former one, the twelve jurors were immediately arrested and imprisoned; their lands and chattels were forfeited to the king, and they became for the future infamous, and no longer, as Bracton expresses it, OTHESWORTH. At a later period the law added to their sentence, with cruel

---

[1] Bracton says, that if perchance the former twelve were not unanimous, but differed in opinion, the second jury might acquit some and condemn others, as happened in the case of Albert Earl of Somerset. This looks as if a verdict might be taken from less than twelve, otherwise the case supposed could not happen; unless the passage means, that at the second trial some of the former jurors might escape by avowing that although they had nominally agreed in the verdict, they had amongst themselves expressed a different opinion. This, however, could hardly have improved their case.—See Bract. 292.

severity, that their wives and children should be turned out of their homes, their houses thrown down, their trees rooted up, and their meadows ploughed.[1]

It clearly appears from Bracton that it was the duty of the recognitors when summoned to serve on a particular assize respecting the disseizin of lands, to make themselves acquainted, by personal inquiry and inspection, with the facts of the case before the day of trial, so that they were not allowed to plead ignorance or mistake if they were afterwards attainted for giving a false verdict.[2] And speaking of cases in which jurors were not liable to a conviction for perjury, the same author says, that if the matter upon which they had given their verdict was one of a secret nature, and known only to a few witnesses, their ignorance was excusable. But if it were of an open and public character, so that all the neighborhood (omnes de patria) knew it, and the jurors alone were in the dark, and had doubts about it, this was culpable ignorance, and they might be attainted for delivering a wrong verdict.[3]

This explains what at first sight appears so repugnant to our ideas of justice, that men should be punished for what might seem to be no more than a mistaken opinion. Originally a wrong verdict almost necessarily implied perjury in the jurors. They were witnesses who deposed to facts within their own knowledge, about which there could hardly be the possibility of error. Thus in questions of disseizin their functions was simply to declare in whose possession of old time they had seen and heard the lands to be. There was no room for difference of opinion here. They had merely to attend to the evidence of their own eyes and ears, and were not, as in modern times, obliged to balance conflicting statements,

[1] Co. Litt. 294, b. Subsequently. this punishment was commuted into a pecuniary penalty.
[2] Bract. 293.   [3] Bracton, 290.

and draw conclusions and inferences from disputed facts. We have seen that in the feudal courts of Palestine a defeated party was allowed in some cases fausser la court; that is, impeach the whole court of false judgment, and challenge each member thereof to mortal combat.[1] And there the court and the witnesses were distinct. In England, the jury and the witnesses were for many years the same, so that it was only just that they should be punished if they willfully gave their evidence, that is their verdict, contrary to what they knew to be the truth. And this seems to have been too common. In the tenth year of the reign of Henry VI. a petition was presented to the Commons, complaining of the disherisons and injustice committed in assizes and other inquests by perjured jurors, and praying that in a writ of attaint the plaintiff may recover his damages against the petit jury, and every member thereof, as well as against the defendant, and that no juror might serve on an attaint unless he had an estate of five pounds a year in the country.[2]

However unconstitutional the practice may have been there is no doubt that in the Tudor reigns juries were summoned before the Star Chamber or Privy Council, and fined for verdicts of acquittal in criminal cases, and sometimes even when they convicted the prisoner. Sir Thomas Smith says that he had seen in his time (that of Elizabeth) an inquest for pronouncing one guilty of treason contrary to the evidence, not only imprisoned, but heavily fined; and another inquest for acquitting another, both fined and "put to open ignominie and shame." But he makes the important admission that "those doings were even then of many accounted very violent, tyrannical, and contrary to the liberty and custom of the realm of England."[3] This arbitrary conduct of the

---

[1] See ante, p. 99.   [2] Rot. Parl. IV. 408, b.
[3] Commonw. of England, III. c. 1. By Stat. 26 Hen. VIII. c. 4, it was

crown was imitated by the courts of law, and several attempts were made by the latter, by the exercise of their own mere authority, to fine and imprison jurors, on the ground that their verdict was false. But it was solemnly decided, in the reign of Charles II., that this was contrary to law. The occasion of this judgment was a case where, on a return to a writ of habeas corpus, it was alleged that the prisoner had been committed to prison, for that being a juryman among others charged at the Sessions Court of the Old Bailey to try an issue between the King and Penn and Mead, upon an indictment for assembling unlawfully and tumultuously, he did, contra plenam et manifestam evidentiam, openly given in court, acquit the prisoners indicted.[1] Chief Justice Vaughan said, "that the court could not fine a jury at the common law where attaint did not lie (for where it did it is agreed they could not), I think to be the clearest position that ever I considered, either for authority or reason of law."

Whatever may have been the effect originally of the second verdict upon the first, there is no doubt that it had at this time long ceased to amount, if unfavorable, to more than a conviction of the jurors, and was of no benefit to the injured party in the way of redress. This was at last attained by the introduction of new trials, which led to the discontinuance of the process by attaint, and it was finally abolished by statute 6 Geo. IV. c. 50. The first instance on record of a new trial being granted occurred in the year 1665,[2] and thereby an immense im-

---

enacted that if any jurors in Wales acquitted any felon, or gave an untrue verdict against the king, contrary to good and pregnant evidence, they should be bound to appear before the council of the marches, there to abide such fine or ransom for their offense as that court should think fit.

[1] Bushell's case, Vaug. 135.

[2] Chief Justice Holt was of opinion that the origin of new trials was more ancient, as we meet with cases in the old books of challenges to jurors, on the ground that they had before been jurors in the same cause. 2 Salk. 648.

provement was effected in the jury system, inasmuch as the measure is remedial, instead of being like the attaint, merely vindictive. Indeed, as has been well said by Blackstone, if every verdict was final in the first instance, it would tend to destroy trial by jury. But no better or more forcible reasons for vesting in courts of law a discretionary power to afford relief against the perverseness or mistakes of juries, by granting new trials, can be given than are contained in the following judgment of Lord Mansfield.[1]

"Whatever might have been the origin of the practice, trials by jury in civil causes could not subsist now without a power somewhere to grant new trials. If an erroneous judgment be given in point of law, there are many ways to review and set it right. When a court judges of facts upon depositions in writing, their sentence or decree may in many ways be reviewed and set right. But a general verdict can only be set right by a new trial; which is more than having the cause more deliberately considered by another jury, when there is a reasonable doubt, or perhaps a certainty, that justice has not been done. The writ of attaint is now a mere sound in every case; in many it does not pretend to be a remedy. There are numberless causes of false verdicts, without corruption or bad intention of the jurors. They may have heard too much of the matter before the trial, and imbibed prejudices without knowing it. The cause may be intricate. The examination may be so long as to distract and confound their attention. Most general verdicts include legal consequences, as well as propositions of fact; in drawing these consequences, the jury may mistake, and infer directly contrary to law. The parties may be surprised, by a case falsely made at the trial, which they had

And Blackstone quotes from the Year Books instances where judgment was stayed, and a new venire awarded, because the jury had eaten and drunk without consent of the judge.

[1] Bright *v.* Eynon, 1 Barr. 290.

no reason to expect, and therefore could not come prepared to answer. If unjust verdicts, obtained under these and a thousand like circumstances, were to be conclusive forever, the determination of civil property in this method of trial would be very precarious and unsatisfactory. It is absolutely necessary to justice that there should, upon many occasions, be opportunities for reconsidering the cause by a new trial."

In theory it is entirely in the discretion of the court sitting in banc to grant or withhold a new trial. But a well understood course of practice has determined the cases in which it will hardly ever be refused. They are these:

1. The want of due notice of trial, unless the defendant has appeared and made defense. 2. A material variance between the issue or paper-book delivered and the record of nisi prius, unless a defense had been made at the trial. 3. Want of a proper jury, as where the jurors were not properly returned. 4. Misbehavior of the prevailing party towards the jury or witnesses. And where hand-bills reflecting on the plaintiff's character had been distributed in court at the time of the trial, and had been sent to the jury, although the defendant denied all knowledge of the hand-bills, and affidavits from all the jurymen were tendered to prove that no such placards had been shown to them, the court refused to admit them (on the general ground that no affidavits on the subject of the cause can be received from the jury), and granted a new trial.[1] 5. The discovery of new and material evidence since the trial, corresponding to the res noviter veniens in notitiam of the Scotch law. 6. Surprise; as, for instance, where a fradulent trick on the part of the plaintiff or defendant has enabled him to obtain the verdict.[2] 7.

[1] Coster v. Merest, 3 Brod. and Bing. 272.
[2] For a recent instance of a new trial granted on the ground of surprise, see Wilkes v. Hopkins, 1 Com. Ben. Rep. 737.

The absence of the attorney, or counsel, or witnesses, under particular circumstances;[1] but the granting of a new trial in these cases is very rare. 8. A subsequent conviction of the witnesses for perjury at the trial. 9. Misdirection by the judge. But the direction of a judge is not to be objected to on account of particular isolated expressions, if upon the whole, and in substance, it leads to a just conclusion, and the proper question for the jury is left to them. 10. The improper admission or rejection of evidence by the judge. On one occasion Lord Ellenborough, C. J., said, "If in this case I had been able to detect any particle of proof that ought not to have been offered to the consideration of the jury, I should have thought such vicious proof would have corrupted the verdict and avoided it."[2] But a new trial will not be granted where evidence has been rejected; and assuming it to have been received, a verdict in favor of the party for whom it was offered would have been manifestly against the weight of evidence, and certainly set aside on application to the court as an improper verdict.[3] In short, the evidence in such a case must be immaterial, and such as ought not, if admitted, to prevent a nonsuit.[4] 11. The finding a verdict without, or contrary to, evidence. But when there is conflicting evidence, it is not usual to grant a new trial unless the evidence for the prevailing party be very slight, and the judge declare himself dissatisfied with the verdict. And a new trial will not be granted on the ground of the verdict being against evidence, where it is for less than twenty pounds, unless some particular right be in ques-

---

[1] Beazley v. Shapley, 1 Price, 201; Warren, v. Fuzz, 6 Mod. 22; and see De Roufigny v. Peale, 3 Taunt. 484.

[2] R. v. Sutton, M. and Sel. 540.

[3] Crease v. Barrett, 1 C. M. and R. 933, where a wider principle asserted by Sir James Mansfield, C. J., in Horford v. Wilson, 1 Taunt. 14, is said to have been "laid down much too generally."

[4] Doe d. Welsh v. Langfield, 16 M. and W. 516.

tion, independent of the amount of damages. But the rule does not apply where there has been a misdirection by the judge, however small the amount of damages may be.[1] 12. Misbehavior of the jury, as in casting lots for their verdict, provided this can be proved without resorting to the affidavits of the jurors themselves, which can in no case be admitted.[2] 13. Excessive damages.

A jury who understand their duty ought to follow the direction of the presiding judge on questions of law, and if they disregard it, and the court think that the judge was right, they will award a new trial. But to this there is a limit. Juries may baffle the court by persisting in the same opinion, and in such cases it has been the practice for the latter ultimately to give way. Thus in an action tried before Lord Mansfield the dispute was as to the proper time of presentment of a bill of exchange; and the jury found for the defendant. A new trial was granted, and, contrary to the direction of the judge, the verdict was again in favor of the defendant. The court then awarded a third new trial, but the same result followed, upon which they refused further to interfere.

[1] Haine v. Davis, 4 Ad. and Ell. 896.
[2] Vaise v. Delaval, 1 Term R. 11, where Lord Mansfield, C. J., said, "in every such case the court must derive its knowledge from some other source; such as from some person having seen the transaction through a window, or by some such means."

CHAPTER IX.

JURY IN CRIMINAL CASES.

SECTION I. *Ancient Mode of presenting Offenses.*

IN considering the judicial system of the Anglo-Saxons incidental mention was made of their manner of trial in criminal cases. The accused had to clear himself by compurgation, and if this failed, owing to his being unable to obtain the requisite number of persons prepared to swear to their belief in his oath of innocence, he was obliged to undergo the ordeal, which consisted of hot iron, boiling water, or the corsnaed, as has been previously explained. We find no trace of anything like a jury empaneled to try offenders before the time of the Normans. Nor for many years after the Conquest do the scanty notices which occur in the old chronicles of persons convicted and punished for crime, furnish a hint of the existence of such a tribunal. The only modes of trial in such cases of which Glanvill speaks, are the judicial combat, compurgation, and the ordeal of hot iron where the suspected person was a freeman, and of water where he was a "villian."[1] The judicial combat took place where an accuser came forward to make the charge; and compurgation, or the ordeal, where the accusation rested, not on the assertion of a single prosecutor, but on the fama publica of the neighborhood.[2]

---

[1] Tract de Leg. XIV. c. 1.

[2] Glanvill's expression is, that in such a case the accused per legem apparentem purgandus est, which is the usual way of speaking of compurga-

At an earlier period, William Rufus, wishing to extort money, caused fifty persons of reputed wealth to be accused of stealing the king's deer, and required them to prove their innocence by undergoing the ordeal of hot iron. Providentially (or owing most probably to some device with which we are unacquainted) they all escaped unhurt, and the king enraged, impiously exclaimed, "MEO judicio a modo responderetur non DEI, quod pro voto cujusque hinc inde plicatur."[1] This shows that faith in the ordeal was even then wearing out, when such language could be applied to it, although it still lingered amongst us for some time longer.

In the reign of Henry II. (A. D. 1177), the Earl of Ferrers having been murdered in London by some midnight assassins, the king ordered several citizens to be seized, and amongst others, one named John Old. He had to undergo the water ordeal, but failed, and then offered fifty pounds to save his life; but the king did not venture to take money for so notorious a crime, and ordered him to be hanged.[2]

With respect to the accusation of criminals amongst the Anglo-Saxons, the law of Ethelred has been previously noticed, which imposed upon the twelve senior thanes of each hundred the duty of discovering and presenting the perpetrators of all crimes within their district. They were to act the part of public prosecutors, and the accused had to clear himself by the usual method of compurgation, failing which, he must submit to the ordeal. This office, however, seems to have fallen into abeyance, at all events after the invasion of the Normans; and accusations of crime were left to the general

gation. He, however, distinctly mentions per Dei judicium as one of the modes of proof.

[1] Eadmer. Hist. Nov. II. 48.
[2] Rog. Hoved. ann. 1177.

voice of the neighborhood denouncing the guilt of the suspected person.[1]

It was a consequence of the peculiar system of society in England in early times, that system which by the institution of the frithborh rendered every man a surety for the conduct of his neighbor, and, therefore, responsible to a certain exent for offenses committed by him, that each community had a direct interest in discovering and bringing to justice malefactors. Besides, who were so likely to know the character of a man as his neighbors? who was so likely to be guided aright in their suspicions as to the author of a crime committed amongst themselves? Still, however, the inconvenience must have been felt of trusting to public rumors to indicate the criminal. It might be too vague and indefinite to warrant the apprehension of any one—and different persons might entertain and express different suspicions. Or again, parties might be fearful or unwilling to make themselves conspicuous as accusers, especially after the introduction of trial by battle, which compelled them to support their charge by single combat. Accordingly we find that this led to legislative interference. The constitutions of Clarendon (A. D. 1164) provided that where a party was suspected whom no one dared openly to accuse, the sheriff, on the requisition of the bishop, should swear twelve lawful men of the neighborhood or vill, in the presence of the bishop, and these were "to declare the truth thereof according to their conscience."[2] This seems evidently to mean, not only that the twelve jurors were to discharge the office of accusers, from which pri-

---

[1] Si nullus appereat certes accusator, sed fama solummodo publica accusat, tunc ab initio salvo accusatus attachiabitur.—Glanv. XIV. c. I.

[2] Et si tales fuerint, qui culpantur, quod non velit vel non audeat aliquis eos accusare, vicecomes, requissitus ab episcopo, faciet jurare duodecim legales hominis de vicineto seu de villa, coram episcopo quod vide veritatem secundum conscientiam suam manifestabant.—Const. Claren. Art. VI.

vate individuals had shrunk, but also to try the truth of the accusation, and pronounce upon the guilt or innocence of the accused. The two functions, however, in early times were almost if not altogether identical. We must remember what has already been said respecting the vorath of the Anglo-Saxons.[1] The office of accusers and triers originally led to the same result, namely, the judgment of God by the ordeal, to which the accused was remitted as the decisive test of his innocence or guilt. Thus we find the following entry in the reign of John: Henricus de Ravesne est captus et malecreditus a juratoribus et quatuor villatis proximis juratis, de latrocinio et burgleria; PURGET SE PER AQUAM. This in a remarkable manner agrees with the result of an unsuccessful attempt at compurgation amongst the Anglo-Saxons. But the ordeal was now falling into disuse. The clergy had declared against it; and in the third year of the reign of Henry III. the justices in eyre for the northern counties were ordered not to try persons charged with crime by the judgment of fire or water.[2] Soon afterwards it so wholly disappeared, that Bracton, who wrote his treatise in that reign, makes no allusion to the subject.

At a parliament held at Clarendon in the reign of Henry II. it was enacted that if any one were accused of murder, robbery, arson, coining, or harboring of felons, by the oaths of twelve knights of the hundred, or in default of knights, by the oaths of twelve free and lawful men, and of four men of each vill of the hundred, he was to undergo the water-ordeal, and if the result of that was unfavorable, he was to lose a foot. But even though successful at the ordeal, if he had been accused of murder or any grievous felony " by the community of the county, and the lawful knights of the county" (per commune comitatus et legalium militum patriæ), he was obliged

[1] See ante, p. 66.   [2] Dugd. Orig. Jur. 87.

nevertheless to leave the kingdom within forty days, and abjure the realm. Here we see what a weighty effect was given to an accusation by the country (per patriam), which to a certain extent countervailed even the proof of innocence afforded by the ordeal. It proves also how much the confidence of the leading men of the nation in the efficacy of that mode of trial was shaken, since they felt that it was safer to remove from the kingdom those who were pointed out by common fame as guilty of atrocious crimes, even although the ordeal declared them innocent.

The accusation by the commune comitatus was nothing more than the knowledge of the neighborhood, which was constantly invoked to decide questions of disputed right, applied to criminal cases, and the Statutes of Clarendon merely threw the responsibility upon a smaller number. The form of proceeding was soon afterwards modified by an ordinance of Richard I. (A. D. 1194), which provided that four knights should be chosen for each county, who when duly sworn were to choose two for each hundred or wapentake. These took a similar oath, and each pair chose ten knights, or in default of knights, ten "lawful and free men," out of each hundred or wapentake so that the twelve might present the crimes and arrest the criminals within their district.[1]

In the reign of Edward I. the bailiffs of each bailiwick, in order to be ready for the periodical circuits of the justices in eyre, were required to choose four knights, who again were to choose twelve of the better men (duodecim de melioribus) of the bailiwick, and it was the duty of the latter to present all those who were suspected of having committed crimes.[2] Each of them took the following oath:

"Hear this, ye Justices! that I will speak the truth of that which ye shall ask of me on the part of the king, and

---

[1] Roger Hoved. 423.   [2] Fleta, lib. I. c. 19.

I will do faithfully to the best of my endeavor. So help me God, and these holy Apostles."

A list was then put into their hands, or they were informed by the justices of the crimes and offenses of which they were to take cognizance (capitula coronæ), and they were charged to answer truly and faithfully and openly on all the matters respecting them.[1]

In consequence of the oath which they took they were called the jurata patriæ, or often simply juratores, and for a long time seem to have united the two functions of a grand jury to accuse, and a petit jury to try the accused. It was also their duty to present any cases of suspicious death which occurred within their jurisdiction, especially where no one came forward to "appeal," *i.e.* accuse another as the perpetrator, or if the person suspected had fled from justice, and was not forthcoming to meet the charge; in both which cases the hundred was amerced in a fine.[2] We find numerous entries in the Rotuli Curiæ Regis such as the following:

Juratores dicunt quod in bosco de Cesterhunt fuit quidam homo inventus occisus et nescitur quis fuerit.

Upon this the court pronounced that it was a case of murder, and the entry on the rolls is Judicium murdrum.[3]

If the malefactor was known or suspected, they presented him thus: Juratores dicunt quod in villa de Sterteford quædam fœmina inventa fuit mortua, et pro morte ejus rectati fuerunt Norman et uxor ejus. Et Abbas de Waltham replegiavit eos.[4]

---

[1] The words in Fleta are: Statim deliberentur iis capitula coronæ, which might seem to imply that a book or list of these capitula was given to the jurors; but we can hardly suppose that any but a very few in those times were able to read. Bracton says, capitula illis duodecim proponenda sunt, from which we may infer that the articles were read to them. Fleta gives a list of these capitula, amounting to 136 in number.

[2] Rot. Cur. Reg. I. 168, 173.   [3] Ibid. 161.   [4] Ibid. 163.

The subject of the Grand Jury, which arose out of the system here detailed, will be discussed in the next chapter.

SECTION II. *Rise and Growth of the Jury System for the Trial of Accusations.*

I do not think it is possible to determine the exact period when the change took place, whereby a person accused of a crime by the inquest of the hundred was entitled to have the fact tried by another and different jurata. Most probably there was no sudden alteration in the system, but in proportion as compurgation and the ordeal fell into disrepute, the necessity would be felt of substituting some other mode of determining whether the accusation of the jurors representing the patria was well founded or not. No tribunal would seem so proper for this purpose as one similar to that which made the charge, for the advantage would thus be secured of having the fact tried by neighbors who were most likely to know all the circumstances of the case. And even in Glanvill's time we find that a "jury of the country" was employed to determine by their testimony or verdict, whether a suspected person had fled, and been arrested after hue and cry raised. If so, he was compelled to clear himself by the legitima purgatio, or compurgation by witnesses. In some such way as this I conceive that trial by jury in criminal cases may have originated, and it certainly was in operation at the time when Bracton wrote, in the reign of Henry III. But even then the same jury sometimes discharged both functions of accusers and triers. Thus the seneschal of Robert Fitz Roger was presented by the jurors of a township in Northumberland for amercing the tenants illegally, and without

---

[1] Si hoc per juratam patriæ fuerit in curia legitime testatum.—Tract. de Leg. XIV. 3.

proper trial, nec per pares suos. This he denied, and put himself for trial upon the same jurors of the township who acquitted him; and the entry of the record thus proceeds, et prædicti juratores sint in misericordia quia contrarium præsentaverint in veredicto suo.[1]

At first, even after the principle was admitted that the trial of offenses fell within the cognizance of a jury, the accused was not entitled to it as a matter of right, but rather by the king's grace and favor, to be purchased by the payment of a certain sum of money or a gift of chattels, the value of which varied according to the circumstances of the case. Many entries in our old records prove this to have been the fact. Thus in the reign of John, at an assize held at Staffordshire, Robert the son of Robert de Ferrariis appealed or challenged Ranulph de Tattesworth for assaulting and wounding his man Roger, and robbing him of his cloak, sword, and bow and arrows; and "the same Roger offered to prove this by his body as the court should determine: and Ranulph came and denied the charge, word for word, and offered to the lord the king a marc of silver to be allowed to have an inquisition by lawful knights whether he were guilty thereof or not." The offer was accepted, and the jury acquitted the accused.[2]

In another instance, in the reign of Henry III., we find a suspected party offering to the king fifteen marcs to be allowed to have an inquisition made "by the jurors of the county and all the nearest townships, Barton excepted."[3]

We here see that the neighboring townships were associated with the jury in the inquest; and this was by no means an unusual practice. But they were not con-

---

[1] Rot. It. Northumb. 21 Hen. III.
[2] Rot. Itin. Staff. 9 Joh. Idem Hugo dat domino Regi catalla sua quæ capta fuerunt cum eo pro habenda inquisicione,—Rot. It. Salop. 5 Joh.
[3] Rot. It. Westmore. 40 Hen. III.

sidered part of the jury, but seem rather to have assisted in the character of witnesses, and to have constituted part of that fama publica of which, although Virgil describes it as

—malum quo non aliud velocius ullum,

our forefathers entertained by no means so unfavorable an opinion. That is, I think, clear, from the heading of several ancient records. Thus, one is entitled "Hundredum de Erminton venit PER DUODECIM,"[1] and yet the entry goes on to state, that "the twelve jurors and four nearest tithings say, on their oath, that the aforesaid Richard is not guilty." In another instance we have the names of the witnesses given, who said that they saw the murder which was the subject of inquiry committed by the prisoner, "and, moreover, the four nearest townships testify the same, and the twelve jurors also say that he is guilty thereof. And he denies the charge against them all. But because he was taken in the fact, and all say with one voice that he is guilty, it is adjudged that he can not clear himself, and, therefore, let him be hanged."[2]

In the time of Bracton, that is, about the middle of the thirteenth century, the usual mode of determining innocence or guilt was by combat on appeal. But in most cases the appellee had the option of either fighting with his adversary or putting himself upon his country for trial. Where, however, murder was committed by secret poisoning, the party accused of the crime was in general not allowed to choose the latter alternative, but was compelled, if he denied the charge, to defend himself by combat; "because," says Bracton, "the country

---

[1] Rot. It. Devon. 33 Hen III. Another form of entry is, Respondet per duodecim.—See Rot. It. Essex, 19 Hen. III.
[2] Rot. It. Glouc. 5 Hen. III.

can know nothing of the fact.¹ But in some cases of this kind the appellee was allowed to make his election, and the reason assigned by Bracton is, that this was of necessity, on account of the inconvenience which would ensue if a man were always obliged to defend himself against the charge by mortal combat; for in a case of secret poisoning the accuser might have to employ a hired champion to fight for him (there being no witness of the deed whom he could put forward), which could not be allowed.

And there were some presumptions of guilt which the law regarded as conclusive, and would not allow to be rebutted. For instance, if a man were found standing over a dead body with a bloody knife in his hand he was estopped from denying that he had murdered him; and could neither clear himself by combat nor put himself upon the country.² So also in the case of a man found murdered in a house where he had slept, whose inmates made no hue and cry, and could show no wounds or other marks of violence sustained by them in defending him from the assassin.

It is obvious that this rule of regarding certain appearances against the accused not merely as presumptions, but as conclusive evidences of guilt, indicates a very defective system of jurisprudence, and must have often led to acts of gross injustice. Of all kinds of evidence that which is called circumstantial requires to be

---

[1] Lib. III. c. 18. Bracton adds: Nisi per præsumptionem et per auditum vel per mandatum, quod quidem non sufficit ad probationem pro appellante, nec pro appellato ad liberationem. This seems to mean that the case of secret poisoning was one of which nobody could have personal knowledge except the accused; and that however far back the rumor of the prisoner's guilt was traced, it would be found to rest solely on presumption and conjecture; for there is no doubt that, as a general rule, hearsay evidence was thought a sufficient ground for a verdict.

[2] Mortem dedicere non poterit, et hæc est constitutio antiqua, in quo casu non est opus alia probatione.—Bract. lib. III. c. 18.

examined with the most searching care, and ought to be acted upon with the most hesitating caution. It has been often said, that circumstances can not lie; but the application of this maxim frequently involves a practical fallacy. The circumstances themselves, if proved, must, of course, be taken to be true, but their real bearing upon the question of innocence or guilt depends wholly upon the aspect in which they are viewed in relation to the accused. The appearance of a picture varies to the eye according to the light in which it is placed and the point of view from which the spectator beholds it, and yet the painting remains all the while the same. So the inference to be drawn from admitted facts, with reference to the guilt or innocence of a party, varies according to the explanation which can be given of the relation in which he actually stands towards them; but the rule of law in Bracton's time prevented the accused from giving this explanation, and the consequence must have been in many cases judicial murder. The annals of the criminal jurisprudence of all countries abound in examples of mistaken inferences of guilt.[1]

It seems, however, there in some cases where the circumstances raised a violent presumption of guilt, the justices might direct an inquiry by a jury, although Bracton says it would be scarcely possible for the accused to escape conviction, on account of the strong presumption against him. And in answer to the objection, that

[1] Staunford, who wrote his Pleas of the Crown in the time of Hen. VII., after quoting Bracton respecting the nature of these presumptions, says: "Britton agrees with him: so that it appears by Bracton and Britton, that in ancient times some of these presumptions were so vehement that they were as condemnation to the other party without any other trial, but they are not so at this day, for trial he shall have notwithstanding such presumption; but not by battle."—Lib. III. c. 16. And he adds: "the mainour in an appeal of death is a bloody knife with which being taken he shall be ousted of his wager of battle, and so it shall be in an appeal of robbery."

he can not be pronounced not guilty of a deed done so secretly that the country can know nothing of the matter, he says that the country (*i. e.*, the jury) sufficiently acquits when it does not expressly convict.[1]

If the accused person put himself upon a jury for trial he was not allowed to choose the patria of any hundred he preferred, but the justices assigned for the purpose any set of twelve they pleased from amongst those who represented each hundred. Reeves assumes that these were identical with the juries who presented the crimes and offenses of their respective districts. He says,[2] " Here, then, do we see the office of the twelve jurors chosen out of each hundred at the eyre : they were to digest and mature the accusations of crimes founded upon report and the notorious evidence of the fact ; and then again, under the direction of the justices, they were to reconsider their verdict, and upon such review of the matter they were to give their verdict finally."

But I incline to think that this view is incorrect, and that in the account which Bracton gives of the mode of proceeding we recognize the existence of a second and different jury, as the triers of the truth of the charge brought by the presentment of the country (fama patriæ) against the accused.

But whether this was so or not in Bracton's time, it is quite clear that the separation of the accusing from the trying jury existed in the reign of Edward III., for a statute of that monarch provides that " no indictor shall be put in inquests upon deliverance of the indictees of felonies or trespass, if he be challenged for such cause by him who is indicted." [3]

Reeves may have been misled by seeing that in Brac-

---

[1] This is clearly inconsistent with what Bracton says about the case of secret poisoning. But it requires only a slight acquaintance with our early jurisprudence to be satisfied that it was a system full of anomalies."

[2] Hist. Eng. Law, II. 33.   [3] 25 Edw. III. c. 3.

ton the jury are supposed to have a previous knowledge of the case;[1] but this proves nothing more than that the original principle of the system was still preserved, and the verdict was simply the testimony of witnesses.

This plainly appears from the oath taken by the twelve jurors:

"Hear this, ye justices! that we will speak the truth of those things which ye shall require from us on the part of our lord the king, and will by no means omit to speak the truth, so help us God!"

Upon this one of the justices charged them, saying, "N. who is here present accused of such and such a felony comes and denies it wholly, and puts himself upon your tongues concerning this for good and for evil; and therefore we charge you by the faith which ye owe to God, and by the oath which ye have taken, that ye make us to know the truth thereon, and omit not, for fear or love or hate, but having only (the fear of) God before your eyes, to say if he be guilty of that which is charged against him, and ye shall not find him guilty (non incumberetis eum) if he is free from or innocent of the crime."

If the justices had any doubt or suspicion as to the source from which the twelve jurors obtained the information on which they founded their verdict, it was his duty to interrogate them on the subject. Perhaps (says Bracton) one or more of them might say that they learnt it from one of their fellow-jurors, and he on being questioned might say that he had heard it from such a one, and so the inquiry might be pursued, until perchance the report was traced to some worthless person of no credit. And if a grave crime had been committed, the author of

---

[1] If the accused were suspected of other crimes besides the one that was the subject of the particular inquiry, the jury were told to say whether he were guilty de hoc quod ei imponitur, vel de aliis maleficiis vel non.—Bract. III. c. 18.

which was unknown, and the judge suspected the jurors of being influenced by any desire to conceal the truth, he might examine each of them separately, and so endeavor to make them declare what they knew.

Here it seems that the jury were acting rather as accusers than as triers, and at all events we see that they did not give their verdict upon evidence taken in court, but upon the private knowledge or belief which each had beforehand of the commission of the offense in question. In this respect they acted precisely similar to the assize in civil cases.

In the reign of Edward III. trials by jury in criminal cases were nearly if not quite the same as at the present day. As an instance may be mentioned the trial of Sir Thomas de Berkeley by a jury of twelve knights, on the charge of having abetted the murder of Edward II.[1]

Although the qualifications of previous knowledge on the part of jurors empaneled to try a prisoner had long fallen into desuetude, the fiction was still kept up by requiring them to be summoned from the hundred where the crime was alleged to have been committed, until the passing of Stat. 6, Geo. IV. c. 50, by which the sheriff is now obliged only to return for the trial of any issue, whether civil or criminal, twelve good and lawful men of the body of his county qualified according to law.[2]

SECTION III. *Trial by Jury in Criminal Cases in Jersey.*

Considering how intimate the connection was between

---

[1] 4 Edw. III. 1330. Rot. Parl. II. 57.

[2] The qualification of a common juror to try cases, both civil and criminal, depends upon Stat. 6, Geo. IV. c. 50, and is as follows: He must possess an annual income of ten pounds issuing from lands of freehold, copyhold, or customary tenure, or of ancient demesne, in fee simple, fee tail, or for the life of himself or some other person; or of twenty pounds from leasehold property, the term being twenty-one years or longer, or determinable on any

Normandy and England, it is interesting to observe how far the judicial proceedings in the two countries resembled each other; and we have unusual means of making ourselves acquainted with the practice of the former, inasmuch as although it has long been obsolete in France, the criminal law of Normandy is still preserved in the Channel Islands. In Jersey, for instance, the Grand Coutumier is the chief authority appealed to, and it forms the basis of the criminal jurisprudence of the island. It has been previously stated that this compilation does not date earlier than the middle of the thirteenth century, and that it is probable that many of the usages therein mentioned were copied from England. Let us see what was the mode of procedure in Normandy in criminal cases, availing ourselves of the account which Sir Francis Palgrave gives of it:[1]

"According to the law of Normandy, criminals were convicted or absolved by an inquest, composed of twenty-four good and lawful men of the country summoned by the sergeant from the neighborhood where the murder or the theft had been committed. The officer is directed to select those who are 'believed to be best informed of the truth of the matter, and how it happened.' None were to be adduced whose integrity or credibility might be reasonably distrusted, either by the accuser or the accused. Known friends or declared enemies, and near relations of either party, were excluded from the inquest, and they were to be brought into court suddenly and without notice, so that they might not be bribed, intimidated, or corrupted. Before the culprit was put upon his trial, a preliminary inquest

---

life or lives; or he must be a householder rated and assessed to the relief of the poor on a value of not less than £20 (except in Middlesex, where the value is to be not less than £30); or he must occupy a house containing not less than fifteen windows.

[1] Eng. Commonw. I. 244.

was taken by four knights, who were questioned touching their belief of his guilt; and, in their presence, the bailiff afterwards interrogated the twenty-four jurors, not as composing one body, but privately and separately from each other. They were then assembled and confronted with the culprit, who could challenge any one for lawful cause; and if the challenge was allowed, the testimony of that juror was rejected. The judge then 'recorded,' or declared the verdict, in which twenty, at least, were required to concur."[1]

At the present day the criminal procedure in Jersey is as follows:[2]

The only court with criminal jurisdiction is the royal court, which is composed of the bailly, or judge appointed by the crown, and twelve jures justiciers, or sworn justices, who are elected by the general body of ratepayers throughout the island, and hold office during their lives.[3] This royal court as at present constituted was established by a charter of King John, which has been confirmed by successive sovereigns. Its jurisdiction extends over all crimes and offenses whatsoever, except high treason, and laying violent hands on the king's ministers whilst in the exercise of their office, which by the charter are reserved for the cognizance of the king in council. When a party has been arrested he is brought, in the first instance, before the court, which is sufficiently

---

[1] "In Brittany, at an early period, judgments were given by the Scabini, upon the evidence of the twelve witnesses who were first examined, and afterwards sworn, and this took place in the 'Mallum,' before the Missus of Nominoe, king or duke of the Bretons; the whole process of the Carlovingian jurisprudence was forced upon this Celtic people."—Ib. II. cxcii.

[2] I have derived my information on this subject from the evidence collected by the Commissioners for inquiring into the Criminal Laws in the Channel Islands (1846).

[3] The royal court has also cognizance of all civil causes arising within the Island.

formed by the bailly and two jurats, and if the offense is of such a nature that it can not be disposed of summarily, the prisoner is called upon to plead to the act of accusation or indictment framed by the attorney-general. If the plea is not guilty, the court makes an act permitting the attorney-general d'informer; the effect of which is to enable him to give evidence in support of the charge, and the prisoner to call witnesses for his defense. The evidence is then taken and reduced into writing before the bailly or lieutenant bailly and two jurats, and when the whole is complete, and the case ready for trial, a jury, called the enditement, is convened by the vicomte (or sheriff), acting under a mandate from the bailly. This is composed of the constable and twelve police-officers of the parish where the crime is alleged to have been committed, and the court must now consist of the bailly and seven jurats. No fresh oath is administered to the jury, and the accused is allowed to challenge them, but on specific grounds. The whole of the proceedings and evidence previously taken are then read by the attorney-general to the jury, the counsel for the defense is heard, and the attorney-general in reply. The jury retire to consider their verdict, in the custody of the vicomte, who takes with him and lays before the jury the indictment and written depositions, that they may refer to them if necessary. When the jury return into court, if they are unanimous, the constable delivers the verdict, which if they find the prisoner guilty, is in the following form: L'accuse est plutot coupable qu'innocent du crime mis a sa charge. If innocent, the verdict is, plutot innocent que coupable. If the jury are not unanimous, each juror in rotation delivers his opinion secretly to the bailly and jurats, and the opinion of the majority is announced by the bailly as the verdict. If the prisoner is declared more innocent than guilty, he is forthwith discharged. If he is found more guilty than innocent, the court pronounce him to be criminally indicted. He is then entitled to appeal to the grande enquete, or jury of twenty-four; or he may waive this right, and submit to judgment. If he appeals, he is remanded to prison until the grand inquest is called.

Within two or three days the court meet, constituted as before. Twenty-four men selected by the attorney-general from amongst the most intelligent inhabitants of the parish wherein the alleged crime has been committed, and the two adjoining parishes, eight from each, are summoned to serve as a jury, and also a few supplementary jurymen from each parish, in case of challenges, sickness, or absence of those who are intended to form the jury. The prisoner may challenge any of them, but only on specific grounds. When the jury is complete they are sworn "to declare well and faithfully what they shall find in their conscience relative to the crime of which the party is accused, namely, whether he is more guilty than innocent, to charge or discharge him, and that they will do so without favor or partiality, as they shall answer it before God." Precisely the same form is then gone through which had been previously observed at the first trial. On the return of the jury into court with the vicomte, if they are unanimous, the foreman delivers the verdict; if they differ, they each deliver their opinion to the bailly secretly; and if twenty out of the twenty-four concur in finding the accused more guilty than innocent, he is declared by the bailly duly attainted and convicted of the offense for which he had been indicted, and sentence is immediately passed. If, however, five or more out of the twenty-four concur in finding the accused more innocent than guilty, he is forthwith discharged.

The bailly and jurats decide all questions of law, and the jury questions of fact. The prosecutor is not allowed to adduce fresh evidence after the enditement or petit jury have met to try the accused, but the latter is sometimes permitted to call evidence in support of his defence before the grande enquete after he has been indicted by the petit jury.

We see in these proceedings an apparent inversion of our own forms. The petit jury seems to have been originally in the nature of a jury d'examen, like our grand jury, and the grande enquete performs the office of our petit jury. There is, however, this material difference, that all the evidence both for and against the prisoner is laid before the enditement, and unless he appeals from their verdict it is conclusive, so that judgment may be passed upon it, which, of course, is not the case with the finding of the grand jury in England. It certainly is a very objectionable part of the practice, that the petit jury should be composed of police-officers who have just been active in detecting the offender, and procuring evidence to convict him; and also that witnesses are not examined viva voce in their presence when they act as an enditement. There also results this anomaly, that if six members of the first jury declare a man not guilty, he is nevertheless condemned, whereas if subsequently five members only of the second declare him not guilty, he is acquited, although the evidence presented to each jury is identically the same. And both these contradictory verdicts remain for all time recorded on the rolls of the court.

CHAPTER X.

THE GRAND JURY AND OTHER MATTERS RELATING TO CRIMINAL TRIALS.

SECTION I. *The Grand Jury.*

AN indictment is a written accusation of one or more persons of high treason, felony, or a misdemeanor, preferred before and presented upon oath by twelve or more, not exceeding twenty-three good and lawful men of the county duly sworn, who are called the Grand Jury. They are, therefore, the accusing jury, as distinguished from the petit or trying jury. It has been said by an eminent legal writer, that the existence of two juries is, "though one of the most important, yet certainly one of the most obscure and inexplicable parts of the law of England."[1] I do not, however, think that the latter part of this remark is true. On the contrary, it seems to me to have been the natural result of the state of things which has been detailed in the preceding chapter. We see that when the justices in eyre paid their periodical visits to the counties, they caused to be summoned before them twelve knights,[2] or other good and lawful men, for each hundred, and charged them upon their oaths to inquire respecting crimes and offenses committed within their respective hundreds or wapentakes, so that they might be ready to present to the

---

[1] Note by Professor Christian to Blackstone, III. 367.
[2] Milites. See a dissertation on the meaning of this word in the Appendix.

court the suspected persons at a future day fixed by the justices. It has been shown that these jurors were the representatives of and substitutes for the fama patriæ, or public rumor, by which in old times when a man was assailed he was said to be male creditus (corresponding to the tyht-bysig of the Anglo-Saxons), and was thereupon arrested and put upon his trial. I have said also that for some time there appears to have been no difference between this accusing jury and the trying jury; nor can the exact period be determined when they became separate and distinct. Most probably, however, this happened when the ordeal fell into desuetude, and was no longer resorted to as a means of testing the truth of the accusation. For, as has been already explained, the consequence of a criminal charge in Saxon, as well as in Norman times, was an appeal to compurgation or the ordeal, and when these modes of trial were abandoned, it was necessary to find some other substitute for them. What, then, was more natural than that the jurata patriæ, borrowed as to its form from the grand assize, and already employed as a tribunal for the discovery of truth in civil cases, should be made use of for the same purpose in criminal?

It was at an earlier period made imperative by statute, that these presentments should rest upon the finding of twelve men at least. Thus by 13 Edw. I. c. 13, it was enacted that sheriffs in their "tourns" should cause their " inquests of malefactors to be taken by lawful men, and by twelve at the least, which shall put their seals to such inquisitions; and those that shall be found culpable by such inquests they shall take and imprison, as they have used aforetimes to do." And to prevent persons being put upon their trial owing to false and malicious accusations, to gratify private revenge, it was enacted in the reign of Edward III. (A. D. 1368), that "no man be put to answer without presentment before justices or matter of record, or by due process and writ original, according to the old law of the land." And it had been previously provided by 1 Edw. III. st. 2, c. 17, that all sheriffs, bailiffs, and others whose office it was to take indictments should do so " by roll indented, whereof the one part shall remain with the indictors, and the other part with him that taketh the inquest; so that the indictments shall not be embezzled, as they have been in times past, and so that one of the inquest may show the one part of the indenture to the justices when they come to make deliverance.

It will have been noticed that the twelve jurors mentioned as indictors by Bracton, were limited to the cognizance of offenses within their own hundred; and the next question to consider is, how the practice arose by which, as at the present day, one body of grand jurors, consisting of twelve at least, came to represent the whole county, and presentments for separate hundreds were discontined. We have no precise information on the subject, but it is perhaps not impossible to trace the steps by which the change was effected. I believe the first notice of a Grand Inquest occurs in the Liber Assisarum for the 42nd year of the reign of Edward III. A commission of oyer and terminer had been issued to Throp. and Lodel, justices, for the counties of Essex, Hertford, Cambridge, Norfolk, and Suffolk; and when at Chelmsford they called upon the bailiffs of each hundred of the county to return their inquest or panels. And afterwards "the sheriff returned a panel of knights, which was the grand inquest (le grande enquest)." Most probably it was the duty of this grand inquest to inquire at large for every hundred in the county, in case there should be any omissions or malpractices on the part of the hundredors who took the smaller inquests; and as the latter were frequently called upon to sit on assizes and juries in civil causes, this double office would be felt to be a burden from which they would be glad to escape, by throwing the duty of making presentments as much as possible upon the knights of the grand inquest. Thus the presentments by the knights, instead of being merely, as at first, supplemental to those of the hundredors, gradually usurped altogether the place of the latter; and the system of the grand jury as it at present exists was fully developed.'

It was formerly deemed felony, if not high treason, for any of the grand jury to divulge the names of the persons whom they were about to present.[2] It was also not unusual to fine them for non-presentments or concealments of offenses within their cognizance; but of this practice Sir Matthew Hale expresses his strong disapproval, saying that it is not warrantable by law, and that "it is of very ill consequence; for the privilege of an Englishman is, that his life shall not be drawn in danger without presentment or indictment; and this would be but a slender screen or safeguard, if every justice of the peace, or commissioner of oyer and terminer, or jail delivery, may make the grand jury present what he pleases, or otherwise fine them." Sir Matthew Hale, however, makes a distinction in favor of the right of the Queen's Bench to fine for an improper presentment or non-presentment; for he says, "there is no parity of reason or example between inferior judges and that court which is the supreme ordinary court of justice in such cases."[3]

The mode in which the grand jury is summoned and performs its functions, is the following:

---

[1] See Reeves's Hist. Eng. Law, Vol. III. 133.
[2] Lib. Assis. 27, 5.
[3] Hale, P. C. II. 161. In Rot. Parl. I. 121, b. (A. D. 1293) we find an instance of a juror committed to jail on the testimony of his fellow-jurors, for procuring a false presentment to be made by them, so as to conceal a felony concerning which plenam scivit veritatem.

The sheriff of each county is directed, by a precept issued to him for that purpose, to return twenty-four or more persons, out of whom the jury is to be taken and sworn; and "if there be thirteen or more of the grand inquest, a presentment by less than twelve ought not to be; but if there be twelve assenting, though some of the rest of their number dissent, it is a good presentment."[1] The number sworn, however, must not exceed twenty-three. In a case that occurred within the last few years, Lord Denman, C. J., said:[2] "The court has no doubt that twenty-three is the limited number. It is a matter of practice proved by authorities in the only way in which proof can be given of a point of that kind which has been undisputed." The reason of this is that twelve agreeing may constitute a majority; for it is a maxim of the English law, as Blackstone says, that "no man can be convicted at the suit of the king of any capital offense [or any felony], unless by the unanimous voice of twenty-four of his equals and neighbors: that is, by twelve at least of the grand jury in the first place assenting to the accusation; and afterwards by the whole petit jury, of twelve more, finding him guilty."

Formerly it was considered necessary that some of the grand jury should be summoned out of every hundred in the county. But this has been altered by statute 6 Geo. IV. c. 50, and the sheriff is now only required to return them from the body of his county. The marshal administers to the foreman of the jury the following oath:

"You, as foreman of this grand inquest for the body of this county of A, shall diligently inquire, and true presentment make, of all such matters and things as shall be given you in charge. The king's counsel, your fellows', and your own, you shall keep secret: you shall

---

[1] 2 Hale's P. C. 161.
[2] R. v. Marsh, 6 Ad. and Ell, 242.

present no one for envy, hatred, or malice; neither shall you leave any one unpresented for fear, favor, or affection, or hope of reward; but you shall present all things truly as they come to your knowledge, according to the best of your understanding: So help you God!"

The rest of the grand jury, by three at a time, in order, are then sworn in the following manner:

"The same oath which your foreman hath taken on his part, you and every one of you, shall well and truly observe and keep on your part: So help you God!"

When the grand jury have been sworn, they receive a charge from the judge who presides in the criminal court, and are instructed by him generally in the duties which they have to perform, and where any of the cases to be brought before them involve difficult points of law, these are explained to them. They then retire to receive the bills of indictment, and examine the witnesses who support the accusation, endorsing on the back of each bill the names of all the witnesses whom they examine in that case. Their duty is to satisfy themselves, from the statements on the part of the prosecution, that sufficient cause appears for calling upon the accused party to answer the charge made against him. If they think that the accusation is unfounded, they indorse on the bill, "Not a true bill," or the letters N. T. B. And if it is not intended to prefer a fresh bill before the grand jury at that assize, the party is discharged for the time; but a bill for the same offense may be afterwards preferred against him at a subsequent assize, if fresh circumstances of suspicion in the meantime arise. If they consider the evidence sufficient to warrant putting the party on his trial, they endorse the words "True bill," or the letters T. B., and the bill being thus found by them becomes an indictment, and the accused is tried by the petit jury.

Of late years an opinion has been frequently expressed,

that the preliminary proceeding by grand jury is useless, and ought to be abolished. And with respect to the district within the jurisdiction of the Central Criminal Court, the idea is perhaps well founded. The legal knowledge and practiced vigilance of the magistrates of the metropolis render it almost superfluous to subject their committals to the supervision of another tribunal, before a prisoner is put upon his trial, and it is a great hardship that busy tradesmen should be taken from their avocations and detained for several days at a time upon an inquiry, which is followed by no useful results so far as respects the jurymen themselves. But the case is very different in the counties which the judges visit in their periodical circuits. The grand jury there consist principally of the landed gentry and magistrates of the county, and it is of the highest importance to secure their attendance on such occasions. They are thus called upon to take their part in the great judicial drama, and see justice administered in its purest and most enlightened form. The committals by each magistrate are exposed to the scrutiny of his neighbors, and a useful lesson is taught to each when bills are thrown out because the evidence is too slight and unsatisfactory to raise any fair presumption of guilt in the accused. For it is no light matter to incarcerate a man on a charge of felony for months previous to his trial, which in many cases must lead to the ruin of his prospects, and then find that the case of suspicion is deemed so weak by the grand jury, that when they assemble they pronounce him entitled to an immediate discharge. Moreover, they hear an exposition of the criminal law from the judge, which must be of essential service to them in the performance of their magisterial duties throughout the year.

But besides all this, the grand jury can often baffle the attempts of malevolence; and who can estimate the blessing to a man unjustly accused of a crime to find himself relieved in so triumphant a manner from the shame and degradation of a trial at the felon's bar? Who, however innocent, with quick and sensitive feelings, would not gladly purchase, at almost any cost short of a compromise of honor, an exemption from such an ordeal? To stand for hours in a crowded court the object of obloquy and suspicion, to catch the whispered comments of the auditory, and see every eye carefully watching each look and gesture, and then to have one's name spread on the wings of the press throughout the world in connection with some odious and disreputable charge, must be a degree of torture sufficient to unnerve the strongest mind. When an application was once made for a new trial, on the ground that excessive damages had been awarded to a plaintiff in an action for a malicious prosecution, he having been tried and acquitted at the Old Bailey, Chief Justice Mansfield in refusing to grant it, said,[1] "The plaintiff is put on his trial at the Old Bailey in the presence of hundreds. What sum would bribe any man to put himself in this situation?"

And there have undoubtedly been periods in our history when it was very necessary that the shield of the grand jury should be interposed between the crown and the subject. If in 1681 the grand jury of the city of London had not resolutely, against the undisguised endeavors of the judges North, Pemberton, and others, refused to bring in a true bill against the Earl of Shaftesbury, it is well nigh certain that that nobleman would have expiated with his life on the scaffold the venial crime of factious opposition to the court. He had been arrested on a charge of high treason, which, however, was a mere pretense, as there was no legal evidence to implicate him; and the bill went before the grand jury. The intention was to remove it when found, as the Parliament was not sitting, to the court of the High Steward,

---

[1] Hewlett v. Cruchley, 5 Taunt. 281.

where Lord Shaftesbury would have been tried by peers selected by the king, and his conviction and sentence would have been inevitable. The counsel for the crown applied that the witnesses in support of the indictment might be examined before the grand jury in open court; the object being to overawe the latter in the discharge of their duty. The foreman reminded the court of the oath which he and his fellows had taken to keep the king's counsel secret, but the judges told him that the king might dispense with secrecy, and disallowed the objection. The witnesses were accordingly openly examined, and the grand jury retired, but soon returned with the word IGNORAMUS written on the back of the bill; upon which we are told that "there was a most wonderful shout, that one could have thought the hall had cracked."[1]

SECTION II. *The Coroner's Jury.*

It has been said of coroners that they are of so great antiquity that their commencement is not known.[2] The name occurs in a rhyming charter granted by the Anglo-Saxon king Athelstan to the monastery of St. John of Beverley, A.D. 925, which contains the following lines:

> If a man be found slain idrunkend,
> Sterved on sain John rike, his aghen men
> Withouten swike his aghen bailiffs make ye fight,
> Nan oyer coroner have ye might:
> Swa mikel freedom give I ye,
> Swa hert may think or eghe see.[3]

In old times the coroner was an officer of some importance, as appears from the way in which Chaucer mentions him in his description of the Frankelein:

> At sessions there was he, lord and sire,
> Full often time he was knight of the shire,
> A shereve had he been, and a coronour,
> Was no where swiche a worthy vavasour.

[1] 8 State Tr. 759–821.   [2] 3 Bulstrode, 176.
[3] Dugd. Monast. II. 130 (Edit. 1817).

It seems that anciently coroners held pleas of the crown, and could pass judgment in criminal cases; but this power was expressly taken from them by one of the provisions of the Great Charter.

We are, however, here no further concerned with the office than as it is connected with the jury system. The earliest statute which regulates and defines the mode of taking a coroner's inquest, is that entitled De Officio Coronatoris, 4 Edw. I. st. 3 (A. D. 1276), and this enacts that when coroners are directed by the bailiffs of the king, or honest men (probi homines) of the county, to go to those who are slain or have died suddenly, or been wounded, or to housebreakers, or to places where treasure is said to be found, they shall forthwith proceed there, and command four of the next towns, or five or six, to appear before them in such a place, and when they are come thither, the coroner upon the oath of them shall inquire, if it concerns a man slain, where he was slain, whether it was in a house, field, bed, tavern, or company, and if any and who were there.

"Likewise it is to be inquired who were and in what manner culpable, either of the act, or of the force; and who were present, either men or women, and of what age soever they be (if they can speak or have any discretion). And how many soever be found culpable by inquisition in any of the manners aforesaid, they shall be taken and delivered to the sheriff, and shall be committed to jail; and such as be found and be not culpable, shall be attached until the coming of the justices, and their names shall be written in the coroner's rolls."

Then there follow a number of minute regulations respecting different kinds of inquiry.

It will be observed, that although the jurors are here required to be summoned from the nearest townships, nothing is said as to their number; and there can be little doubt that at this period it was indeterminate.[1] But afterwards, following the analogy of the jury system in other cases, it became a fixed rule of law that twelve at least must concur in the finding of the inquest, in order that the parties charged thereby may be put upon their trial before a petit jury.[2] The number, however, summoned and assisting at the inquest is immaterial, provided that twelve agree. Where the jury are not unanimous, it is the duty of the coroner to collect the voices, and take the verdict according to the opinion of the majority. If twelve can not agree, the jury are, according to the theory of the law, to be kept without meat, drink, or fire, until they give their verdict; but in practice of course this rule is never enforced so as to endanger life or health. Formerly if they refused to make a legal presentment, it was the custom for the coroner to adjourn them from place to place; but it was said by Chief Justice Holt that it was wrong, and that they ought to be adjourned to the assizes, "where the judge will inform them better."

We have already noticed the mode in which cases of suspected crime were presented originally by the fama patriæ, and afterwards by sworn jurors. And it has been assumed that the instances quoted from the Rotuli Curiæ Regis belonged to that class of presentments made in the manner pointed out by Bracton, when he tells us that twelve jurors were to be charged upon oath by the justices to discover and make known by their verdict on a day certain, all persons suspected of criminal offenses within their hundred or wapentake.[3] Possibly, however, some of these entries may be inquisitions taken by the coroner's jury, for it is obvious that their office closely

---

[1] By the Statute of Marlbridge, 52 Hen. III. c. 24 (A. D. 1267), it was ordained that at the inquests "for the death of a man," all being twelve years of age ought to appear, unless they have reasonable cause of absence.
[2] Smith's case, Combercatch, 386.
[3] Bract. lib. III. fo. 116.

corresponded with that of the jurors or indicators mentioned by Bracton and Fleta. The coroner had a parallel jurisdiction with the twelve sworn hundredors in this respect. It was his duty ex officio to inquire concerning and present all cases of suspicious death, and other matters enumerated by the statute De Officio Coronatoris; and the existence of so many different modes of inquest as were provided for by the hundred jury, the grand jury, and the coroner's jury, proves a laudable anxiety on the part of our ancestors to protect human life and discover and punish crime.

SECTION III. *The Jury de Medietate Linguæ.*

The origin of the jury de medietate linguæ has been generally referred to the reign of Edward III.; and the first mention of it is supposed to occur in the Statute of the Staple, passed in the year 1353. But this is a mistake. In Rymer's Fœdera we find a deed of Inspeximus, or charter of confirmation, granted by Edward III., which recites at length and confirms a charter granted by Edward I. in the thirty-first year of his reign, in which the last-named monarch makes ample provision for the protection and convenience of foreign merchants sojourning within the realm. Amongst other benefits conferred upon them, the charter declares that in all pleas in which merchants are impleaded, except in capital cases, whether they be plaintiffs or defendants, half of the inquest shall consist of foreign merchants residing in the city or town, provided a sufficient number of them can be found, and the other half of good and lawful men of the place where the plea is held. But if six foreign merchants can not be found there, then the number is to be made up of other merchants, and the remaining six are to be other good and sufficient men of the place.[1] The Statute of the Staple, however, of Edward III.[2] was rather more specific in its provisions. It enacted that when both merchants were foreigners, the jury should all be foreigners. Where the one was a foreigner, and the other a denizen, half of the jury should be foreigners and half denizens, and if both were denizens, then all the jury should be denizens.

In the Rolls of Parliament for the year 1308 (2 Edw. II.) occurs a king's writ ordering an action of ejectment for lands in Shropshire to be tried by a jury half English and half Welsh.

At the present day, if an alien be indicted for felony or misdemeanor, he may by proper application to the court require the sheriff or other proper minister to return for one half of the jury a competent number of aliens, if so many there be in the town or place where the trial is had; and if not, then so many aliens as shall be found in the same town or place, if any; and no such alien juror shall be liable to be challenged for want of freehold or other qualification required in denizen jurors, but he may be challenged for any other cause.[3]

It is not necessary that all or any of the alien jurors should be natives of the same country as the prisoner. It is sufficient that they are foreigners.

---

[1] Rymer's Fœd. IV. 362. The charter seems to provide this mode of trial for all merchants as I have given it in the text. The words are ubi mercator implacitatus fuerit vel alium implacitaverit cujuscumque conditionis idem implacitatus exstiterit EXTRANEOUS VEL PRIVATUS......et si de mercatoribus dictarum terrarum numerus non inveniatur sufficiens ponantur in inquisitione ille, qui idonei invenientur ibidem; et residui sint de aliis bonis homnibus et idoneis de locis in quibus illud placitum erit. In 1320 (14 Edw. II.) we have a petition from some Louvain merchants praying that an action about some cloth might be tried by a jury, of which twelve should be foreigners and twelve natives—twenty-four in all. Rot. Parl. I. 382.

[2] 27 Edw. III. c. 8.

[3] 6 Geo. IV. c. 50, § 47.

SECTION IV. *Challenges in Criminal Trials.*

What has been said with respect to all challenges for cause in civil actions, applies equally to criminal trials.[1] But in charges of treason and felony a prisoner is entitled to a peremptory challege, so called "because he may challenge peremptorily upon his own dislike, without showing of any cause."[2] By the common law he might upon an indictment or appeal of death challenge thirty-five, which was one less than the number of three juries. This number was, by Stat. 22 Hen. VIII. c. 14, reduced to twenty in petit treason, murder, and felony; and the right was, by the same statute, altogether taken away in high treason and misprision of high treason; but by Stat. 1 and 2 Phil. and Mary, c. 10, the common law with respect to challenges was revived. And so the matter still stands in the case of treason; but by 6 Geo. IV. c. 50, no person arraigned for murder or felony shall be admitted to any peremptory challenge above the number of twenty; and by 7 and 8 Geo. IV. c. 28, if any person indicted for treason, felony, or piracy, shall challenge peremptorily a greater number of the men returned to be of the jury than such person is entitled by law to challenge in any of the said cases, every such peremptory challenge beyond the number allowed by law shall be entirely void, and the trial of such person shall proceed as if no such challenge had been made.

It has been previously mentioned that a lord of parliament tried by his peers has no right of challenge at all. The reason for which, as given by Coke, is, " for that they

---

[1] Coke says, that where the king is party one shall not challenge the array for favor; for which he assigns the startling reason, "because in respect of his allegiance the sheriff ought to favor the king more." But Hale says expressly that prisoners are allowed to challenge the array for favor.—2 Pt. C. 271.

[2] Co. Litt. 156, b.

are not sworn as other jurors be, but find the party guilty or not guilty upon their faith or allegiance to the king, and they are judges of the fact, and every one of them doth separately give his judgment, beginning at the lowest."

By the common law the king might challenge peremptorily without being limited to any number. But this, says Coke, was mischievous to the subject, tending to infinite delays and danger.[1] It was therefore enacted, by 33 Edw. I. st. 4, that none should challenge for the king except for cause certain, and this is re-enacted, by 6 Geo. IV. c. 50, which provides that the king shall challenge no jurors without assigning a cause certain to be tried and approved by the court.

In the case of a prisoner challenging, he must do so as each juror " comes to the book to be sworn, and before he is sworn ;" but the king need not assign his cause of challenge until the whole panel is gone through, and unless there can not be a full jury without the persons so challenged. And it is then that the counsel for the crown must show cause, otherwise the juror shall be sworn. The practical effect of this rule therefore is, that the crown has the benefit of peremptory challenges, provided it takes care that a sufficient number are left on the panel unchallenged so as to make up a full jury. For as was said by Chief Justice Holt,[2] "cause is not to be shown by the king's counsel till all the panel be gone through ; and then if there be not twelve left to try, they are bound to show cause : that is the law :"—a doctrine which was strenuously but ineffectually impugned by the counsel for O'Coigly, O'Connor, and others, who were tried for high treason in 1798.[3]

When twelve jurors have at last been collected against whom no exception is made, they are sworn separately

---

[1] Co Litt. 156, b.   [2] 12 State Tr. 675.
[3] 26 State Tr. 1231.

according to the following form of oath :—" You shall well and truly try, and true deliverance make, between our sovereign lady the Queen and the prisoner at the bar whom you have in charge; and a true verdict give according to the evidence, so help you God!"

SECTION V. *Question of new Trial in Cases of Conviction of Felony.*

A question of great importance has often been raised, whether in criminal cases there ought not be an appeal from the verdict of the jury on matters of fact. In the English and Scotch law it is unknown, and a conviction of felony can not be questioned by any form of legal process, on the ground that the verdict was not warranted by the evidence. Now as it may be plausibly urged that twelve men are as likely to be mistaken in the effect of evidence in a criminal as in a civil trial, there is an apparent anomaly in allowing a new trial in the one case and not in the other. And certainly if there were no machinery whereby the mistakes of juries in such instances could be corrected other than the courts of law possess, it would be impossible to answer the objection. The defect in the system would be glaring and the evil intolerable. But the constitution provides what may perhaps be considered upon the whole a not inadequate remedy. The prerogative of mercy resides in the crown, and every capital conviction, and indeed every other in which the judge entertains any reasonable doubt as to its propriety, is submitted to the careful and humane consideration of the Secretary of State for home affairs, when, if the evidence upon which the jury have found their verdict appears to be insufficient to sustain it, or fresh facts come to light which tend to establish the prisoner's innocence, a royal pardon is granted, which not only annuls the conviction, but reinstates the party absolutely in all his former civil rights. And if in the course of the trial evidence is admitted against the prisoner as to the reception of which the presiding judge feels a doubt, or any other matter of law arises which he thinks might possibly justify an acquittal, the practice has been not to pass sentence upon a verdict of guilty, but to reserve the point for the consideration of the other judges, and respite the judgment until they have declared their opinion. In this way safeguards are practically thrown round the life and liberty of the subject, which are not contained in the strict letter of the law, for undoubtedly there is no legal obligation either upon the judge to act thus, or upon the crown to rectify mistakes by a pardon.[1] A recent statute (11 and 12 Vict. c. 78) has been passed which has reference to this subject, but it still leaves the matter to the discretion of the judge who tries the case. The statute provides that when any person shall have been convicted of any treason, felony, or misdemeanor before any court of oyer and terminer or jail delivery, or court of quarter sessions, the judge, or commissioner, or justices of the peace before whom the case shall have been tried, may in his or their discretion, reserve any question of law which shall have arisen on the trial for the consideration of the justices of either bench and barons of

---

[1] In the case of the Queen v. Eduljee Byramjee, which was argued before the Judicial Committee of the Privy Council in 1846, upon a petition praying for leave to appeal from a conviction for felony in the Supreme Court of Bombay, the court in delivering judgment said: "The usual practice, where the judgment is not postponed, is, if any objection be taken at the trial which the judge who tries the prisoner does not admit to be valid, but deems worthy of consideration, to reserve it for the opinion of the fifteen judges. If the majority think the objection ought to have been sustained, the judge who tried the prisoner reports to the Secretary of State, and the prerogative of the crown is exercised in such a manner as the advisers of the crown think meet. The prisoner has no legal right, in the proper sense of the term, to demand a reconsideration by a court of law of the verdict, or of any legal objection raised at the trial."—5 Moore's P. C. Cases, 287. The application was refused; and the same result followed in another similar case, the Queen v. Alloo Paroo, (Id. 296), in which the author was counsel.

the Exchequer, and thereupon shall have authority to respite execution of the judgment on such conviction, or postpone the judgment until such question shall have been considered and decided, as he or they may think fit; and in either case the court in its discretion shall commit the person convicted to prison, or shall take a recognizance of bail, with one or two sufficient sureties, and in such sum as the court shall think fit, conditioned to appear at such time or times as the court shall direct, and receive judgment, or to render himself in execution, as the case may be.

Against an unlimited right of appeal in cases of felony upon mere questions of fact there are grave objections:—not the least of which is the certainty that if it were allowed, it would be resorted to, however hopeless the attempt, in every capital case, from the wish to prolong life until the termination of the appeal. This consideration had full weight given to it by the Judicial Committee of the Privy Council in the case just quoted of the Queen v. Eduljee Byramjee. They said, "where persons charged with the commission of felonies have been convicted, it is natural that they should resort to every possible means to escape from the penalty of the law, or to put off to the latest moment the execution of the sentence." But perhaps a course might be adopted which would be more satisfactory than the present method. A fresh trial might be granted upon a certificate of the judge that he was not satisfied with the conviction. This would prevent any abuse of the privilege, and give the prisoner a legal right to have the verdict against him reconsidered. In cases where the judge declined so to certify, there seems to be no reason why an appeal should be allowed; for it might then be assumed with sufficient certainty that the accused was guilty.

In France if the court is unanimously of opinion that the jury are mistaken in their verdict, no judgment is pronounced, but a new trial takes place at the next session before a different jury. When the accused is found guilty by a bare majority, a new trial is granted, if a majority of the court are of opinion that it is advisable. But there can be no new trial when the prisoner is acquitted, whether contrary to the opinion of the court or not. Besides the advantage thus afforded to a prisoner, he has the right of appeal to a cour de cassation to obtain a reversal of his conviction, if any of the formalities imperatively required by the law have been omitted or violated at his trial. But this reversal is not tantamount to an acquittal, for the case is again remitted to the court below, or such court as the cour de cassation appoints.[1] In certain specified instances also a prisoner is entitled to a revision of his sentence, even where his appeal to the cour de cassation is rejected. Such are the convictions of two persons for the same crime where it is clear that one of the two must be innocent. In this case both convictions are annulled, and the accused parties are tried again before a court different from either of those which previously condemned them. So also a revision takes place where sufficient evidence is laid before the appeal court to show that a person for whose supposed death the prisoner has been convicted is still alive. When this happens the cour de cassation designates the court to which is delegated the task of determining whether the fact be so or not, and which, confining its attention exclusively to this question, informs the appeal court of its decision, and then leaves the latter to deal with the case as it thinks fit. Again, if before the execution of the sentence any of the witnesses are prosecuted for perjury, the judgment is respited, and if they are convicted, the cour de cassation annuls the sentence, and remits the case for a second trial before a court different from that which previously had cognizance of it.[2]

[1] Code d'Instruct. Crim. II. chap. I, 2. [2] Id. chap. 3.

CHAPTER XI.

REQUIREMENT OF UNANIMITY IN THE JURY.

SECTION I. *Origin of the Rule as to Unanimity.*

"IF the work of forming verdicts," says Bentham, "had been the work of calm reflection working by the light of experience, in a comparatively mature and enlightened age, some number, certain of affording a majority on one side, viz., an odd number, would on this, as on other occasions, have been provided; and to the decision of that preponderating number would of course have been given the effect of the conjunct decision of the whole."[1]

The origin of the rule as to unanimity may, I think, be explained as follows:

In the assize as instituted in the reign of Henry II. it was necessary that twelve jurors should agree in order to determine the question of disseizin; but this unanimity was not then secured by any process which tended to make the agreement compulsory. The mode adopted was called, indeed, an afforcement of the jury; but this term did not imply that any violence was done to the conscientious opinions of the minority. It merely meant that a sufficient number were to be added to the panel until twelve were at last found to agree in the same conclusion; and this became the verdict of the assize. It might perhaps be unreasonable to require that so large a number as twelve should be the minimum without

[1] Art of Packing as applied to Special Juries.

whose agreement no valid decision could be made; but this is entirely a question of degree, and must depend very much upon the state of society, the amount of intelligence amongst the jurors, and other circumstances of a varying nature. We can easily understand that it would have been improper at that time to allow a single juror, who after all, as has been already fully explained, was nothing more than a witness, to determine a disputed right of possession; and in proportion to the magnitude of the question at issue would the concurrence of several testimonies be felt to be necessary, in order to arrive at a safe conclusion. The civil law required two witnesses at least, and in some cases a greater number, to establish a fact in dispute: as, for instance, where a debt was secured by a written instrument, five witnesses were necessary to prove payment. These would have been called by our ancestors a jurata of five. At the present day, with us no will is valid which is not attested by at least two witnesses. In all countries the policy of the law determines what it will accept as the minimum of proof. Bearing then in mind that the jury system was in its inception nothing but the testimony of witnesses informing the court of facts supposed to lie within their own knowledge, we see at once that to require that twelve men should be unanimous was simply to fix the amount of evidence which the law deemed to be conclusive of a matter in dispute.

Nor is it difficult to discover why the number twelve was chosen for the purpose. Twelve seems to have been the favorite number for constituting a court amongst the Scandinavian nations. We have seen that in the Anglo-Saxon polity the twelve senior thanes were to go out, and the reeve with them, and swear on the relic given to them in hand, that they would accuse no innocent man. Twelve "lahmen" were to administer the law between the British and the Angles. The number of compurgators in cases of importance was usually twelve, so that it became a common expression of Anglo-Norman law to say, that a man freed himself from a charge with the twelfth hand, si sen escundira sei duzime main; and this number prevailed equally on the Continent. Long habit had taught men to regard it as the proper amount of evidence to establish the credibility of a person accused of an offense; and it was natural that the same number should be required when the witnesses came forward, not to speak to character, but facts.[1]

This seems, at all events, to be a more satisfactory explanation than the fanciful one suggested in an old tract, the authorship of which is attributed to Lord Somers. The writer says: " In analogy, of late the jury is reduced to the number of twelve, like as the prophets were twelve, to foretell the truth; the apostles twelve, to preach the truth; the discoverers twelve sent into Canaan to seek and report the truth; and the stones twelve, that the heavenly Hierusalem is built on; and as the judges were twelve anciently to try and determine matters of law; and always, when there is any waging law, there must be twelve to swear in it; and also as for matters of state, there were formerly twelve councilors of state. And anything now which any jury can be said to do, must have the joint consent of twelve, else it is, in construction of law, not the doing of the jury, but of private persons, and void."[2]

But in old times a verdict was sometimes taken from eleven, if they agreed, and in that case the refractory juror was committed to prison.[3] Both verdicts were, how-

---

[1] The rule as to unanimity in the jury is an additional proof that the verdict of the latter was quite distinct from the judicium parium. Amongst the pares who constituted the judges of the county and baronial courts, the opinion of the majority prevailed: vincat sententia plurimorum.—Leg. IIen. I. 5.

[2] Guide to English Juries, by a person of quality. 1682.

[3] Bro. Abr. Jurors, pt. 53. Fitzh. Abr. verdict, 40.

ever, recorded. Thus, in an assize upon a writ of right, between the abbot of Kirkstede and Edmund de Eyncourt, in the reign of Henry III., eleven of the jury found for the abbot and the twelfth for de Eyncourt, and judgment was given according to the verdict of the eleven, quia prædicti undecim concorditer et præcise dicunt.[1] But it was decided in the reign of Edward III. that the verdict of less than twelve was a nullity, and the court said, that the judges of assize ought to carry the jury about with them in a cart until they agreed.[2]

Although the rule is thus shown to have been reasonable in its commencement, it entailed consequences of a very inconvenient nature. In that quaint old book, "The Doctor and Student," written in the reign of Henry VIII., the following question is asked of the lawyer by the divine:

"*Doctor.*—If one of the twelve men of an inquest know the very truth of his own knowledge, and instructed his fellows thereof, and they will in no wise give credence to him, and thereupon, because meat and drink is prohibited them, he is given to that point, that either he must assent to them, and give their verdict against his own knowledge and against his own conscience, or die for lack of meat: how may the law then stand with conscience, that will drive an innocent to that extremity, to be either forsworn, or to be famished and die for want of meat.

"*Student.*—I take not the law of the realm to be, that the jury after they be sworn may not eat nor drink till they be agreed of the verdict; but truth it is, there is a

---

[1] Plac. ann. 56 Hen. III. Rot. 29. So where the jury consisted of eleven and ten found for the plaintiff and one for the defendant, the entry was quia dicto majoris partis juratorum standum est quod prædictus W. recuperet, &c.—Pasc. 14 Edw. I. Rot. 10. Hale. P. C. II. 297. n. (c).

[2] 41 Assis. 11. At the present day a verdict from less than twelve is sometimes taken by consent of both parties.

maxim and an old custom in the law, that they shall not eat nor drink after they be sworn till they have given their verdict, without the assent and license of the justices; and that is ordained by the law for eschewing divers inconveniences that might follow thereupon, and that specially if they should eat or drink at the costs of the parties;[1] and therefore if they do contrary, it may be laid in arrest of the judgment: but with the assent of the justices they may both eat and drink, as if any of the jurors fall sick before they be agreed of their verdict, so sore that he may not commune of the verdict, then by the assent of the justices he may have meat and drink, and also such other things as be necessary for him; and his fellows also at their own costs, or at the indifferent costs of the parties, if they so agree, or by the assent of the justices, may both eat and drink."

The rule, however, in this respect, is different at the present day, for it is only after the judge has summed up and the jury are considering their verdict, that they are prohibited from having " meat, drink, or fire, candle-light only excepted." Otherwise, in cases when a trial extends over several days, it would be physically impossible to enforce abstinence, and prisoners would escape by resorting to the expedient of tedious and protracted delay in their defense. No such lengthened trials were, however, known in the simple times of old. But the reason assigned for the rule in the passage above quoted is not the true one. It arose, no doubt, from the propensity of our ancestors to indulge in excess at their meals; and was dictated by a fear lest jurors should, if they had access when

---

[1] In the time of Elizabeth it was the custom for the successful party to entertain the jury afterwards at dinner: "The party with whom they have given their sentence giveth the enquest their dinner that day most commonly, and this is all they have for their labor, notwithstanding that they come some twenty, some thirty or forty miles or more, to the place where they give their verdict; all the rest is of their own charge."—Smith's Commonwealth, c. 18.

impaneled to food and drink, become incapacitated from a due discharge of their duty. The first mention of the rule occurs, I believe, in Fleta, which was written in the reign of Edward I., and it is there said, that the sheriff is to cause the jurors in an assize to be kept sine cibo et potu until they are agreed.[1] But at that time it was in the option of the justices, either compellere ad concordiam the jury in this way, or to afforce it by adding, as has been previously explained, jurors to the majority, until twelve were found to be unanimous.[2] The expression compellere ad concordiam shows that in Fleta's time a compulsory process might be resorted to in order to produce an unanimous verdict; and this is further shown by the fact, that the dissentient minority were subjected to a fine quasi pro transgressione. But here again we must not forget that the jurors were still regarded merely as witnesses. And if seven men swore positively that they had seen and known the possession of land to be in a particular person, or his ancestors, the presumption was very strong that five other neighbors who professed to be cognizant of the matter must have known the same fact, and therefore, in refusing to concur in the verdict of the majority, they were deemed to be guilty of contumacy, if not willful perjury. But it deserves notice, that by the law of the Saxon Ethelred, which has been already quoted, if two-thirds of the thanes who formed the court or inquest agreed, the remaining one-third who dissented were fined. "Let doom stand where thanes are of one voice: if they disagree, let that stand which

---

[1] It was a law of the Lombards ut judices jejuni causas audiant et decernant. And by one of the laws of Hoel-dda (Leg. Wall. lib. v. § 48), Respondere non teneor post meridiem. . . . ; .nulla causa post meridiem orari debet. Blackstone notices that by the "Golden Bull" of the German empire, if, after the congress was opened, the electors delayed the election of a king of the Romans for thirty days, they were to be fed only with bread and water until the election was made.

[2] Fleta, IV. c. 9.

VIII. of them say. And let those who are out-voted pay each of them VI. half-marks."[1] And the thanes spoken of here were certainly not witnesses, but sat in the capacity of judges.

The above considerations afford, I think, a satisfactory account of the origin of the rule which requires unanimity in the jury. And if the explanation be admitted, the principle involved does not seem to have been unreasonable. The question, however, is very different, whether the rule ought to be retained when the character of the tribunal has changed, and the functions which it has to discharge are no longer the same as they were when it first came into existence. This will be the subject of inquiry in the next section.

SECTION II. *Question of the Reasonableness of the Rule considered.*

In a valuable note to his "Middle Ages," Mr. Hallam, speaking of "the grand principle of the Saxon polity, the trial of facts by the country," says, "From this principle (except as to that preposterous relic of barbarism, the requirement of unanimity) may we never swerve—may we never be compelled, in wish, to swerve —by a contempt of their oaths in jurors, and a disregard of the just limits of their trust!"[2] This is a stern judgment against the policy of the law which requires that a jury, if it delivers a verdict at all, shall be unanimous; and it may be useful briefly to consider whether and how far it is correct.

---

[1] In all the old Scandinavian tribunals the opinion of the majority prevailed. Sed si illi XII. in unum convenire non poterint, major pars prævalebit, et quicquid juramento suo decreverit.—Priv. Civ. Ripensis, ann. 1296. But, as I have previously shown, the twelve in these cases were not "jurymen," but judges.

[2] Supp. Notes, Midd. Ages, p. 262.

The question has been often discussed, and the objection is one not easily answered. In no other tribunal in this country is unanimity essential in order that its decision may be valid. When in any of the courts of common law, or in the court of appeal in Chancery, the judges differ in opinion, that of the majority prevails; or if the numbers on each side are equal, then the maxim of præsumitur pro neganti prevails, and the party who seeks to set the court in motion fails in his application. When the House of Lords sit as a court of appeal, or as a criminal court to try a peer, or in case of impeachment of a commoner, a bare majority of one is sufficient to determine the judgment;[1] and it may be fairly asked, why the rule should be different for twelve jurors, and why, if there be a single dissentient amongst them, no verdict can be given?

One advantage resulting from the rule no doubt is, that if any one juror dissents from the rest, his opinion and reasons must be heard and considered by them. They can not treat these with contempt or indifference, for he has an absolute veto upon their verdict, and they must convince him or yield themselves, unless they are prepared to be discharged without delivering any verdict at all. This furnishes a safeguard against precipitancy, and insures a full and adequate discussion of every question which can fairly admit of doubt; for if all are at once agreed upon the effect of the evidence, it may be reasonably presumed that the case is free from difficulty, and too clear to admit of any difference of opinion.

But, on the other hand, it is impossible to deny that there are very strong reasons to be urged against the continuance of the requirement of unanimity. In the first place, it is quite certain that in many cases the unanimity

[1] In order, however, to convict, the greater number must consist of at least twelve.

is only apparent and not real, and is purchased at the sacrifice of truth. How seldom do we find in the casual intercourse of life that the first twelve men we meet take the same view of a disputed fact; and yet this is the condition which is exacted from that number of persons who meet together for the first time in a jury-box. They are expected to agree in the same conclusion, no matter how intricate may be the circumstances of the case, and obscure the darkness in which it is shrouded, and this too after witnesses on the one side, apparently trustworthy and respectable, have made statements which directly contradict the statements of witnesses equally trustworthy and respectable on the other. Nor must we forget that they have to listen to all the arguments which the practiced ingenuity of counsel can urge, to make them assent to and adopt that view which each is retained to advocate. The natural consequence of this must be, that the mind oscillates and feels a difficulty in coming to a conclusion. Still, however, each individual does come to a conclusion; for the mental balance seldom remains long in a state of equilibrium without inclining to the one side or the other of a disputed question. One reason of this seems to be, that a state of suspense is disagreeable to the human mind. It is mortifying not to be able to form a definite opinion, and to be obliged to content ourselves with the safe but unsatisfactory truism, that "much may be said on both sides." We feel rest in certainty, and uneasiness in proportion as we recede from it. Hence it is not surprising that, however difficult the case and contradictory the evidence may be, each of the twelve should have his own opinion as to the result. But the marvel is, that all should agree in that result,—that the balance of each man's mind should be struck in the same direction,—that all should feel the same cogency of proof,—that no one should be drawn to a conclusion different from that at which his fellows have arrived. The truth is, that verdicts are often the result of the surrender or compromise of individual opinion. One or more jurymen find themselves in a minority, and many causes concur to render them less tenacious of their opinion than we might expect. If the minority is very small, those who form it may reasonably suspect themselves mistaken, and so be more readily disposed to change their views. Besides few like to appear to be obstinate and unyielding. It is an ungracious thing to stand out against numbers, especially when by so doing many others besides one's self are put to inconvenience. Under these circumstances a man will often be persuaded to give way although he remains unconvinced.

But, moreover, there is both truth and force in the following remarks of Bentham: "Though what never can happen is, that by a quantity of bodily pain or uneasiness any real change should be produced in the opinion formed by any human being, on a subject that has no natural connection with that pain or uneasiness, yet what may very easily and will generally happen is, that either by the eventual assurance of any given quantity of pleasure, or, what comes to the same thing, by the assurance of having at command a given quantity of the instruments of pleasure in any shape, or by the eventual apprehension of any given quantity of pain or uneasiness, a disposition may, in a bosom soothed with that assurance or galled by that apprehension, be produced—a disposition—yes, and moreover an effective determination, to submit to that pain for a greater length of time than any during which the same pain will be submitted to by a bosom not acted upon in either way as above."

We thus see how resistance may be overcome, and how unanimity is rendered no longer, what it might well appear to be, an impracticable condition. And this also explains why the inconvenience so seldom occurs, of juries being discharged from giving a verdict because they are unable to agree; a thing which our experience of the diversity of opinion amongst men upon all points which do admit of doubt, would lead us frequently to expect.

But here we are met by a consideration of a very serious kind. Each juryman is bound, under the solemn sanction of an oath, to decide according to his own honest and sincere conviction. He has sworn, that he will well and truly try, and a true verdict give, according to the evidence, so help him God! He can not devolve this responsibility upon another, by adopting without agreeing in the opinion of that other; and so long as he conscientiously thinks differently, he is bound, whatever be the consequences, to adhere to his own opinion. That this is not the common practice with jurors may be admitted; but their duty is not the less clear and imperative. A more lax view of the individual obligation of each is adopted on account of the mischief which results from a final disagreement. But the man who has taken an oath that he will judge fairly between man and man, and who joins in a verdict which is opposed to his own view of the effect of evidence in the case, commits a greivous sin, for which he will assuredly have one day to answer. Since, then, the chances against real unanimity are great, and the temptation to apparent unanimity is strong, ought a rule to be maintained the tendency of which is to bring about such a result? I think not; and in confirmation of this view gladly quote what the Commissioners, appointed in 1830 to report upon the Courts of Common Law, say upon this subject:

"It is essential to the validity of a verdict that the jury should be unanimous; and regularly they are not allowed to be discharged (unless by consent of the parties) until such unanimous verdict has been returned. It is difficult to defend the justice or wisdom of the latter principle. It seems absurd that the rights of a party, in questions of a doubtful and complicated nature, should depend upon his being able to satisfy twelve persons that one particular state of facts is the true one. As it is notorious that upon such questions a body of men so numerous are often found to differ irreconcileably in their views, it is obvious that the necessity of returning in every case a verdict, and an unanimous one, before they separate, must frequently lead to improper compromise among the jurors of their respective opinions.

"There is reason also to apprehend that where any of them happen to be actuated by partial motives, it must tend to produce a corrupt verdict. Indeed, no one can have been much conversant with courts of justice, without having frequently heard the remark (where the verdict has been very long in suspense), that one or other of the contending parties has a friend upon the jury.

"On the other hand, however, the necessity for the unanimity of the jury carries with it one most valuable advantage. In the event of any difference of opinion it secures a discussion. It is not possible to poll the jury at once, and so without further trouble or consideration to come to the conclusion. Any one dissentient person can compel the other eleven fully and calmly to reconsider their opinions.

"But there seems as good reason why, after a certain period of time, sufficiently long for the purpose of reasonable and ample discussion, the jury (if still in disagreement) should not be excused from the necessity of giving a verdict, or why the present principle of keeping them together till unanimity be produced by a sort of duress of imprisonment, should be retained. And the interests of justice seem manifestly to require a change of law upon this subject.

"We propose, therefore, that the jury shall not be kept in deliberation longer than twelve hours, unless at the end of that period they unanimously concur to apply for further time, which in that case shall be granted;[1] and that at the expiration of the twelve hours, or of such prolonged time for deliberation, if any nine of them concur in giving a verdict, such verdict shall be entered on record, and shall entitle the party in whose favor it is given to judgment; and in failure of such concurrence the cause shall be made a remanet."

It seems impossible to answer or evade the force of this reasoning. And yet, although twenty years have elapsed since the above recommendation was made in a report to the crown, signed by some of the most distinguished lawyers of the day, so slow is the march of improvement in the law, that it has never been carried into effect, and the rule as to unanimity remains in all its rigid necessity at the present day. In this case, however, let it be observed that lawyers propose the change —and that, so far, the profession is not answerable for the continuance of a mischief which, in the words of the Report, is injurious to the interests of justice. Why should the perverseness or knavery of a single juryman be allowed to invalidate the verdict which eleven others are agreed to give? Many years ago Professor Christian expressed his opinion that "the unanimity of twelve men, so repugnant to all experience of human conduct, passions, and understandings, could hardly in any age have been introduced into practice by a deliberate act of the legislature;"[2] and it remains to be seen whether the legislature will much longer tolerate such an anomaly.

In order, however, to secure the advantage already hinted at of a due consideration of the opinions of the

---

[1] This proposal is borrowed from the provision to that effect in Stat. 55 Geo. III. c. 42, for extending trial by jury to civil causes in Scotland.
[2] Notes to Blackst. Comm. 3, 375.

minority, I would propose, according to the recommendation of the commissioners, that where the jury can not all agree, a certain period should be allowed to elapse before the verdict of the majority is taken. In Scotland if the jury in a civil case do not agree within six hours after they have begun to consider their verdict, they are discharged by the court, unless they themselves apply for further time to deliberate. It seems to me that an improvement upon this would be to allow the opinions of the majority at the expiration of that or even a shorter period to prevail. If a majority in both houses of Parliament is sufficient to ensure the passing of a law which affects the destinies of the whole empire, why may not a majority determine a question of civil right between party and party? The efficiency of jury-trial in civil causes would be thereby greatly increased, and a temptation would be taken away which it is to be feared too often leads jurymen to trifle with their consciences and their oaths.

The foregoing objections may be said to apply with full force to the requirement of unanimity in criminal trials, but I think notwithstanding that in them it ought to be retained. Considerations must be here placed in the opposite scale which have no place when the decision of civil suits is alone in question. To allow a verdict of "Guilty" to be pronounced by a majority, implies that there is a minority dissentient; that a certain number of the jurors are not satisfied that the charge against the prisoner is proved, or perhaps are entirely satisfied that he is innocent. Now this is not likely to happen except in doubtful cases, for in them only can there exist a real difference of opinion. And how it must paralyze the arm of Justice, when from the very tribunal appointed by law to try the accused, a voice is heard telling her that she ought not to strike![1] Considering the state of

[1] According to the Theory of Probabilities, if p represents the probability

public feeling with respect to capital punishments, would it ever be possible in such a case to carry into ex-

that each juror separately would give a correct decision, and n the number of jurors, then the probability that an unanimous verdict is right, is

$$\frac{p^n}{p^n+(1-p)^n},$$

and the probability that a verdict given by $n-m$ of the jury is right, is

$$\frac{p^{n-2m}}{p^{n-2m}+(1-p)^{n-2m}}.$$

If $p=\frac{3}{4}$, that is, supposing the probability to be that each juror by himself would be right 3 times out of 4, then we have in favor of the probability of an unanimous verdict being right, about 167776220 : 1; of a majority of 8 to 4 being right, about 256 : 1; and of a majority of 7 to 5 about 17 : 1. This shows what an enormous difference there is between an unanimous verdict and that of merely a majority, considered as to their mathematical values.

The following remarks upon the mathematical application of probabilities to such a question as the correctness of a verdict are, in substance, those of Professor Donkin, of Oxford, which have been kindly communicated to me by my friend, Dr. Twiss.

Let there be n possible and conflicting hypotheses equally probable a priori, and let the probability of a certain event, supposing the truth of the first hypothesis, be p_1; and similarly, let $p_2, p_3, \ldots p_n$ be the respective probabilities of the event, on the suppositions of the truth of the other hypotheses. Then if the event in question happens, the a posteriori probabilities of the several hypotheses become proportional respectively to $p_1, p_2, p_3, \ldots p_n$, and therefore if $p_1+p_2+p_3+\ldots p_n = S$, the actual values of these a posteriori probabilities are

$$\frac{p_1}{S}, \frac{p_2}{S} \ldots \ldots \frac{p_n}{S}.$$

Now suppose a question is submitted to a jury of $m+n$ persons, of whom m decide it one way and n the other, and let m be greater than n. Let $x=$the probability that any one juror will give a right decision, and let this probability be the same for all the jurors. The probability that m are right and n wrong is expressed by the formula $x^m(1-x)^n$, and the probability that n are right and m wrong by $x^n(1-x)^m$. Therefore the a posteriori probabilities of the two hypotheses are

$$\frac{x^m(1-x)^n}{x^m(1-x)^n+(1-x)^m x^n}; \text{ and } \frac{x^n(1-x)^m}{x^m(1-x)^n+x^n(1-x)^m}$$

The first of these is the probability that the decision is right.

ecution the sentence of death? And yet to substitute a secondary punishment, on the ground that the verdict was carried by only a majority, would be to acknowledge a lurking and most uncomfortable suspicion that the conviction was wrong. It would be felt to be unsafe to let the law take its course, and therefore the miserable compromise would be attempted of inflicting a minor punishment, as though there could be any middle course open to the executive in the case supposed. If satisfied that the verdict is right, it ought to allow it to be followed by the allotted doom, except so far as mercy may interfere; but if doubt so far prevails as to induce a mitigation of the punishment, there ought to be no punishment at all. The question of innocence or guilt as determined by the verdict of a jury does not admit of degree. We can not therefore graduate the sentence according to the strength or weakness of the proof. The party is either guilty, and ought to be punished according to the nature of his offense, or not guilty, and ought to be set free.

If we suppose $x=\frac{1}{2}$ this formula reduces itself to $\frac{1}{2}$; or, in other words, if it is only an even chance that each juror is right, it is only an even chance that a decision of any majority is right.

But this, I think, shows the fallacy of attempting to draw any practical inferences from such calculations. No one can seriously believe that if there are twelve persons who are each as likely to be right as wrong, and eleven of them agree in the same opinion against one dissentient, the probability remains still as great that they are wrong as that they are right; and yet that is the consequence which flows from the above mathematical formulæ.

The formula given by Laplace, for the probability that a decision given by m jurors against n is right, is

$$\frac{\int_{\frac{1}{2}}^{1} x^m (1-x^n)\, dx}{\int_{0}^{1} x^m (1-x)^n\, dx}.$$

See the subject discussed in the Encyclopædia Metropolitana, Vol. II. 469-70.

But if after a conviction by a majority only the prisoner were pardoned on that account, this would be to give effect to the verdict of the minority, contrary to every rule of principle and reason.

This principle of regulating the punishment pro modo probationum was openly recognized in the criminal law of France, and made the subject of an ordinance in the year 1670. Under that law the judge was required to pronounce a milder sentence when the evidence of guilt was not satisfactory, but still such as to warrant reasonable suspicion; and the consequence was, as we might expect, that deplorable mistakes were committed. M. Oudot mentions a case where three persons were condemned to death by the parliament of Dijon, in 1782, for a robbery attended with violence. The court of appeal (chambre de la Tournelle) at Paris thought that the proofs were stronger against one than against the others, and he was executed, but the others were sentenced to the galleys. In the following year their innocence was completely established by the confession of the real perpetrators of the crime, and the government of the day endeavored to make some reparation to the sufferers by a pecuniary grant.[1]

Now it is no answer to say that a jury might have been equally mistaken as to the guilt of these men; for the question is not whether the evidence was sufficient; but whether, its insufficiency being admitted, the court ought to have acted upon it, and sent the prisoners to the galleys? Surely every one who considers for a moment must see what a practical fallacy such conduct involves.

In Germany, however, the same rule is still in force. Feuerbach, an experienced judge and accomplished jurist of Bavaria, says,[2] that "there the theory has been adopted of extraordinary punishments on the failure of complete legal proof, so that a man of whom it is ad-

[1] Théorie du Jury, chap. 3.   [2] Betracht. über das Geschwornengericht.

mitted that he has not been convicted according to law (nay, perhaps that he is innocent, but involved in suspicion, owing to unhappy accident or the malice of his enemies) must undergo a part, at all events, of the sentence, too little if he is guilty, but far too great if he is innocent. Nay, a further and more dangerous step has been taken; and where strong presumptions exist against the accused, the liability to supicion is made itself an offense!"

Some weight ought also to be given to considerations of humanity. Mercy may plead that where there is a difference of opinion amongst the twelve as to the prisoner's guilt, he ought to have as much benefit from the doubt which is thus proved to exist amongst the jury, as he is entitled to have at the hands of each individual juryman who has a reasonable doubt, in which latter case the juryman is always enjoined to acquit.

Such are the reasons which induce me to think that the rule as to unanimity in the jury ought to be relaxed in civil and retained in criminal cases. In Scotland, however, exactly the reverse has happened. There juries in civil trials, under the system recently introduced, must be unanimous, while the verdict in criminal is determined by the majority. But in the "service of heirs," and other cases which will be noticed hereafter, unanimity is not required; for, as Erskine tells us,[1] "the inquest hath always consisted of an odd number, that an equality of voices might not make the verdict doubtful, sometimes seventeen, sometimes thirteen; but it appears that by the latter practice the number has been fixed to fifteen." And we learn from a passage in Balfour, that in 1554 it was expressly decided that "if the persons of inquest be discrepant, contrare unto other, and equally divided in their deliverance and determination, except only the chancellor (*i. e.* foreman) and odd man of the inquest, who refuses to

[1] Inst. III. t. 8.

give his vote, alleging that none of the said parties has justly decerned in the matter, and that he in his conscience is not persuaded nor inclined to either of their deliverances; in this case he may be charged and compelled by the Lords' letters to deliver with the one half of the assize or with the other, notwithstanding his allegance foresaid."[1]

But whatever may be the practice of other countries in this respect, it would perhaps be not difficult to prove that it is better to allow the opinion of the majority to prevail in both civil and criminal cases, than to demand unanimity in the former. The time is fast approaching, if it has not already come, when trial by jury, like every other part of our legal fabric, will become the subject of public criticism, and I feel persuaded that then it will be found impossible to justify or retain a rule which is opposed to both justice and expediency.

[1] Compare with this the power of the Scandinavian Lawman to determine the judgment or verdict, *ante*, p. 17.

CHAPTER XII.

ON THE PROPER PROVINCE OF THE JURY.

SECTION I. *Powers and Duties of Juries in England.*

IT was very early provided that the jury should not entangle themselves with questions of law, but confine themselves simply and exclusively to facts. This rule was afterwards expressed by the well-known maxim called " that decantatum in our books,"[1] ad quæstionem facti non respondent judices, ad quæstionem juris non respondent juratores; an invaluable principle of jurisprudence, which more than anything else has upheld the character and maintained the efficiency of English juries as tribunals for the judicial investigation of truth. It is obvious, however, that many questions of fact involve also questions of law. Thus if the proposition to be determined be, whether A did or did not make a will; the answer depends, first, upon the fact whether he actually executed a written paper, purporting to be a will; secondly, whether he was competent to make it; and, thirdly, upon the legal effect of the instrument which he signed; and if a jury were called upon to determine by themselves the general question in the above form, they would have to take into account both law and fact, which is beyond the scope of their functions.

So also in the earliest cases to which the assize of Henry II. applied itself, which were chiefly those of disseizin—inasmuch as that term had a technical meaning,

[1] Bushell's case, Vaughan, 149.

and implied a wrongful dispossession,—if the jury assumed that the act, of which they took cognizance, was wrongful, they decided a question of law. And this seems to have frequently occurred, as in the case previously cited from Jocelin de Brakelonde, where the jurors paid no regard to a deed produced on behalf of the convent which established its right, but gave their verdict upon their own view of the facts. And, indeed, upon all general issues; as upon "not guilty" pleaded in trespass, "nul disseizin" in assize, and the like; though it be matter of law whether the defendant be a trespasser or disseizor, in the particular case in issue; "yet the jury find not (as in a special verdict) the fact of every case by itself, leaving the law to the court, but find for the plaintiff or defendant upon the issue to be tried, wherein they resolve both law and fact complicately, and not the fact by itself; so as though they answer not singly to the question what is the law, yet they determine the law in all matters, where issue is joined, and tried in the principal case, but where the verdict is special."[1] To remedy this difficulty it was enacted by Statute 13 Edw. I. c. 30 (A. D. 1285), that the justices assigned to take assize should not compel the jurors to say precisely whether an ouster of possession were "disseizin" or not, so that they were willing to declare the truth of the fact, and ask the assistance of the justices (as to its legal effect).[2] It was, however, provided, that "if they of their own accord will say that it is disseizin or not, their verdict should be admitted at their own peril."

It has been strenuously maintained by some writers that the jury are entitled in all cases, where no special

---

[1] Ibid. 150.
[2] Quo casu si Juratores ignoraverint si manifesta fuerit disseisina vel non, compelli non debent ulterius, sed petere debent instructionem Justiciarorum. Fleta, IV. c. 9.

pleas have been put on the record, to give a general verdict according to their own view of the law, in criminal as well as civil cases. That is, supposing the action to be brought for a libel or an assault, or the indictment to charge a felony or a misdemeanor, and the only plea is not guilty, they assert that the jury are justified in bringing in a verdict of acquittal, notwithstanding they are told by the judge that in point of law there is no defense, provided they think otherwise themselves. But it is impossible to uphold the doctrine. It is founded on a confusion between the ideas of power and right. We shall have occasion to consider the subject with reference to questions of libel hereafter, and here it will be enough to say that, although juries have undoubtedly the power in such cases to take the law into their own hands, and so, it may be, defeat the ends of justice, or do what they believe to be substantial justice, they do so at a sacrifice of conscience and duty. The law can not depend upon the verdict of a jury, whose office is simply to find the truth of disputed facts;—and yet such must be the result, if they may decide contrary to what the judge, the authorized expounder of the law, lays down for their guidance. This would introduce the most miserable uncertainty as to our rights and liberties, the misera servitus of vagum jus, and be the most fatal blow that could be struck at the existence of trial by jury. Can it for a moment be contended that twelve men in a jury-box are to determine that not to be an offense which the law, under a penalty, forbids? May they pronouce that to be manslaughter or justifiable homicide which the law declares to be murder? If so, then they may by their verdict abrogate, by rendering ineffective, every enactment of the legislature, and they become a court of appeal from the solemn decision of Parliament and the Crown. That they can do so is not disputed, but so can the judges give judgments contrary to law, if they choose to disregard their oaths, and yield to the influence of corrupt motives. In both cases the law presumes that men will act according to their duty.

Indeed, it is difficult to understand how any one acquainted with the principles and settled practice of the English law, can assert that it sanctions the doctrine which is here combated. Why should all demurrers be withdrawn from the cognizance of a jury, if when they try issues of fact they may also determine the law? Why should a bill of exceptions tendered at a trial, in consequence of some supposed misdirection of the judge in point of law, be argued before the court alone? Why should there ever be special verdicts in which the jury find merely the facts, and leave the conclusion of law to be drawn by the judges themselves? And even if the jury do intermix with the facts so found legal inferences, the court pays no attention to the latter, but decides according to its own view of the law. Moreover, it is the constant practice for the courts to grant new trials in civil cases (and in misdemeanors where there has been a conviction), if the jury have given a verdict contrary to what the presiding judge has correctly laid down to be the law. And the care taken in very early times to relieve the jury from the danger of giving a verdict upon a mistaken view of the law, as has been shown above, proves that it never was intended that they should determine legal questions for themselves. For formerly, in finding a general verdict, either for the plaintiff or the defendant in civil cases, or a verdict of " not guilty " in criminal, a jury was exposed to the risk of an attaint if it decided contrary to law,[1] especially after that had been explained to them, and laid down by the court. Now,

[1] See Litt. Sect. 368, where Coke says, "although the jury, if they will take upon them (as Littleton here saith) the knowledge of the law, may give a general verdict, yet it is dangerous for them so to do, for if they do mistake the law, they run into the danger of an attaint; therefore to find the special matter is the safest way where the case is doubtful."

however, that attaint has been abolished, there is no mode of punishing a jury; and the remedy for an improper verdict in civil actions is a new trial. But in trials for felony, if jurors choose to assert contrary to law by a verdict of not guilty, that, admitting all the facts to be proved, no legal offense has been committed by the prisoner, he must inevitably escape; for there can be no second trial, he having been already once in jeopardy upon the charge. And it is to be feared that this has too often happened in trials for murder arising out of a duel. The law of England is clear and explicit, that death occasioned by a duel is murder; and yet, notwithstanding the numerous trials which have taken place for this offense, how few have been the convictions! The facts have generally been beyond dispute, and the jury can not have meant by their verdict of acquittal to throw discredit on the evidence; but, influenced by the maxims which pass current in the world as the code of honor, they have determined that killing another in a fairly-fought duel is not murder. It is not likely that such a false notion would now be countenanced by any jury, for happily the current of opinion has set with irresistible force against duelling; and there is, we may hope, little danger of their not being willing to vindicate the law; but past experience incontestably proves how the law may be warped by juries, when its stern mandates are opposed to their own prejudices, and their duty comes strongly into conflict with their feelings. And when they choose to trifle with the obligation of their oath, and take the law into their own hands, there is some truth in the retort made by Colonel Lilburne upon the judges at his trial in 1649, "You that call yourselves judges of the law are no more but Norman intruders; and in deed and in truth, if the jury please, are no more but cyphers, to pronounce their verdict,"—a doctrine which provoked Mr. Justice Jermin to exclaim, "Was there ever such a damnable blasphemous heresy as this is, to call the judges of the law cyphers?"[1]

It can not therefore be denied that in all criminal cases the jury do virtually possess the power of deciding questions of law as well as of fact. This is an anomaly, but it can only occur when they forget and violate their duty. The theory of our constitution admits several anomalies, against the inconvenience arising from which the only safeguard is the settled course of usage, and the good sense with which the objectionable power is exercised. Thus the Crown possesses the undoubted prerogative of interposing its veto upon every bill which has passed the two houses of Parliament; and if this were often or indiscreetly exercised, legislation would be brought to a standstill, and the monarchy placed in imminent peril. But no one fears that any such obstruction will take place. The theory is corrected by the practice. A mathematician can demonstrate that a bridge built in a particular form can not stand; but it does stand nevertheless: and why? because the force of friction, which has not been taken into account, supplies the power requisite to sustain the fabric. Now, what friction is in physical science, usage is in the affairs of men.

In civil actions, where the question to be determined is one in which legal inference is inextricably mixed up with fact, the modern practice is for the jury to find a general verdict for the plaintiff, subject to the opinion of the court, upon a special case stated by the counsel on both sides. The first instance of this, of which we have notice, occurred, I believe, in the reign of Charles II. And it is by no means unusual, in such cases, to put the court so far in the place of the jury as to enable it to draw such

---

[1] Practical effect was once given to the idea of the supremacy of juries by a Colonel Martin, who was tried at Reading, and who caused the jury to put on their hats, telling them that it was their right, inasmuch as they were the chief judges in the court.—See 4 State Tr. 1381.

inferences of fact as they may think a jury would have, or ought to have drawn. But upon the inconvenience of this part of the arrangement, English judges have expressed a strong opinion. Thus the late Mr. Justice Bayley, writing to Chief Commissioner Adam, said:[1]

"Facts only, and not evidence, ought to be stated, and whatever inferences ought to be drawn, should be drawn by the jury, not by the court; but of late years. practically, an incorrect and slovenly mode has been adopted, of leaving it to the court to draw such inferences as the court shall think the jury ought to have drawn. The consequence is, that if the case is turned into a special verdict, it becomes necessary to reform it, and to apply to the court to draw the proper inferences. This practice, however, leads to inconvenience, and upon principle can not be supported." And in the case of Arkwright *v.* Gell,[2] it was said by the court: "A special case was reserved at the trial for the opinion of the court, stating a great number of documents and facts upon which the court are not merely to give their judgment on matters of law, but to take the office of the jury by determining whether any and what inferences of fact ought to be drawn from the facts stated. This course leads to one great inconvenience, as it tends to confound the rule of law with an inference of fact only, which inference might have been varied by a very slight circumstance."

It may, perhaps, in strictness be said that a large portion of the duties of juries is not confined to the determination of matters of fact. I allude to their power of awarding compensation by way of damages. This is a judicial act. They first find the facts upon which they are to exercise a discretionary judgment with respect to the

---

[1] See Adam on Trial by Jury (in Scotland), p. 392.

[2] 5 Mees and Wels. 227, and see Brockbank *v.* Anderson, 7 Man. and Gr. 313

amount which they think fit to award. It is obvious that this is a very different function from merely deciding upon the effect of evidence as to whether such and such allegations have been satisfactorily proved. We can easily conceive that their duties might be limited exclusively to this, and that when they had informed the court of their opinion, the latter might be called upon to say what amount of compensation the justice of the case required. But this would clearly be no question of law. That presupposes a definite and general rule to be applied in all similar cases alike. Damages, however, must vary according to the circumstances of each particular case. While therefore juries in dealing with questions of compensation act not merely as triers of fact, judges would be unable to determine the amount without departing from their character of being solely expounders of the law.

The question of what is the province of the jury in determining actions for libel, gave rise to one of the most memorable conflicts of opinion in our legal history. And although, as it was afterwards made the subject of a declaratory act of Parliament, this question may be thought to possess no longer any practical importance, it may be interesting to give a short review of the struggle, especially as some misconception prevails as to what was the real object and effect of the act. I venture to think that it fell far short of the view contended for by those who opposed Lord Mansfield, and that it by no means asserted the doctrine laid down by Lord Camden, Erskine, and Fox, namely, that the question of whether the matter in a publication is libelous or not, is one for the consideration solely of the jury, with which the court has no right to interfere. This I believe to be contrary to all legal principle and authority; and it is not difficult to show that such never has been, nor is now, the law of England.

In the early part of 1770, Woodfall, the printer of "The Morning Advertiser," was tried before Lord Mansfield, for having published in his paper what was alleged to be a libel: and the Chief Justice told the jury that " all they had to consider was, whether the defendant had published the letter set out in the information, and whether the innuendoes imputing a particular meaning to particular words, as that " the K—" meant his majesty King George III.; but they were not to consider whether the publication was, as alleged in the information, " false and malicious," these being mere formal words; and that whether the letter was libelous or innocent was a pure question of law, upon which the opinion of the court might be taken by a demurrer, or a motion in arrest of judgment." The jury found the defendant " Guilty of the printing and publishing ONLY;" but the court afterwards rejected this verdict as ambiguous, and ordered that there should be a new trial.

In another case, Rex v. Miller, which occurred the same year, Lord Mansfield said,[1] " The direction I am going to give you is a full conviction and confidence that it is the language of the law. If you by your verdict find the defendant not guilty, the fact established by that verdict is, he did not publish a paper of that meaning; that fact is established, and there is an end of the prosecution. You are to try that fact, because your verdict establishes that fact, that he did not publish it. If you find that, according to your judgment, your verdict is final; and if you find it otherwise, it is between God and your consciences; for that is the basis upon which all verdicts ought to be founded; then the fact finally established by your verdict, if you find him guilty, is, that he printed and published a paper, of the tenor, and of the meaning, set forth in the information; that is the only fact finally established by your verdict; and

[1] 20 State Tr. 892-3.

whatever fact is finally established, never can be controverted in any shape whatever. But you do not, by that verdict, give an opinion, or establish whether it is or not lawful to print or publish a paper of the tenor and meaning in the information; for supposing the defendant is found guilty, and the paper is such a paper, as by the law of the land may be printed and published, the defendant has a right to have judgment respited, and to have it carried to the highest court of judicature."

The doctrine here laid down by this great and venerable judge, the greatest who has ever sat on the English bench, exposed him to much but most unmerited obloquy. To say nothing of the virulent invectives of that common slanderer, Junius, who pretended to believe that Lord Mansfield was engaged in a grand conspiracy against the liberty of the press, he was assailed by Lord Chatham, in the House of Lords, in a manner which drew from him an eloquent and striking reply. He said:[1]

"His lordship tells the house that doctrines no less new than dangerous in their nature have been inculcated in the Court of King's Bench, and that particularly in a charge which I delivered to the jury on Mr. Woodfall's trial, my directions were contrary to law, repugnant to practice, and injurious to the dearest liberties of the people. This is an alarming picture, my lords, it is drawn with great parade, and colored to affect the passions amazingly. Unhappily, however, for the painter, it wants the essential circumstance of truth in the design, and must, like many other political pictures, be thrown, notwithstanding the reputation of the artist, among the miserable daubings of faction.

"So far, in fact, my lords, is the charge without foundation, that the directions now given to juries are the same that they ever have been. There is no novelty in-

[1] 16 Parl. Hist. 1302.

troduced, no chicanery attempted, nor has there, till to serve some interested purposes of late, been any outcry raised against the integrity of the King's Bench."

A few days afterwards Lord Mansfield informed the House of Lords that he had left a paper with the clerk of the house, containing the judgment of the court in the case of the king against Woodfall, and that their lordships might read it and take copies of it if they pleased. Lord Chatham bitterly attacked the Chief Justice, affirming that his conduct in giving judgment in the case was irregular, extrajudicial, and unprecedented; and Lord Camden, on the following day said, " I consider the paper delivered in by the noble lord as a challenge directed personally to me, and I accept of it; he has thrown down the glove, and I take it up. In direct contradiction to him, I maintain that his doctrine is not the law of England." He then proposed a series of questions as to the exact meaning of the opinion contained in the judgment, and asked Lord Mansfield to answer them, but the latter refused to recognize his opponent's right thus to catechize him, and the subject was no further pursued.[1]

It was, however, revived in 1874, on the trial of the Dean of St. Asaph, who was prosecuted for publishing a dialogue between a gentleman and a farmer, written by Sir William Jones.[2] Mr. Justice Buller told the jury that it was no part of their duty to form any opinion as to the character of the paper alleged to be libelous; upon which Erskine, who was the Dean's counsel, moved for a new trial, on the ground of misdirection, and urged the opposite view upon the court in a remarkably able

---

[1] The conduct of Lord Mansfield on this occasion has been censured as wanting in spirit. I think, however, that it was dignified and proper. A political opponent has no right to demand from a judge categorical answers to questions framed for the express purpose of throwing odium upon the judgment-seat.

[2] 21 State Tr. 847–1046.

XII.] POWERS AND DUTIES OF JURIES. 227

argument. Lord Mansfield delivered judgment, and showed that in every trial for libel since the revolution (and to go further back for precedents would be useless) the practice of the courts of law had been uniform on this point; and that the direction of every judge had been substantially the same as that of Mr. Justice Buller, which was then objected to. After citing the case of Rex v. Francklyn,[1] where the Craftsman, a celebrated party paper, written in opposition to the ministry of Sir Robert Walpole, was prosecuted, and the verdict was guilty, he thus proceeded:

"I recollect one case afterwards, in which, to the great mortification of Sir Philip Yorke, then attorney-general, the Craftsman was acquitted; and I recollect it from a famous witty and ingenious ballad that was composed on the occasion by Mr. Pulteney. Though it be a ballad, I will cite a stanza from it to show you the opinion upon this subject of the able men in opposition, and the leaders of the popular party in those days. They had not an idea that the jury had a right to determine upon a question of law, and they rested the verdict on another and better ground:

> For Sir Phillip well knows
> That his innuendoes
> Will serve him no longer
> In verse or in prose;
> For twelve honest men have decided the cause,
> Who are judges of fact, though not judges of laws.[2]

Now which of these two great lawyers, Lord Mansfield and Lord Camden, was right? It has been said by high

---

[1] 17 State Tr. 625.

[2] It is said Lord Mansfield quoted these lines wrongly, and that they run thus in the original ballad, printed in 1754:

> "For twelve honest men have determined the cause,
> Who are judges alike of the facts and the laws."

However this may be, there can be no doubt that Lord Mansfield's version is the legally correct one.

authority, that the doctrine of the former was contrary to law as well as liberty, and that his argument for making the question of "libel or not" exclusively one of law, that the defendant may demur, or move in arrest of judgment, and so refer it to the court, admits of the easy answer, that although there may be a writing set out in the information as libelous, which it would under no circumstances be criminal to publish, yet that an information may set out a paper the publication of which may or may not be criminal, according to the intention of the defendant and the circumstances under which it is published.¹ But Lord Mansfield never meant to withdraw from the consideration of the jury the attending circumstances of the publication. He always told them that they exclusively were to determine whether the meaning of the innuendoes, as alleged in the indictment, was proved: and this they could hardly do without considering the context of the objectionable passage and surrounding circumstances of the case. And, as to the question of intention, the same same great judge seems to have laid down the law with perfect correctness, as a brief consideration will show.

In most criminal cases the question of legal guilt depends upon the intent as a matter of fact, which the jury can alone determine. Thus, for instance, the killing a man is murder, if death or grievous bodily harm is intended by the blow; but it may be the result of mere accident and mischance. This involves no question of law, but is a fact for the jury to decide. There are, however, some actions from which the law presumes criminality independent of the intention of the party doing them. Such is the case where a man intending to commit another felony, in the execution of his purpose undesignedly kills a man. Here the law implies malice, and the offense is murder. So if two persons mutually agree to com-

¹ Lord Campbell's Lives of the Chief Justices, II. 480.

mit suicide together, and take poison, or attempt to drown themselves together, but only one of them dies, the survivor is guilty of murder. So also if death ensues from the grossly unskillful treatment of a medical practitioner, he is guilty of manslaughter. The fact of his not having intended to kill his patient is no defense; if he had, the offense would have been murder; but the act is notwithstanding criminal in a less degree, because the law presumes that a man must intend the natural consequences of his own acts. In a case of this kind the rule was thus clearly laid down by Lord Lyndhurst: "I shall leave it to the jury to say, first, whether death was occasioned or accelerated by the medicines administered; and if they think it was, then I shall tell them, secondly, that the prisoner is guilty of manslaughter, if they think that in so administering the medicines, he acted with a criminal intention, or from very gross ignorance."[1]

Now to apply these remarks to the question of libel. In Woodfall's case Lord Mansfield told the jury what seems to be undoubtedly the law, that where an act, in itself indifferent, if done with a particular intent, becomes criminal, there the intent must be proved and found; but where the act is in itself unlawful (*i. e.* prima facie and unexplained), the proof of justification or excuse lies on the defendant; and in failure thereof the law implies a criminal intent. In the latter case the intention is immaterial, and therefore not a question of fact in issue, for the crime consists in publishing a libel; a criminal intention in the writer is no part of the definition of the crime of libel at the common law.[2] Surely, therefore, according to all principle and analogy, when the jury have found the fact of the publication, and the meaning

---

[1] R. *v.* Webb, 1 Moo. and Rob. 410.
[2] See the opinion of all the judges delivered to the House of Lords in 1789. 22 State Tr. 300.

of the innuendoes as applicable in the sense given to them in the indictment or information, and nothing remains but the question of whether such a publication, with such a meaning attached to its language, is an offense against the law—this is as much within the province of the court to determine, as to determine that death, when it ensues from a given state of facts, amounts to manslaughter. Suppose the publication of a libel of the most seditious kind, about the meaning of which there can not be the possibility of a doubt,—has not the law clearly defined the quality of this act to be criminal? and by making juries judges of the quality of such an act, are we not in effect substituting their voice for the voice of the law? It may be, and generally is, essential to ascertain many circumstances of fact connected with the libel, as, for instance, whether it is explained away by the context; whether it is a mere quotation used for the purpose of refutation, and matters of this kind, which are all properly for the jury; but when these have been ascertained by the verdict, it would seem that the law, as expounded by the judge, ought then to step in and declare whether it does or does not permit such and such a publication under a given state of things to take place with impunity. In other words, the law must ultimately determine whether it is a libel or not. If this be not so, the conclusion seems inevitable—that of no publication, no matter how treasonable, seditious, or blasphemous it may be, can illegality be predicated as a matter of law, but it must depend upon the varying caprice of twelve men in a jury-box. And that the view here taken is correct, seems to follow from the unanimous opinion of all the judges, delivered to the House of Lords in 1789, in answer to the following question:

"On the trial of an information or indictment for a libel, is the criminality or innocence of the paper set forth in such information or indictment as the libel, matter of fact, or matter of law, where no evidence is given for the defendant?"

To this the judges replied:

"We answer, That the criminality or innocence of any act done (which includes any paper written) is the result of the judgment which the law pronounces upon that act; and must therefore be, in all cases, and under all circumstances, matter of law, and not matter of fact; and this, as well where evidence is given, as where it is not given for the defendant: the effect of evidence given for the defendant as to this question being nothing more than to introduce facts or circumstances into the case which the prosecutor had left out of it, upon which it will still be for the law to pronounce whether the act done be criminal or innocent."

To this it is no answer to say, that in all general verdicts the jury do in reality take the question of law into their own hands: as, for instance, when, as they undoubtedly have the power of doing, they pronounce a man "Not guilty" of murder who has deliberately killed another in a duel. No lawyer will contend that such a verdict is not contrary to law, although the jurors are dispunishable for it, and there is no remedy. It will be at once admitted that they ought, in such a case, to follow the direction of the judge telling them that death by duelling is murder.

And so also it would seem that the direction of the judge ought to guide them with respect to what kind of publications the law regards as criminal. But the hypothesis against which we are arguing assumes that the jury, and not the law, is to decide this, and therefore it follows that there ought to be no direction to them whatever on the subject.

Nor could it be urged against the validity of the doctrine maintained by Lord Mansfield, that the question of criminality depended upon whether the libel was true or not, and that this is a fact which can be found by the jury alone: for until the passing of " Lord Campbell's Libel Act"[1] in 1843, which provides that the truth may be inquired into, but shall not amount to a defense, unless it was for the public benefit that the matters stated in the indictment should be published,—the truth of the libel complained of was, in a criminal proceeding, no defense at all; and hence arose the oft-repeated, but much misunderstood maxim, " The greater the truth, the greater the libel;" the meaning of which is, that a man is perhaps more likely to be provoked to commit a breach of the peace when the matters alleged against him are true, then when they are false; as in the latter case he can afford to treat the slander with contempt.

The question, however, was at last taken up by the Legislature, and was supposed to be finally settled by the Act known as "Fox's Libel Act," passed in 1792.[2] It is entitled "An Act to remove doubts respecting the functions of Juries in cases of Libel:" and it declares and enacts that the jury may give a general verdict of guilty or not guilty upon the whole matter put in issue upon the indictment or information, and shall not be required or directed by the court or judge before whom it shall be tried to find the defendant guilty, merely on the proof of the publication of the paper charged to be a libel, and of the sense ascribed to the same in the indictment or information

Provided that on every such trial the court or judge before whom it shall be tried, shall, according to their discretion, give their opinion and direction to the jury on the matter in issue, in like matter as in other criminal cases.

Provided also that nothing therein contained shall prevent the jury from finding a special verdict in their discretion, as in other criminal cases.

---

[1] 6 and 7 Vict. c. 75.   [2] 32 Geo. III. c. 60.

Provided also that in case the jury shall find the defendant guilty, he may move an arrest of judgment, on such ground and in such a manner as by law he might have done before the passing of the act.[1]

"By this bill," says Lord John Russell,[2] "juries were constituted judges of the law as well as of the fact, that is to say, they were entitled to decide not only whether the writing in question had been published or no, but also whether it were libelous." But this is a mistake. No such power is conferred upon juries by the statute in question, and they are no more entitled since its passing to take the law into their own hands in cases of libel, than in those of murder, or any other alleged crime. An attentive perusal of the provisions of the act will show that it does no more than place trials for libel on the same footing as trials for other offenses; and it in no respect absolves a jury from the duty of obeying the direction of the judge as to the legal character of the writing which is the subject of inquiry. If authority is wanted for this assertion it is easily supplied. In the case of R. v. Burdett,[3] tried in the year 1820, Mr. Justice Best said, "It must not be supposed that the statute of George the Third made the question of libel a question of fact; if it had, instead of removing an anomaly, it would have created one. Libel is a question of law, and the judge is the judge of the law in libel, as in all other cases; the jury having the power of acting agreeably to his statement or not. All that the statute does is to prevent the question from being left to the jury in the manner in which it was left before that time. Judges

---

[1] In 1793 Lord Abercromby, one of the Lords of Session in Scotland, said, "Our law in this respect has always been different from the common law of England, where in the case of libel the jury till a late period were judges of fact, but not of the law. With us even in matters of libel the jury have always determined both as to the law and the fact."—23 State Tr. 114.

[2] Essay on English Government, p. 391.   [3] 4 Barn. and Ald. 131.

are in express terms directed to lay down the law as in other cases. In all cases the jury may find a general verdict; they do so in cases of murder and treason; but then the judge tells them what is the law, though they may find against him, unless they are satisfied with his opinion."

What seems to have been really objectionable in the practice of the court previous to the statute was the course of directing a verdict of guilty to be found on the mere proof of the publication of the document alleged to be a libel, and truth of the innuendoes, and then putting the defendant to the necessity of moving in arrest of judgment, on the ground that it sufficiently appeared on the face of the record that the matter complained of was no libel. If in the opinion of the judge the use of the words in question, admitting them to be proved, did not amount to an offense, the defendant was entitled to an acquittal at once and to have the direction of the judge to that effect, as in all other trials where the law does not hold the act charged to be criminal. "According to the practice," say the Commissioners on the Criminal Law,[1] "in the case of libel, a general verdict of guilty was required to be found in all such cases; the jury were not allowed to exercise any option, and the inference of guilt was, so far as regarded malice, required to be made, without the sanction of the judge's opinion that it was one warranted by the facts. It was, we apprehend, with a view to the removal of these anomalies, that the Libel Act was passed, without any intention to enlarge the province of juries by investing them with any judicial authority to determine what shall constitute a libel. By the second section (of the Act) the court shall, according to their discretion, give their opinion and direction to the jury on the matter in issue between the king and the defendant, as in other criminal cases. As a general rule,

[1] Sixth Report, 1841.

so far as our experience extends, it is usual for the judge to inform the jury in respect of the legal quality of all the facts proved, or which the evidence tends to prove, so far as the legal quality of such facts is essential to the issue; that is to the guilt or innocence of the accused." The learned Commissioners state distinctly, that the statute leaves the question of libel or no libel a mere question of law; and they add, with perfect truth, that to make so important a question as that of libel an exception to the rule that ad quæstionem facti respondent juratores, ad quæstionem juris judices, would constitute an anomaly, and an unfortunate one; for no other case can be selected in which the just application of the law to the facts is so difficult; and consequently none in which the delegation of the duty to a jury would be more likely to occasion confusion and inconvenience.

SECTION II. *Distinction between the Office of the Judge and that of the Jury.*

The distinction between the province of the judge and that of the jury is, in the English law, clearly defined, and observed with jealous accuracy. The jury must in all cases determine the value and effect of evidence which is submitted to them. They must decide what degree of credit is to be given to a witness, and hold the balance between conflicting probabilities. The law throws upon them the whole responsibility of ascertaining facts in dispute, and the judge does not attempt to interfere with the exercise of their unfettered discretion in this respect. But, on the other hand, the judge has his peculiar duty in the conduct of a trial. He must determine whether the kind of evidence offered is such as ought or ought not to be submitted to the jury, and what liabilities it imposes. When any questions of law arise, he alone determines them, and their consideration is absolutely withdrawn from the jury, who must in such cases follow the direction of the judge; or if they perversely refuse to do so, their verdict (in civil cases) will be set aside, and a new trial granted. If, in order to determine this, it is necessary to have recourse to evidence, as for instance, to show that a proposed witness is incompetent, this evidence must be received by the judge, and adjudicated upon by him alone. The rule can not be better or more concisely enunciated, than as laid down in a recent case: "If the evidence offered at the trial by either party is evidence by law admissible for the determination of the question before a jury, a judge is bound to lay it before them, and to call upon them to decide upon the effect of such evidence: but whether such evidence when offered is of that character and description which makes it admissible by law, is a question which is for the determination of the judge alone, and is left solely to his decision."[1]

The construction of written documents (except in the case of innuendoes in libel) is entirely for the court, who must determine what the legal effect of the instrument is. But where it contains words of technical art, or which have by local usage a particular meaning, this is submitted to the jury, who pronounce what that meaning is; and then the judge, having had the language thus as it were translated to him, defines the legal consequences which flow from the document itself.[2] This rule applies also in general to the case of letters which have passed between the parties, out of which an agreement is to be collected; but where they are written in such a manner as to be capable of different constructions, and can be explained by other transactions and circumstances,

---

[1] Lewis *v.* Marshall, 7 Man. and Gra. 743, and see Bartlett *v.* Smith, 11 Mees. and Wels. 485.

[2] See Neilson *v.* Harford, 8 M. and W. 806; Hitchin *v.* Groom, 5 C. B. 519.

the whole evidence must be left to the jury to decide upon, for they are to judge of the truth or falsehood of collateral facts which may vary the sense of the letters themselves; but if they are not capable of explanation by any other circumstances, then the construction of them, like deeds or other written agreements, is a mere matter of law for the court.[1]

A good illustration of the difference between the functions of the judge and those of the jury is afforded in the case of an action for a malicious prosecution. Here the question always is, whether the defendant had "reasonable and probable cause" for procuring the arrest of the plaintiff. Now this is a mixed question of law and fact. The jury are merely to determine the truth or falsity of the facts alleged by the defendant in justification of his conduct, but the result of those facts, supposing them to be proved, that is to say, the question of whether they do or do not amount to what the law deems to be reasonable and probable cause, is for the judge alone.[2] Nor does it make any difference in principle if the case be one in which the question of reasonable or probable cause depends not upon a few simple facts, but upon facts which are numerous and complicated, and upon inferences to be drawn therefrom; it is still the duty of the judge to inform the jury that, if they find the facts proved, and the inferences to be warranted by such facts, the same do or do not amount to reasonable or probable cause, so as thereby to leave the question of fact to the jury, and the abstract question of law to the judge. It is, no doubt, attended with difficulty to bring before the jury all the combinations of which numerous

---

[1] See per Buller, J., Macbeath *v.* Haldimand, 1 T. R. 182.

[2] Sutton *v.* Johnstone, 1 T. R. 493, 510, 784. In Beckwith *v.* Philby, 6 Barn. and Cress. 638, Lord Tenterden said, that whether there was any reasonable cause for suspecting that a plaintiff had committed a felony, was a question of fact for the jury.

facts are susceptible, and to place in a distinct point of view the application of the rule of law, according as all or some only of the facts and inferences from facts are made out to their satisfaction; but the task is not impracticable, and it must be performed by the judge who endeavors correctly to administer the law.[1]

Let us illustrate this part of our subject by a few more examples.

Littleton says that executors shall have free entry, egress, and regress, to carry out of the house the goods of their testator "by reasonable time," and upon this Sir E. Coke makes the following comment:[2] "This reasonable time shall be adjudged by the discretion of the justices before whom the law dependeth, and so it is of reasonable fines, customs, and services, upon the true state of the case depending before them; for reasonableness in these cases belongeth to the knowledge of the law, and therefore to be decided by the justices. How long it should endure is not mentioned in the law, but is left to the discretion of the justices."[3] It must not, however, be taken for granted that the question of reasonableness is, in all cases, one for the court and not for the jury. The

---

[1] Panton v. Williams, 2 Q. B. 169. With reference to the judgment of the Exchequer Chamber in this case, from which the observations in the text are taken, Lord Denman, C. J., said in Rowlands v. Samuel, 11 Q. B. 41, n. (a): "I regret that it was not brought before the House of Lords. That case, however, does not lay down as a rule, that the judge is to submit each particular fact to the jury, but not only that he is to look at all together, ask the jury which is proved, and decide according to the result, whether probable cause is shown or not. As to single facts, what law can he resort to in directing the jury? How can he lay down, as a general proposition of law, what particular fact shows probable cause under the circumstances of an individual case? The fact which is probable cause in one case is not in another. What general rule can there be? There is, on any view, a difficulty; but the Court of Exchequer Chamber having decided as they did, I have always endeavored to follow their ruling."

[2] Co. Litt. 56, b.

[3] "Quam longum esse debet non definitur in jure, sed pendet ex discretione justiciariorum."

true rule, in this respect, was laid down by Lord Mansfield when he said, with reference to the reasonable notice required to be given by the holder of the bill, when dishonored by the acceptor, to the drawer or indorser: "What is reasonable notice is partly a question of fact and partly a question of law. It may depend in some measure on facts; such as the distance at which the parties live from each other, the course of the post, &c. But wherever a rule can be laid down with respect to this reasonableness, that should be decided by the court, and adhered to by every one for the sake of certainty."[1]

The meaning of Lord Mansfield in the passage just quoted is, that whenever from a given state of facts found by a jury to be true, the law has settled that a certain inference shall be drawn, it is the duty of the court to pronounce what that legal inference is, and not leave it to the jury to determine. In other words, if a statutory enactment, or uniform course of decisions, has put a particular construction on proved or admitted facts, it is the province of the judge to declare that construction where the circumstances of the case are such that it applies to them. For example, the law has decided, that if the holder of a bill of exchange gives notice of its dishonor by the next day's post to a drawer or indorser living at a different place, this is a reasonable notice. "It is," says Abbot, C. J., "of the greatest importance to commerce, that some plain and precise rules should be laid down, to guide persons in all cases, as to the time within which notice of dishonor of bills must be given. That time I have always understood to be the departure of the post on the day following that on which the party receives the intelligence of the dishonor."[2] This, then, being the rule, the only question for the jury in such a case

[1] Tindall v. Brown, 1 T. R. 168.
[2] Williams v. Smith, 2 B. and Ald. 500.

would be, whether the letter giving the notice was, in fact, posted not later than the following day.

So, in other instances, it is for the judge applying his knowledge of the law to determine whether an alleged custom is reasonable or not; but the facts, unless they are set forth with sufficient clearness and precision on the record, and are undisputed, must be first submitted to the jury to be found by them, before the judge can pronounce his opinion upon their legal effect. "For issues may be joined on things which are partly matters of fact and partly matters of law; and then when the evidence is given at the trial, the judge must direct the jury how the law is; and if they find contrary to such direction, it is a sufficient reason for a new trial."[1] The judgment from which these words are taken was delivered in a case where the defendants in an action of trespass justified under a plea alleging a custom for the inhabitants of a town to walk and ride, at all seasonable times in the year, over certain arable land which had been used as a public place of resort. But the court said, that as it appeared on the face of the record that corn was growing on the land, this was sufficient to enable it to determine that the time when the trespass was committed was not a seasonable time; and the plea was held to be bad. So it was decided by the court, that a custom for "the poor, necessitous and indigent householders," residing within a particular township, to cut and carry away rotten boughs and branches in a close was bad, on account of the uncertain description of persons in respect of whom the right was claimed; and a verdict which found the custom to be as alleged, was set aside as being contrary to law.[2]

Let us next take the case of an action brought for necessaries supplied to an infant. Is the judge or the jury

[1] Per Curiam, in Bell *v.* Wardle, Willes. 206.
[2] Selby *v.* Robinson, 2 T. R. 758.

to decide what are necessaries? Formerly it seems to have been thought that this was exclusively the province of the judge: and in an old case, where a plaintiff sued a retainer of the Earl of Essex, "for the price of a satin doublet and hose with sleeves and gold lace, a velvet jerkin and hose, and a fustian doublet and cloth hose," and the defendant pleaded infancy, to which the plaintiff replied, that the apparel was delivered to him for his necessary dress during the time of his service, whereupon the defendant demurred (*i.e.* denied that the replication was a sufficient answer in point of law to his plea); the court finding that the defendant was described in the declaration as a gentleman, "agreed clearly that the satin, lace, and velvet, were not necessary apparel for a gentlemen; and therefore the action would not lie for so much but only for the residue."[1] And at the present day, if the articles furnished are manifestly such as can not possibly come under the category of necessaries, the question would not be left to the jury at all, but the plaintiff would be nonsuited.[2] "Suppose," said the court on one occasion lately, "the son of the richest man in the kingdom to have been supplied with diamonds and race-horses, the judge ought to tell the jury that such articles can not possibly be necessaries."[3]

But, if the articles are not of this description, then the question arises whether they were bought for the necessary use of the infant, in order to support himself properly in the degree, state, and station of life in which he moves; for the word necessaries is not confined to such things only as are needed for the support of life, but embraces what is fit and suitable to maintain a person in his particular grade; and this is for the jury to decide.[4]

---
[1] Gouldsborough, 168.
[2] Brooker *v.* Scott, 11 Mees. and Wels. 67.
[3] Wharton *v.* Mackenzie, 5. Q. B. Rep. 612.
[4] See per Parke, B., in Peters *à* g.leming, 6 Mees. and Wels. 47.

SECTION III. *Mixed Questions of Law and Fact.*

So far the rule seems clear, and such as may be acted upon without much difficulty. But there are classes of cases where the circumstances are so numerous and varying as to prevent the deduction of any definite inference of law; and where the inference necessary to support a verdict must be drawn by the jury themselves from the facts in evidence before them. Such, for instance, is the question of whether a party has acted with due caution in a matter involving certain legal liabilities.

It has been said that "fraud and covin is always a question of law; it is the judgment of law on facts and intents."[1] But this is, perhaps, too broadly stated. It is no doubt true that there are cases in which the law implies fraud from certain facts, irrespective of any intention in the party to commit an actual fraud. Thus, if a tradesman conveys away the whole of his effects, this is considered an act of bankruptcy, as being fraudulent against his creditors. The conclusion here is one of law, and applies to all such assignments, whatever the object may be which the assignor has in view. So also, if he departs the realm to avoid a criminal prosecution for murder, this is an act of bankruptcy, because the necessary consequence must be to delay his creditors, although such may not be his intention at all. But there are many cases where the fraud, in law as well as in fact, depends wholly on the intention; and this must always be a question for the jury. A more correct rule was given by Mr. Justice Buller, when he said, "Fraud is sometimes a question of law, sometimes a question of fact, sometimes a mixed question of law and fact."[2]

This phrase, "mixed question of law and fact," is frequently used, but it is deficient in that clearness and pre-

---

[1] Per Lord Ellenborough, in Doe d. Otley *v.* Manning, 9 East, 64.
[2] Eastwick *v.* Cailland, 5 T. R. 426.

cision at which legal expressions should aim. Every complicated proposition may be resolved into several distinct ones, each of a simpler nature than the general one —and upon the proper solution of these the answer to the whole depends. This answer is the result of all the particular answers to the separate questions into which the general one has been divided. Now each of these may be made to fall within its appropriate category, whether of law or fact, and ought to be answered either by the judge or by the jury accordingly. If the proposition is carefully analyzed there ought to be no difficulty in assigning the different elements of which it is compounded to their proper tribunal for determination. Some may be questions of law, and others questions of fact; but no one of them, if rightly framed, need or ought to involve both. After all have been answered, then the result is the inference to be drawn from the whole; and must be submitted to the jury, or decided by the judge, according to the nature of the case. If the law has defined the legal import and quality of the facts found by the jury in answer to the separate questions, it is the province of the court to pronounce that as the consequence of their finding; but if the circumstances are such as to exclude the application of any general rule of law, the inference must be one merely of fact, and is to be drawn by the jury. So that here again the question ultimately is either one of law or one of fact, but not mixed up of both. The true meaning of the expression, therefore, really amounts to no more than this, that there are some questions which can not be properly answered without first determining some matters of fact and ascertaining some point or points of law.

SECTION IV. *Presumptions of Law and Fact.*

In almost all cases where the evidence is what is called

circumstantial, that is, where the mind must be guided to a conclusion by observing the relation which certain proved facts bear to each other, independently of any direct evidence of the ultimate fact which is the object of inquiry, it must be left to the jury to deduce the proper inference. "In a great portion of trials," said Lord Tenterden, "as they occur in practice, no direct proof that the party accused actually committed the crime is or can be given; the man who is charged with theft is rarely seen to break the house or take the goods; and in cases of murder, it rarely happens that the eye of any witness sees the fatal blow struck, or the poisonous ingredients poured into the cup. In drawing an inference or conclusion from facts proved, regard must always be had to the nature of the particular case, and the facility that appears to be afforded, either of explanation or contradiction."[1] Where the connection between certain facts is such that the one may be generally inferred from the other with a great degree of probability, the inference is usually called a presumption; and this is more or less cogent, according as experience has shown the more or less frequent co-existence of the phenomena in question. And, as was well said by the eminent judge who has just been quoted, "It is one of the peculiar advantages of our jurisprudence that the conclusion is to be drawn by the unanimous judgment and conscience of twelve men conversant with the affairs and business of life: and who know that where reasonable doubt is entertained, it is their duty to acquit; and not of one or more lawyers, whose habits might be suspected of leading them to the indulgence of too much subtlety and refinement." I have already pointed out the peculiar danger attaching to this kind of evidence,[2] and need only add here that in criminal cases the safest rule in applying it seems to be to consider not only whether it sufficiently supports the

[1] R. v. Burdett, 4 Barn. and Al. 161. [2] See *ante*, pp. 203--4.

hypothesis of guilt, but also, whether it is inconsistent with the hypothesis of innocence.

But there is a somewhat larger class of presumptions, corresponding to the præsumptiones juris of the Roman law, where the law itself presumes the existence of certain facts until the contrary is proved. These cases therefore fall within the consideration of a jury only if evidence is offered to rebut the legal presumption. If not, the latter is deemed to be, and is acted on by the court as conclusive. Such is the presumption that a person who has been abroad for the space of seven years, and has not been heard of within that time, is dead: that a child born in wedlock is legitimate: that official acts have been duly executed; that a person in possession of land is seized in fee: as against the writer, that a letter was written on the day on which it is dated; that the holder of a bill of exchange or promissory note gave value for it. Such also was the rule of the Roman law where two persons died very nearly at the same time, and there was no evidence to show which survived the other.[1]

Besides these there is a limited class of presumptions, the præsumptiones juris et de jure of the Roman law, which are absolute and conclusive in their nature, and may not be rebutted by evidence to the contrary.[2] They are in reality valid conclusions of law, and, therefore, can

[1] No definite rule has been adopted by our own law on this subject. See the case of General Stanwix in R. *v.* Dr. Hay, 1 W. Black. 641. Where a father and son, joint tenants, were hanged in the same cart, and the question was whether the wife of the son was entitled to dower, the jury found that the son survived the father, as he appeared to have struggled the longest. Cro. Eliz. 503.

[2] Conjectura vel a LEGE inducitur vel a JUDICE. Quæ ab ipsa lege inducitur, vel ita comparatur, ut probationem contrarii haud admittat, vel ut eadem possit elidi. Priorem doctores præsumptionem juris et de jure; posteriorem præsumptionem juris appellant. Heinecc. Elem. Jur. Civ.—The Lex here mentioned corresponds to our "Court"; the Judex to our "Jury.

not be submitted to the cognizance of a jury. They are founded on reasons of convenience, and amount to no more than this, that the law has said that certain consequences shall be deemed to flow from given premises, although no such consequences may have, in fact, resulted from them. Such was the old rule of law that a child born of a mother whose husband lived within the realm, or inter quatuor maria, as it was called, was conclusively held to be legitimate. So at the present day, if a man marries a woman visibly pregnant, it is a conclusive inference of law that the child afterwards born is legitimate. Formerly this class of presumptions was more numerous than in latter times, when the tendency has been to adopt a more rational rule, and consider them conclusive only in absence of proof to the contrary. But there are several statutes which proceed upon the old principle. Such is that which interposes a bar to the recovery of debts after a certain period has elapsed, upon the presumption that payment has been made; and that which, in cases of prescription prevents a disturbance of the right by presuming a grant from the owner of the fee.

SECTION V. *Utility of Written Pleadings.*

The English system of pleading is, in theory, admirably adapted for civil trials by the intervention of a jury; or perhaps it would be more correct to say, it has grown as an offshoot out of that system. For when the true principles of pleading are kept in view, a more efficacious instrument for enabling the jury to discharge their peculiar functions can hardly be imagined. The plaintiff makes a written statement of his cause of complaint, and to this the defendant puts in an answer, which consists, at his option, either of a denial of the facts alleged on the other side, or an admission of them with the addition of some other facts which, in his opinion, justify his conduct. Or he asserts, that taking all that is said by the plaintiff to be true, it gives the latter no legal right of action. In this case he is said to demur, and the question is obviously one of law, ready at once for the decision of the court. But if there is no demurrer, then the plaintiff must either reply or demur to the fresh matter of fact alleged by the defendant; and here again the defendant must either rejoin in like manner as he answered before, or he must demur. And so the pleadings proceed until the dispute between the parties ultimately resolves itself into the assertion of some fact or facts, by the one side, which are denied by the other, and it is the province of the jury to determine by their verdict which is right; or else a question of law is raised for the decision of the court. No matter how complicated the transaction may have been, it will generally be found, that the real points in dispute are few, and it is of immense importance to have these distinctly evolved, and presented for decision in a precise and categorical form. This is done by the preliminary operation of written pleadings, which have fallen into disrepute solely on account of the grievous abuses which have crept into and deformed the system. If the true principle of pleading were kept steadily in view, and the system freed from the oppressive technicality which now disgraces it, it would well deserve the eulogium passed upon it by Sir Thomas Smith, in his "Commonwealth of England," written in the reign of Elizabeth. "Having seen," he says, "both in France and other places, many devices, edicts, and ordinances how to abridge process, and to find how that long suits in law might be made shorter, I have not perceived or read, as yet, so wise, so just, and so well-devised a mean found out as this is by any man among us in Europe. Truth it is, that when this fashion hath not been used, and by those to whom it is new, it will not be so easily understood, and, therefore, they may peradventure be of contrary judgment; but the more they do weigh and consider it, the more reasonable they shall find it." When trial by jury in civil cases was introduced into Scotland, in the year 1815, it was immediately discovered that some such mode of preparing the issues of law and fact was indispensable. To leave the whole circumstance of an involved and intricate transaction at large to the jury, without telling them on what specific points their opinion was required, was to impose upon them a task to which they were inadequate; and error and confusion would have been the result. Hence it became necessary, as we shall presently see, to frame distinct issues, in the shape of questions, to be submitted to the jury, and these questions, when properly drawn, embrace seriatim all the facts really in dispute.[1]

[1] *Qualifications of Common Jurors, and Exemptions from serving on Juries in England.* Stat. 6 Geo. IV. c. 50, §§ 1, 2 enacts: " That every man except as hereinafter excepted between the ages of twenty-one years and sixty years residing in any county in England, who shall have in his own name or in trust for him within the same county ten pounds for the year above reprizes in lands or tenements, whether of freehold, copyhold, or customary tenure, or of ancient demesne, or in rents issuing out of any such lands or tenements, or in such lands, tenements, and rents taken together in fee simple, fee tail, or for the life of himself or some other person, or who shall have within the same county twenty pounds by the year above reprizes in lands or tenements held by lease or leases for the absolute term of twenty-one years or some longer term, or for any term of years determinable upon any life or lives, or who being a householder shall be rated or assessed to the poor rate, or to the inhabited house duty in the county of Middlesex on a value of not less than thirty pounds, or in any other county on a value of not less than twenty pounds, or who shall occupy a house containing not less than fifteen windows, shall be qualified and shall be liable to serve on juries for the trial of all issues joined in any of the King's Courts of Record at Westminster, and in the superior courts, both civil and criminal, of the three counties palatine, and in all courts of assize, nisi prius, oyer and terminer, and jail delivery, such issues being respectively triable in the county in which every man so qualified respectively shall reside, and shall also be qualified and liable to serve on grand juries in courts of sessions of the peace, and on petty juries

CHAPTER XIII

THE JURY SYSTEM IN SCOTLAND.

SECTION I. *Jury Trial in Civil Cases.*

IF we could be quite sure that the book called "Regiam Majestatem" gives a true account of the old law of Scotland, and was generally received as an authority in the courts there, we might safely assume

for the trial of all issues joined in such courts of session of the peace, and triable in the county, riding, or division in which every man so qualified respectively shall reside, and that every man (except as hereinafter excepted), being between the aforesaid ages, residing in any county in Wales, and being there qualified to the extent of three-fifths of any of the foregoing qualifications, shall be qualified and shall be liable to serve on juries for the trial of all issues joined in the courts of great sessions, and on grand juries in courts of sessions of the peace, and on petty juries for the trial of all issues joined in such courts of sessions of the peace in every county in Wales in which every man so qualified as last aforesaid respectively shall reside.

II. "Provided always that all peers, all judges of the King's Courts of Record at Westminster, and of the courts of great session in Wales, all clergymen in holy orders, all priests of the Roman Catholic faith who shall have duly taken and subscribed the oaths and declarations required by law, all persons who shall teach or preach to any congregation of protestant dissenters whose place of meeting is duly registered, and who shall follow no secular occupation except that of a schoolmaster, and producing a certificate of some justice of the peace of their having taken the oaths and subscribed the declaration required by law, all sergeants and barristers-at-law actually practicing, all members of the society of doctors of law and advocates of civil law actually practicing, all attorneys, solicitors, and proctors duly admitted in any court of law or equity, or of ecclesiastical or admiralty jurisdiction, in which attorneys, solicitors, and proctors have usually been admitted, actually practicing, and have duly taken out their annual certificates, all officers of any such courts actually exercising the duties of their

that trial by an assize of twelve jurors in civil cases was almost coæval in Scotland with the establishment of that institution in England. But it is doubtful whether the book in question is what it professes to be. The best lawyers do not regard it as an authority, and we must receive with caution its statements as to the proceedings by assize in Scotland in ancient times.[1]

respective offices, all coroners, jailers, and keepers of houses of correction, all members and licentiates of the Royal College of Physicians in London actually practicing, all surgeons being members of the Royal College of Surgeons in London, Edinburgh, or Dublin, and actually practicing, all officers in his majesty's navy or army on full pay, all pilots licensed by the Trinity House of Deptford, Stroud, Kingston-upon-Hull, or Newcastle-upon-Tyne, and all masters of vessels in the buoy and light service employed by either of these corporations, and all pilots licensed by the lord warden of the Cinque Ports, or under any act of parliament or charter for the regulation of pilots of any other port, all the household servants of his majesty, his heirs and successors, all officers of customs and excise, all sheriffs' officers, high constables, and parish clerks, shall be and are hereby absolutely freed and exempted from being returned, and from serving upon any juries or inquests whatsoever, and shall not be inserted in the lists to be prepared by virtue of this act as hereinafter mentioned; provided also that all persons exempt from serving upon juries in any courts aforesaid, by virtue of any prescription, charter, grant, or writ, shall continue to have and enjoy such exemption in as ample a manner as before the passing of this act, and shall not be inserted in the lists hereinafter mentioned."

[1] The date and authenticity of the Regiam Majestatem have been a subject of much controversy amongst Scotch lawyers. All admit that it is so identical with Glanvill's treatise, that the one must have been copied from the other. But the question is, Which is the original and which is the copy? Skene Dalrymple, and other writers of eminence, declare themselves in favor of the prior claim of the Scotch work, and maintain that it is a genuine code of the laws of Scotland, promulgated by David I., who reigned from 1124 to 1153. On the other hand, Craig, Lord Stair, Lord Hales, and others, are of opinion that the Regiam Majestatem was copied from Glanvill, interpolated with matters relative to Scotland, and imposed upon the nation as a capitulary of one of their ancient kings. See Ross's Lectures on the Law of Scotland (Edinburgh, 1822), II. 60–64. This writer thinks it evident that the Scotch work was copied from Glanvill, "and afterwards adapted to the meridian of Scotland by the insertion of so many chapters and the interpolation of particular parts;" and he says that the laws of Scotland and England were nearly the same in the time of Henry II. when

It is transparently clear that the "Regiam Majestatem" is the same work as Glanvill's treatise, "De Legibus," and that the differences which occur between the two versions are merely colorable and verbal. Indeed, the very words of the English author are for the most part used in the former work, to describe what purports to be the proceeding by an assize in Scotland.

Thus, according to the "Regiam Majestatem," the claimant of land there, at the close of his pliant, demanded an assize in the following terms: "I ask the assize of that village, and placing myself in the protection of God, and of the assize of the village, on account of my petition, and of the persons known to me as respectable, that they may not proceed in the said case."[1] Twelve lawful men, de vicineto vel de curia, were thereupon chosen, who swore in the presence of the parties, "that they would recognize which of them had the better right in his demand." The provisions with regard to the original selection, and if necessary, addition of jurors who knew the facts in dispute, are the same in the two treatises, as also the definition of the kind of knowledge which was deemed sufficient. This will plainly appear from the following extract from an ancient vernacular translation of the original Latin, of the Scottish treatise:

"The assize passand fordward, to take inquisition of the mater; either the richt of the parties is well knawn to the assisours, or some of them his knawledge thereof,

---

Glanvill wrote his treatise. It seems that commissioners had been more than once appointed by the old Scotch parliaments to revise the Regiam Majestatem, and other ancient books, but no report was ever made by them; nor was any parliamentary ratification given to their labors. "So that," says Professor Erskine, in his "Principles of the law of Scotland," "none of these remains are received as of proper authority in our courts." The Regiam Majestatem is so called from the two words with which it begins.

[1] Peto assisam talis villæ, et pono me in Deum et assisam villæ super petitione meâ, salvis mihi suspectis personis, ne procedant in dicta causa.

and some are ignorant, or all ignorant. Gif nane of them knawes the trueth, and in the court testifies the samine be their great eath; other persons sall be chosen in their place, untill sic men be chosen quha knaws the veritie. Bot gif some of them knawes the trueth, and some knawes nocht; they quha are ignorant being repelled, others sall be admitted be the court, untill twelve men be found all aggreand together. All the assisours sall sweare, that in that mater or debate, vpon the decision quhere they are chosen; they sall nocht laine nor conceale the trueth wittinglie, nor na falset say. It is required of them wha sweares, to the effect they may have knawledge of the mater quhilk is in question, that they knaw the veritie, be sight, or be hearing of themselves, or be narration of their fathers, or be sic sure tokens and arguments to the buhilk they will give, or may give, als great faith as to their awin proper (doings or sayings)."[1]

When the verdict was given, the presiding judge (called Dumester) pronounced the doom or judgment of the court, either for the demandant or the tenant (defendant), as the case might be. If the jurors were accused of having sworn falsely, this was tried by an "attaint," that is, a jury of twenty-four lawful men; and if found guilty they were deprived of all their personal property, imprisoned for a year at least, and rendered forever infamous. This punishment was confirmed by various penal statutes, passed in the reigns of James III. and James IV.[2] The same rules that we find in Glanvill were laid down with respect to the judicial combat, where the defendant preferred that mode of trial, or consanguinity between the parties, prevented the assize.[3]

---

[1] Reg. Maj. Book, I. c. 12.

[2] Jac. 3 Parl. VI. c. 47; Parl. VIII. c. 63. Jac. 4. Parl. III. c. 35.

[3] Reg. Majest. Lib. III. c. 29. Quon. Attach. c. 31. It was enacted by Stat. Jac. 6 Parl. XIV. c. 12, that no person without the king's license should fight any "singular combat," under pain of death and confiscation of all his movables.

We must not, however, confound this mode of trial with that per pares, which, as Lord Ivory says, "continued to prevail in the whole civil courts of Scotland, down to the old court of the Session."[1] This writer speaks of the trial per pares as trial by jury, but I believe this is a mistake. The reasons for maintaining that the judicium parium was quite different from the jury system, have been detailed in a previous part of the present work, and they apply equally to the trial per pares in Scotland. The latter were nothing more than the suitors, or homage of the baronial and other territorial or local courts, and they discharged the functions of both judge and jury, being, in fact, the whole court presided over by an officer who seems to have been closely analogous to the lawman of the Swedish and Norwegian tribunals. Lord Ivory himself admits that the province of the judge seems only to have been to preside in court, and "informe the soytours (suitors,) gif they be ignorant, of the law anent wordes (interlocutors) or decreits."[2] And, what still more strongly proves the point I contend for, he quotes a passage from Glassford, who says that the judgment or sentence of the suitors "was not merely a verdict, making way for sentence by the judge, but was the interlocutor or judgment of court on the whole matter referred." But with reference to criminal trials the word "peers" is used in a more general sense in the old Scotch law, "that na man should thole judgment, or be judged be ane man of inferior estate, than his awin peir; that is, ane earle, be earles; ane baron, be barons; ane vavassour, be vavassours; ane burgess, be burgesses. Bot ane man of inferior estate may be judged by men of greater estate."

But independently of the trials before the suitors of the baronial and other courts, and without insisting upon the

---

[1] Form of Process, II. 272.
[2] Quon. Attach. c. 16 § 5.

authority of the Regiam Majestatem, there undoubtedly existed in Scotland in ancient times trial by jury in some cases of a civil nature, and its form seems to have closely resembled that which prevailed in England. Thus, Spottiswood says, that in those days all acts of spoliation, intrusion, and others of that nature, were precognosced by a verdict of twelve men best knowing the land, whose declaration being presented to the judges they used to determine; and he cites from a Book of Decrets and Acts, a case in the year 1469, respecting the right to certain lands, where the parties of their own consent named twelve persons, who, being sworn, gave their " deliverence," *i.e.* verdict, as follows : " We decree and deliver after our knowledge and understanding, that in no time bygone we heard ever that the laird of Samuelston had possession of the said lands with mannor, pasture, &c.; and that Nicol and his predecessors have ever been in peaceable possession of these lands." After which deliverance, says Spottiswood, the Lords decerned Samuelston to desist therefrom in time coming.[1]

Moreover, we learn from Lord Kaimes,[2] that the ancient records of the sheriffs and other inferior courts of Scotland when searched, prove that civil causes in them were tried by juries; and there is an Act of the year 1587, expressly appointing molestations to be tried by a jury before the sheriff. The same writer tells us, that, conjecturing that the old form of jury trials might wear out more slowly in shires remote from the capital, he made diligent search, and discovered a book of the sheriff's court of Orkney, beginning July 3, 1602, and ending August 29, 1604, in which all the processes, civil as well as criminal, were tried by juries.

And the form of procedure in Scotland known by the name of " service of heirs," has always required the aid

[1] Ivory's Form of Process, II. 274.
[2] Historical Tracts, Vol. I. 273, 274.

of an inquest, or jury; whose number, says Erskine, "has alway consisted of an odd number, that an equality of voices might not make the verdict doubtful."[1] This number has for a very long period been fixed at fifteen. Also in all cases where a person was to be declared incapable of acting from "furiosity," or fatuity, or a widow's right to dower was to be ascertained, and in striking the "fiars" of the different counties, the verdict of a jury has been indispensable.

Unlike, however, what happened on this side the border, no general development of the jury system in civil trials took place in Scotland; and it gradually fell into such complete disuse and oblivion, that it came almost to be a question whether it had ever existed there at all.

Lord Kaimes endeavors to account for this result by the following theory. He says, that the maxim of our forefathers seems to have been, that though questions of law might be trusted to a single judge, matters of proof (*i.e.*, disputed facts) are safest in the hands of a plurality; but where the judges of a court were sufficiently numerous for this purpose, there was no need of the intervention of a jury.[2] The Court of Session in Scotland was instituted in 1532, and consisted of fifteen members; the object being to relieve the king and council of the load of business growing daily upon them. "One thing," says Lord Kaimes, "we are certain of, without

---

[1] Inst. Book III. c. 8.

[2] Historical Tracts, Vol. I. 270–273. Few will be disposed to agree with Lord Kaimes' view where he says: "Juries were never employed in any British court where the judges were sufficiently numerous to act the part of a jury. Juries, for example, were never employed in parliament, nor in processes before the king and council. And in England when the court last named was split into the King's Bench, the Exchequer, and the Common Pleas, I am verily persuaded that the continuance of jury trials in these new courts was owing to the following circumstances, that four judges only were appointed in each of them, and but a single judge in the circuit courts."

the necessity of recurring to a conjecture, that the daily council, which came in the place of the session, and equally with it consisted of many judges, had not from the beginning any jury trials, but took evidence by witnesses, and in every cause gave judgment upon the proof, precisely as we do at this day. These facts considered, it seems a well-founded conjecture, that so large a number of judges as fifteen, which constitute our present Court of Session, were appointed with a view to the practice of the preceding courts, and in order to prevent the necessity of trying causes by juries. In the former court, viz., the daily Council, we find it composed of bishops, abbots, earls, lords, gentlemen, and burgesses; in order, probably, that every man might be tried by some, at least, of his own rank; and in examining the records of this court, we find at first few sederunts, but where at least twelve judges were present. This matter is still better ordered in the present Court of Session. Nine judges must be present to make a quorum; and it seldom happens in examining any proof that the judges present are under twelve in number. This, I am persuaded is the foundation of a maxim which among us passes current, without any direct authority from the regulations concerning the jurisdiction of this court. It is said to be the grand jury of the nation in civilibus, and it is supposed that its privilege to take proof without the aid of a jury proceeds from this branch of its constitution."

It seems to me to be an answer to this ingenious theory, that in criminal trials in Scotland juries have never been discontinued. But if the fact of a court being composed of judges sufficiently numerous to act the part of a jury satisfactorily accounts for the disuse of the latter, we should certainly expect to find, that after the institution of the Court of Session it was no longer employed in criminal cases. For surely the judges of that court were as competent to deal with the proof of matters of fact in criminal as in civil trials. The rules of evidence are the same in both cases, and the object in view is alike the same; namely, to ascertain the truth where there is a conflict of proof.

Let us, however, now turn our attention to the system as it exists at the present day. In the year 1787, Lord Swinton, one of the judges of the Court of Sessions, published a pamphlet, recommending the introduction of jury trial into Scotland, in certain specified civil actions; and Lord Mansfield, who had retired from the chief justiceship, and was then upwards of eighty years of age, was applied to for his opinion. This great jurist accordingly penned, for the private information of Lord Henderland, another of the Scotch judges, the following weighty remarks "every line of which," says Lord Campbell, "is worth a subsidy."[1]

"Great alterations in the course of the administration of justice ought to be sparingly made, and by degrees, and rather by the court than by the legislature. The partial introduction of trial by jury seems to be big with infinite mischief, and will produce much litigation.

"Under the words proposed, it may be extended almost to anything; reduction, restitution, fraud, injury. It is curious that fraud, which is always a complicated proposition of law and fact, was held in England as one of the reasons for a court of equity, to control the inconveniences of a jury trying it. The giving it to the desire of both parties might be plausible; but where only one desires that mode of trial it is a reason against granting it, because many causes and persons have popular prejudices attending them which influence juries.

A great deal of law and equity in England has arisen to regulate the course and obviate the inconveniences

---

[1] Lives of the Chief Justices, Vol. II. p. 555.

which attend this mode of trial. It has introduced a court of equity distinct from a court of law, which never existed in any other country, ancient or modern; it has formed a practice by the courts of law themselves, and by acts of parliament, bills of exceptions, special verdicts, attaints, challenges, new trials,[1] &c.

"Will you extend by a general reference all the law and equity now in use in England relative to trials by jury? The objections are infinite and obvious. On the other hand, will you specify particularly what their system should be? The Court of Session and the judges of England, added together, would find that a very difficult task."

When Lord Grenville was minister, in 1806, he brought in a bill for extending trial by jury to civil causes in Scotland. He introduced the measure by an able speech, and the bill was printed and circulated throughout the country. His plan was to engraft the jury system on the Court of Session; and he was led to believe that the ordinary mode of pleading in that court by summons and defenses would at once afford the means of bringing cases to an issue fit to be tried by a jury.

At this time the arrear of appeals from the Court of Session to the House of Lords had become overwhelming, and hence the necessity, not only of clearing off that arrear, but also of devising means, if possible, for preventing future accumulation. Many of these appeals turned upon mere questions of fact, the mode of examining which produced immense volumes of evidence, much of which was irrelevant, and much inadmissible. It was thought,

---

[1] Lord Campbell adds: "These principles were unfortunately overlooked in the year 1807, when jury trial exactly according to the English model, with its unanimity, special verdicts, and bills of exceptions, was introduced into Scotland. The experiment, I am afraid, has proved a failure, and Lord Mansfield's predictions have been fatally verified." This, as will hereafter appear, is very different from the opinion of Chief Commissioner Adam, derived from the result of his own extensive experience.

therefore, that if such questions were tried by a jury, many cases would not be appealed at all, and the judicial machinery of the Scotch courts would be materially improved, especially in respect of the law of evidence.

Lord Grenville, however, soon afterwards, with his ministry of "All the Talents," was removed from power, and the bill was dropped.

The subject was again revived by the Report of the Law Commission, appointed in 1808, in which a modified opinion was given in favor of some measure of a similar kind. A majority of the commissioners thought "that under proper regulations it might be for the utility of the subjects within Scotland to introduce this mode of trial into the proceedings of the Court of Session to a certain extent, by conferring on the court, as now divided, a power to direct an issue or issues to be tried in any cause, upon a question or questions of fact, by a special order to be made for that purpose; and also to direct that the same should be tried either before a judge or judges of the Court of Session, or before the Court of Justiciary, or before the Court of Exchequer, as the Court of Session in its subdivision should deem most expedient."

No practical result followed from this suggestion until several Scotch appeals in 1812, which turned upon facts alone, caused considerable difficulty and embarrassment in the House of Lords, and directed the attention of those most conversant with appeals to trial by a jury, as a possible remedy for the evil. At that time Mr. (afterwards Chief Commissioner) Adam had the largest amount of this kind of practice, and he was led particularly to consider the subject, with a view to some practicable measure. Ultimately he drew up a paper, in which the whole question wrs reviewed, and this was submitted by him to Lord Chancellor Eldon. A draft of a bill was afterwards prepared, which was brought into

Parliament by Lord Eldon in 1815, and before the end of the session it became law. The Act of Parliament is 55 Geo. III. c. 42; and as the measure was intended only as an experiment, the term of its operation was limited to seven years.

This act provided for the establishment of a court and the appointment of one chief and two other judges to be called "The Lords Commissioners of the Jury Court in Civil Causes," whose functions were limited to the trial of issues directed by the Court of Session and sent to the Jury Court. New trials were to be allowed by the Court of Session on the grounds of the verdict being contrary to evidence—misdirection of the judge—undue admission or rejection of evidence—excess of damages—res noviter veniens ad notitiam (that is, evidence discovered subsequent to the trial which could not have been previously foreseen or known), or "such other cause as is essential to the justice of the case,"—but the granting or refusing a new trial was not to be subject to review or appeal to the House of Lords.[1] Bills of exceptions were also allowed, and in fact the object of the act was to "give to Scotland the form, the machinery, the principles, the rules, and the practice of the common-law courts of England in respect to all that related to the trial of matters of civil right by jury."[2] But at the same time no alteration whatever was made in the municipal law of Scotland as regarded the rights of the parties in a suit.

The jury were to consist of twelve jurors drawn by ballot, and their verdict must be unanimous; but it was wisely provided that if a jury impaneled shall not agree

---

[1] This power of granting new trials was afterwards, by 59 Geo. III. c. 35, § 16, exclusively vested in the Jury Court.

[2] Adam on Trial by Jury, p. 241. No mention is made in this Act of special verdicts, but they were recognized as existing in practice in Scotland by 59 Geo. III. c. 35, § 20. Chief Commissioner Adam says it was unnecessary to introduce them by legislative enactment, as being "inherent to trial by jury."

in their verdict within the space of twelve hours (now limited to six) from the time they shall be enclosed to consider of their verdict, they shall be discharged by the court from delivering their verdict, unless they themselves apply for further time ; and the Court of Session may thereupon order another jury to be summoned to try the cause de novo. The form of oath to be administered to the jurors was prescribed by the act, and is as follows :

"You swear by God, and as you shall answer to God at the great day of judgment, that you shall well and truly try these issues (or this issue), and a true verdict give according to the evidence."

The original act was amended, and further provisions applicable to the subject, were introduced by 59 Geo. III. c. 35, and afterwards by 6 Geo. IV. c., 120, and 13 and 14 Vict. c. 36, which last acts contain regulations respecting the mode in which pleadings are to be drawn and issues framed. Also by 11 Geo. IV. and 1 Will. IV. c. 69 (1830), trial by jury in Scotland was united with the ordinary jurisdiction of the Court of Session, and the Jury Court established by 55 Geo. III. c. 42, ceased to exist.

It was not likely that so great an innovation could be introduced without strong prejudice and opposition on the part of a nation so tenacious of its usages as the Scotch. One of the ablest of their lawyers has thus described their feelings on the subject:[1] "The people were taught to believe that all their native jurisprudence was in danger of being subverted by the introduction of English law, and this raised an obstinate spirit of resistance against whatever was peculiarly English. The necessity of unanimity in juries, with the number of twelve instead of fifteen, proved, for a long time, a great

---

[1] "Examination of the objections stated against the Bill brought into the House of Lords in the 6 Geo. IV." By Professor Bell.

obstruction to the adoption of jury trial as established in England. Even when those difficulties were at last surmounted, fears for the law still furnished the honest a pretended ground of much opposition, although the case of perfect adaption to their purpose, with which even these English pecularities have been found to work among us, may be a lesson against violent prejudice and outcry in matters of this kind.

"It was not yet perceived that a new sort of knowledge—a more correct analysis of the substantial grounds of action and defense—a better foresight of the general issue, more accurate habits, more vigilant attention, were necessary than before. Every one was offended that he was not held as competent now to conduct judicial proceedings as formerly, and yet could not help feeling that error, and embarrassment, and danger attended every step of their proceedings. It was difficult for the new system to become popular."

Independently of prejudice and dislike, a great and serious difficulty in the way of successful experiment lay in the nature of Scotch pleadings. We must remember that the English system of pleading has grown up side by side with the jury. It has been modified by the exigencies of the tribunal to which it is adapted, and has for centuries been molded in a form, the professed object of which is to evolve clearly and distinctly the issues of fact to be determined by the jury. Most faulty, indeed, the system has become, and legal subtlety has rendered it too often an engine of odious chicane, which is a disgrace to English jurisprudence, but in theory it is what I have previously described; and if its true purpose had been always kept in view, it would not have fallen into the bad repute under which it now deservedly suffers, and which it will be difficult for it to survive. But in Scotland there was no apparatus of pleading ready to meet the wants of the new-comer; and without some mode of raising specific questions of fact asserted on one side and denied on the other, trial by jury would be a useless mockery.

Now in Scotland every civil action is commenced by a Summons, which calls the opposite party into court, to meet and answer the claim of the pursuer (*i.e.*, plaintiff, corresponding exactly to the Greek term $\Delta\iota\omega\kappa\omega\nu$). This, until very lately, in technical language must have been "libeled," that is, have all the grounds of action stated in it, and causes of action of a very heterogeneous nature may be included in the same summons.[1] But, now, by a recent statute (13 and 14 Vict. c. 36), it is provided that the summons shall not contain any statement whatever of the grounds of action: but the allegations in fact which form those grounds shall be set forth in an articulate condescendence together with a note of the plaintiff's pleas in law, and these shall be annexed to the summons and be held to constitute part of it ; and the defenses (*i.e.* pleas) to such summons shall be in the form of articulate answers to the condescendence. Also, where necessary, there shall be appended a statement of the allegations in fact on which the defendant rests his defense, and a note of his pleas in law. Previously to this act the instrument called "defenses," too frequently deserve the description given of it by Chief Commissioner Adam, as " a vague oratorical pleading;"—and it contained a reservation to add and eik afterwards, if necessary. As it was formerly almost impossible to collect with sufficient certainty from the summons and defenses what were the real points in dispute between the parties, it became usual for the plaintiff to put in a condescendence or specification of facts on his part, which was followed by answers on the part of

---

[1] Thus, sending a challenge to fight a duel (an actionable offense by the law of Scotland), assault and slander have been united in the same action. Haslop *v.* Staig, 1 Murray, 16. And of another defamation, adultery and assault. Kirk *v.* Guthrie, 1 Murray, 271.

the defendant. "A condescendence should disclose with precision and in full all the facts of the case, and consequently all the grounds of action on which the pursuer relies. The answers to the condescendence on the part of the defender should deny with precision the allegations of the pursuer, and should aver on his own part all those facts and grounds of defense on which he relies." Chief Commissioner Adam adds, " Supposing these last-mentioned legal instruments to be executed strictly and correctly in pure averment of fact, it is hardly possible to conceive any pleadings better adapted to secure a correct distribution of justice." And, I believe, the effect of the late act has been greatly to improve the form of the condescendences and defences.

This mode of pleading was the ancient form adopted in the Court of Session, when trial by jury in civil actions formed no part of the judicial system of Scotland. But however perfect it might be in theory, it has been found defective in practice. And the same writer, who has eulogized the principle on which the instruments ought to be framed, thus describes their actual operation: "The language of pure averment has not been observed, the style of the paper is argumentative, observations on the bearings of the facts are introduced, legal reasoning is superadded, material facts are often omitted, or an unfair gloss put upon those which are stated, owing to the attention being withdrawn from fact to argument. Thus the security against surprise is diminished, and repeated amendments of the condescendences and answers become necessary, creating at once much delay and great additional expense. Thus the frame of these instruments, as here described, present difficulties of the most serious nature in preparing the question or questions for trial by jury."

To meet this difficulty, and obtain a means of evolving with precision the real facts in dispute, the Scotch Jury

Act (55 Geo. III. c. 42) provided that the Court of Session should direct an issue or issues to be tried. It therefore became necessary to frame the statements of the parties in that shape; and for this purpose advocates were appointed to discharge the office of Clerks of the Issues, and raise the proper questions out of the pleadings and exhibits in the cause, acting under the superintendence of a judge, whose duty it was to revise and consider with them the form of the issues, and to sign them when finally settled. The counsel and agents of the parties attended the clerks and the judge, "discussing the subject, not in formal argument, but in quiet conversation."[1] In such a system it is obvious that expedition will principally depend upon the nature and extent of the admissions which each party is disposed to make; and on this subject the late Chief Commissioner says, "There is one part of the proceeding which will always require deliberation, namely, the obtaining the admissions which preface the issues. Admissions save much time at trials, secure against failures in matters of formal proof, and save much expense to parties. When the agents and their employers meet to settle admissions, the proceeding is always abortive; but when the clerks interpose, when they reason with the parties, and show them that no advantage can be taken by the one over the other, the obtaining admissions very rarely fails of success."

Now, however, by the recent Act, the office of Issue Clerk and that of Jury Clerk are abolished, and their duties are performed by any of the clerks of Session. And where in the course of any cause before the Court of Session matter of fact is to be determined, and an issue is to be adjusted with reference thereto, the plaintiff must prepare and deliver ('lodge in process") the issue he proposes, and the defendant any counter issue required by the nature of his defense. And the Lord Ordinary

[1] Adam on Trial by Jury, 21.

before whom the cause depends appoints the parties to attend him for the adjustment of the issues; but if at a second meeting they are not adjusted and settled by consent, he reports the matter to the Inner House, or court, by whom the issues are then adjusted.

The system of pleading, therefore, in Scotland, to meet the requirements of the system, is, when properly drawn, shortly as follows. A correct technical summons with condescendences ; correct technical defenses, containing answers in which the admissions and denials are distinct and articulate; and when there are separate defenses, the facts on which they rest must be averred simply and correctly and without argument. Afterwards in order to frame an issue, whether general or special, the contents of the condescendence and answers, together with those of the exhibits, are drawn to a point or points, and put in the shape of a question as a general issue, or of questions as special issues, as the case may admit or require.

The form of such an issue (or issue of style as it has been called)[1] in the case of an action brought by a father in consequence of a cart driven by a servant of the defendant running over his child on the highway, is as follows:[2]

It being admitted that William Wilson was servant to the defendant, Thomas Harvie, from Whitsunday to Martinmas, 1826:

It being also admitted that on the 16th day of September, 1826, in the street in the city of Glasgow called Gallowgate, a cart, the property of the defender passed over and caused the death of the pursuer's son ; and that at the time it so passed over the child the said cart was under the management of the said William Wilson:

Whether the death of the said child was caused by the fault, negligence, or want of skill on the part of the said William Wilson, to the loss, injury, and damage of the pursuer?[3]

Damages laid at £1000.

[1] By issue of style is meant a formula or precedent of an issue.

[2] By the English law the father could not bring an action for such an injury unless the child were also his servant. If not, the child must bring the action in his own name, but he might appear by his father as his prochein amy.

[3] Compare with this case Lynch v. Nurdin, 1 Q. B. 29, where defendant

It may be useful to give two more examples of this kind of pleading.

The following is an issue in an action for reduction (*i. e.* setting aside instruments alleged to have been forged, or fraudulently obtained):

It being admitted that the pursuer is heir of provision of the late Peter Lyon, and that on the 25th day of March, 1831, the said Peter Lyon granted the two bills Nos. 4 and 5 of process, for the sums of £200 and £20 respectively.

Whether at the time of granting the said bills, or either of them, the said Peter Lyon was a minor, and granted the said bills, or either of them, to his enorm lesion?

Or,

Whether, at the time the said bills, or either of them, were or was granted, the said Peter Lyon was engaged in trade, and granted the said bills in the course of, or for the purpose of carrying on the said trade?

Whether the said bills, or either of them, were or was granted in security of payment of a debt or debts due by the father of the said Peter Lyon? and, Whether the said Peter Lyon viciously intromitted with the funds of his said father?

In an action for defamation brought by a parishioner against a Presbyterian minister:

Whether, on or about the 21st day of March, 1821, at Aross, in the island of Mull, at a meeting of the Presbytery of Mull, the defender did falsely, maliciously, and injuriously say and allege, that the pursuer had been guilty of a gross violation of the Sabbath-day by having, after coming out of church, on a Sunday recently before the said 21st day of March, taken his fishing-rod, or other implement, for killing fish, and gone out to take fish, and had been employed in fishing during a part of that day, or did use or utter words to that effect, to the injury and damage of the pursuer?

Whether, on or about Sunday the 5th day of July, 1821, at or near the parish-church of K., at the celebration of the sacrament in the said parish-

---

left his horse and cart unattended in the street, and plaintiff, a child seven years old, got upon the cart in play, and another child incautiously led the horse on, whereby the plaintiff was thrown down and hurt. It was held that the defendant was liable for his negligence, although the plaintiff was a trespasser and contributed to the injury by his own act. The plaintiff appeared in this action by his mother and guardian. As to the liability of a master in such cases for the negligence of his servant according to the English law, see Brucker *v.* Fromont, 6 T. R. 659, Croft *v.* Alison, 4 Barn. and Al. 590.

church, the defendant did falsely and injuriously say to N. S., elder of the said parish, that the pursuer had been guilty of the said offense, and did direct the said N. S. to prevent the pursuer from advancing to the communion-table, or did use or utter words to that effect, to the injury and damage of the pursuer?

Damages laid at £500.[1]

It is important however to notice, that at the trial of a cause where the question for the jury is put in the form of a general issue, as for instance, "whether the deed in question is or is not the deed of the party?" where of course there may be a great variety of grounds on which the deed may be denied, as non-execution, fraud, duress, erasure,—reference must be had to the previous pleadings, to ascertain what grounds have been there averred; for to these the party is limited. In other words, he can not travel out of the record, but must confine himself to the allegations on which he has chosen to rest his case in the summons or defenses, condescendences or answers.

The late Chief Commissioner Adam bears a high testimony to the conduct of juries in Scotland during the time that he presided over them, a period of full twenty years; and says, that they were distinguished for intelligence, attention, and impartiality. With reference to the much-disputed question of requiring unanimity in a verdict, he says, that during all that period only one instance happened of a jury separating after being inclosed for several hours without agreeing on their verdict, and this was in 1830, just before the merger of the Jury Court in the Court of Session.[2] The cause was tried a second time, and the new jury found a verdict which was not disturbed. Upon this point Mr. Adam gives it as his decided opinion, that "notwithstanding the appre-

---

[1] See Macfarlane's Notes on Issues in Jury Cases (Edinburgh, 1849), a work in which the subject is most ably discussed and practical forms are given. To the kindness of this gentleman I am indebted for some valuable information and remarks.

[2] Irvine v. Kilpatrick, ultimately determined in the House of Lords. 7 Bell's Appeal Cases, 186.

hensions which arose in men's minds by requiring that the jury should be unanimous, experience has proved that it is a most practicable and certainly a most beneficial regulation."

Of misconduct on the part of Scotch juries he also knew of only one case, which happened during the last year of the existence of the "Jury Court," when a jury was accused of having drawn lots for their verdict. And this was made the ground of application for a new trial, but the court unanimously refused to grant it, as the charge could not be satisfactorily established without the evidence of the jurors themselves as to what passed while they were in deliberation; and to admit this would be contrary to all principle and authority, both in England and in Scotland.[1] Since that time I believe that no other instance of alleged misconduct on the part of Scotch juries has occurred.

With reference to the question of how the new system has worked since its introduction into Scotland, there is some difference of opinion. In an able article which appeared in "The Edinburg Review," in the year 1830, the writer, speaking of the objections which had been urged against it, says, "The experience of the last fifteen years has silenced them all; and has most fully demonstrated, not only that there is nothing in the circumstances of Scotland repugnant to jury trials, but that it is in the very situation in which this mode of trial is chiefly required. The time of the Court of Session and of the House of Lords has been wasted on no cases of mere evidence; such cases have been satisfactorily tried, or have been saved from the necessity of trial, by one or both of the parties discovering, when the matter in dispute was brought to a precise point by an issue, that there

---

[1] Stewart *v.* Frazier, March, 1830. That such is the rule in England, see Owen *v.* Warburton, 1 Bos. and Pull. N. R. 326; Vaise *v.* Delaval, 1 Term. Rep. 11.

was nothing to try; there has not been one moment's demur with any one jury; there have not probably been above a dozen of new trials, and not half a dozen of successful bills of exception; such progress has been made in the service of issues, that very few cases can now occur for which the right one, and this commonly a general one, is not prepared; and whatever inconveniences have occurred, have arisen from the novelty of the institution, and not from anything essential to it."

This is, however, too flattering a picture. Trial by jury in civil cases can not be said to be popular in Scotland. It is looked upon there as an exceptional proceeding, attended with expense, uncertainty, and delay In the Sheriff's Courts there is no jury in civil actions, but the proofs are taken by commission, which is also still resorted to in the Court of Session, if the parties prefer that mode of inquiry. In that case the court decides upon the evidence so obtained. But of late years I believe, the opinion of many has been in favor of allowing the judge to hear the evidence himself, and decide the facts as well as the law, so as to supersede the use of either a commission or a jury. And the late act (13 and 14 Vict. c. 36) facilitates the accomplishment of this view, for it provides that if the parties to a cause consent, the Lord Ordinary may, unless the court on his report deem it imprudent and improper, try the issue without a jury, taking evidence and hearing counsel as nearly as may be in the manner of an ordinary jury trial.

For the existence of the unfavorable feeling which has just been mentioned it is, perhaps, not difficult to account. In the first place, the new system had to encounter all the opposition which is felt to innovations upon old established forms. Practitioners and judges had to go, as it were, to school again, and disliked the trouble of having to master the details of a new mode of procedure. This prejudice has not yet died away, and many of those who prophesied failure have not been indisposed to realize their predictions by discountenancing as much as possible the jury trial. Besides this, the want of experience on part of the judges in dealing with a somewhat complicated system, transplanted from England with all the refinements of special verdicts, bills of exceptions, and motions for new trials, has led to many miscarriages, causing both expense and delay. Misdirections have been frequent, and mistakes made, which have severally tried the patience and the pockets of the litigant parties. Thus, in one case the Court of Session held that it was proper to be tried by a jury, and sent it before two juries successively, whereas the House of Lords on appeal decided that it ought never to have been submitted to a jury at all, on the ground that, taking his own statement to be true, the plaintiff was out of court.[1] It must not, however, be supposed that mistakes of this kind never happen in England. But here, from long experience of the advantages of the system, the public are less sensitive respecting its defects, just as we are less disposed to criticize with harshness the failings of a familiar friend than those of a new acquaintance. And if it is persevered in north of the Tweed there seems no reason to doubt that much of the disfavor now felt towards it will gradually be removed. The recent Act has already remedied many of the evils complained of, and experience will suggest practical improvements whereby the system may be made more efficient by being freed from unnecessary technicality, and thus become better adapted for its object; which is simply to ascertain the truth of disputed facts.

SECTION II. *The Assize in Criminal Trials.*

According to immemorial usage in Scotland, criminal

[1] Irvine *v.* Kilpatrick, before quoted, p. 321.

charges there have always been tried by an assize or jury of fifteen. In the collection of ancient laws and treatises on the laws of Scotland by Skene, in 1609, we are told that " the justice eyre should be holden twice in the year, for it is statute and ordained that the justice and his deputes should have two head courts yearly, universally in all parts, once on the grass, and once on the corn (query, spring and autumn?) both in the inland and also in the isles." The mode of obtaining information and presentment of crimes was called taking up dittay, and this was anciently done in each vill or town, either by authority of the justiciar through an inquest of three credible persons and the headsman of the place (a sort of grand jury), or, as Baron Hume thinks more probable, the charge of conducting the inquisition fell principally on the sheriff and the justice clerk, or his deputies.[1] This was, however, altered in 1587, when a new arrangement of the circuit eyres (or ayres as it is written) was made. It was then provided that there should be appointed by the King's commission so many persons in each shire or burgh, " being known of honest fame," who were to be " constant and continual uptakers of dittay" wherein they might proceed at their discretion, either by sworn inquest or on the information of persons duly sworn, or on their own proper knowledge. Ultimately, however, the method of taking up of dittay was abolished by Stat. 8 Anne, c. 16, which devolved the making of presentments on the justices of peace at quarter sessions, or at meetings to be held by them twice in the year for that special purpose. But in practice this duty has been allowed to fall into the hands of the sheriff, whose office was new modelled in 1748, and he has the obligation imposed upon him of inquiring into the circumstances of every crime committed in his sher-

---

[1] See Hume's Comment. on the Criminal Law of Scotland, II. 23.

iffdom as soon as his fiscal or the party lays any complaints before him.

With regard to the assize or trial-jury, the ancient proceeding before them is thus concisely described in Skene's collection: "If the person attached compeers in the court, and being accused has no relevant exception or reasonable defense, of necessity he should pass to the knowledge of an assize, conform to the laws of the realm, at the which time the whole assizors should be called and the absent amerced (Jac. VI. Parl. 11. c. 76). And the party accused should be heard to propose all and sundry his lawful defenses against the whole assizors, or any of them, to repel them, as he may best of the law, and stay them to pass upon his assize."

This and what follows afterwards respecting the trial and verdict, is substantially the same as the practice at the present day, which we now proceed to consider. But first as to the jurors of assize.

The sheriff of each county makes up a roll or list of persons within his county duly qualified to serve as jurors, whose names are inserted in a book, called The General Jury-Book, which is open to the inspection of any person on the payment of one shilling.[1] After this list has been entered in the General Jury-Book, the sheriff selects from it the names of all persons qualified to be special jurors, and enters them in another book, called The Special Jury-Book, which is also open to inspection on payment of the same fee. When the day of trial arrives, the jury, whose number is fifteen, are chosen by ballot out of an assize, which in general contains forty-five names, taken

---

[1] The jury-process in criminal cases in Scotland is now regulated by 6 Geo. IV. c. 22. The qualification of a common juror is an estate of inheritance in land of the yearly value of £5, or personal property to the extent of £100. This was fixed by Stat. 6 Ann. c. 26. Butchers are excluded from serving (See Bell's Dict. of the Law of Scotland). It is a popular notion that tney can not act as jurymen in criminal trials in England, but this is a mistake.

from the two lists. One-third of the jury are chosen from the special, and two-thirds from the common list.[1] Each prisoner, and the prosecutor also, is entitled to challenge five jurors peremptorily, that is, without assigning any reason; and any number, if he can show good legal cause for so doing. Of the five special jurors, however, not more than two can be peremptorily challenged by either the prisoner or the prosecutor.

A landed proprietor, or landed man, as he is called in the Scotch law, has a right to be tried by a jury the majority of whom are landed men. To entitle him, however, to this privilege he must have been infeft in lands, and it can not be claimed by one who is merely the eldest son or heir-apparent of a landed proprietor. By a late statute (11 and 12 Vict. c. 78), it is enacted that one list of assize or jurors shall be sufficient for the trial of all accused parties at each "diet" or each circuit court during its sittings.

After the jury have been duly balloted for, and have taken their places in the box, they are sworn by the clerk of court in the terms of the following oath:

"You fifteen swear by Almighty God, and as you shall answer to God at the great day of judgment, you will truth say and no truth conceal,[2] in so far as you are to pass on this assize."

By a recent statute (11 and 12 Vict. c. 79, 1848) the prisoner (or, as he is called in Scotland, "panel") must be called upon to state any objection he may have to the relevancy, *i.e.*, legal sufficiency of the "libel" (corres-

---

[1] In former times the presiding judge nominated the jury of fifteen from the forty-five persons contained in the list of assize.

[2] These words, "and no truth conceal," have evident reference to the fact, that the jury formerly proceeded upon their own knowledge of the case, and were witnesses as well as triers. We may compare with this the ne nænne sacne forhelan, which was part of the old Anglo-Saxon oath, as has been previously noticed.

ponding to our indictment),[1] and the question of relevancy must be disposed of by the court before he is called upon to plead Guilty or Not Guilty; "and in case the

[1] The term indictment is not unknown to the Scotch law. Libels in fact are of two kinds, either "indictments" or "criminal letters." The former are in use only in the High Court of Justiciary, and are signed by the Lord Advocate or his deputy. They are in form addressed to the prisoner. The latter to which the term libel is usually applied, are used in the Circuit Courts of Justiciary and Sheriff's Courts, and like English indictments speak of the prisoner in the third person.

The libel is in a syllogistic form. The major premiss consists of the general allegation, that the offense with which the prisoner is charged is in its nature a crime against the law, and the minor is the assertion that the prisoner committed that offense.

HERCULES JAMES ROBERTSON, ESQUIRE, ADVOCATE, SHERIFF OF RENFREWSHIRE, To   Officers of Court, jointly and severally hereby specially constituted:—WHEREAS, it is humbly meant and complained to me by ROBERT WYLIE, Writer in Paisley, and ROBERT RODGER, Writer there, joint Procurators Fiscal of the Sheriff Court of Renfrewshire, acting for the Upper Ward of said Shire, for the public interest, upon PETER M'KELLAR, now or lately gamekeeper, and now or lately residing at or near Broom, in the Parish of Mearns and Shire of Renfrew: THAT ALBEIT, by the laws of this and of every other well-governed realm, ASSAULT, especially when committed to the injury of the person, and by a person who has been previously convicted of Assault, is a crime of an heinous nature, and severely punishable: YET TRUE IT IS AND OF VERITY, that the said Peter M'Kellar is guilty of the said crime aggravated as aforesaid, actor, or art and part, IN SO FAR AS, on the
                Seventh day of June, Eighteen Hundred and Fifty, or on one or other of the days of that month, or of May immediately preceding, or of the bypast days of July immediately following, and within or near a pasture field at or near the mansion house of Broom, in the Parish of Mearns aforesaid, then and now or lately possessed by Allan Pollock, junior, residing there, and seventy or thereby yards from the said mansion-house, the said Peter M'Kellar did, wickedly and feloniously, attack and assault John Lennox, bleacher, now or lately residing at or near Hazleden, in the Parish of Mearns aforesaid, and did with a stick or other similar weapon, strike him on the breast and across the knees, or other parts of his body, and did knock him twice to the ground, and the said John Lennox having got up and proceeded towards the road or pathway leading from the said mansion-house of Broom to the porter's lodge of Broom, situated at or near the old Kilmarnock road, the said Peter M'Keller did, time aforesaid, upon or near

libel shall be found relevant the same shall be read, unless such reading shall be dispensed with by the panel; and the panel shall then be called upon to plead to the

> the said road or pathway from the mansion-house of Broom aforesaid, and three hundred and twelve yards or thereby distant from the said mansion-house, in the Parish of Mearns aforesaid, again, wickedly and feloniously, attack and assault the said John Lenox, and did, with a stick, or other similar weapons, strike him repeatedly on the left shoulder and arms, or other parts of his body; by all which the said John Lenox was hurt, bruised, and injured in his person; and the said Peter M'Kellar has been previously convicted of assault; And the said Peter M'Kellar having been apprehended and taken before John Willox, Esquire, one of her Majesty's Justices of the Peace for Renfrewshire, did, in his presence, at Pollokshaws, on the
>   Eighth day of June, Eighteen Hundred and Fifty,
> emit and subscribe a Declaration; and the said Peter M'Kellar having thereafter been taken before John Dunn, Esquire, one of my Substitutes, did, in his presence at Paisley, on the said
>   Eighth day of June, Eighteen Hundred and Fifty,
> emit and subscribe another Declaration: WHICH DECLARATIONS, as also a medical report or certificate, bearing to be dated "Pollokshaws, 8th June, 1850," and to be signed "Thos. Corbett, Surgeon," as also an extract or certified copy of a conviction for the crime of assault, obtained against the said Peter M'Kellar, before the Sheriff Court of Argyleshire, at Inverary, on the
>   Eleventh day of June, Eighteen Hundred and Forty-two,
> as also extracts or certified copies of three several convictions for the crime of assault, obtained against the said Peter M'Keller, before the Sheriff Court of Stirlingshire at Stirling, on the
>   Twentieth day of May, Eighteen Hundred and Forty-five,
> Thirteenth day of September, Eighteen Hundred and Forty-five, and
>   Thirty-first day of January, Eighteen Hundred and Forty-eight,
> respectively, as also an extract or certified copy of a conviction for the crime of assault, obtained against the said Peter M'Kellar, before the Justice of Peace Court of Renfrewshire at Johnstone, on the
>   Sixteenth day of April, Eighteen Hundred and Forty-nine,
> as also an extract or certified copy of a conviction for the crime of assault, obtained against the said Peter M'Kellar, before the Justice of Peace Court of Renfrewshire, at Pollokshaws, on the
>   Fourth day of May, Eighteen Hundred and Fifty,
> being to be used in evidence against the said Peter M'Kellar at his trial, will, for that purpose, be in due time lodged in the hands of the Clerk of Court, in order that he may have an opportunity of seeing the same: ALL WHICH, or part thereof being found proven by the verdict of an Assize, or admitted

libel, and in case he shall plead Guilty the court shall proceed to pass sentence, and in case he shall plead Not Guilty the court shall remit him, with the libel as found relevant, to the knowledge of an assize, and the case shall be otherwise proceeded with in ordinary form."

Formerly the prisoner was called upon to plead first, and he was then asked by the judge whether he had any objection to offer to the relevancy of the libel. In England and Ireland he first pleads, and if there is a fatal error on the face of the indictment, he may take advantage of it at any stage of the proceedings either before conviction, or afterwards in arrest of judgment, or after judgment by writ of error. If before, the judge determines it at the time,[1] or reserves it in his discretion for the consideration of the Court of Criminal Appeal, lately instituted by the Act 11 and 12 Vict. c. 78. If after, the only resource is to bring a writ of error upon the judgment, provided the objection appears upon the record, that is, the face of the indictment;—for if not, as has been before mentioned, the prisoner has no right after a verdict of Guilty to have the question considered. But in any case where the objection appears on the face of the record, the prisoner is entitled to a writ of error, even although the judge at the trial refuses to reserve

---

by the judicial confession of the said Peter M'Kellar, in a court to be held by me or my Substitute, the said Peter M'Keller OUGHT to be punished with the pains of law, to deter others from committing the like crimes in all times coming.

HEREFORE, &c.

[1] By the most wholesome provision of an Act passed in the present year, 1851 (14 and 15 Vict. c. 100), the court at any criminal trial in England or Ireland may amend variances between the indictment and evidence offered in proof thereof in matters not material to the merits of the case, and by which the accused can not be prejudiced in his defense ; and it may then either proceed with or postpone the trial to be had before the same or another jury, as the court shall think reasonable. Section 24 of this Act prevents in future indictments from being held insufficient for certain trivial defects and omissions, in the section specified.

the point, and determines it against him. And this writ of error is brought in and the case argued before the Court of Queen's Bench, and if the judgment there is unfavorable it may be carried to the House of Lords, whose judgment, as being that of the Supreme Court of Appeal in the kingdom, is final and irreversible. Moreover, it is now enacted that if on a writ of error brought in any criminal case, the Court of Error shall reverse the judgment, it shall be competent either to pronounce the proper judgment, or remit the record to the court below, in order that such court may pronounce the proper judgment.[1]

In Scotland the interlocutory judgment given upon the question of relevancy is final; and after conviction no objection to the libel can be received in arrest of judgment; for the time for making such objection is when the relevancy of the libel is under consideration.[2] This is surely an improvement upon the English practice.

When the assize has been once sworn, they must, as in England, be kept by themselves apart, and no extraneous intercourse whatever is allowed. In the case of any sudden interruption from unavoidable accident, as the illness of a juryman or the prisoner, there can be no adjournment, nor any continuation of the trial with the same assize, but the jury must be discharged, and a new jury balloted on a subsequent occasion from the same assize to try the case afresh.[3]

Having heard the whole of the evidence, and the summing up of the judge, and chosen their chancellor or foreman, the jury are inclosed to consider their verdict. An act passed in the year 1587, directs that "the clerk

---

[1] 11 and 12 Vict. c. 78, § 5.
[2] For an account of the interlocutor of relevancy, see Baron Hume's Commentaries, II. 285; and the trial of Carnegie, in the year 1728, for the murder of the Earl of Strathmore. 17 State Tr. 134.
[3] Alison's Crim. Law, II. 631.

of the Justiciarie sall enclose the said assyse them alane, or in ane house by thamselfis, and suffer na personen to be present with thame or repair to thame in ony wyse, nather clerke nor utheris, under pretense of farder informatioun, resolving of ane dout, or ony uther culler or occasion qhatsumever. But that the said hous be holden fast, and na man present thairin bot the said assaisirs (assizors), and that they be not sufferit to cume out of the said hous for qhatsumever caus, or to continew the geving of their sentence to an uther tyme ; bot that they be inclosit as said is, unto the tyme they be fully agreit, and returne thair answir be the mouth of the said chancellair to the judge."

The assize must remain inclosed, as directed by the act, until a majority have agreed upon their verdict. Formerly this must have been delivered in writing, but the frequent escape of guilty parties in consequence of inaccuracies in the mode of framing the verdict, and the rule that no parol statement of the jury could be received to explain their meaning, led to the passing of an act, 54 Geo. III. c. 57, which provided that where the jury was unanimous a viva voce verdict might be given. This was followed by 6 Geo. IV. c. 22, which enacted that all verdicts in criminal cases, whether the jury are unanimous or not, shall be returned by the mouth of the chancellor of the jury, unless when the court shall direct written verdicts to be returned. This statute also provides, that in all cases of verdicts being returned by the mouth of the chancellor, when the jury are not unanimous in their verdict, the chancellor shall announce the same, so that an entry thereof may be made in the record. And soon afterwards an act was passed (9 Geo. IV. c. 29), which provides that verdicts in writing shall be discontinued in all cases where the verdict is returned before the court adjourns.

A written verdict therefore in practice is now quite

obsolete, but formerly in such a case the chancellor from the jury-box, in the presence of his fellow-jurors and in open court, delivered the verdict sealed to the presiding judge. The latter opened it, and, after reading it, handed it to the clerk, who engrossed it verbatim on the record.[1]

A written verdict could in no case be altered, amended, or varied: but a parol verdict may be explained, and its legal import discussed, between the court and the jury before it is finally recorded. This obviates many difficulties, and furthers the ends of justice, which was frequently defeated by technical objections taken to the mode in which the jury had expressed their verdict in writing. Where, however, a written verdict was delivered, the jurors present might declare that it was not their verdict, or that it contained a material omission or error. This they might prove by their oaths; but they could not object to the verdict as having been irregularly and improperly obtained from them.

According to the present usage the jury are asked by the clerk if they are agreed upon their verdict, and the chancellor (*i.e.* foreman) then announces it aloud. It is in general either "Guilty;" or "Not Guilty;" or "Not Proven." It may however be a special verdict, finding certain charges proven and the remainder not proven.

With reference to the question of the efficiency of trial by jury in Scotland, Mr. Alison thinks that the qualification of jurors is too low, and that they are hardly equal to the due discharge of their important functions. He says "The qualification of £200 for an ordinary juryman has been found both in the civil and criminal courts, to have brought a class into the jury-box incapable, in a great variety of cases, of understanding the intricate and important questions which are submitted to them for decision. They become utterly confounded, in particular, if the pro-

---

[1] Alison's Crim. Law, II. 639.

ceedings are protracted to any considerable length, and, after four or five hours' attention to the evidence, are generally guided by the most able speech which is addressed to them on its import. Verdicts in consequence, both in the civil and criminal courts, have become much more uncertain than formerly; and the opinion has extensively spread among practical men, that if you can only protract the proceedings to a certain length, or the case is one of any considerable intricacy, little reliance can be placed on the verdict of the jury being conformable to the evidence which has been laid before them."[1]

[1] Alison's Crim. Law of Scotland, II. 385.

In England and Wales the total number of persons committed in 1850 for alleged offenses was 26.813. The result of the proceedings consequent thereon was as follows:

Not prosecuted and admitted evidence	141	
No Bills found against	1,458	
Not Guilty on Trial	4,639	
Acquitted and Discharged		6,238
Acquitted on the ground of Insanity	26	
Found Insane	12	
Detained in Custody		38
Sentenced to Death	49	
" Transportation	2,578	
" Imprisonment	17,602	
" Whipping, Fine, &c.	307	
Pardoned without sentence	1	
Convicted		20,537
Total Committed		26,813

With respect to the question of the greater certainty of convictions following commitments, the tendency during the last five years to a decrease in the proportion acquitted is confirmed by the Returns for 1850. In the three years ending with 1845 the proportion was stationary at 28·6 per cent.; for the five subsequent years it has been, in 1846, 27·6 per cent.; in 1847, 25·1 per cent.; in 1848, 24·4 per cent.; in 1849, the same; and in 1850, 23·2 per cent. The proportion in 1850 is comprised of 0·5 per cent. discharged by reason of no prosecution, including those admitted evidence, 5·4 discharged, no Bill being found; and 17·3 acquitted and discharged on trial by the petty jury. This increase, says Mr. Redgrave, of the Home

282   THE JURY SYSTEM IN SCOTLAND.   [CH.

SECTION III. *The Verdict of Not Proven.*

It is a peculiarity of the Scotch jury system in criminal trials that it admits a verdict of Not Proven, corresponding to the Non Liquet of the Roman law. The legal effect of this is equivalent to Not Guilty; for a prisoner in whose case it is pronounced can not be tried again. According to the homely but expressive maxim of the law, no man can be made to "thole an assize" twice. It is worth considering whether it is advisable to retain in Scotland or introduce in England this kind of verdict. Sir Walter Scott applied to it the term "bastard," and I think this not unaptly describes its nature. It is, in fact, a sort of compromise between

Office, who compiled the Tables, in the proportion convicted, appears coincident with the diminished severity of the punishments inflicted. In 1850, of those convicted one in 419 only had judgment of death passed or recorded against them, and one in 79 alone was sentenced to transportation.

In Scotland, the total number of persons committed for trial, or bailed, in 1850, was 4,468, with the following results:

Discharged without Trial by the Lord Advocate and his Deputies	660
Discharged from other causes	163
Not Guilty on Trial	35
Not Proven on Trial	223
Found Insane	6
Total Discharged or Acquitted	1,087
Convicted	3,363
Outlawed	18
Total	4,468

In Ireland, the total number of persons committed in 1850 was 31 326 Of these 14,218 were acquitted, and 17,108 convicted.

conflicting opinions, and affords a convenient refuge where the mind is in doubt as to the effect of evidence. It can not be denied that such a verdict correctly in-

Comparative Table, showing the Number of Convictions and Acquittal Ireland for Seven Years, with the rate per cent. of each on the ? Number of Offenses.

YEARS.	Convicted.	Acquitted.	Total.	Rate per cent.	
				Convicted.	Acquitted.
1844..	8,042	11,406	19,448	41·35	58·65
1845..	7,101	9,595	16,696	42·53	57·47
1846..	8,639	9,853	18,492	46·72	53·28
1847..	15,223	15,976	31,209	48·81	51·19
1848..	18,206	20,316	38,522	47·26	52·74
1849..	21,202	20,787	41,989	50·49	49·5
1850.	17,108	14,218	31,326	54·61	45·39

Considered as to the class of crime, the following are the results:

Class.	Convicted.	Acquitted.
1. Offenses against person	38.31	61.69
2. Offenses against property with violence.	47.52	52.48
3. Offenses against property without violence	61.27	38.73
4. Malicious offenses against property	49.78	50.22
5. Forgery and offenses against currency	49.60	50.40
6. Miscellaneous offenses	37.99	62.01

With reference to this subject, it will be interesting to cite what Quetelet, a writer of great eminence, says of the operation of trial by jury in Belgium. The following extract is translated from his work, Sur la Théorie des Probabilités, published in 1846. We must bear in mind, that the jury in criminal cases was not adopted in Belgium until 1830; and Quetelet begins by quoting a passage from a work written by him in 1829:

"'In 1826 our tribunals condemned 84 individuals out of 100 accused, and the French tribunals 65: the English tribunals have also condemned 65 per cent. during the last twenty years. Thus, out of 100 accused, 16 only have been acquitted with us, and 35 in France, as in England. These two latter countries, so different in manners and in laws, however, pro-

dicates the result at which we arrive in cases where some crime has been committed, and circumstances of grave suspicion, which yet do not amount to proof, point to a particular person as the perpetrator. And we are often justified in holding this opinion even where the verdict of Not Guilty has been given. We thereby mean to imply that the fact of the innocence of the accused is not established to our satisfaction, while, on the other hand, we can not say that we are convinced of his guilt. And this state of mind occurs with reference to many things which do not readily, if at all, admit of demonstration. The verdict of Not Proven, would, perhaps, correctly express

nounce in the same manner on the fate of the unfortunate submitted to their judgments; whilst our kingdom, so similar to France by its institutions, acquits a half less of the accused. Should the cause of this difference be sought in the fact, that we have not the institution of the jury, which our neighbors have? We think it is so.

"'Let us examine, in fact, what is passing before the correctional tribunals where the judges only give sentence, as in our tribunals. We shall find in France the same severity as with us. Of 100 accused only 16 are acquitted.

"'Let us examine the tribunals of police simply,—the same severity; of 100 accused, only 14 are acquitted. The preceding will lead us, then, to the conclusion, that when 100 accused come before the tribunals, whether criminal or correctional. or simple police, 16 will be acquitted if they have to be dealt with by judges, and 35 if they have to be dealt with by a jury.'

"Such were the conclusions I came to from the first statistical documents on crime which were published in France and Belgium. I did not then know that the following year would realize my conjectures in the most brilliant manner. The revolution of 1830 detached Belgium from the kingdom of the Netherlands, and gave it the institution of the jury. Immediately the acquittals took the same course as in France.

"The chances of acquittal for one accused were then doubled in Belgium by the sole fact of the institution of the jury; and of 100 accused, 16 who would have been condemned by the system in operation anterior to 1830, were returned to society. Is this a benefit? is it an evil? I confine myself to giving over this remarkable fact to the meditation of the legislator."

the opinion of many as to the existence of apparitions, or the alleged facts of animal magnetism. We feel disinclined to believe them, and yet the evidence for them is so strong that it seems almost impossible to explain them on the hypothesis of either imposture or delusion.

Now, if by the verdict of not guilty a jury were understood affirmatively to declare that, they in their consciences believed the prisoner to be innocent of the crime imputed to him, it is clear that they could only pronounce it where they had no moral doubt on the question, and must in other cases, where this doubt was felt, resort to some such mode of expression as "not proven," to indicate the effect of the evidence upon their minds. But this is not the meaning of "not guilty." It does not necessarily imply more than that the legal evidence is not sufficient to produce that degree of certainty which would justify or render safe a conviction. And a proof of this is furnished by the fact, that this verdict is returned in cases where the guilt of the accused is notorious, but owing to some technical difficulty or mistake the jury are directed to acquit. They do not thereby say that he has not committed the crime, but merely that it is not legally proved that he has. There is, therefore, nothing in the verdict which need alarm the most scrupulous conscience, for it may be, and, indeed, ought to be, given whenever a jury is not fully and beyond all reasonable doubt satisfied of the guilt of the accused. And we must remember that the law presumes every man to be innocent who is not proved to be guilty, so that the jury do no more than their strict duty when they declare him to be not guilty whom the evidence falls short of convicting, however dark and unfavorable may be their suspicions respecting him.

Such, then, being the case with respect to the verdict

of Not Guilty, it is not difficult to show that there are grave objections against that of Not Proven. In the first place, it favors too much the natural indolence of the human mind, which thus escapes the necessity of coming to a definite conclusion upon doubtful facts. There must be always a strong temptation to adopt it where there is much suspicion, but a deficiency of legal proof. But is this fair towards the accused? Surely if the evidence does not establish the charge against him, he is entitled to an absolute acquittal. But although the verdict of "Not Proven" is so far tantamount to an acquittal, that the party can not be tried a second time, it falls very far short of it with regard to the effect upon his reputation and character. He goes away from the bar of the court with an indelible stigma upon his fame. One hardly sees how he can afterwards hold up his head amongst his fellow-men, when there stands recorded against him the opinion of a jury, that the evidence respecting his guilt was so strong that they did not dare to pronounce a verdict of acquittal. So that many of the evil consequences of a conviction follow, although the jury refuse to convict. When Sir Nicholas Throckmorton was tried and acquitted by an English jury in the first year of Mary's reign, he said, "It is better to be tried than to live suspected." But in Scotland a man may be not only tried but acquited, and yet live suspected, owing to the sinister influence of a "Not Proven" verdict. This is a state of things which ought not to exist. It occasions too much peril to innocence, when, as often happens, circumstances have woven a dark web of suspicion around it. For it may be feared that a jury will too readily resort to such a verdict where they find a difficulty in coming to a definite conclusion. At the same time it must be admitted that there are cases in which a jury, even where they can not convict, are almost justified in recording their sense of the impression which the evidence has left upon their minds. Such was the famous trial in Scotland, in 1839, of the soi-dissant Earl of Stirling, charged with having forged, and knowingly uttered as forged, certain documents in support of his claim to the peerage. The unanimous verdict in that case of Proven as to several of the documents being forgeries, and by a majority Not Proven as to the prisoner having forged them, or uttered them knowing them to be forged, was a merciful one, of which, I think, the accused could have no reason to complain, especially after Lord Meadowbank's charge to the jury. That learned judge said:

"Gentlemen, the prisoner may have been the dupe in all these transactions, and so his counsel, I think, endeavored to persuade you that he had been. This is possible, no doubt; but we have only an ingenious surmise in support of the proposition, while you have it clearly made out, that the only person who enjoyed the fruits of the imposition is the prisoner himself, and but one very trifling piece of evidence that can be alleged to support the theory of the learned counsel. . . . Our business is to do justice, and you in particular have to weigh the evidence calmly and deliberately; and, should you doubt of that evidence being sufficient to bring the charges here made home to the prisoner, to give him the full benefit of that doubt. But to entitle you to do so, these doubts must be well considered, and the circumstances on which they are founded deliberately weighed. To doubts that are not reasonable you have no right whatsoever to yield. You are not entitled to require at the hand of the prosecutor direct proof of the facts laid in his charge. In no case can such be exacted. The circumstances laid in evidence must be put together, and it is your duty then to consider what is the rational and reasonable inference to be drawn from the whole of them

—in short, whether it be possible to explain them upon grounds consistent with the innocence of the party accused; or whether, on the contrary, they do not necessarily lead to a result directly the reverse."

CHAPTER XIV.

JURIES IN THE UNITED STATES.

BY Article III. of the Constitution of the United States of America, it is provided that "The trial of all crimes, except in the cases of impeachment, shall be by jury, and such trial shall be held in the state where the said crimes shall have been committed; but, when not committed within any state, the trial shall be at such place or places as the Congress may by law have directed.

And Article V. of the Amendments to the Constitution enacts, that "No person shall be held to answer for a capital or otherwise infamous crime, unless on a presentment or indictment of a grand jury, except in cases arising in the land or naval forces, or in the militia when in actual service in time of war or public danger; nor shall any person be subject for the same offense to be twice put in jeopardy of life or limb."

By Article VI.: "In all criminal prosecutions the accused shall enjoy the right to a speedy and public trial by an impartial jury of the state and district wherein the crime shall have been committed."

By these enactments trial by jury in criminal cases was embodied in, and made part and parcel of, the Constitution of the United States when they broke off from, and established their independence of, the mother-country. But it is somewhat remarkable that the original Articles are wholly silent on the subject of trial by jury in civil actions—a principle of jurisprudence so familiar to the Anglo-Saxon mind, that we might have supposed it would be deemed an essential element in the fundamental laws of the new republic. And this omission was eagerly seized on by the enemies of the constitution as a handle for attack. They argued that silence upon this point, coupled with the language of the original Articles, that "the supreme court shall have appellate jurisdiction, both as to law and fact," was equivalent to a proof that the abolition of the civil jury was intended; and a long and vigorous controversy arose upon the subject. The view of those who, while the plan of the Constitution was under discussion, contended that omission amounted to abolition, was ably combated in "The Federalist," in a paper which the late Mr. Justice Story describes as a monument of admirable reasoning and exalted patriotism.[1] The real fact was, that the diversity of the institutions on this point, of the different states that composed the Union, induced, if it did not compel, the eminent men who framed the Constitution, to leave the subject to the discretion of Congress. The writer in "The Federalist" maintained that trial by jury was in no case abolished by the Constitution, and that in controversies between individuals the institution would remain precisely in the situation in which it was placed by the constitutions of the different federal states. He pointed out the great variety in the forms of judicial procedure which existed in those states, and said: "From this sketch it appears that there is a material diversity, as well in the modification as in the extent of the institution of trial by jury in civil cases in the several states; and from this fact these obvious reflections flow; first, that no general rule could have been fixed upon by the convention which would have corresponded with the circumstances of all the states; and, secondly, that more, or at least as much, might have been hazarded by taking

[1] Commentaries on the Const. III. 633.

the system of any one state for a standard, as, by omitting a provision altogether, and leaving the matter, as has been, to legislative regulation." After stating his conviction that there were many civil cases in which trial by jury was ineligible, and pointing out the difficulties in the way of establishing it, the writer says, "The best judges of the matter will be the least anxious for a constitutional establishment of the trial by jury in civil cases, and will be the most ready to admit that the changes which are continually happening in the affairs of society may render a different mode of determining questions of property preferable in many cases in which that mode of trial now prevails."

Notwithstanding, however, these reasons, public opinion was not satisfied, and various state conventions proposed different plans for the adoption of some general rule on the subject. The result was, that in the first session of Congress, the following amended article was proposed and carried, and is incorporated into the constitution: "In suits at common law, where the value in controversy shall exceed twenty dollars, the right to trial by jury shall be preserved. And no fact tried by a jury shall be otherwise re-examined in any court of the United States than according to the rules of the common law." "This," says Mr. Justice Story, "is a most important and valuable amendment, and places upon the high ground of constitutional right the inestimable privilege of a trial by jury in civil cases—a privilege scarcely inferior to that in criminal cases, which is conceded by all to be essential to political and civil liberty."[1] And, on one occasion, the supreme court, in pronouncing judgment on an appeal in a civil suit, observed: "The trial by jury is justly dear to the American people. It has always been an object of deep interest and solicitude, and every encroachment upon it has

[1] Story's Commentaries, III. 638.

been watched with great jealousy. The right to such a trial is, it is believed, incorporated into, and secured in every state constitution in the Union."[1]

The limits of the present work preclude me from enumerating the minute differences in the jury systems of the different states; but I may here mention a few of the leading principles enunciated by the federal constitutions. Most of them declare that the right of trial by jury shall remain inviolate. That of New Jersey provides that the legislature may authorize the trial of civil suits, when the matter does not exceed fifty dollars, by a jury of six men. In Connecticut, Indiana, and Mississippi, the jury are empowered, in all prosecutions or indictments for libels, to determine the law and the facts under the direction of the court, and the truth of the alleged libel may be given in evidence. In New Hampshire the constitution provides, that the legislature may make such regulations as will prevent parties from having as many trials by jury in the same suit or action as had before been allowed and practiced, and extends the civil jurisdiction of justices of the peace to trials of suits where the sum demanded in damages does not exceed four pounds. One article is as follows: "In order to reap the fullest advantage of the inestimable privilege of the trial by jury, great care ought to be taken that none but qualified persons should be appointed to serve; and such ought to be fully compensated for their travel, time, and attendance." The constitution of Maryland declares, that in controversies respecting property, and in suits between man and man, the ancient trial by jury is preferable to any other, and ought to be held sacred. That of Missouri provides that, in prosecutions for crimes, slaves shall not be deprived of an impartial trial by jury.[2] I do not find this humane and equitable enactment in the constitution of

[1] Story's Commentaries, III. 638.
[2] This was written before the abolition of slavery.

any other slave-holding state. In Tennessee the judges "shall not charge the juries with respect to matters of fact, but may state the testimony and declare the law." In Iowa, whose constitution dates from 1846, the General Assembly may authorize trial by a jury of a less number than twelve in inferior courts. In Wisconsin (1848) a jury trial in civil suits may be waived by the parties, in all cases, in the manner prescribed by law.

Throughout the Union, in all trials, whether civil or criminal, unanimity in the jury is essential. Offenses are brought under the cognizance of a petit jury by the presentment of a grand jury, as in England. The qualification of a juror varies in different states. In New York he must be subject to assessment for personal property belonging to him, or for land in his possession, which he holds under contract for purchase, upon which improvements have been made of the value of one hundred and fifty dollars, or have a freehold estate of the same value. The jury-lists are made up by persons called supervisors in New York, select men in New England, trustees in Ohio, and sheriffs in Louisiana and other states. The differences between the method here and in America of obtaining grand and petit jurors are not of sufficient importance to justify detail in a work like this, which does not profess to be a practical treatise on the law of juries; and I need only refer the reader to the Code of the State of New York, which has lately been there adopted, and where ample and minute information will be found upon the subject of the jury system in that state.[1] I

---

[1] In 1873, the legislature of the State of New York enacted that "the previous formation or expression of an opinion or impression in reference to the circumstances upon which any criminal action at law is based, or in reference to the guilt or innocence of the prisoners, or a present opinion or impression in reference thereto, shall not be a sufficient ground of challenge for principal cause to any person who is otherwise legally qualified to serve as a juror upon the trial of such action: provided the person proposed as a juror, who may have formed or expressed, or has such opinion or impression

may mention, however, that by that code juries de medie-tate linguæ and trials by a jury at the bar of the court, are abolished; also a jury trial may be waived by the consent of both parties in actions arising on obligations, and with the assent of the court in other actions. In such cases the trial of questions of fact is to be had by the court, or, in some cases, by referees, and it is then conducted in the same manner as a trial by the court.

The question of the political and social influence of the jury as one of the institutions of the United States will be noticed hereafter.

as aforesaid, shall declare on oath that he verily believes that he can render an impartial verdict according to the evidence submitted to the jury on such trial, and that such previously formed opinion or impression will not bias or influence his verdict, and provided the court shall be satisfied that the person so proposed as a juror does not entertain such a present opinion as would influence his verdict as a juror."—Laws of N. Y., ch. 475, p. 1133. And see Morgan's Best on the Principles of Evidence, vol. I., p. 38.

CHAPTER XV.

TRIAL BY JURY IN FRANCE AND OTHER PARTS OF THE CONTINENT.

SECTION I. *Trial by Jury in France.*

TRIAL by Jury in France owes its birth to the Revolution of 1789. Prior to that period criminal charges were tried by judges, who decided both law and fact. These sat either singly or collectively, and the preliminary proceedings were carried on in secret; a system of which a more detailed account will be given when we come to speak of it as existing in Germany. This procédure secrète was borrowed from the Inquisition, which was introduced into France in the thirteenth century, not long before the judicial tribunal or parliaments of Paris and Toulouse were established by Philip the Fair. It soon found favor with the judges and lawyers, who were for the most part ecclesiastics, but was, as might be expected, unpopular with the nation; so that more than two centuries elapsed before it became general throughout the kingdom, by virtue of a royal ordinance issued in 1539, at the suggestion of the Chancellor Poyet, who became the victim of his own measure.[1] It will be sufficient here to say, that the system was made an engine of grevious injustice and horrible torture both moral and physical. The latter was only abolished in 1780, a few years before the storm of the first revolution burst over France.

Trial by jury in criminal charges was established in

[1] Meyer, Inst. Judic. liv. iv. c. 14. Bernardi, Orig. de la Legislat. Franc. c. 10. Oudot, Théorie du Jury.

France by a law of the Constitutent Assembly, on the 16th of September, 1791. But it soon became a mockery; for although by a law of 1793 it was enacted, that the extraordinary tribunals there established should proceed only upon the verdict of a jury, they soon, during the reign of terror, became permanent commissions, which dispensed with even the form of a jury, and committed murder by wholesale, refusing even the aid of advocates to the accused. When this frightful period had passed away, trial by jury again emerged, and several modifications were made in the system. By the law of 18 Fructidor, An. VI. it was enacted, that no verdict that was not unanimous should be given sooner than after a deliberation of twenty-four hours.

When Napoleon had determined to furnish a code to France, he caused the draft of his Code d'Instruction Criminelle to be submitted to the different courts throughout the kingdom, in order that their opinions might be ascertained. The number that replied to the invitation was seventy-three. Of these twenty-two declared themselves in favor of the retention of trial by jury, thirty desired its abolition, and twenty-three expressed no definite opinion on the subject. The reasons assigned by the opponents of the system were in substance these: They said that the institution was well enough for the English, who were used to it, but was unsuited to the French character and habits. The laboring population had neither sufficient leisure to serve, nor enlightenment to discharge the duties of jurymen. The middle classes, from whom alone they could be chosen, were averse to undertaking so troublesome an office, and becoming the judges of their fellow-citizens; and carried this feeling so far as to be disposed to acquit even the guilty; so that the consequence would be an impunity for crime.[1]

[1] See Oudot, Théorie du Jury, p. 207.

Napoleon, however, resolved to retain the jury trial, but at the same time took care that the selection of jurors should be, to a certain extent, under the control and influence of the executive. In 1808 he promulgated his Code d'Instruction Criminelle, which embodied the whole of the French criminal law.

There is in France no grand jury or jury of accusation at all. It did exist there from 1791 until 1808, when it was abolished by the Code Napoleon. How, then, was its place supplied, and what is the machinery for bringing to trial those who are suspected of crime? The code delegated this duty upon two different officers, the one the procureur du roi, the other the juge d'instruction. The procureur was to act the part of a public prosecutor attached to the court of the district over which its jurisdiction extended. And it is declared to be the duty of all magistrates and functionaries within that district to inform him of any crime that may be committed of which they have information. He ought, in cases of heinous crime, to repair to the spot, and there collect the evidence as to the fact and mode of its perpetration, examining witnesses and reducing their depositions to writing. He is empowered to order the arrest of the accused, and interrogate him as to his guilt. The evidence thus obtained is all written down, and forms when duly signed the procès-verbal, which is then transmitted, with all the papers and documents in the case, to the juge d'instruction. In each arrondissement there is one of these appointed by the government, and taken from amongst the judges of the civil court, to serve in that capacity for three years. In Paris there are (or were) six of these judges, or, as we may call them, justices. The Code expressly provides, that in the exercise of their functions as a judicial police, these magistrates shall be under the surveillance of the procureur général of the cour royale. In all cases of flagrant and heinous crime they are em powered to act of their own authority, precisely in the same way as the procureurs just mentioned, but may require the presence of the latter to assist them. In other cases, however, they can not proceed without communicating with the procureur, and must act according to his directions.

It is the duty of the juge d'instruction, from time to time, and at least once a week, to report his proceedings to a chambre du conseil, composed of three magistrates, and if they are of opinion, when the whole case is before them, that the accused ought not to be prosecuted, they order him to be discharged, or hand him over to the correctional police, if they think the offense is one that may be dealt with summarily. But if they think that he ought to be put upon his trial before a jury, it is the duty of the procureur then to transmit the whole of the proceedings to the procureur général of the cour royale. This officer must, within five days after receiving the case, make a report thereupon to a section of the cour royale, specially constituted for the purpose, who after duly considering the matter amongst themselves, finally determine whether the accused ought or ought not to be put upon his trial. If they decide in favor of the former course they remit the case to the assize court, and the procureur général draws the indictment or acte d'accusation as it is called, which is a long and rhetorical instrument, more like the inflamed speech of an advocate than a grave judicial document, in which are detailed all the circumstances attending the alleged crime, or, in the language of the Code, "the fact and all the circumstances which may aggravate or diminish the penalty."[1] It concludes with the words:

"In consequence N. is accused of having committed

---

[1] Le fait et toutes les circonstances qui peuvent aggraver ou diminuer la peine.

such a murder, such a theft, or such another crime under such and such circumstances."[1]

Such is an outline of the preliminary process whereby in France a person accused of a crime is brought to trial. And in principle it seems to differ little or not at all from commitments by magistrates in this country, excepting always the important fact, that here such commitments are always submitted to the scrutiny of a grand jury before the trial can take place. There is one kind of proceeding, indeed, in which amongst us the grand jury is dispensed with; and that is where a criminal information has been obtained in the Court of Queen's Bench. But this occurs only in the case of minor offenses, known as misdemeanors—not felonies—and it is never granted without first calling upon the accused to show cause to the contrary. He has the opportunity of denying or explaining the charge against him by affidavit. The whole matter is fully discussed in open court before four of the judges, and a strong case must be made out by the prosecutor before they will allow the usual and ordinary course to be departed from of preferring a bill before a grand jury. It is entirely in their discretion to grant or withhold the rule—that is, order for the information to issue; and it is hardly possible to conceive a tribunal more admirably fitted to determine whether the circumstances of the case are such as to justify the application.

The want of a tribunal corresponding to our grand jury has been strongly felt and deplored by some of the ablest of the French jurists. M. Berenger, the author of some valuable treatises on criminal law and procedure, says,[2] that a jury d'accusation would bestow inestimable

---

[1] En conséquence N. est accusé d'avoir commis tel meurtre, tel vol, ou tel autre crime, avec telle et telle circonstance.

[2] Of the jury, such as it should be in France. Du jury tel qu'il doit être en France.

advantages; the chief of which would be the abolition of secret investigations, which are the disgrace of legislation in France. The witnesses would go before a jury instead of giving their evidence in the private room of a juge d'instruction. The proceedings would be oral and their length curtailed, and the accused would be relieved from a voluminous mass of documents artfully prepared to make out a case of guilt. He adds, that the suppression of the "jury d'accusation" in 1808 rendered it necessary almost to double the judicial staff. It covered France with an army of substitutes, increased the number of justices (juges de première instance), and of assistants and deputies of the procureurs généraux; and, in short, so complicated the machine of justice, as to cripple and impede all its movements.

M. Oudot, in his "Théorie du Jury," fully adopts these sentiments, and declares his opinion that a "jury d'accusation" is the sole means of preserving innocent persons from accusations the object of which is to gratify party spirit and malevolence. Alluding to its original institution in 1791, and suppression by Napoleon in 1808, he quotes the following passage from Berenger: "The jury of accusation was dreaded as an obstacle to despotism, the elements of which were being prepared, and this shade which it caused ought to render it dear to the friends of liberty."[1]

With respect to the trial jury some modifications and changes took place in the provisions of the Code, between the time when it was published, in 1808, by Napoleon and the revolution of February, 1848. The system in France was until the overthrow of the monarchy at the latter period, substantially as follows.

According to the Code no one could discharge the office

---

[1] On redoutait le jury d'accusation comme un obstacle au despotisme dont on preparait les éléments, et cet ombrage qu'il causait doit le rendre cher aux amis de la liberté.

of juror who was not thirty years old, and in full possession of civil rights. Persons seventy years of age were excused, if they so desired. It is curious that in the Code Napoleon the liability to serve as a juryman is treated as a privilege or right conferred, while with us it is looked upon as a burden from which persons are glad to claim exemption. But the explanation of this is, I think, not difficult. In England we are so habituated by the experience of centuries to the system, that the proceedings are regarded almost with indifference, and our faith in the perfect fairness of criminal trials is so profound, that it never occurs to any one to imagine that he can individually advance the cause of justice, or is called upon to protect his fellow-countryman, when accused, by serving upon the jury that is to try him. We look upon the summons to attend as jurymen as a disagreeable interruption of our private avocations, being entirely satisfied that the prisoner will be justly, as well as mercifully dealt with under the care of the presiding judge, whoever may compose the jury. But in France this mode of trial was a novelty. It imparted a sense of dignity and power to be called upon to adjudicate upon questions of life and liberty, and to exercise functions which had hitherto been confined to judges and parliaments. This raised the participator in such a right, not only in his own estimation, but in that of his fellow-citizens, and consequently the office was felt to be a distinction and an honor.

According to the Code, the right of acting as jurors was confined to the members of the electoral colleges— that is, those who enjoyed the electoral franchise, which was then of a limited nature—and certain other functionaries and persons whose status afforded a presumptive assurance of respectability and character—such as retired military and naval officers, physicians, licentiates of law, and notaries.

The principal changes that have been introduced into the system since the revolution of February, 1848, are contained in the law of the 7th of August in that year, and are as follows. The primary lists of jurors include all Frenchmen not being employed in domestic service, who are thirty years old, and in the possession of civil and political rights; but it is an essential qualification that they are able to read and write. And the law excludes bankrupts, and persons who for any crime have been sentenced to more than one year's imprisonment, except in the case of political offenses, where conviction does not entail this consequence, unless it is so expressly stated in the sentence. Also state officers, public functionaries, priests, and national schoolmasters. Persons of the age of seventy years, and workmen or laborers who live by daily toil, and can prove that the service would be too burdensome to them, are excused if they so desire. The primary lists are prepared by the mayors of districts, and finally made up and completed by the 15th of September each year. On or before the 1st of November, each mayor sends his list to the prefect, who forms out of them a general list for the department over which he presides. Smaller lists are them made from the general one, not by the prefect, but by a commission consisting of local officers of each district; and these, together with a reserve list, are sent by the prefect to the assize courts of his department. From them, ten days before an assize commences, the president of the court draws openly by lot the names of thirty-six persons, and six supplemental ones, to form the jury panel for the assize.

Each person thus chosen by lot receives due notice to attend on a fixed day, but, except in the case of extraordinary assizes, or, as we should call them, special commissions, no one is obliged to serve on juries at more than one assize each year. At the time of trial the names are thrown into a box or urn, and twelve are ballotted for to compose the jury. Both the prisoner and the procureur général have each the right of peremptory challenge, until only twelve names remain, and they are not allowed to declare the grounds on which they object to any of those whom they challenge;[1] the words of the law being, "Neither the prisoner nor his counsel, nor the procurer-general, will be allowed to expose their motives for the objection."[2]

The course of procedure at the trial is as follows:[3]

The president, at the sitting of the court, addressing the jury, says, "You swear and promise before God and man to examine with the most scrupulous attention the charges which shall be brought against N, and that you will not betray either the interests of the accused, nor those of society which accuses him; that you will not communicate with any one until after the delivery of your verdict (déclaration), nor listen to hatred or malevolence, nor to fear or affection; that you will decide according to the charge and the kind of defense, following the dictates of your conscience and your sincere conviction, with the impartiality and firmness which befit men who are just and free." Each of the jurors is then separately called upon by the president to take the oath, which he does by raising his hand, and saying the words "Je le jure." After the evidence both for and against the prisoner has been heard, the president sums up the case, and directs the attention of the jury to the principal points. He then submits to them the question which they have to try in the following terms:

[1] L'accusé, son conseil, ni le procureur général, ne pourront exposer leurs motifs de recusation.

[2] In the above account I have stated the law as it was last settled; but so many and so rapid are the changes that take place in France in this æra of revolutions, that it is hardly possible to know what institution exists there. At present (December, 1851) military despotism seems to have superseded all constitutional liberty. [3] Code d'Instruction Crim. liv. II.

"Is the accused guilty of having committed the crime, with all the circumstances contained in the indictment (acte d'accusation)?"

Or, if in the course of the inquiry, aggravating circumstances have been proved which are not mentioned in the indictment, he asks them in addition the question: "Has the accused committed the crime, with such and such circumstances?" And if the defense consists in asserting the existence of a fact which in the eye of the law justifies the deed, he asks, "Is such a fact proved?"

The president then informs the jury that if a majority of them are of opinion that there are extenuating circumstances in favor of the accused, they are to declare it by stating, "By a majority (we think that) there are extenuating circumstances in favor of the accused." The questions for their consideration are then given to them by the president in writing, as well as a copy of the indictment and original procès-verbal, and they are told by him that they must vote by secret ballot, and if they find the prisoner guilty by a bare majority they must state this in their verdict.

The jury then retire to their room under the guard of an officer, and choose a foreman, or chef des jurés, but, in default of any such choice, the first called into the jury-box by lot acts as foreman. It is his duty to read aloud to his fellow-jurymen the following notice, which is always posted up in the room:

"The law does not require of jurors an account of the means whereby they are convinced. It only prescribes to them rules for their guidance as to the fullness and sufficiency of a proof: it enjoins them to ask themselves, in silence and apart, and seek in the sincerity of their conscience, what impression the proofs brought against the accused, and those for the defense, have made on their reason. The law does not say to them, 'You shall take as true every fact attested by such or such a number of witnesses;' nor, on the other hand, does it say, 'You shall regard as not sufficiently established every proof which shall not consist of such a procés-verbal, such documents, such testimony, or such evidence.' It puts to them only this question, which includes the full extent of their duties: ' Have you a sincere conviction?' It is essential not to forget that the jury are to concern themselves solely with facts; and they fail in their duty when they take into consideration the penal consequences which will follow upon their verdict. Their mission has not for its object the prosecution nor the punishment of offenses; they are called upon simply to decide whether the accused is or is not guilty of the crime with which he is charged."

But notwithstanding these words of excellent advice to jurors as to their duty in bringing in a verdict, it is notorious that they do regard, and are influenced by, the amount of punishment which the law affixes to a crime. Cambacérés declared that "the jury always examine what will be the result of their verdict;"[1] and in a speech in the Chamber of Deputies in 1831, M. Barthe said: " It is said that the jury ought to know nothing but the facts. Before the reality all this theory disappears. The jury are not ignorant of the penalty, and the greater the penalty is, the more difficult it is for them to agree among themselves upon the question against the prisoner which is submitted to them."[2] M. Guizot also expresses the same opinion: " I know that when the jury pronounce a fact crime or delinquency, they think strongly of the penalty which is attached to it."[3] But this is by no means

---

[1] Les jurés examinent toujours quel sera le résultat de leur déclaration.

[2] On dit que les jurés ne doivent connaitre que les faits. Devant la réalité toute cette théorie disparait. Le jury n'ignore pas le peine, il la prend en considération, et plus la peine est grand, plus il est difficile avec lui-meme pour résoudre contre un accusé la question qui lui est soumise.

[3] Je sais que, quand le jury déclare un fait crime ou délit il pense forcement à la peine qui y est attachée.

peculiar to France. It is the instinct of human nature, where the feeling of pity is often stronger than that of stern duty, and especially amongst the class from which jurors in criminal trials are usually taken. The same occurs in England, and must be the case wherever juries exist. And the knowledge of this fact leads to an important practical conclusion. It teaches the lesson that penal laws must not be too severe, so as to revolt the sense of the people; otherwise they will be rendered nugatory by verdicts of acquittal.

The mode in which the jury vote in coming to a decision, is regulated by a law of the 13th of May, 1836, and is as follows. Each juryman receives in turn from the foreman a slip of paper, marked with the stamp of the court, and containing these words; "On my honor and conscience my verdict is......." He is then to fill up the blank space with the word Yes! or No! upon a table so arranged that none of his colleagues can see what he writes, and afterwards hand the paper closed up to the foreman, who is to deposit it in a box kept for the purpose. A similar operation must be gone through on the questions of whether there are extenuating or aggravating circumstances or not; whether the fact admits of legal excuse; and whether the prisoner was competent to distinguish right from wrong when he committed the act. The foreman must next draw out the slips of paper and write down the result, without, however, stating the number of votes on each side, except when there is a majority of only one for a conviction. The slips of paper must then be burnt in the presence of the jury.

The cases in which a new trial must, and those in which it may be granted, have been already noticed in a previous part of the present work.[1]

Such is an outline of the jury system in France; and as regards the trial of ordinary offenses and crimes against

[1] See *ante*, pp. 193, 194.

society, as distinguished from those against the state, it seems to have worked upon the whole well. But great complaints have long been made, and not unjustly, that the influence of the executive has by means of the prefects, who are its creatures, been unduly felt in the selection of jurors. Whatever may have been the form of government in that country since the Revolution of 1789 (and the changes are almost too numerous to reckon), it has always been actually ruled by a bureaucracy, which radiating from the metropolis as a common center, spreads like a net-work over the provinces, and is in immediate and direct dependence upon the state. But even the degree of interference hitherto exercised does not satisfy the present ruler of France. In a pamphlet recently published, which is supposed to have been written with the sanction, if not by the direction, of Prince Louis Napoleon, the author declares that the system must be pushed still further. He says:

"We loudly and at once proclaim that the cause which has overturned everything, constitutions and governments, is the predominance of parliamentary power, and the neglect of the part which executive authority has played and must ever play in France. That part is the primary condition of our national existence, and it can not be overlooked in our political institutions. The constant tendency of royalty in France has been to introduce unity in all things, in the territory, in the organization of the clergy, in the judicial body, in the administration, in the army, in the laws, and to subject everything, in different degrees, to its direction and to its authority."

Juries have not escaped the effects of this all-absorbing spirit of state-meddling, and the consequence is, that they have been generally found pliant instruments to achieve victory for the ministry of the day, in political prosecutions. Every Englishman must have been struck by the facility with which verdicts against the press have been obtained in France, so that even before it was laid prostrate and trampled upon by the iron heel of military despotism, its liberty was in constant jeopardy. It was strange to see the people so eagerly seconding, by convictions, the efforts of governments to silence journals which were hostile to its policy. In 1851, a French jury found a verdict of Guilty against a writer, for advocating, in an argumentative article, the abolition of capital punishments!

On the occasion of the conviction of the newspaper called the "Evénement," one of the other French journals, the "Presse," thus wrote on the 15th of September, 1851:

"The 'Evénement' appeared yesterday before the Court of Assize of the Seine, presided over by M. Perrot de Chezelles. The 'Evénement' was suspended. The responsible editor was condemned to nine months' imprisonment, and 3,000 francs fine. The author of the article, M. F. Victor Hugo, was condemned to 2,000 francs fine, and nine months' imprisonment..... The 'Evénement' will have four of its editors in prison! Where will the Government stop in this path? It will not stop —it can not. The 'Réforme' has been condemned; the 'Peuple' has been condemned; the 'Vote Universel' has been condemned; the 'Presse' has been condemned; the 'Siécle' has been condemned; the 'République' has been condemned: the 'Assemblée National' only escaped condemnation by submission. And then came the turn of the 'National,' of the 'Ordre,' of the 'Gazette de France,' of the 'Journal des Débats,' and of the 'Union'..... Compression is a ball which runs down an inclined plane. It is not journals which are prosecuted, but the liberty of the press. The journals which now applaud or are silent will find this, but it will then be too late..... In a short time we shall be obliged to employ as extracts from inviolable writers (alluding to a quotation given from a pamphlet by Prince Louis Napoleon in 1834) what we dare not write ourselves. Such is the state in which the liberty of the press stands in France on the 15th of September, 1851."

To this it was plausibly answered that the convictions only proved that the journals were unpopular with the public. The "Journal des Debats" said, "It is useless to conceal the fact—we are not popular. Public opinion is in one of those periods of reaction which generally follow popular commotion; the experience and the fear of disorder generally compel it to such extremes. We have no doubt that under the last monarchy the newspaper articles such as are now most severely punished would have been acquitted by the jury..... It is from the great mass of society that our judges are taken. It is not the speech of the public prosecutor that produces the condemnation of a journal; it is the feeling which is abroad. That feeling is now against us." But in the time of the French monarchy verdicts were given against the press which could never have been obtained in England since the Revolution of 1689; and this is only to be explained on two grounds; first, that the government has influence in the selection of jurymen; and, secondly, that freedom of political discussion is neither properly understood, nor sufficiently valued in France.

Such unhappily is that country. With Freedom, Equality, and Fraternity on her lips, she is at heart servile, and worships the idol of power if it only bears a dazzling front, and flatters the national vanity by display and parade. Let one of her own jurists describe what was her real state in 1818, notwithstanding her constitutional charter and liberal institutions; and there is no reason to believe that it is in any degree improved since then. M. Berenger thus writes:

"We are content to place a magnificent frontispiece

before the rubbish of despotism; deceitful monument, whose aspect charms, but freezes with terror when we penetrate into it. Under liberal appearances, with the pompous words, jury, public debates, judicial independence, and individual liberty, we are gradually conducted to the abuse of all these things, and to the contempt of all our rights. An iron rod takes the place of the wand of justice."[1]

The especial want of France is to become habituated to the great Anglo-Saxon principle of self-government. A German writer, in an able review of the jury system lately introduced into his own country, contrasts England with France in this respect, and says, emphatically,[2] "True freedom such as we mean has its home in England, and finds its self-government in its immediate development; it is there that the whole liberty of the nation is built up out of a system of separate liberties;" and he points out that the German character has many close affinities to the English in its feeling of brotherhood and local and family attachments.

In France there is no civil jury. It has been proposed and deliberately rejected.

In 1790, when the whole subject of an organic change in judicial proceedings was under the consideration of the Constituent Assembly, the question of the introduction of jury trial in civil actions was brought forward and duly discussed. Thouret, who acted as the reporter of the committee on that occasion, was strongly opposed to

[1] Nous nous sommes contentes de placer un magnifique frontispiece devant les décombres du despotisme; monument trompeur, dont l'aspect séduit, mais qui glace d'effroi, quand on y pénetre.—Sous des apparences liberales, avec les mots pompeaux des jures, des débats publics, d'independance judiciaire, de liberté individuelle, nous sommes doucement conduits a l'abus de toutes ceschoses et au mépris de tous les droits : une verge de fer nous tient lieu de baton de justice. De la Justice Criminelle en France. 1818.

[2] Gneist, Die Bildung der Geschwornengerichte in Deutschland. (Berlin, 1849).

the project, and declared that it would jeopardize the existence of trial by jury altogether. In this he was warmly supported by Regnier, who said, that if they established it they would expose themselves to the reproaches of future ages, by decreeing a principle of which the execution was impracticable. Robespierre, on the other hand, advocated its adoption—chiefly as a means of counteracting what he called the aristocratic spirit which was beginning to display itself. The Abbe Sieyès had a plan of his own in favor of the scheme, and this he proposed to the Assembly, but without success; and the project was almost unanimously rejected.

In 1793, during the sitting of the Convention, Hérault de Séchelles presented the report of the committee which had, like that of the Constituent Assembly, been appointed to take into consideration judicial reform, and they declared that they were adverse to the institution of the jury in civil causes. Barrére and other speakers opposed this view, and spoke in favor of its introduction; but Robespierre now gave it only a faint support, and proposed that the question should be adjourned. Couthon called the idea of a jury in civil cases merely a fine dream, and caricatuted the system as absurd and impracticable. The matter was again referred to the committee, and Hérault de Séchelles afterwards at some length explained the reasons which induced himself and his colleagues to reject the proposal; and which will be more fully noticed in the last chapter of this work. The result was, that the Convention adopted the view of the committee, and, in accordance with it, enacted that a number of judges should be appointed for the trial of civil causes under the name of public arbitrators. I am not aware that the subject has been again revived; but since the Revolution of February, 1848, a proposal was made in the assembly to submit questions hitherto dealt with summarily by the correctional police, to a jury trial; but this plan met with little favor, and was rejected.

SECTION II. *The Jury in other parts of the Continent.*

Trial by Jury in criminal cases was introduced into Belgium in 1830, at the time of the revolution, when that country separated from Holland. It is based upon the provisions of the Napoleonic Code. In Holland the system does not exist.

It was introduced into the kingdom of Greece in 1834, and is expressly retained by one of the articles of the new constitution granted in 1843.

In Portugal it was partially adopted in 1832, and more fully developed by a law of 1837. In 1838 the number of the jury was limited to six. In 1840 fresh modifications were introduced. The verdict, whether of acquittal or conviction must be that of two-thirds of the jury at least, but it is the duty of the judge, if he thinks it incorrect, to annul it, and refer the question to another jury.

Trial by jury was established in Geneva by a law of the 12th of January, 1844. The system there has this peculiarity, that the law recognizes a distinction between a verdict of guilty " under extenuating circumstances," and one with the words, " under very extenuating circumstances." The effect of either is to prevent the sentence of death or imprisonment for life from being passed; and of course in the case of the latter verdict the punishment is slighter than when the former is returned. In 1844 a person was tried for housebreaking and stealing, and two questions were put to the jury: first, whether the prisoner had himself stolen the articles? secondly, whether he was the accomplice of some person unknown, who was the actual thief? The jury answered the first in the negative and the second in the affirmative, adding, " under extenuating circumstances." The court thereupon sentenced the prisoner to five years' imprisonment. He appealed to the cour de cassation, on the ground that the second question ought not to have been put as he was not charged as an accomplice in the indictment, and the court set aside the verdict. He was then tried before another jury, who found him guilty of having stolen the property of the prosecutor "under very extenuating circumstances," and the court, although they had sentenced him to five years' imprisonment when he had been convicted only as an accomplice, now sentenced him to three years' imprisonment when convicted as a principal, because the second jury had accompanied their verdict with the last mentioned words.

When the court are unanimously of opinion that a verdict of guilty is wrong, they have the power of annuling it, and remitting the case to be tried by a fresh jury. The prisoner may also appeal to the cour de cassation, not upon the merits, but upon questions of informality or defects vitiating the trial.

In Sardinia jury trial has been lately introduced; and on the 23rd of May, 1850, the archbishop of Turin (M. Franzoni), who refused to appear, was tried and found guilty by a jury of an offense against the respect due to the laws, by publishing a circular in which he ordered the clergy not to recognize the jurisdiction of the secular tribunals.

CHAPTER XVI.

INTRODUCTION OF TRIAL BY JURY INTO THE CRIMINAL PROCEDURE IN GERMANY.

SECTION I. *System of Criminal Procedure which Trial by Jury was intended to supersede.*

BEFORE detailing the change which has taken place in the judicial system of Germany by the recent introduction of trial by jury, I think it will be interesting and useful to give an account of the mode of criminal procedure which it was intended to supersede. It is thus only that we can fully appreciate the evils of which it is the appropriate remedy, and the yearning desire for its adoption which has long been felt and expressed by the ablest and most influential of the German jurists. The subject has occupied the minds of profound thinkers and writers in Germany for many years, and it would be hardly an exaggeration to say, has produced what may be called a jury literature. The works with which I am most familiar, and of which I have in the present chapter chiefly availed myself, are those of Welcker,[1] Mittermaier,[2] Gneist,[3] and Goetze.[4]

It appears that criminal processes not very dissimilar

---

[1] Staats-Lexicon, Vol. VII. Art. Jury.

[2] Die Mündlichkeit die Oeffentlichkeit und das Geschwornengericht (1845). Mittermaier is professor at Heidelberg, and one of the most distinguished jurists and writers in Germany. The above work is a storehouse of valuable learning in the criminal procedure of different countries. He has announced for publication a new work on the subject, which I regret has not appeared in time for me to make use of it.

[3] Die Bildung der Geschwornengerichte in Deutschland (Berlin, 1849).

[4] Ueber die Preussichen Schwurgerichte und deren Reform (Berlin, 1850).

to our own were not altogether unknown in Germany before the introduction of the jury system, properly so called, into the Rhenish provinces in 1798. We find several instances of offenses tried before a court consisting of a presiding officer and a certain number of burgers summoned for the occasion. And it is remarkable that the number of these burgers was most frequently twelve. Thus a Swabian ordinance of the year 1562, declared, "that the burgomaster and council of the four judicial districts should summon so many 'jurymen' (urtheiler), as that each court might be provided with twelve good and fit (tüchtigen) jurymen." In Emmendingen the tribunal was composed of twelve persons, the headmen of the surrounding villages. In Oppenau and Oberkirch the burgers chose a number of their fellow-citizens to act as jurymen for a certain period, and these were known by the name of Twelve-men (zwölfer), because that was the number required to constitute a court.

Welcker gives us the record of a criminal trial at Durlach, in the grand duchy of Baden, in 1748, where one Pfeiffer sat as president, and twelve citizens as jurymen, or blutrichter as they are called. The prisoner, who was charged with theft, was defended by an advocate, and at the close of the case the public were excluded from the room where the proceedings took place, and the door was closed while the jurors gave their votes. These, however, were not confined to the question of innocence or guilt, but embraced the punishment to be suffered, if they were satisfied that the accused was guilty. This was the case in the present instance, and the votes of each of the twelve jurymen or judges is recorded, together with the reasons which influenced the sentence for which he voted. The reasons were different, but the sentence was unanimous—and it was—Death.

Sometimes the number of jurors was twenty-four, as in Hauenstein, to whose inhabitants an old charter of 1442 secured the right of "being tried in all cases by a court consisting of their equals, and by no stranger." In Friburg the tribunal was composed of thirty burgers, of whom six were town-councilors, and twenty-four masters of guilds or companies.

Many of the popular courts continued until a recent period. Thus in Constance the mode of trial by burgers was suppressed by an imperial ordinance of Austria, in 1786. It ceased at a still later period at Offenburg, Genenbach, Zell, and the district of the Hammersbach Thal. And at Überlingen, the town-councillors in a body, presided over by the syndic or mayor, acted as a jury in criminal cases until the end of the German Empire in 1803.

Publicity was another important feature of these tribunals. They were often held in the open air, with the blue vault of heaven their only canopy, which seems to have been the judgment-hall amongst the Israelites of old. "And Deborah, a prophetess, the wife of Lapidoth, she judged Israel at that time. And she dwelt under the palm-tree of Deborah between Ramah and Bethel in Mount Ephraim: and the children of Israel came up to her for judgment."[1] The famous Vehmgericht of Westphalia was in like manner held under an old tree in the open air, but no strangers were permitted to approach the mysterious precincts. Indeed this custom of judicial sittings sub dio, continued, according to Welcker, to exist in many places in Germany until the beginning of the present century.[2]

The opposite system to that which we have just considered, where citizens are entitled to be tried in open court by their peers, chosen out of the whole body of

---

[1] Judges IV. 4, 5.
[2] See Zentner, Das Geschwornengericht. and Staats-Lexicon, VII. 693-4.

the community, is one in which the process of investigation is secret, and life and liberty depend on the sentence of a judge or judges appointed by the state, and removable at the pleasure of the sovereign. This engine of tyranny and oppression gradually superseded in Germany the old popular judicature, and the struggle there has been to restore what was thus lost, and re-establish it with the improvements suggested by the example of those countries where a more enlightened civilization prevailed. England has chiefly supplied the model for imitation in this respect, and to her the nations of the Continent have looked when engaged in the great task of judicial reform. We complain amongst ourselves, and justly, of the abuses which have crept in and deformed our courts of equity and law. We groan beneath the evils of Chancery chicane, and are indignant at the costly frivolities of special pleading. These have, in the course of ages become such, as to amount in many cases to a positive denial of justice; and the recoil in the public mind is such as to threaten the very existence of our legal institutions. But let us not too sweepingly or hastily condemn. Let us see the nature of the criminal procedure under which Germany suffered, and thankfully contrast with hers our own happier lot.

It need be no matter of surprise that the Germans should ardently desire a change in their mode of conducting criminal inquiries. Amongst them a prolonged system of moral torture was, and still is, except where the jury trial has been introduced, resorted to with the professed view of extracting a confession of guilt from the accused; the consequence of which is that the unhappy prisoner, against whom no crime has yet been proved, remains for years in prison, subject to all the appliances which perverted ingenuity can devise to induce him to criminate himself. Worn out by harassing examinations, which are conducted by officials who visit his cell at all hours of the day and night, and who scruple not to employ the most disgusting tricks to entrap him into admissions; his brain reeling with fright at dressed-up apparitions, or the sudden sight of a bleeding corpse or moldering remains, and his mind weakened by solitary confinement, he not unfrequently prefers death upon the scaffold, and seeks by a false confession to escape the horrors of his protracted trial.[1]

The following is the account which Fauerbach, one of the most accomplished jurists of Germany, gives of the mode of criminal procedure there:[2]

"The accused is separated from his judges; they see him not; they hear him not; only through the medium of third persons does his voice and the cry of his defense reach them. They hear not the witnesses who speak for or against him; the living words of his lips must first be reduced to the cold form of a written record before they can touch the feelings of those who have to pronounce his doom. The investigation itself is as mysterious from the beginning to the end as is the ultimate decision. Without support, without an advocate, the accused stands alone before the inquisitor, who, has, perhaps, already condemned him in his heart, who puts forth all his strength to prove him guilty, because his reputation is enhanced by the number of convictions he can obtain. The law, indeed, prescribes that the officer shall deal impartially to discover innocence as well as guilt; it forbids him to use any stratagem which may entrap the innocent, or extort by compulsion what ought to be only a voluntary confession, and to record

[1] If any one wishes to see with what burning indignation German writers speak of the secret inquisitorial system in the criminal jurisprudence of their country, let him read the article on the jury by Welcker, a jurist of considerable repute, in the Staats-Lexicon. The style, however, is by no means attractive. The sentences are of suffocating length, and the constant accumulation of epithets gives the whole an air of rhetorical exaggeration.

[2] Betracht über das Geschwornengericht.

everything faithfully, without addition, omission, or alteration. But what are laws whose requirements are not fulfilled; which the honest need not, and the dishonest trangress with impunity? The notary, when he is there, is generally a dependent creature, who puts down what the inquisitor bids him write; the accused lets the one say, and the other write, what they please, either from fear, or because in his ignorance he does not suspect the importance which the judge may attach to a circumstance more or less. In order to subject the inquisitor to a species of control, sometimes two or more assessors are appointed, who, however, for the most part, hardly know why they accompany him; and after all, do nothing more than add their signatures to the copy of the examination. Thus the whole process has a veil of dark suspicious secrecy. Out of his lonely cell, the prisoner is led to the equally lonely examination chamber—that workshop where the arrows are forged which are directed against liberty and life. Except by special favor he neither sees nor knows who are his accusers; nor does he see the witnesses against him except when they are suddenly confronted with him in order to induce a confession. . . . Our ancestors saw a criminal brought before the tribunal of justice in the morning, and hanging on the gallows a condemned malefactor in the evening. But we regard it as a model of speedy justice if the proceeding is finished at the end of half-a year; nor are our feelings shocked if the accused lingers in prison for two years—and how often is it not much longer during the inquiry?[1] Our rules of process have imposed heavy weights upon the course of investigation, which impede, if they do not absolutely prevent it, from proceeding accurately and straight.

"Every circumstance, no matter how unimportant, with reference to the main point of the inquiry, must be

[1] In the case of 2,388 persons arrested and subjected to judicial interroga

traced out in all its accidental turnings and windings before the examining judge ventures to declare the process closed. . . . A second mode adopted for protecting innocence from danger is the most anxious limitation of the proofs of guilt. Where no ordinary understanding using the utmost caution entertains a doubt, there the judge must still doubt when the question is whether he shall pronounce a malefactor guilty. As if the conclusion at which the mind arrives as to the fact of a crime having been committed, rested upon proofs different from those which establish any other historical fact, the full legal proof of guilt is made to consist entirely of certain specified presumptions, which afford no more certainty than evidence which is excluded. Thus the conviction of an offender (independently of the separate proof of the corpus delicti [Thatbestand]) depends upon his having been fool enough to perpetrate the deed before the eyes of at least two unexceptionable witnesses, or upon his weak and good-natured readiness to accuse, or (according to the English expression) criminate himself by his own confession."

In the passage just quoted Feuerbach alludes to the tories in the Duchy of Baden, in the year 1837, the periods of inquiry (that is trial) respectively were as follows:

4 months in the case of 995 persons.
6 . . . . 274 "
8 . . . . 327 "
10 . . . . 228 "
12 . . . . 179 "
14 . . . . 151 "
16 . . . . 68 "
18 . . . . 35 "
20 . . . . 36 "
22 . . . . 56 "
24 . . . . 6 "
A still longer period . 33 "

2,388

factitious value given in Germany to different kinds and degrees of evidence. Witnesses are divided into two classes, sufficient, and insufficient or suspicious.[1] The latter are persons under the age of eighteen, accomplices, the injured party, informers, except such as are officially bound to inform, persons of doubtful character, and persons in any way connected with or hostile to the party affected by their testimony. Children under eight years of age, and persons directly interested in the result of the trial, are incompetent witnesses.

So far the classification is not open to much exception. But mark the absurdity which follows! The evidence of two sufficient witnesses, that is, witnesses who do not fall within the category of suspicious or incompetent, is taken as proof; that of one sufficient witness as half proof. The testimony of two suspicious witnesses, if agreeing, is considered equal to that of one sufficient witness. A confession made before two sufficient witnesses in the absence of the judge is only half proof, and requires to be confirmed by other evidence. And these rules are applied with mechanical regularity to all the complicated and difficult questions connected with the discovery of crime.

Thus we see a kind of arithmetical calculation made to usurp the place of moral probability, and technical rules substituted for the exercise of the reasoning faculties. The degree of conviction which a particular class of proof is à priori assumed to inspire, is expressed by a formula, which is acted upon without reference to the real effect produced upon the mind. It is like throwing evidence respecting an alleged murder into a machine, and then deciding whether it has been committed or not, according to the result that comes out. It is a consequence of this mode of procedure, that in Bavaria and most other

---

[1] See the interesting preface by Lady Duff Gordon to her translation of Feuerbach's Criminal Trials.

German states a prisoner is not executed until he has confessed his crime. This seems to me to be one of the severest censures upon the system, for it implies that those who uphold it have little confidence in the efficacy of their rules as to proofs and half proofs for discovering the truth. They therefore endeavor to obtain assurance from the lips of the accused himself. But the means by which they extort this are such as to deprive it of half its value, and often rendered it the most unsafe species of evidence to rely upon.

But it is not in Germany alone that the system has prevailed. It was in full force in France under the old inquisitorial process which preceded the establishment of the jury there. And the reason seems to be that in both countries the people had nothing to do with the administration of justice, which was left wholly to officials and a professional class. Casuistical subtlety was thus brought into play, and the theories of the closet were applied to the ever-changing circumstances of fact.

If we contrast this artificial and unreal method of dealing with evidence with the practice of our own courts, we shall see at once how enormous is the advantage of the latter. The jury are fettered by no rules whatever in considering the effect and weight of the evidence they have heard, but have simply to determine whether or not they are convinced by it. For this no juridicial refinements are needed; indeed, here they can properly have no place; but each individual must satisfy himself by the aid of his own common sense, whether the proof is such as to leave no reasonable doubt upon his mind. We have indeed rules—and some of them arbitrary and unreasonable—for excluding evidence from the consideration of the jury, but none which prescribe the amount of belief which evidence when once admitted must produce.

Let us now look at the practical working of the German system, and cite a few instances of recent occurrence. Some years ago a highway robbery and murder was committed on the road leading from Cassel to Fulda, and a poor schoolmaster was taken up on suspicion of being the assassin. He was thrown into prison, and after he had been there wearied by solitary confinement, interrupted only by attempts to extort from him an avowal of guilt, suddenly in the dead of midnight there appeared before him a figure like a ghost, in a sheet stained with blood, which with awful threatenings commanded him to confess. The horror-stricken wretch obeyed, and upon the strength of that confession he was condemned to death. Before, however, the sentence was executed, the real murderer was discovered, and the life of the innocent man was saved. But it was too late: he left his prison indeed, but it was only to become the inmate of a madhouse. The ghost had been dressed up by the authorities for the occasion, and they no doubt prided themselves upon the success of their stratagem, until the Providence of God revealed the truth.[1]

Again, in the month of February, 1830, a Danish ambassador, named Von Qualen, was found dead in a garden at Cutin, in the duchy of Oldenburg, and the snow on the ground was covered with blood from his body. The surgeons who examined it at first were of opinion that death was caused by a fall, but afterwards they thought he had been murdered. Two servants of the deceased, both of whom had hitherto borne unimpeachable characters, were arrested, although there were no tangible grounds of suspicion against them. During six long years they remained in prison, and in that time had to undergo upwards of eighty examinations, which when taken down filled six thousand pages. At last the Facuity of Jurists, to whom the case was referred, pronounced their judgment, which was, that "not only the

[1] Annalen der Kurhess. Criminal Justiz.

accused were to be released, as entirely innocent, but their claims to compensation for their long imprisonment were expressly reserved to them." Against this judgment, however, the public prosecutor appealed, and the two victims, who had been in the meantime set at liberty, were again incarcerated. In 1837 the Court of Appeal at Oldenburg gave judgment in the case; and as regarded one of the accused, confirmed the decree of the Faculty of Jurists; but condemned the other to pay the costs of his maintenance in jail, and half the expense of the process against him![1] Well may Welcker, when narrating this instance of prostituted justice, indignantly exclaim: " And until the eighth year,—Yes! I say, until the eighth year, in Germany—the Germany of the nineteenth century—in the ordinary course of law, could such a criminal process—such a frighful martyrdom of inquiry—continue against these hapless and innocent men!"[2]

He mentions also a case that occurred in recent times in the Grand Duchy of Hesse, where, after the ordinary means employed to bring about a confession had failed, the magistrate caused the back of the accused to be seared with a hot iron, and after having allowed him to satisfy his famished appetite with salt food he deprived him of water wherewith to slake his raging thirst. This however was carrying the system too far, and the official who had thus exercised his diabolical ingenuity " to discover the truth," was dismissed from his post."[3]

In the year 1830, a person named Wendt, living at Rostock, in the Duchy of Mecklenburg, was accused of poisoning his mother and his wife, and of attempting to poison his mother-in-law and several other persons, and also of arson. In 1834, the Faculty of Jurists at Gottingen acquitted him of the first charge, but found him guilty on the others, and condemned him to be broken

---

[1] Bauer's Strafrechtsfälle, II.   [2] Staats-Lexicon, VII. 709.
[3] Welcker quotes as his authority Demme's Annalen, VIII. 162.

on the wheel. The case, however, was referred to a similar faculty at Heidelberg, who, in 1836, with precisely the same materials before them, pronounced him innocent of all the crimes except that relating to his wife, about which their judgment seems to have been equivalent to a verdict of "not proven;" and with respect to that they ordered him to pay the costs of the proceeding. On appeal to the Supreme Tribunal at Parchim, that court, in 1838, declared him innocent on all the charges, and reversed the decision of the Heidelburg jurists as to costs. In 1839, a prisoner under sentence of death, confessed that he was the perpetrator of the crimes of which Wendt had been accused, and of which he was the victim; for the long-protracted trial destroyed his health and reduced him to beggary.[1]

SECTION II. *Introduction of the Jury Trial in Criminal Cases.*

When the French during the war of the revolution made themselves, in 1798, masters of the provinces bordering the Rhine, they introduced there trial by jury in criminal cases, which had been established in France by a decree of the Constituent Assembly, on the 16th of September, 1791. The institution took vigorous root, and flourished so as to outlive the ephemeral possession of the soil by the invaders. At the close of the war part of these provinces were united to Prussia, where the old system of judicature prevailed. The hatred felt throughout Germany at the French name was at this period intense, and the people were anxious to obliterate all traces of the military inundation which had swept over them, and to restore the old landmarks of German nationality. Prussia, therefore, looked with no favor upon a tribunal which was the offspring of French dom-

[1] Demme's Neue Annalen.

ination, but the inhabitants of the Rhineland clung to it with the affection of men who knew by experience the benefits it conferred. The government now adopted a wise course. They appointed a commission of five persons, well qualified for the task, two of them natives of Rhenish Prussia, and three of Prussia Proper (the latter members of the Supreme Court at Berlin), who were thoroughly to investigate the practical working of the system, and ascertain by personal inquiry what were the views and wishes of the inhabitants of Rhenish Prussia on the subject. After a long and deliberate inquiry, the Commissioners made their report in 1819, and they were unanimous in favor of the continuance of the jury trial.[1] The Prussian government acquiesced, and the institution was preserved as it exists at present. An exception, however, was made that same year in the case of trials for political offenses, which were removed from the cognizance of a jury; and this, no doubt, was a serious encroachment upon the rights which it is the object of the system to secure.

The other provinces of the Rhine, such as Rhenish Hesse and Bavaria, also retained the same mode of trial, and their attachment to it has increased with time. In the words of Welcker, "they cling to it as firmly as to their religion."[2]

In Prussia Proper, the political convulsions of 1848 led to the grant of a constitution, which was proclaimed on the 5th of December in that year, and it contained the promise that jury trial should be introduced into the courts of criminal justice. This promise was fulfilled by the promulgation of a law on the 3rd of January, 1847, which established the new system, and regulated its mode of action by a number of provisions taken chiefly without

---

[1] Gutachten der konigl. preuss. immediat justiz commission über das Geschworengericht. 1819.

[2] Staats-Lexicon, VII. 753.

any material variation from the Code Napoleon. The qualifications of jurors were made to depend upon a certain rate of assessment to taxes, or the presumed possession of a certain intellectual capacity. The latter included attorneys and notaries, professors, physicians and surgeons, and all official persons who have property to the amount of 500 thalers, or are immediately nominated by the king. Every juryman must be at least thirty years old, and in the full enjoyment of civic rights; and he must also have resided a year in the district for which the list is made up.

The lists are prepared by proper officers in September every year, and are then for three days open to public inspection. The objections to any names must be made within the same period, and are decided upon by the persons who prepared the particular lists. These are then submitted to the president of the ministry, who out of them frames smaller lists for each jury district. He chooses sixty names for every assize, and these are reduced to thirty-six by the presiding judge, not however in the way of selection, but by ballot, while the public prosecutor and the prisoner have each the right of rejection or "challenge," to which the only limit is that twelve must be left.

It would occupy too much space to detail all the minute regulations of the law of the 3rd of January, 1849, establishing the jury trial in criminal cases throughout the Prussian dominions. And it is the less necessary to do so, as many modifications are already projected, the suggestions of both theory and experience.[1] It will be sufficient here to state generally, that there is no jury of accusation corresponding to our grand jury, and that the number of the trying jury is twelve, who may give a verdict by a majority. If, however, the numbers are seven to five the judges who preside at the trial must decide it

[1] See Gneist, Die Bildung der Geschworeng. in Deutschland.

themselves according to a plurality of opinions.[1] And where the jury are unanimous in a verdict of guilty, but the court is satisfied that they are mistaken, it may annul the verdict and order a fresh trial. But if the same verdict is returned a second time it is final.

By a law of the 15th of April, 1851, political offenses were withdrawn from the cognizance of juries in Prussia.

The jury system in criminal trials was adopted in Bavaria and Hesse, in 1848. In Wurtemberg and Baden, in 1849. In Austria at the beginning of 1850; and the first trial by jury took place at Vienna in the autumn of that year. In Hanover and many of the smaller states it either has been already, or is about to be introduced.

Eagerly as trial by jury was demanded in Germany, and gladly as the concession has been received, experience has already proved that institutions, like trees, when transplanted do not flourish with the same vigor as when growing in their native soil. An ordinance can not supply that which usage and habit alone can give. The effective working of a system like the jury depends in an especial manner upon circumstances which can not be made the subject of legislation.[2] It takes its coloring and complexion, and, indeed, all its vitality, from the intellectual and moral character of the people, in whose hands it is placed as a plastic instrument for good or evil. And the character of a nation is the growth of ages influencing much more than influenced by institutions adopted from without. I by no means say that there is anything in the German mind antagonistic to a

---

[1] So tritt das Gericht selbst in Berathung und entscheidet nach Stimmenmehrheit über den von den Geschworenen nur mit einfacher Mehrheit festgestellten Pukt. § III. der Verordn. 3 Jan. 1849.

[2] Die blosse Einfuhrung neuer liberalen Formen und die Nachahmung gerichtlicher Einrichtungen fremder Länder nicht hinreicht, wenn diese Formen nicht in den Sitten des Volkes wurzeln und ihre belebende Kraft durch gewisse Zustände erhalten. Mitiermaier, Die Mündlichkeit &c. p. 75.

full and fair development of all the advantages of the jury trial. But time alone can show whether this is so or not. The danger, I think, is, lest in their love for theory and passion for the ideal, they become too impatient of defects which ought to be remedied, not by the abstract rules of philosophic principle, but the homely suggestions of practical experience. Moreover, many questions of difficulty must of necessity arise, which will make the Germans at first dissatisfied with the tribunal. The province of the jury and that of the judge may be clearly defined on paper, but this will not prevent collisions from occurring, from time to time, between them, which will engender a spirit of opposition, and cause the people to look upon the latter with suspicion and mistrust. Juries will now and then return absurd verdicts, which will tend to bring the institution into contempt. Some instances of these have already happened, and are noticed by Goetze, vice-president of the royal Supreme Court at Berlin, in his short treatise, published last year, "Ueber die Preussischen Schwurgerichte und deren Reform." It would be easy to match such cases by similiar blunders on the part of English juries; but here we make allowances as for the faults of an old friend, and their occurrence hardly excites more than a passing smile. We know that they are mere exceptions, and can afford to excuse them. Not so in Germany, where as yet it can scarcely be known whether they will prove the exception or the rule. Many reasons of this kind concur to abate the enthusiasm with which the Germans regarded the jury trial when at a distance. They now begin to scan more narrowly the system. Goetze has done this in the work already mentioned, and Professor Gneist in an elaborate treatise has pointed out its defects, and suggested a great variety of amendments in the shape of a new projet de loi (𝕲𝖊𝖘𝖊𝖙𝖟𝖊𝖓𝖙𝖜𝖚𝖗𝖋). He says that the institution has not been greeted with the applause that had been expected. What would a year previously have been met with acclamation is now received with unmistakable coldness. He attributes this chiefly to the nature of the property qualification required for serving on the jury, which makes it too much of a class interest, and to the interference of government in the preparation of the lists. But there can be no doubt that the new system is a valuable boon and an immense improvement upon the former procedure. All friends of constitutional freedom and enemies of judicial oppression must wish well to the great experiment; and we may hope that amongst a people so truthful, so honest, and so enlightened as the Germans, trial by jury will soon become one of their most efficient as well as cherished institutions.

CHAPTER XVII.

ILLUSTRATIONS OF TRIAL BY JURY IN THE CASE OF ENGLISH STATE PROSECUTIONS

I PROPOSE, in the present chapter, to illustrate the improvement which has taken place in the conduct of criminal proceedings in this country, by a few examples of trials at different periods of our history. As juries are drawn from the mass of the people, and from no distinct class or body having interests separate from those of the rest of the nation, they may be fairly deemed to represent the average state of public feeling and spirit; and the verdicts they give are a tolerably correct index of the opinions entertained by society on questions affecting the rights and liberty of the subject. But in former times the proper province of the jury was not sufficiently understood, and the rules of evidence were so loose and defective, that a prisoner stood in great jeopardy where the court, acting in obedience to the known wishes of the crown, strove to obtain a conviction.

Sir Nicholas Throckmorton's case deserves to be mentioned, as betokening the commencement of a more manly spirit in juries, which had in state prosecutions previously been so accustomed to yield a servile deference to the authority of those in power, as to render trial by jury little better than a mockery. For, as Hargrave says,[1] "in ancient times, and more especially in the reign of Henry VIII., when from the devastation

---

[1] See 1 State Tr. 407 (Howell's Edit.).

made by civil wars amongst the ancient nobility, and other causes disturbing the balance of the constitution, the influence of the crown was become exorbitant, and seems to have been in its zenith, to be accused of a crime against the state and to be convicted were almost the same thing. The one was usually so certain a consequence of the other, that exclusively of Lord Dacre's case, who was tried by his peers and acquitted in the reign of Henry VIII., and that of Sir Nicholas Throckmorton in the reign of his daughter Mary, the examples to the contrary are very rare."

Sir Nicholas Throckmorton was tried in the year 1554 (the 1st of Mary), by a common jury before commissioners at Guildhall, on a charge of high treason, for conspiring and imagining the death of the Queen, and intending to depose and deprive her of her royal estate, and also traitorously devising to take violently the Tower of London. In many respects the trial is remarkable, as showing the contrast between the mode of conducting a criminal prosecution then and at the present day. The attorney-general, Griffin, was of course one of the counsel for the crown, but he was led by Sergeant Stanford,[1] who took precedence of the Queen's first law-officer. The commissioners and the counsel catechised the prisoner much in the same way as is still customary in France and Belgium, and sought to entrap him into unfavorable admissions, notwithstanding the affecting appeal made by him to their sense of justice and fair play. He said:

"I pray you remember that I am not alienate from you, but that I am your Christian brother—neither you so charged but you ought to consider equity, nor yet so privileged, but that you have a duty of God appointed you how you shall do your office; which if you exceed

[1] Stanford, or as the name was written, Staundforde, was the author of a learned work, called Pleas of the Crown.

will be grievously required at your hands. It is lawful for you to use your gifts, which I know God hath largely given you, as your learning, wit, and eloquence, so as thereby you do not seduce the minds of the simple and unlearned jury, to credit matters otherwise than they be. For, master Sergeant, I know how by persuasions, enforcements, presumptions, applying, implying, inferring, conjecturing, deducing of arguments, wrestling and exceeding the law, the circumstances, the depositions and confessions, unlearned men may be enchanted to think and judge those that be things indifferent, or at the worst oversights, to be great treasons; such power orators have, and such ignorance the unlearned have. Almighty God by the mouth of his prophet doth conclude such advocates to be cursed, speaking these words, 'Cursed be he that doth his office craftily, corruptly, and maliciously.'"

This address does not seem to have had much influence upon the learned sergeant, who opened the case against the prisoner by asking him the following question:

"How say you, Throckmorton, did not you send Winter to Wyat into Kent, and did devise that the Tower of London should be taken, with other instructions concerning Wyat's stir and rebellion?"

Throckmorton admitted that he had said to Winter that Wyat was desirous to speak with him, but denied that he had concerted with them any plot for taking the Tower. Upon this Stanford read a confession made by Winter, although he was alive and might have been called so as to give his evidence in the presence of the prisoner; and then triumphantly turning to the jury he exclaimed:

"Now, my masters of the jury, you have heard my sayings confirmed with Winter's confession; how say you, Throckmorton, can you deny it? if you will, you shall have Winter justify it to your face."

Throckmorton, however, said that as there was nothing

material in the confession to implicate him, he might safely admit the whole to be true, although he might truly deny some part of it. Sergeant Dyer then adduced another confession of an alleged co-conspirator named Croftes, and proceeded to state the substance of it, when Sir Nicholas Throckmorton interposed, and took a most just and reasonable objection, saying:

"Master Croftes is yet living, and is here this day; how happeneth it he is not brought face to face to justify the matter, neither hath been of all this time? Will you know the truth? either he said not so, or he will not abide by it, but honestly hath reformed himself."

But this argument had no effect, and the next step was to read a confession by one Vaughan, of a damnatory nature against the prisoner; after which Sir Thomas Bromley, lord chief justice of England, who was one of the commissioners, said to him:

"How say you, will you confess the matter? and it will be best for you."

Throckmorton.—"No, I will never accuse myself unjustly; but inasmuch as I am come hither to be tried, I pray you let me have the law favorably."

Vaughan was then called, and being sworn, gave his evidence vivâ voce. Throckmorton admitted that some part of his confession previously read was true, "as the name, the places, the time, and some part of the matter." This made the attorney-general turn triumphantly to the jury and exclaim, "So you of the jury may perceive the prisoner doth confess something to be true." The questioning of the accused was resumed, and the confessions of other persons, not produced as witnesses, implicating him, were read. He took several objections in point of law, and amongst them this, that only one witness had appeared against him, whereas the law required that there should be two to justify a conviction on a charge of high treason. He therefore desired that the Court would read the statute relating to that crime to the jury; but Chief Justice Bromley answered, "No! for there shall be no books brought at your desire; we know the law sufficiently without book." After some altercation between the court and the prisoner, the attorney-general interrupted them, saying, "I pray you, my Lord Chief Justice, repeat the evidence for the Queen, and give the jury their charge; for the prisoner will keep you here all day." But Throckmorton felt that he was speaking for his life, and was not inclined tamely to surrender his right to be heard. At last, after some home thrusts had been made by him at Mr. Attorney, the latter, losing his temper, said:

"I pray you, my lords, that you the Queen's commissioners suffer not this prisoner to use the Queen's learned counsel thus; I was never interrupted thus in my life, nor I ever knew any thus suffered to talk as this prisoner is suffered: some of us will come no more at the bar, an we be thus handled."

At last Chief Justice Bromley summed up the case, and Throckmorton afterwards addressed the jury in an earnest speech, saying, "The trial of our whole controversy, the trial of my innocency, the trial of my life, lands, and goods, and the destruction of my posterity forever, doth rest on your good judgments." The jury then retired, and after deliberating for several hours, returned into court with a verdict of Not Guilty. Upon this the Lord Chief Justice, with the most marked impropriety remonstrated with them in a threatening tone, saying, "Remember yourselves better. Have you considered substantially the whole evidence as it was declared and recited? The matter doth touch the Queen's highness and yourselves also;—take good heed what you do." But the jury were firm, and Whetston, the foreman, answered, "We have found him not guilty, agreeable to all our consciences."

Bromley, C. J.—" If you have done well, it is the better for you.

But it was not better in a pecuniary sense for the jury. The attorney-general immediately rose, and thus addressed the court:

"And it please you, my lords, forasmuch as it seemeth these men of the jury, which have strangely acquitted the prisoner of his treasons whereof he was indicted, will forthwith depart the court, I pray you for the Queen that they and every one of them may be bound in a recognizance of £500 a piece to answer to such matters as they shall be charged with in the Queen's behalf, whensoever they shall be charged or called."

The court, however, went further than even this monstrous request asked them to do; for according to the report of the trial, being dissatisfied with the verdict, they committed the jury to prison. Four of the number were soon afterwards discharged, on humbly admitting that they had done wrong; but the remaining eight were brought before the Star-Chamber and most severely dealt with. Three were adjudged to pay £2,000 each, and the rest £200 each.

It is unnecessary to point out the irregularities and injustice in the conduct of this trial, which, thanks to the firmness and honesty of the jury, terminated in an acquittal. To use the words of the accomplished editor of Criminal trials,[1] "With the exception of the arraignment, we look in vain for any similarity to our present system of criminal procedure. Instead of a statement of the facts of the case by the queen's counsel, for the assistance of the court and jury in attending to the evidence, we find only repeated protestations of the guilt of the prisoner; and, instead of being calmly called

---

[1] D. Jardine, Esq. The observations of this author are always interesting, and his work is a valuable manual for those who wish to make themselves acquainted with our old criminal jurisprudence.

upon by the court for his defense when the case for the prosecution is closed, we see the prisoner, from the beginning to the end of the trial, literally baited with questions and accusations by the court and the counsel, repeatedly urged both to confess his guilt, and required to answer separately to each piece of evidence as it is produced. Throckmorton was a man of great talents and of singular energy of mind; and his activity and boldness gave him unusual advantages in his altercations with the judges and counsel; but a man of less firmness of nerve, though entirely innocent, would, under such circumstances, have been utterly unable to defend himself."

It is, perhaps, not fair to complain of the confessions of absent parties being received in evidence as any special hardship in this case; for the proper rules and principles of evidence at this time were so little understood, that almost anything was considered admissible, whether hearsay or not. I have selected the trial as an example, not only of the firmness of a jury when the government was despotic in its character, but also of the mode in which state prosecutions were then carried on, that we may feel and appreciate the change which has taken place. But it was not until the æra of the Revolution, in 1689, that this change became effective and real.

The next trial to which I shall advert as illustrating the improper practices resorted to in former times to obtain a conviction, and, at the same time, showing the necessity then of an institution like the jury to serve as a bulwark against the attacks of the crown and the servility of the judges, it that of Penn and Mead, who were indicted at the Old Bailey, in the year 1670 (28 Charles II.) for having, with divers other persons to the jurors unknown, unlawfully and tumultuously assembled and congregated themselves together in Gracechurch Street, in London. The indictment then set forth that Penn, by agreement, wish, and abetment of Mead, in the open street, did preach and speak to the persons in the street assembled, by reason whereof a great concourse and tumult of people a long time did remain and continue, in contempt of the king and his law, and to the great terror and disturbance of many of his liege people and subjects.

The real ground of the prosecution in this case was the dislike felt by the government against the Protestant Non-conformists, to whom Penn and Mead belonged, being both Quakers, a sect which at that time had lately come into existence; and owing to their extraordinary dress, demeanor, and doctrines, they were looked upon as fanatics of a pestilent kind. Their meeting-houses were shut up by the authorities, and they were commanded not to assemble and preach in the streets. But, as Neal, the historian of the Puritans, says, "In imitation of the prophet Daniel, they would do it more publicly because they were forbid. Some called this obstinacy, others firmness; but by it they carried their point, the government being weary of dealing with so much perverseness."

The following account of the trial is taken from a narrative written by Penn and Mead themselves;[1] and of course some allowance must be made for possible exaggeration on their part. But there can be no doubt that the proceedings were conducted with unseemly harshness, and the jury were threatened by the court in a manner subversive of every principle of justice.

The trial took place before the lord mayor, recorder, and aldermen; and after two or three witnesses had proved the fact that Penn had preached to the people, and that Mead was there, the recorder summed up the case to the jury, and they were told to consider their

[1] See 6 State Tr. 951-69.

verdict. They retired to a room up-stairs, and in the words of the narrative, "After an hour and a-half's time, eight came down agreed, but four remained above; the court sent an officer for them, and they accordingly came down. The bench used many unworthy threats to the four that dissented; and the recorder, addressing himself to Bushel, one of the jury, said, "Sir, you are the cause of this disturbance, and manifestly show yourself an abettor of faction; I shall set a mark upon you, sir!"

Sir J. Robinson (Alderman).—"Mr. Bushel, I have known you near this fourteen years; you have thrust yourself upon this jury, because you think there is some service for you: I tell you, you deserve to be indicted more than any man that hath been brought to the bar this day."

Bushel.—"No, Sir John; there were threescore before me, and I would willingly have got off, but could not."

Alderman Bloodworth.—"I said, when I saw Mr. Bushel, what I see is come to pass; for I knew he would never yield. Mr. Bushel, we know what you are."

May.—"Sirrah, you are an impudent fellow. I will put a mark upon you."

The jury were then sent back to consider their verdict, and after some considerable time they returned to the court. Silence was ordered, and the jury were called by their names.

Clerk.—Are you agreed upon your verdict?"

Jury.—"Yes."

Clerk.—"Who shall speak for you?"

Jury.—"Our foreman."

Clerk.—"Look upon the prisoners at the bar. How say you? Is William Penn guilty of the matter whereof he stands indicted in manner and form, or not guilty?"

Foreman.—"Guilty of speaking in Gracechurch Street."

Court.—"Is that all?"

Foreman.—" That is all I have in commission."

Recorder.—" You had as good say nothing."

May.—" Was it not an unlawful assembly? You mean he was speaking to a tumult of people there."

Foreman.—" My lord, this is all I had in commission."

The narrative then thus proceeds: " Here some of the jury seemed to buckle to the questions of the court; upon which Bushel, Hammond, and some others, opposed themselves, and said they allowed of no such word as an unlawful assembly in their verdict; at which the recorder, mayor, Robinson, and Bloodworth, took great occasion to vilify them with most opprobrious language: and this verdict not serving their turns, the recorder expressed himself thus:

Recorder.—" The law of England will not allow you to part till you have given in your verdict."

Jury.—" We have given in our verdict, and we can give in no other."

Recorder.—" Gentlemen, you have not given in your verdict, and you had as good say nothing; therefore go and consider it once more, that we may make an end of this troublesome business."

Jury.—"We desire we may have pen, ink, and paper."

Their request was complied with, and the jury again retired; and after a short interval returned into court with their verdict written. They found Penn "guilty of speaking or preaching to an assembly met together in Gracechurch Street;" and Mead not guilty. This put the court into a passion, and the recorder said:

".Gentlemen, you shall not be dismissed till we have a verdict that the court will accept: and you shall be locked up, without meat, drink, fire, and tobacco; you shall not think thus to abuse the court; we will have a verdict, by the help of God, or you shall starve for it."

Penn.—" My jury, who are my judges, ought not to be thus menaced; their verdict should be free, and not compelled; the bench ought to wait upon them, but not forestal them. I do desire that justice may be done me, and that the arbitrary resolves of the bench may not be made the measure of my jury's verdict."

Recorder.—" Stop that prating fellow's mouth, or put him out of the court."

The jury were again directed to retire to their room; but Penn made a spirited remonstrance. He said: "The agreement of twelve men is a verdict in law, and such a one being given by the jury, I require the clerk of the peace to record it, as he will answer at his peril. And if the jury bring in another verdict contradictory to this, I affirm they are perjured men in law. You are Englishmen (turning to and addressing the jury); mind your privilege; give not away your right."

The court then adjourned to the next morning, which was Sunday, when the prisoners were brought to the bar, and the jury sent for. They still persisted in their verdict, that Penn was only guilty of speaking in Gracechurch Street, which was of course no legal offense.

Clerk.—" What say you? Is William Penn guilty of the matter whereof he stands indicted, in manner and form aforesaid, or not guilty?"

Foreman.—" Guilty of speaking in Gracechurch Street."

Recorder.—" What is this to the purpose? I say I will have a verdict." And speaking to Bushel, he said: "You are a factious fellow; I will set a mark upon you; and whilst I have anything to do in the city, I will have an eye upon you."

Mayor.—" Have you no more wit than to be led by such a pitiful fellow? I will cut his nose."

Penn.—" It is intolerable that the jury should be thus menaced: is this according to the fundamental laws? Are not they my proper judges by the Great Charter of England? What hope is there of ever having justice done, when juries are threatened, and their verdicts rejected? I am concerned to speak, and grieved to see such arbitrary proceedings. Did not the lieutenant of the Tower render one of them worse than a felon? And do you not plainly seem to condemn such for factious fellows, who answer not your ends? Unhappy are those juries who are threatened to be fined, and starved, and ruined, if they give not in verdicts contrary to their consciences."

Recorder.—" My Lord, you must take a course with that same fellow."

Mayor.—" Stop his mouth; jailer, bring fetters, and stake him to the ground."

Penn.—" Do your pleasure; I matter not your fetters."

Recorder.—" Till now I never understood the reason of the policy and prudence of the Spaniards in suffering the Inquisition among them: and certainly it will never be well with us till something like unto the Spanish Inquisition be in England."

Again the jury were commanded to retire, and consider their verdict, although the foreman protested, saying, " We have given in our verdict, and all agreed to it and if we give in another, it will be a force upon us to save our lives."

Next day they returned into court, when the following scene took place.

Foreman.—" Here is our verdict in writing, and our hands subscribed."

The clerk took the paper, but was prevented by the recorder from reading it; and he commanded the clerk to ask for a positive verdict.

Foreman.—"That is our verdict; we have subscribed to it."

Clerk.—" How say you? Is William Penn guilty, &c. or not guilty?"

Foreman.—" Not guilty."

Clerk.—" How say you? Is William Mead guilty, &c. or not guilty?"

Foreman.—" Not guilty."

Clerk.—" Then hearken to your verdict; you say, that William Penn is not guilty in manner and form as he stands indicted; you say that William Mead is not guilty in manner and form as he stands indicted; and so you say all."

Jury.—" Yes, we do so."

The court then commanded that every juror should distinctly answer to his name, and give in his separate verdict, which they unanimously did, saying, Not guilty " to the great satisfaction of the assembly."

Recorder.—" I am sorry, gentlemen, you have followed your own judgments and opinions, rather than the good and wholesome advice which was given you; God keep my life out of your hands; but for this the court fines you forty marks a man, and imprisonment till paid."

Upon this Penn came forward, and said:

" I demand my liberty, being freed by the jury."

Mayor.—" No, you are in for your fines."

Penn.—" Fines, for what?"

Mayor.—" For contempt of court."

Penn.—" I ask, if it be according to the fundamental laws of England, that any Englishman should be fined or amerced but by the judgment of his peers or jury; since it expressly contradicts the 14th and 29th chapters of the Great Charter of England, which say, 'No freeman ought to be amerced but by the oath of good and lawful men of the vicinage.'"

Recorder.—" Take him away, take him away; take him out of the court."

Penn.—" I can never urge the fundamental laws of England, but you cry, 'Take him away! take him away!' But it is no wonder, since the Spanish Inquisition hath so great a place in the recorder's heart. God Almighty, who is just, will judge you all for these things."

"They then," says the narrative, "hauled the prisoners in to the bale dock, and from thence sent them to Newgate, for the non-payment of their fines; and so were their jury. But the jury were afterwards discharged upon an Habeas Corpus, returnable in the Common Pleas, where their commitment was adjudged illegal."[1]

In addition to what has been said in a previous chapter, as to the illegal custom of fining juries for their verdicts, we may here mention that in the reign of Elizabeth, in a case where three persons had been indicted and tried for murder, and the jury found them guilty of manslaughter only, against the direction of the court, and apparently against the evidence also, all the jurors were committed and find, and bound over in recognizances for their good behavior.[2] And in the reign of James I. it was held by the lord chancellor, the two chief justices and the chief baron, that when a party indicted is found guilty on the trial, the jury shall not be questioned; but when a jury has acquitted a felon or traitor against manifest proof, they may be charged in the Star-Chamber, "for their partiality in finding a manifest offender not guilty."[3] This doctrine was extended to the case of fining the grand jury when they ignored a a bill; and an instance of it occurred, in 1667, when Chief Justice Kelying fined a grand jury of the county of Somerset for refusing to find a true bill of murder against a man; but "because there were gentlemen of repute in the county, the court spared the fine."[4] This case, however, and several others in which the same

---

[1] See Bushell's case, Vaughan, 135. *Ante*, p. 154.
[2] Yelverton, 23. Noy, 48.   [3] 12 Co. Rep. 23.   [4] 2 Keble, 180.

judge was concerned, were brought before the House of Commons, and the conduct of the chief justice was condemned, the house resolving "that the precedents and practice of fining or imprisoning jurors for verdicts is illegal." Finally, in 1670, it was solemnly decided by the Court of King's Bench, that the practice was contrary to law.[1]

But juries during the seventeenth century were not always so courageous in resisting the threats and bullying of the court. The infamous Jefferies found little difficulty in persuading them to convict during his bloody assize, or "campaign," as it was not unaptly called by his master, King James II., in the west of England, after the suppression of the Duke of Monmouth's rebellion. There are few more affecting trials on record than that of Mrs. Alice Lisle[2] indicted in 1685 for high treason, in having "traitorously entertained, concealed, comforted, upheld and maintained" one Hicks (a dissenting minister), well knowing him to be a false traitor, and to have levied and raised rebellion and insurrection against the king. So ran the indictment; but the real fact was, that Mrs. Lisle had received Hicks in her house after the battle of Sedgmoor, at which he had been present with the insurgents. The whole gist of the accusation consisted in the allegation that she knew at the time that he had been out with the rebels; and this most certainly was not proved, whatever suspicions there might be on the subject. But Jefferies was not to be balked of his prey. His conduct throughout the trial was disgraceful to humanity; browbeating the witnesses

---

[1] Mr. Jardine says (Criminal Trials, p. 118) that in some extreme cases where juries obstinately persist in giving a verdict contrary to the direction of the court in matters of law, they are even at the present day liable to be fined; and he supports this assertion by a quotation from Hawkins's Pleas of the Crown. But this is very questionable in point of law, and certainly would never now be attempted in practice.

[2] 11 State Tr. 298–382.

when they did not swear quite up to the mark, and straining every point against the prisoner. The animus of the judge was plainly seen even in the affectation of impartiality with which he closed his address to the jury on summing up the case. He said:

"Gentlemen, upon your consciences be it; the preservation of the government, the life of the king, the safety and honor of our religion, and the discharge of our consciences as loyal men, good Christians, and faithful subjects, are at stake; neither her age nor her sex are to move you, who have nothing else to consider but the evidence of the fact you are to try. I charge you, therefore, as you will answer it at the bar of the last judgment, where you and we must all appear, deliver your verdict according to conscience and truth. With that great God, the impartial judge, there is no such thing as respect of persons; and in our discharge of our duty in courts of justice, he has enjoined us, his creatures, that we must have no such thing as a friend in the administration of justice; all our friendship must be to truth, and our care to preserve that inviolate." Bishop Burnet gives the following account of the verdict of the jury: "Though it was insisted on as a point of law, that till the persons found in her house were convicted, she could not be found guilty, yet Jefferies charged the jury in a most violent manner to bring her in guilty. All the audience was strangely affected with so unusual a behavior in a judge. Only the person most concerned, the lady herself, who was then past seventy, was so little moved at it, that she fell asleep. The jury brought her in Not guilty. But the judge in great fury sent them out again. Yet they brought her in a second time Not guilty. Then he seemed as in a transport of rage. He upon that threatened them with an attaint of jury. And they, overcome with fear, brought her in the third time, Guilty."

Poor Mrs. Lisle was executed—but her attainder was reversed in the following reign by an Act which recited that she had been convicted by a verdict injuriously extorted and procured by the menaces and violences, and other illegal practices of George Lord Jefferies, baron of Wem,[1] then lord chief justice of the King's Bench.

The trial and conviction of Mrs. Gaunt, on a charge of the same kind, was a fit sequel to that of Mrs. Lisle—and fills up the measure of our disgust at proceedings in which murder was committed under the form of law.

The trial and conviction of Baxter, in 1685, were also disgraceful to both judge and jury. The latter had been carefully selected by the sheriffs, who were the tools of the government, and willingly seconded Jefferies in his eagerness for a conviction.

It is refreshing after this to turn to cases where the jury both understood and performed their duty. Such was that when Sir Hugh Campbell was tried in Scotland, on a charge of high treason, in 1684, and the lord justice-general by repeated questions endeavored to induce a witness for the crown to say something unfavorable to the prisoner. The scene is thus described in Wodrow's "History of the Sufferings of the Church:"[2]

"After silence, the justice-general interrogates Ingrham again: who answered, he had said as much as he could say upon oath. And the justice-general offering a third time to interrogate Ingrham, Nisbet of Craigentinny, one of the assizers, rose up and said, 'My lord justice-general, I have been an assizer in this court above twenty times, and never heard a witness interrogate upon the same thing more than twice; and let Cesnock's persuasion be what it will, we who are assizers, and are to cog-

---

[1] He is so styled in the Act; but it seems that the letters patent, if any were in preparation, elevating him to this dignity, were never formally made out. In a book printed in 1687, a dedication appeared addressed to Jefferies by the titles of "Earl of Flint, Viscount Wycomb, and Baron Wem."

[2] 10 State Tr. 970.

nosce upon the probation upon the peril of our souls, will take notice only to Ingrham's first deposition, though your lordship should interrogate him twenty times.' The justice-general answered him with warmth, 'Sir, you are not judges in this case.' The laird of Drum, another of the assizers, presently replied, 'Yes, my lord, we are only competent judges as to the probation, though not of its relevancy.' Whereupon the whole assizers rose up, and assented to what those said. The justice-general, in a great heat, said, 'I never saw such an uproar in this court, nor, I believe, any of my predecessors before me; and it is not us you contemn, but his majesty's authority.'"

The trial and acquittal of the Seven Bishops in 1688 is a glorious example of the benefits of trial by jury.¹ There can not, I think, be a doubt that the obsequious judges at that time (always excepting Mr. Justice Powell) would have found them guilty if the decision had rested with them. The bishops were indicted for a conspiracy, the alleged overt act of which was the composition and publication of a seditious libel under the form of a petition to the King (James II.). After the case had proceeded at great length, and some evidence to prove the publication, about which there was a great difficulty, had been supplied by the opportune arrival of the Lord President of the Council, the lord chief justice, Sir R. Wright, said: "Truly, I must needs tell you that there was a great presumption before, but there is a greater now, and I think I shall leave it with some effect to the jury. I can not see but here is enough to put the proof upon you." After the case had been summed up, and the opinions of the several judges given upon the point of law, as to whether the petition in question was a libel or not, the chief justice said to the jury:

¹ 12 State Tr. 183–431.

"Gentlemen of the jury, have you a mind to drink before you go?"

Jury.—"Yes, my lord, if you please."

Upon this wine was sent for, and the jury having refreshed themselves, retired to consider their verdict. They stayed in deliberation all night, "without fire or candle," and the next morning came into court with a verdict of Not Guilty; "at which there were several great shouts in court, and throughout the hall." The shouts, says Kennett, were carried on through the cities of Westminster and London, and flew to Hounslow-heath, where the soldiers in the camp echoed them so loud that it startled the king, who was then in Lord Feversham's tent. He sent to know what was the matter, and the earl came back and told him, "It is nothing but the soldiers shouting upon the news of the bishops being acquitted." The king replied, "And do you call that nothing? but so much the worse for them."

The king might well ask whether it was nothing, when the army proclaimed by huzzas its sympathy with a verdict which rescued the Church of England from its hostile grasp. It was the death-knell of all his hopes, and told him, with a voice that could not be mistaken, that Protestant England would not submit her neck to the dominion of an alien pontiff, or her liberties to the caprice of a bigoted monarch.

Bishop Burnet tells us of a jury in his time who were shut up a whole day and night, and those who were for an acquittal yielded to the fury of the rest, only that they might save their lives, and not be starved.[1] At the present day, when the jury in a criminal

---

[1] Not long ago a special jury at Salisbury, who were shut up to consider their verdict, sent a message to the Sheriff, saying that they had already used as fuel the chairs, and were on the point of burning the tables in their room. On one occasion lately a facetious judge being asked by a juror on retiring, whether he might have a glass of water, decided that he might, saying, that in his opinion water was not drink.

trial can not agree upon a verdict, they are discharged as soon as the confinement and abstinence become seriously injurious to health; and this is generally certified to the court by a medical man. But it may well be doubted whether the rule as to their being kept "without meat, drink, or fire," ought not to be relaxed. It is difficult to see what harm can possibly result from their being supplied with a moderate degree of food and the warmth of fire during their deliberation. The interruption of their ordinary occupations, and the loss of time and inconvenience occasioned by their attendance at the trial, are quite a sufficient stimulus to induce them to come quickly to an agreement, without adding the pangs of hunger, and thirst, and cold. And it seems absurd, if not worse, to try and starve men into unanimity in a matter in which their consciences are concerned. The result must often be that the strongest stomach, instead of the wisest head, carries the day. I feel persuaded that if we first heard of the existence of this custom in a book of travels relating to some distant country, we should denounce it as utterly unreasonable; and nothing but long usage could reconcile us to its continuance amongst us. For my own part, I am unable to devise an argument defending it. The possibility of excess seems to be the only pretext for the rule; but this is a chimerical apprehension, since it is always in the power of the court to take care that the food and drink supplied shall be of the most temperate kind. It may possibly be said, that even this to some common jurors would be a temptation to prolong the sitting; but when we consider the detriment to their own private affairs which absence causes, such a case can only be a rare and exceptional one.

As a refreshing contrast to the mode of conducting state prosecutions in old times, we can not do better than carefully peruse the trials of Hardy, Horne Tooke, and others, indicted in 1794, for high treason; and also those of Thistlewood, and Ings, indicted in 1820, for the same offense. The circumstances, however, of the cases at these two periods were very different. Hardy, Horne Tooke, Holcroft, Thelwall, and others, were tried for constructive treason, in conspiring to subvert the govment, by attending illegal meetings, and inciting the people to send delegates to a convention, with intent that the persons to be assembled at such convention might wickedly and traitorously, without, and in defiance of, the authority and against the will of the parliament of this kingdom, subvert and alter the legislature, rule and government of the realm, and depose the king from the royal state, title, power, and government thereof.[1] The prisoners were, at their own wish, tried separately; and the occasion afforded Erskine an opportunity for the display of his unrivalled eloquence, and the achievement of his most brilliant triumphs. He was counsel for Hardy, whose trial came on first, and it will be forever memorable from the noble oration of the impassioned advocate who defended him. Erskine then eclipsed himself, and made a speech not unworthy of comparison with any ever delivered by Demosthenes or Cicero. It is impossible to give a notion of its excellence by mere extracts; it would be like offering a few bricks as a specimen of a house. Nor is this the place for criticising the mighty effort. But one passage I may cite to show the boldness of his language, and the spirit with which juries can be addressed when a question of political freedom is at stake. It is as follows:

"I will say anywhere, without fear,—nay, I will say here, where I stand,—that an attempt to interfere, by despotic combination and violence, with any government which a people choose to give to themselves, whether it be good or evil, is an oppression and subver-

[1] State Trials, Vols. XXIV. and XXV.

sion of the natural and unalienable rights of man; and though the government of this country should countenance such a system, it would not only be still legal for me to express my detestation of it, as I here deliberately express it, but it would become my interest and my duty. For, if combinations of despotism can accomplish such a purpose, who shall tell me what other nation shall not be the prey of their ambition?—Upon the very principle of denying to a people the right of governing themselves, how are we to resist the French, should they attempt by violence to fasten their government upon us? Or, what inducement would there be for resistance to preserve laws, which are not, it seems, our own, but which are unalterably imposed upon us?— The very argument strikes as with a palsy the arm and vigor of the nation. I hold dear the privileges I am contending for, not as privileges hostile to the constitution, but as necessary for its preservation; and if the French were to intrude by force upon the government of our own free choice, I should leave these papers, and return to a profession, that, perhaps, I better understand."

The result was, that Hardy was acquitted, and the government were ill-advised enough to persist in the other prosecutions, which, as might be expected, terminated in its defeat. Thistlewood and his companions, called the "Cato-street Conspirators," were determined rebels, who had all but succeeded in surprising and assassinating the ministers of the day at Lord Harrowby's house in Grosvenor-Square.[1] They were convicted and executed as they deserved; and I only allude to their trials as good examples of the fair and temperate mode in which they are now conducted. But for this purpose any of the trials during the last hundred years may be

---

[1] 33 State Tr. 681–1566.

taken at random, and they, perhaps better than any argument or theory, will serve to display the inestimable benefits of the system in cases affecting reputation, liberty, or life.

CHAPTER XVIII.

THE JURY CONSIDERED AS A SOCIAL, POLITICAL, AND JUDICIAL INSTITUTION.

AN institution like the jury, existing for ages amongst a people, can not but influence the national character. And it is not difficult to point out proofs of this. If Englishmen are distinguished for one moral feature more than another, it is, I think, a love for fair play, and abhorrence of injustice. Now the very essence of the jury trial is its principle of fairness. The right of being tried by his equals, that is, his fellow-citizens, taken indiscriminately from the mass, who feel neither malice nor favor, but simply decide according to what in their conscience they believe to be the truth, gives every man a conviction that he will be dealt with impartially, and inspires him with the wish to mete out to others the same measure of equity that is dealt to himself.

But we must not suppose that it is trial by jury in criminal cases only that exercises a beneficial influence, or that it can safely stand alone. In his able and philosophical work, " De la Démocratie en Amérique,"[1] M. de Tocqueville avows his conviction that the jury system, if limited solely to criminal trials, is always in peril. And the reasons he gives for this opinion are well worthy of consideration. He says that in that case the people see it in operation only at intervals, and in particular cases; they are accustomed to dispense with it in the ordinary affairs of life, and look upon it merely as one means, and not

[1] Tom. II. 188.

the sole means of obtaining justice. But when it embraces civil actions, it is constantly before their eyes, and affects all their interests; it penetrates into the usages of life, and so habituates the minds of men to its forms, that they, so to speak, confound it with the very idea of justice. The jury, he continues, and especially the civil jury, serves to imbue the minds of the citizens of a country with a part of the qualities and character of a judge; and this is the best mode of preparing them for freedom. It spreads amongst all classes a respect for the decisions of the law; it teaches them the practice of equitable dealing. Each man in judging his neighbor thinks that he may be also judged in his turn. This is in an especial manner true of the civil jury; for although hardly any one fears lest he may become the object of a criminal prosecution, everybody may be engaged in a law suit. It teaches every man not to shrink from the responsibility attaching to his own acts; and this gives a manly character, without which there is no political virtue. It clothes every citizen with a kind of magisterial office; it makes all feel that they have duties to fulfill towards society, and that they take a part in its government; it forces men to occupy themselves with something else than their own affairs, and thus combats that individual selfishness, which is, as it were, the rust of the community. Such are some of the advantages which, according to the view of this profound thinker, result from trial by jury in civil cases.

But, moreover, it is one great instrument for the education of the people. "This is, in my opinion," says M. de Tocqueville, "its greatest advantage."[1] He calls it a school into which admission is free and always open, which each juror enters to be instructed in his legal rights, where he engages in daily communication with

[1] "C'est là, à mon avis," says M. de Tocqueville, "son plus grand avantage."

the most accomplished and enlightened of the upper classes, where the laws are taught him in a practical manner, and are brought down to the level of his apprehension by the efforts of the advocates, the instruction of the judge, and the very passions of the parties in the cause. Hence, says M. de Tocqueville,[1] "I regard it as one of the most efficacious means that society can employ for the education of the masses."

It is also no mean advantage of the system, that it calls upon the people largely to participate in judicial functions; and this makes them in a great degree responsible for the purity of the proceedings of the courts of law. Such, indeed, was the case at Athens of old, but public morality was there at a low ebb: and the capital error was committed of lessening the sense of responsibility, by distributing it amongst a crowd of dicasts, who decided causes with the feelings and passions of a tumultuous assembly, rather than the grave austerity of a court of justice. From the first of these evils England has been preserved by Christianity; and the second has been avoided by limiting to twelve persons in each case the investigation of disputed facts, and decision respecting innocence or guilt. We are so familiar with the system, that we can hardly appreciate its full value. And yet it must react upon and influence the tone of public feeling, when so large a portion of the community are frequently called upon to discharge the important functions that devolve upon juries; when they have so often to promise, under the awful sanction of an oath, to lay aside anger, and hate, and fear; nor allow themselves to be swayed by love or friendship while they address themselves to their solemn duties: when they witness the unwavering firmness and stern impartiality with which justice is administered, and listen to the calm and passion-

---

[1] "Je le regarde comme l'un des moyens les plus efficaces dont puisse se servir la société pour l'éducation du peuple."

less recapitulation of the evidence by the presiding judge, in whose hands the balance is held so evenly, that it is often difficult to discover to which side his own individual opinion inclines, and impossible to know which he wishes to succeed.

The jury may also be considered in another point of view. It is a political institution of the highest value.— "The jury," says M. de Tocqueville,[1] "is emphatically a political institution. The man who judges in criminal cases is, then, really a master of society. The institution of the jury places the people themselves, or at least one class of citizens, upon the seat of the judge. The institution of the jury, then, actually places the direction of society in the hands of the people, or of this class."

The basis, and as it were taproot, of that enlightened freedom which distinguishes the Anglo-Saxon race, is the principle of self-government. It is astonishing how little the crown or the executive interferes with the internal regulation of the affairs of Englishmen. Municipal institutions in our towns spread over the kingdom a number of small parliaments, in which the representatives of each locality, annually elected by the rate-payers, discuss and decide upon the business which interests the inhabitants with as much independence as the House of Commons itself. If any act of illegal usurpation were attempted, they would instantly become the centers of resistance round which the people would rally. The borough funds are administered by each corporation, and the police act under its orders with as little control by the government as though the latter did not exist. Almost every man has an opportunity of making

---

[1] " Le jury, est avant tout une institution politique. . . . L'homme qui juge au criminel est donc réellement le maître de la société. L'institution du jury place le peuple luimeme, ou du moins une classe de citoyens, sur le siége du juge. L'institution du jury met donc réellement la direction de la société dans les mains du peuple, ou de cette classe."—De la Démocratie en Amérique, Tom. II. 184–186.

his voice heard and his influence felt in all questions of local interest. And if he fails in his opposition to measures to which he is adverse, it is only because he is outvoted by a majority of his fellow-citizens. A field for active exertion is thus afforded to those busy spirits which take delight in the excitement of public business and popular harangues, and a safety-valve is opened through which escapes the vapor of ill-humor, which, if pent up altogether, might explode in sedition or treason. This it is which, combined with the enjoyment in ample measure of the political franchise, places the liberties of the country in a position of stable equilibrium, and enables the vessel of the State to ride at anchor and in safety, while the storm of revolution sweeps with whirlwind violence over Europe.

Now it is obvious that trial by jury is in direct harmony with and encourages the exercise of this habit. Its very nature consists in making the people the arbiters in questions affecting their property, liberties, and lives. "It is to trial by jury," says one whose opinion is entitled to the greatest weight on such a question,[1] "more than even by representation (as it at present exists)[2] that the people own the share they have in the government of the country; it is to trial by jury, also, that the government mainly owes the attachment of the people to the laws; a consideration which ought to make our legislators very cautious how they take away this mode of trial by new, trifling, and vexatious enactments."

On the continent however, and especially in France, although there trial by jury does partially exist, self-government is practically unknown. Centralization swallows up and absorbs all freedom of local action. The government stretches out its polypus arms in every di-

[1] Lord John Russell, On the English Government, p. 394
[2] That is in 1823.

rection, and hardly anything is too minute and unimportant for its grasp. The people do not manage their own affairs, but are treated like children, fit only to be "under tutors and governors."[1] The consequence is, that the executive is made responsible for every real or imaginary evil; discontent at its measures smolders in the hearts of the population, and the riot of a mob leads to the overthrow of a throne. "The more contracted power is," says Dr. Johnson, "the more easily it is overthrown. A country governed by a despot is an inverted cone. Government there can not be so firm as when it rests upon a broad basis gradually contracted, as the government of Great Britain." The history of France during the last sixty years abundantly proves this. The government there, under whatever form, whether that of Directory, Consulship, Empire, Restoration, Monarchy of the Barricades, Republic, or the Army, which is its present phase, has always been essentially despotic in its character. It has ruled by a system of paid employés in immediate dependence upon itself. The provincial functionaries, such as prefects and subprefects, and mayors of arrondissements, are mere puppets whose strings are pulled by the executive in Paris. In no country is the system of police surveillance and espionage more thoroughly understood or constantly practiced. No public meetings are convened as in England to take into consideration the measures of government, and if necessary organize a peaceful opposition to

---

[1] Il est évident que la pluplart de nos princes ne veulent pas seulement diriger le peuple tout entier; on dirait qu'ils se jugent responsables des actions et de la destinée individuelle de leurs sujets, qu'ils ont entrepis de conduire et d'éclairer chacun d'eux dans les differents actes de sa vie, et au besoin, de le rendre heureux malgré lui-meme. De leur coté les particuliers envisagent de plus en plus le pouvoir social sous le meme jour; dans tous leur besoins ils l'apellent à leur aide, et ils attachent à tous moments sur lui leurs regards comme sur un precepteur ou sur un guide.—De Tocqueville, Démocratie en Amérique.

them. The people are not, except in the solitary instance of dropping their individual votes into the ballot-box when the period of an election comes round, made parties to the management of their own interests. Hence there is, properly speaking, no public opinion in France, the influence of which can be felt by statesmen, and enable them to forecast the measures which will be best suited for the wants and most in accordance with the real wishes of the nation. Hence also results the startling paradox, that the French of all people in the world are the most impatient of constitutional control, and the most servilely submissive to despotic power.

But how, it may be asked, is this consistent with the assertion that the institution of the jury, which does exist in France, is conducive to self-government? The answer is, that its tendency is thwarted by opposing influences. It is but of recent introduction, and has not grown with the growth and strengthened with the strength of the French people. It has been adopted from without, and there has not yet been time for it to counteract the results of centuries. In order to become the champion of freedom, it ought first to be its child. A nation must be accustomed to and familiar with the use of free institutions, to derive full benefit from the jury trial. As the people are thereby invested with the most important part of the judicial office, the right of determining questions of innocence and guilt, they must be fitted for their task in order to discharge it well. But how can this be if they have been brought up in habits of servile dependence upon the will of the government, acting everywhere and in everything through its official myrmidons? This serves partly to explain the fact to which I have before adverted, that French juries actively seconded the government in its attacks upon the liberty of the press, and have thus conspired with it against their own freedom.

But there is also another reason for the apparent anomaly. There is no doubt that the jury in any shape, if left to itself, is antagonistic to arbitrary power. Hence, in all the continental nations where it has been introduced, the governments have endeavored to retain some influence over its decisions by entrusting the formation of the primary lists of the jurors, out of whom the particular twelve are to be selected, to their own officers. Between such employés and our own sheriffs there is really no analogy. A French prefect is the nominee and paid servant of the government. He may be dismissed by it at any moment, and has, therefore, a direct and palpable interest in obeying the suggestions of those upon whom his tenure of office depends. But the sheriffs in this country are in no sense the creatures of the crown or the government. In the first place they receive no salary or pay of any kind, but, on the contrary, serve at a heavy expense to themselves. The office is in reality a burdensome one—and so would be felt were it not for the honor and position it confers for the time being. It is held only for a year, and the crown selects for it one of three persons in each county whose names are selected and presented by the judges. The sheriff is, in fact, in his ministerial capacity merely the officer of the courts of law for executing their writs and process; and as such he is amenable to their summary jurisdiction, and may be fined by them for neglect of duty.

We can, therefore, at the present day afford to smile at the danger with which we are threatened by a French writer, M. Oudot, when he points out as a defect in our system, which may be attended with the gravest consequences, the fact that the nomination of the sheriffs charged with the selection of juries belongs to the crown. He says, "If the minister could succeed in corrupting the judges who present the candidates for the office of sheriff, he might inflict a mortal blow upon the independence of the jury."[1] But it can not be denied that there have been times when the apprehension was by no means chimerical, not, indeed, that the judges might be corrupted in selecting candidates for the office, but that the sheriffs themselves, might yield in the performance of their duties to the influence of favoritism and power. Under the Tudor princes it was no uncommon thing to tamper with the sheriff in order that he might return a panel favorable to the wishes of the crown; and refractory juries were summoned before the Star-Chamber or Privy Council, and there reprimanded, and sometimes punished with fine and imprisonment. Thus it was that, in the eloquent words of Mr. Hallam,[2] "That primæval institution, those inquests by twelve true men, the unadulterated voice of the people responsible alone to God and their conscience, which should have been heard in the sanctuaries of justice, as fountains springing fresh from the lap of earth, became like waters constrained in their course by art, stagnant and impure."

But we must not exaggerate the extent or effect of this interference. The Star-Chamber never ventured to deprive the subject of his general right to trial by jury. The exercise of the powers of that unconstitutional tribunal was wholly exceptional. It did not pretend to assume cognizance of the great mass of offenses known to the law, but was the instrument whereby the crown gave effect to its own prerogative, the nature of which was in those days little understood, nor was its power confined within any definite limits. At an earlier period we find a formal attempt made in a single instance (at least I know of no other), to abrogate by law the claim

[1] Théorie du jury.
[2] Const. Hist. Eng. I. 316, 3rd edit. In Lodge's Illustrations and the Paston Correspondence we find numerous examples of improper solicitation by persons interested of the jurors returned on the panel.

of a citizen to be tried by a jury of his countrymen. The rolls of Parliament for the reign of Edward IV. contain a petition from two persons, Henry Bodrugan and Richard Bonethon, praying that their conviction might be annulled.[1] An act had been passed in the fourteenth year of that reign, which authorized the justices of the King's Bench to examine them on a charge of felony, and provided, "that if the said Henry and Richard were by their examination found guilty, they then should have such judgment and execution as they should have had if they were of the same attaint by the trial of twelve men, and like forfeiture to be in that behalf." The accused parties refused to appear, and were convicted by default. They therefore petitioned the crown that the judgment might be annulled, on the ground that a trial by justices in this mode was unknown to the law of England, and was a novel and dangerous innovation. The king granted their prayer, and thus affirmed the principle of the indefeasible right of the subjects of this realm to be tried, as they have heretofore been accustomed, by a jury of their peers.

And it would be difficult to conceive a better security than this right affords against any exercise of arbitrary violence on the part of the crown, or a government acting in the name of the crown. No matter how ardent may be its wish to destroy or crush an obnoxious opponent, there can be no real danger from its menaces or acts so long as the party attacked can take refuge in a jury fairly and indifferently chosen. If the law of the land is that the question of guilt is in all cases to be decided by such a tribunal, the people must conspire against themselves before monarch or minister can injure their property or unjustly abridge their individual freedom. To use the words of Bourguignon, when speaking of the jury in his excellent memoir on the means of improving that system in France: "Leur indépendance ne peut être dangereuse parceque leur pouvoir n'est qu'instantané : ne tenant à aucune corporation ils ne peuvent avoir d'autre intérêt que celui de la justice ; on ne saurait faire servir le pouvoir qui leur est confié, à un système général d'oppression ou de tyrannie, puisque, pour les séduire, il faudrait séduire la masse entière des bons citoyens, et leur faire préférer l'intérêt des oppresseurs à leur propres intérêts."

Hence it is that the nations of the Continent have so ardently desired to obtain this mode of trial amongst themselves, and have put it in the van of their demands in all revolutionary movements. It is no exaggerated statement of the Danish jurist, Repp, when he says, "All modern nations (Europeans and Americans at least), in as far as they dare express their political opinions, though disagreeing in many other points in politics, seem to agree in this: that they consider trial by jury as a palladium, which lost or won, will draw the liberty of the subject along with it. In the many constitutions which have been projected or established in the nineteenth century, most other things were dissimilar and local; this alone was a vital point, a punctum saliens from which it was expected that the whole fabric of a liberal constitution would be spontaneously dated."[1]

Take, for instance, the freedom of the press. This, which we justly prize as one of the first of social blessings, is chiefly indebted to the jury for its vigorous existence. Every state-trial for a seditious libel in this country is an appeal from the government to the people. They by their representative twelve determine in each case, under the guidance of a judge, the degree of license which is allowable in the discussion of public questions; and their liberty is thus placed directly in their own hands. A tyrannical minister in a country whose constitution is

[1] Historical Treatise on Juries in Scandinavia.

nominally free may, through the agency of servile and corrupt tribunals, establish despotism under the form of law. But how can he accomplish this when, instead of judges removable at pleasure, he has to obtain the concurrence of independent citizens, taken at random from the community? They will not forge chains to enslave themselves. They will not pronounce a publication to be criminal because it reflects upon a government whose conduct they feel ought to be subject to their censorship and control. The press, therefore, that mightiest agent for good and evil of modern times, has a peculiar interest in the preservation of a tribunal which gives it the right of saying Provoco ad populum, when the arm of the executive is stretched out to destroy it.

Moreover, it is no light matter in a constitutional point of view, for the people to repose undoubting confidence in their legal tribunals. Political grievances are really often of far less practical importance than judicial. It is a much less evil to be deprived of an electoral vote than to be exposed to the danger of an unfair trial upon a false accusation, or to have one's property at the mercy of an adversary who is rich enough to bribe a venal judge. No whisper of such a suspicion is ever breathed in this country, and the consequence is a feeling of security and confidence in the upright administration of the law which nothing can shake. This is said to have been in a remarkable manner exemplified during the great Rebellion of 1642. Then, although the kingdom was rent asunder by civil wars, and Royalist and Roundhead fought desperately for their opposite political creeds, the ordinary functions of the courts of justice were neither changed nor suspended. The judges went their circuits, and held their assizes: and juries determined questions of property and life as in times of profound tranquillity; nor did either party attempt to interfere with proceedings which both felt alike an interest in protecting. In the later years of ancient Rome the corruption of the legal tribunals was notorious. No reader of Cicero requires to be reminded of this; and it was one of the most efficient causes which led to the downfall of the Republic; for liberty became valueless when the fountains of justice were poisoned at their source.

An opposite evil may, indeed, arise in times of popular excitement. Jurors drawn from the masses of the people, and under the influence of the same passions as their neighbors and fellow-citizens, may paralyze the arm of government by refusing to bring in verdicts of guilty where the charge is that of sedition or treason, although the case against the accused is clearly proved. This has happened at different times in this country, and it might be carried to such an extent as to render a state-prosecution a hopeless attempt. But the evil suggests its own remedy. It may, I think, be safely asserted, that when this universal disinclination to convict exists, even where the evidence is clear, it is time to change the measures which have provoked such a humiliating result. It is worse than useless to persist in a course of policy which renders the executive powerless, and gives a triumph to the mob in every verdict of acquittal. The tack of the vessel must be altered when she can make no headway in the course that has been hitherto steered.

With respect to the jury system as a means of protecting innocence, it may be safely averred that it is the rarest of accidents when an innocent man is convicted in this country.' To say that it never happens would be to give to a human tribunal the attribute of infallibility, to fly in the face of recorded facts. But so long as man's judgment is liable to error, such cases must now and then occur, whatever precaution is taken to prevent them. And before such a catastrophe can happen in

· For tables of the numbers of acquittals and convictions in the United Kingdom during the last few years, see APPENDIX.

our own courts, how strong must be the evidence which implicates the accused! The committing magistrate, the grand jury, the petit jury, and the presiding judge, must all, in different degrees, have concurred in bringing about the result. I say the presiding judge, for if he has grave doubts as to the prisoner's guilt, it is always in his power, and indeed it becomes his duty, to point out to the jury what the circumstances are which may make it unsafe for them to bring in a verdict of guilty; and it is well known that such an intimation is hardly ever disregarded.

But can it with equal truth be asserted that juries never acquit in ordinary cases when they ought to condemn? I fear not. This is no doubt the vulnerable point of the system, that feelings of compassion for the prisoner, or of repugnance to the punishment which the law awards, are sometimes allowed to overpower their sense of duty. They usurp in such cases the prerogative of mercy, forgetting that they have sworn to give a true verdict according to the evidence. But it is an error at which humanity need not blush: it springs from one of the purest instincts of our nature, and is a symptom of kindliness of heart which as a national characteristic is an honor. In some parts of Ireland, indeed, we can not doubt that unwillingness to convict has proceeded from sympathy with crime; but those cases are exceptional. The state of Ireland is abnormal. Her social system is disorganized; and so long as murders can be there committed in broad day in the face of many bystanders, and no attempt be made to prevent the crime or arrest the assassin, we can not hope that juries will be found less ready to secure impunity to guilt. When in respect of any class of offenses the difficulty of obtaining convictions is at all general in England, we may hold it as an axiom, that the law requires amendment. Such conduct in juries is the silent protest of the people against its undue severity. This was strongly exemplified in the case of prosecutions for the forgery of bank-notes, when it was a capital felony. It was in vain that the charge was proved. Juries would not condemn men to the gallows for an offense of which the punishment was out of all proportion to the crime; and as they could not mitigate the sentence they brought in verdicts of Not Guilty. The consequence was, that the law was changed; and when secondary punishments were substituted for the penalty of death, a forger had no better chance of an acquittal than any other criminal. Thus it is that the power which juries possess of refusing to put the law in force has, in the words of Lord John Russell,[1] "been the cause of amending many bad laws which the judges would have administered with professional bigotry,[2] and above all, it has this important and useful consequence, that laws totally repugnant to the feelings of the community for which they are made, can not long prevail in England."

It would be strange indeed if we were dissatisfied with a tribunal which is one of the objects most prized by those nations on the continent who possess it, and most coveted by those who do not. Let us listen to the language used by a German judge on opening an assize court in Rhenish Bavaria, in 1834:[3]

"As often as the day again appears, on which jurors meet for the discharge of their important functions, earnest thoughts must throng upon the mind of every reflecting person who understands how to judge of and lay to heart the higher relations of the social union. The first impression certainly amongst us all is a feeling of joy that we are still in possession of an institution which

---

[1] Essay on English Government, p. 393.

[2] This expression is rather harsh, for it must be remembered that the judges are bound to administer the law as they find it. They are not responsible for its undue severity. This is the fault of the legislature. So that, "professional bigotry" really can mean nothing more than "conscientious regard for their duty and their oaths."

[3] See Staats-Lexicon, Vol. VII. Art. Jury.

the freest nations of two hemispheres regard as their most precious jewel, and watch over with jealous eyes—an institution which calls on the unprejudiced, independent citizen to be the judge of his equal;—which surrounds the holiest rights of man—the rights of liberty and honor—with the strongest guards which human foresight could devise, when it freed the verdict of guilty or not guilty from the trammels of legal technicality, and entrusted it to the conscience of chosen men, who taken from the midst of the population, and from all classes of the community, offer every possible guarantee for a discerning and impartial administration of justice. The people who possess such an institution stand higher than those who are still without it. They are less in their nonage, and more free. The citizen who from time to time is summoned from the round of his usual avocations to the judgment-seat, must feel himself in a high degree honored and elevated by the trust reposed in him. He becomes more conscious of his worth as a man and a citizen. He gains both in experience and intelligence. Rightly, therefore, may a certain degree of pride mingle with the feeling of joy of which I have spoken."

Such sentiments could only spring from a deep conviction of the worth of the object they applaud. And this conviction was no doubt strengthened by the contrast that exists between trial by jury and the mode of criminal procedure in the other German states, of which we have already spoken. But such contrast enhances the value of the testimony.

It must, however, be admitted that it is not in its criminal functions that the jury has been exposed to the attacks of those who question its title to public favor. No voice worth noticing has been raised against it in this aspect, although it has often been said in jest, that an innocent man would prefer being tried by a judge, and a guilty one by a jury, who would be more likely to blunder into an acquittal. But its merits as a tribunal for the decision of civil actions have been more freely canvassed; and here we can not appeal to the desire of the continental nations to adopt the institution as a testimony on its behalf; for in no instance have they introduced into their courts trial by jury in civil cases. They have looked at it only as a means of protection against false charges of crime, and have not ventured to submit to its decision complicated questions of property or contract, where facts asserted on one side are denied on the other.

In the speech made by Hérault de Séchelles, when he presented the Report of the Jurisprudence Committee to the French National Convention in 1793, he said:

"It is not the same in civil affairs as in criminal. In criminal matters where the law is deficient, the accused is discharged of right, because his crime not being found in the law is no longer considered as crime; it is only a question then of acquitting or condemning him. But in a civil process, a party may make a just demand for the most legitimate rights, and it is possible that the law may be silent. In this case what shall the judge do? shall he send away a plaintiff whose moral right is clear, a victim of the imprévoyance of the civil law? But there is a more urgent reason because it belongs to the nature of things. It is, that in almost all lawsuits it is impossible to distinguish the fact and the right, which usually are mixed together; and the one can not be preserved or apprehended without the other. But further: in criminal matters you rise from the fact to the law; in civil, from the law to the fact: so that it would be necessary in civil matters to place the judge in the first order and the jury in the second. The example of the English is opposed; but it is a fact, that they groan under a civil jurisprudence which is at the same time slow and circuitous. . . .

"The institution of the civil jury has appeared to us

impracticable, and those who are obstinate in supporting it have not enough, perhaps, reflected upon the nature of the jury. The jury in criminal matters, as in civil affairs, only decides upon the facts, not upon the law Or if it should be possible to find in each contestation the means of declaring a fact, if there exists not a law for each contestation, as there exists one for each crime, how would the judges act charged with applying the law? They would decide then according to their own opinion. But if they did not see the fact like the juries, or if, as it more often happens, the matter can be considered under different bearings, if it presents different consequences, then the judges would be themselves juries, or rather the juries would be useless. It would be a monstrous thing in civil matters that the judges could annihilate by their opinion the declaration of the the jury; it would be doing away with the jury itself. Shall it be said, then, that in this case the office of the judge will be useless? But then they make the juries judges of facts as well as law; which is repugnant to the nature of things; then they are simply judges, and there are no more juries."

And one of the ablest and most philosophical jurists of modern times, Meyer, expressly points out the civil jury as one of the defects of our judicial system.[1] After admitting in terms of warm eulogium the advantages of the jury as a tribunal for criminal inquiry, he says that no reason exists for entrusting the examination of facts in a civil action to persons who are not familiar with the conduct of such actions. But the grounds alleged by Meyer for his opinion are so weak, that it is surprising to find them brought forward by a writer of his reputation. His argument is this. A civil proceeding not only possesses much less interest for those who investigate it, but presents much greater variety than

[1] Orig. des Instit. Judic. II. c. 21

one of a criminal nature; and a juryman can not be expected to give as much attention to a question which has not the same degree of importance as those of the latter kind. There may be motives why a defendant in a civil cause should not wish to give a complete answer to the action, but may find his advantage in being defeated. For instance, he may be in possession of a guarantee or indemnity which he can enforce against a third party; and he may, in collusion with the plaintiff, submit to an adverse verdict, in order to share with the latter the proceeds of the guarantee, which he can afterwards recover against the guarantor! And Meyer asks how such a manœuvre can be discovered by a jury, which is not like a permanent judge conversant with actions, and can have no motive for suspecting the parties? It is hardly necessary to answer such reasoning as this; but it may be asked in reply, what motives a judge any more than a jury could have for imagining that a case so utterly improbable would happen. And if it did, the judgment of a court must be the same as the verdict of a jury. If a party declines to defend a suit, the plaintiff must succeed, whatever may be the nature of the arrangement between them with respect to ulterior proceedings. No court of law or equity can eke out for a man a defense of which he refuses to avail himself. And, besides, Meyer forgets that the guarantor in such a case could immediately, after being called upon to pay the money, bring an action against the party whom he indemnified, and recover the whole amount he had been compelled to pay; so that there can be no imaginable reason why the defendant in the first suit should collude with the plaintiff to the injury of the guarantor. A man is not likely to agree to divide a sum with A, when by so doing he renders himself liable to pay the whole amount to B. But, moreover, we are told by the same author, that the whole proceeding of trial by jury in civil suits is illusory.

The jury, he says, give their verdict after the whole case has been summed up by the presiding judge; and that verdict may be set aside by the court above, and a new trial ordered on various grounds; which have been previously explained. Of what value, then, he asks, is a mode of trial which is submitted to the censorship of a superior tribunal, not only in matters of form, but upon the merits, as in the case of questions as to the sufficiency of evidence and excessive damages? What is the liberty of a jury which sees a first verdict annulled, because it is not approved of by the presiding judge, and which knows that after a second trial the verdict will be brought under the consideration of the same judges who have already invalidated the decision arrived at in the first? Is not the intervention of the jury in civil questions, subject to the correction of a permanent tribunal, the means of throwing ridicule on the institution, and inspiring a doubt of its utility, even in criminal proceedings?

Now, strangely enough, the objections which are here urged by Meyer against trial by jury in civil cases will, to most minds, I think, appear to be some of the chief recommendations of the system. I need not repeat here the language of Lord Mansfield, which has been already quoted, respecting the necessity of not allowing verdicts in the first instance to be in all cases final, and subject to no power of revision or possibility of reconsideration. It would be much easier to argue in favor of admitting such a power in criminal cases, than to deny its advantages in civil. The supervision of verdicts, as it is exercised by the courts of law in this country, not only does not render the jury trial illusory, but increases its efficiency in a remarkable degree. Whatever might be the nature of the tribunal, it would be an intolerable hardship if no means existed of correcting its mistakes, which must sometimes inevitably occur in the course of investigating difficult and complicated questions of fact. The decision of a court consisting of one or more judges, to whom alone Meyer would intrust this task, is surely liable to error; and yet either its decision must be in all cases irreversible, or if not then, according to his argument, its powers are nugatory, and its proceedings illusory.

But although it is easy to answer the above objections, it can not be denied that plausible arguments may be urged against the fitness of a jury to determine the intricate questions that often arise in civil actions. Nor will it be thought a sufficient answer to say that the system has in this country antiquity to recommend it. We live in times when this plea is treated with small respect. A better reason for the continuance of an institution must be given than that it has been handed down to us by our forefathers, although this alone ought to raise a presumption in its favor, and throw upon the opponent the burden of proving his objection. The many evils which have long deformed our jurisprudence have produced in the public mind a feeling of jealousy and discontent at the state of the law, which is not likely to be restrained by the reflection that the present generation is no worse off in this respect than those which have preceded it. That man must be a careless observer, who thinks that a remedy will be found in mere palliatives, or that mischief can be arrested by a few slight changes. The machinery of our law is too complicated, and its working too expensive, to suit the wants of the present busy age; and it must be effectually amended, or it will run the risk of being rudely overthrown.

At times impatient murmurs may be heard against the ignorance or perverseness of juries, and their verdicts are unfavorably contrasted with what are supposed likely to have been the decisions of a learned and clear-sighted judge. Within the last few years an innovation has taken place of an important kind. The act establishing the county courts has substituted single judges for juries in all cases within their jurisdiction where neither of the litigant parties claims to have the cause heard before the latter tribunal. But a still greater change consists in the number of the jurors. The old immemorial twelve are no longer required, but the jury is limited to five, whose verdict determines the facts in dispute. The reason of this, no doubt, has been a conviction on the part of the legislature, that the great majority of causes which would be tried in the county courts were likely to be of too trifling a nature to justify them in throwing the burden of attendance upon a larger number. But in selecting an uneven number like five, and still requiring their verdict to be unanimous, they seem to have been impressed with the idea, that in case of difference of opinion there must necessarily be a majority, who are more likely to influence the dissentients than where the numbers are equally divided. The allowing judges to decide both facts and law in claims limited to a certain amount, is nothing more than extending to civil cases the principle which entrusts magistrates with the power of summary conviction in minor offenses.

In the outlines of a proposed code lately put forth by the Society for Promoting the Amendment of the Law, one of the articles is, "All questions of fact shall be determined by the judge, unless either party shall require them to be determined by a jury." This corresponds with the provision in the New York code previously quoted, which enables the parties in a cause, by mutual consent, to dispense with a jury. And certainly, as regards the public, no fair objection can be taken to such a plan; for volenti non fit injuria; and there seems no reason why, if both parties desire it, they should not be at liberty to forego a jury trial. But an additional burden would thereby be thrown upon the judges; and this deserves consideration, as will be noticed hereafter. The opponents, however, of the civil jury say—and it may be admitted—that juries are sometimes mistaken, and their verdicts wrong. I believe that this happens much less frequently than the objection implies; and chiefly in those cases where there is such a conflict of evidence and probabilities as would render it difficult for any tribunal, however constituted, to arrive at the truth. The presiding judge has, by the tendency and bias of the remarks which he makes in summing up, the means of influencing and guiding them to a right result; and they have generally the good sense to avail themselves of all the help afforded by his perspicacity. And in the power of granting a new trial, the court possess an effectual, though, it must be confessed, an expensive remedy, against verdicts in civil cases which are manifestly improper. True it is that causes are sometimes submitted to the decision of juries with which they are unfitted to deal. Such are questions arising out of long and complicated accounts, and other matters of a like kind; but these ought never to be brought before them. The only proper tribunal for such inquiries is the forum domesticum of the arbitrator; and experience ought by this time to have taught parties the folly of incurring in those cases the costs of appearing in court, where the almost inevitable consequence is, that the cause is referred to arbitration, after much unnecessary expense and delay. It would not be difficult for an opponent of the system to cite ludicrous examples of foolish verdicts, but they would be a very unfair sample of the average quality; and nothing can be more unsafe than to make exceptional cases the basis of legislation. In a country like this, which is one vast hive of commerce and manufactures, and where so large a proportion of civil actions arises out of transactions in trade, it may be with certainty affirmed, that the persons most likely to understand the nature, and arrive at the truth of the dispute between litigant parties, are those who are conversant with the details of business, and engaged in similar occupations themselves. And such are the men who constitute our juries. It may well be doubted whether Lord Mansfield would have been able to elaborate from the principles of the common law, cramped and fettered as it was by the technicalities of a bygone time, the noble system of mercantile law, which has immortalized his name, without the assistance of juries of merchants, who so zealously co-operated with him in the task of applying the legal maxims of the days of the Henrys and Edwards to questions arising upon bills of exchange, charter-parties, and policies of insurance. Nor must we forget the many other advantages of this mode of trial, which have been already noticed in an earlier part of the present chapter.

It was said of Socrates that he first drew philosophy from the clouds, and made it walk upon the earth. And of the civil jury it may be also said, that it is an institution which draws down the knowledge of the laws to the level of popular comprehension, and makes the unlearned understand the nature and extent of their legal rights and remedies.

Supposing, however, we were to abolish it, what tribunal are we prepared to substitute in its place? Are we to throw the burden upon the judges, and make them like the Scabini of the Franks, decide disputed facts, as well as expound the law? But it may well be doubted whether this would in the end more effectually secure the great object of judicial inquiry, namely, the discovery of truth. To say nothing of the exhaustion of mind which would be felt by a judge called upon in the rapid succession of causes tried at nisi prius to weigh contradictory evidence, and balance opposing probabilities,—although it may sound paradoxical, it is true, that the habitual and constant exercise of such an office tends to unfit a man for its due discharge. Every one has a mode of drawing inferences in some degree peculiar to himself. He has certain theories with respect to the motives that influence conduct. Some are of a suspicious nature, and prone to deduce unfavorable conclusions from slight circumstances. Others again err in the opposite extreme. But each is glad to resort to some general rule by which in cases of doubt and difficulty, he may be guided. And this is apt to tyrannize over the mind when frequent opportunity is given for applying it. But in the ever-varying transactions of human life, amidst the realities stranger than fictions that occur, where the springs of action are often so different from what they seem, it is very unsafe to generalize, and assume that men will act according to a theory of conduct which exists in the mind of the judge.

I am satisfied also that the concurrence of the people in the administration of the law, through the medium of the jury, greatly increases the respect and reverence paid to the judges. In deciding upon facts, opinions will necessarily vary, and judges, like other men, are liable to be mistaken in estimating the effect of evidence. Every one thinks himself competent to express an opinion upon a mere question of fact, and would be apt to comment freely upon the decision of a judge which on such a question happened to be at variance with his own. It is easy to conceive cases where much odium would be incurred, if, in the opinion of the public, the judge miscarried in a matter which they thought themselves as well able to determine as himself. From this kind of attack the judge is now shielded by the intervention of the jury. He merely expounds the law, and declares its sentence; and in the performance of this duty, if he does not always escape criticism, he very seldom can incur censure. So that De Tocqueville is strictly right when he says, "Le jury qui semble diminuer les droits de la magistrature, fonde réellement son empire: et il n'y a pas de pays où les juges soient aussi puissans que ceux où le peuple entre en partage de leurs priviléges."

But, moreover, the tendency of judicial habits is to foster an astuteness, which is often unfavorable to the decision of a question upon its merits. No mind feels the force of technicalities so strongly as that of a lawyer. It is the mystery of his craft, which he has taken much pains to learn, and which he is seldom averse to exercise. He is apt to become the slave of forms, and to illustrate the truth of the old maxim—qui hæret in litera hæret in cortice. Now a better corrective for this evil could hardly be devised than to bring to the consideration of disputed facts the unsophisticated understandings of men fresh from the actual business of real life, imbued with no professional or class prejudices, and applying the whole power of their minds to the detection of mistakes, or the disentanglement of artifice and fraud. The jury acts as a constant check upon, and corrective of, that narrow subtlety to which professional lawyers are so prone, and subjects the rules of rigid technicality to be construed by a vigorous common sense.

And there is good sense in the following quaint remarks taken from the pamphlet already quoted, which is attributed to Lord Somers:[1] "If judges had power of both determining the matter of fact, and also the matter of law, as must, if there were no juries, their latitude of erring, &c., must then be the greater, and their doing wrong or mischief might be the more, inasmuch as they might wrong one then in both the fact and law; and their encouragement so to do would be improved, since then it must be harder to detect them, as whether erred in the fact, or in the law, or partly in both; like as it's easier seeking a bush than a wood. . . . But were judges presumed saints, and never so upright, &c., yet who can imagine, but at a trial when witnesses are all examined, and

---

[1] Guide to English Juries, by a Person of Quality.

evidence all given, the jury being so many persons, and probably knowing something of the matter before, they may, all assisting one another, better observe, remember, and judge upon the whole matter, than any one or two, &c., others, though called judges? Certainly one may do more with help than without. So the proverb is—Ne Hercules quidem contra duos; oculi plus oculo vident. Two to one is odds at foot-ball. And, non omnes sed pauci decipi aut decipere possunt. The fewer may the more easily deceive or be deceived. Quandoque bonus dormitat Homerus. Nemo sine crimine vivit. Humanum est errare. It's natural for man to err. None's without fault; and the surest foot may slip."

If common jurors are sometimes found deficient in intelligence, the true remedy is not to abolish the system, but to improve it by educating the people so as to make them more fit to discharge the duties which it imposes. The more we train and discipline their minds, and above all, the more we teach them to act upon Christian principles, so that they may undertake the office under a deep and solemn sense of responsibility, and with a conscientious reverence for their oaths, the more excellent an instrument for the ends of justice will the jury become. And the converse of this is equally true. Where the mental capacity of a nation is mean, or the standard of public morality is low, and the obligation of an oath is lightly felt, no worse machinery could be devised for judicial investigations. It is invidious to specify instances, but it is easy to see that there are countries where trial by jury, even in criminal cases, must be a doubtful experiment, and in civil, at present, beyond all question a failure.[1]

The late change in the law, whereby parties in an ac-

[1] I may mention British India as a country where I believe it would be very unsafe to entrust questions to the decision of a native jury. All who have had much practice in Indian appeals must be painfully aware how little

tion are made admissible witnesses for themselves, has, I think, increased the importance as well as the difficulty of the office of the jury. It is remarkable that our great legal optimist, Blackstone, pointed out, a century ago, "the want of a complete discovery by the oath of the parties," as one of the defects of our jury system. He said:

"This each of them is now entitled to have, by going through the expense and circuity of a court of equity, and therefore it is sometimes had by consent, even in the courts of law. How far such a mode of compulsive examination is agreeable to the rights of mankind, and ought to be introduced in any country, may be matter of curious discussion, but is foreign to our present inquiries. It has long been introduced and established in our courts of equity, not to mention the civil law courts; and it seems the height of judicial absurdity, that in the same cause between the same parties, in the examination of the same facts, a discovery by the oath of the parties should be permitted on one side of Westminster-Hall, and denied on the other: or that the judges of one and the same court should be bound by law to reject such a species of evidence, if attempted on a trial at bar; but, when sitting the next day as a court of equity, should be obliged to hear such examination read, and to found their decrees upon it. In short, within the same country, governed by the same laws, such a mode of inquiry should be universally admitted, or else universally rejected."

I am by no means disposed to deny that the admission of parties to give evidence in a cause in their own behalf will facilitate the ends of justice, by promoting the discovery of truth; but without doubt the temptation to perjury is thereby increased, and the task of the jury will be often rendered more difficult and delicate. Even

reverence the natives have for truth, even when guarded by the sanction of an oath. An attempt, however, has been made partially to introduce the system in India, in civil cases. See Reg. VI. of 1832, Sec. iii.

stopping far short of perjury, a man is naturally inclined to give an undue coloring to the merits of his own case; his memory is sharpened as to points favorable to him, and his wishes often make him put an interpretation upon the words used in a verbal contract or other transaction to which he is a party, which he is apt to confound with the words actually uttered on the occasion. All this will impose upon the jury the task of deciding more frequently than heretofore between opposite and conflicting statements, and require more than usual caution and intelligence on their part. The same difficulty, however, would occur if any other tribunal were resorted to, and therefore it can be no valid argument against the use of the jury in civil causes.

The great object of all ought to be to increase the efficiency of this mode of trial by educating the people. And by education I do not mean merely the sharpening of the intellect, but the teaching them to act upon religious principle. It has been strongly said, that "the whole establishment of King, Lords, and Commons and all the laws and statutes of the realm, have only one great object, and that is, to bring twelve men into a jury-box." This is hardly an exaggeration. For to what end is the machinery of the constitution employed but to give every man his due, and protect all in the enjoyment of their property, liberty, and rights? And the twelve men in the jury-box are in this country the great court of appeal, when in the case of the humblest as well as the most exalted citizen, these or any of these are attacked. Long may it be so! and while other nations are heaving with the throes of revolution, and regard their polity with discontent, long may the characteristics of England be her attachment to the institutions handed down to us by our forefathers—her confidence in the pure and upright administration of justice —and her reverence for the law.

INDEX.

Afforcement of jury, 105.
Althing, 27.
America, jury in, 289.
Anglo-Saxons, jury unknown to, 45, 46.
    Tribunals of, 52–54.
        Numerical divisions how maintained, 54–55
        Witnesses amongst, 70–76.
        Publicity of proceedings, 72.
Arimannen, 19, 35.
Asega, 22.
Assise of Henry II., 101.
    Its origin, 110–113.
    Its subsequent history, 112–115.
    Difference between assisa and jurata, 115–123.
Assisa vertitur in juratam, 115.
Assises de Jerusalem, 95, 96.
Asworen eth, 25, 66.
Attaints, originally in nature of new trial, 149
    Punishment by, 152.

Battle, trial by, 81.
Belgium, jury in, 312.
Boni Homines, 36, 38.
Bot, 4.
Borh, 50.
Burhgemote, 54

Capitula Coronæ. 164.

Challenges in civil trials, 145–149.
   In criminal, 191–2.
Chamber de la Tournelle, 213.
Compurgators amongst the Anglo-Saxons, 61–70.
   Their usual number, 63.
   Difference between them and a jury, 69–70.
   Instance of suit decided by, 84–86.
Conquest, Norman, meaning of term, 75–9.
Coroner, when jury returned by, 142.
Coroner's jury, 186.
Corsnead, 68, 159.
Cour de cassation, 196.
Curia regis, 82, 104, 110, 111.
Cyre-ath, 65, 130.

De Medietate Linguæ jury, 189
Dicasts of Athens, 7, 135.
Ding, 34.
Dingmänner, 34.
Distringas, 140, 145.
Dumester, 252.

Ealder-man, 54.
Echevin, 36–57.
Elisors, 132, 142.

Fá, 49.
Fama publica. 159. 167.
   Patriæ, 170, 179, 188.
Fausser la Court, 99, 153.
Forath or Vorath, 66.
Folgarii, 55.
France, trial by jury in, 295.
   No grand jury in, 297.
   Question of civil jury considered and rejected, 305
   Want of self-government in, 308, 357.
Frank-pledge, system of, 53.
Frithborh, 47, 50.
Frosta-thing, 16.

Gau, 532, 94.
Gemot, 33, 56, 57, 76.
Geneva, trial by jury in, 312.
Gerefa, 33, 53.
Germany, system of criminal procedure in, 314.
   Introduction of trial by jury in, 325.
Godi, Icelandic, 27.
Graf, 33.
Grâgas, 27.
Grand Coustumier 4, 173.
Grand Assise. See Assise.
Grand Enquête, 176, 177.
Grand Jury, 178.
   Its use considered, 184.
   Does not exist on Continent, 297.
Greece, jury in, 312.
Gula-thing, 16, 18.

Hallmotes, Anglo-Saxon, 92.
Hlaford, 63, 67.
Hundred Court, 53.
Hundredors, 73, 148.

Iceland, legal tribunals in, 28.
Issues for jury trial in Scotland, 265.
   Forms of, 266, 267.

Jefferies, Chief Justice, his conduct at trial of Mrs. Lisle, 345–6.
Jersey, trial by jury in, 173.
Judex Quæstionis, 10.
Judices Pedanei, 38.
Judicium Parium, not trial by jury, 91, 92, 199.
   Applies to members of feudal and county courts, 94.
Jurata, its origin and nature, 116–118.
Jurata patriæ, 93, 117, 164, 179.
Jurors, originally mere witnesses, 105, 106.
   Gradually ceased to be so, 124–128.
   Fluctuations in numbers of, 108–109.

Personal knowledge originally required, 135–138.
Might give verdict upon their own knowledge against evidence of witnesses, 136.
Change in this respect, 137.
Disagreeing minority punished, 109.
Kept sine cibo et potu, 202.
Jury, theories as to origin, 3–6.
Its proper functions, 7, 9.
Unknown to Anglo-Saxons, 45.
Not introduced by William the Conqueror. 82
Panel tampered with, 141.
Fined for verdict, 153.
In criminal cases, 165.
Proper province of, 216.
Powers of in cases of libel, 223.
Considered as a political institution, 357.
Advantages of jury in civil cases, 373, 377.
Jury de Medietate linguæ, 189.
Justiciars appointed, 81.

Kions-neffn, 24.

Lahmen, 56.
Landgericht, 33.
Laugrettomen, 16–18.
Laudatores, 62.
Law and fact, 242.
Legitima purgatio, 165.
Lex Terræ, 106.
Lex Servilia, 145.
Libel, province of jury in, 223–235.
Fox's libel act, 232.
Scotch term for indictment, 274–5.
Logman, 17, 18.

Mægas, 52.
Magna Charta, 91, 92.
Mallum, 7, 33.

Mansfield, Lord, his ruling in cases of libel, 224.
Manung, 70.
Marken, 32.
Milites, 118.
Missus, 43.
Nämbd in Sweden, 19, 20, 21, 30.
Nefndarmen, 16.
New trial in civil cases, 154, 156.
   Question of, in cases of felony, 193.
Nisi Prius, meaning of term, 140.
Non Liquet, 10.
Normans, legal changes introduced by, 81.
   Examples of Anglo-Norman trials, 82–90.
Norse Thing, 7.
Not Proven, verdict of, 280.

Ordeal of three kinds, 67–68.
Oath of Anglo-Saxon witnesses, 74.

Pares. See Judicium Parium.
Pleadings, system of written, 246.
Portugal, jury in, 312.
Presentment, ancient mode of, 159–161.
Press, freedom of, 364.
Presumptions of guilt in old times conclusive, 168.
   Of law and fact, 243.
Probi homines, 22, 90, 112, 187.

Rachinburgen, 6, 19, 35, 38.
Recognitors of assize, 107.
Recusatio judicis, 146.
Regiam Majestatem, date and authenticity of book discussed, 249.
Rim-ath, 130.
Russell, Lord John, his view of utility of jury, 358, 368.
Russia, twelve sworn jurors in, 31.

Sachibaro, 34.
Sandemænd, 23, 25, 26.

Sardinia, jury in, 313.
Scabini, 6, 10, 36-38, 57.
Scandinavia, so-called "juries" in, 14, 15.
Scir-gemot, 54.
Scotland, jury-system in civil cases, 249-271.
    Assize in criminal trial, 271-2.
Secta, 56, 94.
    Mode of trial by, 128.
Sheriff, 140, 143.
    Tampered with, 361-2.
Six-hyndesmen, 62.
Special jury, earliest notice of, 143.
    Form of striking, 144.
    Cost of, 145.

Tales de circumstantibus, 143.
Tenmannetale, 51.
Thanes acting as judges or accusers, 56, 57.
Tingmænd, 23.
Triers, 148, 149, 170, 223.

Unanimity of jury, origin of rule, 197.
    Reasonableness of rule, 203-215.
    Not required in Scotland in criminal trials, 280.
    Nor in France or elsewhere on Continent, 195-6.
United States, jury in, 289.

Venire facias, 122, 139, 141.
Verdict, originally nothing more than the conjoint testimony of the jury, 11.
    Jury fined for, 154.
Varthing, 26, 27.
Vorath, 66-7, 162.

Wapentake, derivation of word, 53.
Wergild, 48, 51, 52, 61, 80.
Witan, 54.

www.ingramcontent.com/pod-product-compliance
Lightning Source LLC
Chambersburg PA
CBHW020322170426
43200CB00006B/237